FAMILY CARE OF SCHIZOPHRENIA

THE GUILFORD FAMILY THERAPY SERIES
ALAN S. GURMAN, EDITOR

Family Care of Schizophrenia:
A Problem-Solving Approach to the Treatment of Mental Illness
Ian R. H. Falloon, Jeffrey L. Boyd, and Christine W. McGill

The Process of Change
Peggy Papp

Family Therapy: Principles of Strategic Practice
Allon Bross, Editor

Aesthetics of Change
Bradford P. Keeney

Family Therapy in Schizophrenia
William R. McFarlane, Editor

Mastering Resistance: A Practical Guide to Family Therapy
Carol M. Anderson and Susan Stewart

Family Therapy and Family Medicine: Toward the Primary Care of Families
William J. Doherty and Macaran A. Baird

Ethnicity and Family Therapy
Monica McGoldrick, John K. Pearce, and Joseph Giordano, Editors

Patterns of Brief Family Therapy: An Ecosystemic Approach
Steve de Shazer

The Family Therapy of Drug Abuse and Addiction
M. Duncan Stanton, Thomas C. Todd, and Associates

From Psyche to System: The Evolving Therapy of Carl Whitaker
John R. Neill and David P. Kniskern, Editors

Normal Family Processes
Froma Walsh, Editor

Helping Couples Change: A Social Learning Approach to Marital Therapy
Richard B. Stuart

FAMILY CARE
OF SCHIZOPHRENIA

*A Problem-Solving Approach
to the Treatment of Mental Illness*

IAN R. H. FALLOON
JEFFREY L. BOYD
CHRISTINE W. McGILL

*University of Southern California
School of Medicine*

THE GUILFORD PRESS

New York   London

© 1984 The Guilford Press
A Division of Guilford Publications, Inc.
200 Park Avenue South, New York, N.Y. 10003

Printed in the United States of America
Second printing, April 1987

LIBRARY OF CONGRESS CATALOGING IN PUBLICATION DATA

Falloon, Ian R. H.
  Family care of schizophrenia.

  (The Guilford family therapy series)
  Bibliography: p.
  Includes index.
    1. Schizophrenia—Treatment. 2. Schizophrenics—
Family relationships. 3. Family psychotherapy.
4. Behavior therapy. I. Boyd, Jeffrey, L. II. McGill,
Christine W. III. Title. IV. Series. [DNLM: 1. Behavior
Therapy. 2. Family Therapy. 3. Schizophrenia—therapy.
WM 203 F196f]
RC514.F325   1984   616.89'8206   84-10835
ISBN 0-89862-049-X (cloth)
ISBN 0-89862-923-3 (paper)

PREFACE

The family has been scapegoated as a major contributor to the pathogenesis of schizophrenia. The behavioral family therapy approach challenges these long-standing notions and instead posits the family as the major resource for the community management of schizophrenia and other severe mental illnesses. Through enhancing the problem-solving functions of the family as a unit behavioral family therapy appears to improve the ability of the family to modulate environmental stress and its impact on family members. This appears to be associated with a reduced risk for florid episodes of schizophrenia in a vulnerable family member, who has previously suffered from that disorder. Furthermore, the problem-solving model serves as a structure for planning and achieving functional goals for all family members.

This volume describes the rationale, the techniques, and the efficacy of behavioral family therapy in the context of comprehensive community management of schizophrenia. The first section is devoted to developing the assumptions that underlie the behavioral family therapy model. The lack of evidence for a specific family etiology and the consistent, yet puzzling findings from genetic studies are discussed. Family and environmental stress factors, including "expressed emotion" and life events, are examined in the context of family coping behavior, and the enormous burden of family care giving. It is assumed that every member of a family is doing his or her utmost to cope with the environmental stresses he or she is facing. Traditional community rehabilitation methods are described. The need for family-based interventions that harness the full range of resources that are available in the community is expounded. Such approaches look beyond the interpersonal transactions of the family system to broader community systems, and to the intrapersonal and biological functions of the patient and his or her family members. Family therapy in its various guises is explored in Chapter 5. Methods that derive from social casework, multiple groups, systems theory, and psychosocial and educational approaches are compared. A common thread of effective family problem solving appears to weave these often disparate approaches together. The final chapter in this section outlines the development of behavioral family therapy to its current form.

The second section of this book is dedicated to an explicit description of the specific strategies employed in behavioral family therapy. Detailed illustrations of all aspects of the treatment program are provided as a therapy manual. The importance of the functional analysis of family behavior is stressed throughout. The aim of the therapist is to build upon the strengths of the family to help them overcome the weaknesses in their problem-solving activities. The straightforward nature of the structured problem-solving approach leads to family education about schizophrenia and communication issues commanding much greater space in this volume, although both these facets of the program are considered important only when they clearly contribute to family problem solving.

The final section deals with the evaluation of the efficacy of behavioral family therapy in the comprehensive community management of schizophrenia. The criteria upon which any innovative approach can be judged involve considerations of effectiveness and costs. An extensive controlled trial of behavioral family therapy was sponsored by the National Institute of Mental Health from 1978 to 1983. The family therapy approach proved more effective than more traditional individual supportive psychotherapy when both were combined with optimal drug therapy, rehabilitation counseling, and crisis management. Not only did the family therapy appear to reduce the clinical morbidity of schizophrenia, such as florid exacerbations and negative symptoms, but it enabled patients to use a lower dose of neuroleptic drugs. Improvements in social functioning of index patients were substantial, leading to restoration of normal patterns of work and social functioning. The benefits to family members were substantial, with improved physical and emotional health and a reduction in the burden associated with caring for the index patient. An analysis of the factors that may have contributed to the superiority of behavioral family therapy supported the view that the reliably measured improvements in family problem solving and coping functions were the prime mediators of change. Finally, a cost–benefit analysis showed that the family approach, despite being home-based, resulted in substantial cost savings for the community. Thus, it may be concluded that behavioral family therapy is a significant therapeutic advance in the mental health field.

A multitude of talented people participated in the development of this family therapy approach, and subsequently in the family research project. Several deserve special thanks for their efforts and support:

Robin Skynner, Isaac Marks, Julian Hafner, and Michael Crowe, who offered support and advice during the formative stages of these methods. Robert Liberman, Francis Lillie, and Robert Aitchison made major contributions to refining the structured problem-solving techniques. Ralph Talbot and Ruby Palmer assisted in the further development of the home-based approach. Howard Moss, Javad Razani, Alexander Gilderman, Jeri Doane, Jean Pederson, Christine Vaughn, David Lukoff, John Strang, George Simpson, Malcolm Williamson, Michael Goldstein, Cathy Wood-Siverio, Grant Marshall, Robert Miles, and Kim Shirin contributed to the research project. Valuable comments on the book manuscript were made by Robert Liberman, Alan Gurman, Edward Harpin, and Manhal Al-Khayyal. Virginia Cardin and Neil McDonald provided assistance in editing and with the research. Finally, we would like to thank the many warm, loving, creative families, who graciously invited us into their homes to share the joy and anguish of coping with mental illness.

CONTENTS

SECTION ONE

FAMILIES AND SCHIZOPHRENIA

CHAPTER 1

FAMILIAL STUDIES OF THE ETIOLOGY
OF SCHIZOPHRENIA

The association between family disturbance and schizophrenia has a long history. However, the exact nature of this relationship remains essentially unresolved. The tendency for schizophrenia to run in families, although not striking overall, is nonetheless pronounced in many families. But is this finding the result of genetic inheritance or associated with distorted family communication, or perhaps a combination of both? Clearly an understanding of the pathogenesis of this disorder may assist in developing effective therapeutic strategies, including family psychotherapies. Furthermore, because the prevalence of schizophrenia in more than one family member is relatively low, it may be illuminating to examine those families in which schizophrenia does not show a familial incidence. Factors that may serve to "protect" family members from developing schizophrenia may again provide valuable information to the therapist, who may seek to fashion similar "protective" mechanisms in the families he or she is treating. This chapter will review the many studies of family communication and genetics in schizophrenia, as well as longitudinal studies of children who are at risk for developing schizophrenia because they have a parent suffering from the disorder.

Because much of this research is highly technical, we will attempt to glean from it the implications that are of particular relevance to clinical interventions. However, it is important for the clinician to understand that the strengths of these guidelines lies in the scientific rigor whence they are derived. The development of the behavioral family therapy approach to the treatment of schizophrenia has been derived from this empirical approach. This itself has been a problem-solving exercise, whereby all possible strategies for intervening in family systems to enhance the mental health of all family members have been carefully evaluated and the best combination of interventions painstakingly shaped into a viable and effective treatment approach that continues to be reviewed for further refinement. This progressive revision of therapeutic strategy, based on a critical assessment of empirical evidence, is at the heart of behavioral psychotherapy. It is a method we hope to foster throughout this book in the hope that readers will not merely accept our approach uncritically, but may be able to develop even more effective methods for dealing with their own patients.

ETIOLOGICAL STUDIES OF FAMILY INTERACTION

The long association between observed disturbances in family relationships in familes in which a member has been diagnosed as having schizophrenia has led to the inevitable conclusion that these disturbances may have preceded the onset of illness and contributed to it. These hypotheses owe much to the impact of psychoanalysis, particularly after World War II when a remarkable surge in the popularity of this approach resulted from its utility in understanding and treating the traumatic stress reactions in military personnel. Freud's study of paranoia in the celebrated Schreber case clearly implicated the harsh child-rearing methods of a tyrannical father in the development of a delusional disorder in his son (Schatzman, 1971). However, Freud did not believe that psychoanalysis could assist in the treatment of schizophrenia. Nevertheless, a gallant few of his followers attempted to adapt the methods of psychoanalysis, particularly the development of close transference relationships, to the plight of institutionalized persons suffering from schizophrenia. Sullivan (1927) attempted to develop a surrogate family type of milieu for schizophrenic patients at the Shepherd–Pratt Clinic with an aim to provide a corrective "family" experience for his patients while they were inpatients. Frieda Fromm-Reichmann (1948) conducted heroic efforts to assist severely disturbed schizophrenic patients and clearly demonstrated that these individuals were accessible to psychosocial interventions if therapists were patient, tolerant, and willing to persist and to accept very limited goals. Unfortunately, she will be best remembered for her description of the potential role of mothers in the etiology of schizophrenia. The so-called "schizophrenogenic mother" became the battle cry upon which the family was implicated as a major factor in driving family members into the fearsome world of schizophrenia. This emotional child-abuse paradigm had profound ramifications in the subsequent development of community treatment approaches that are still prevalent today. However, attention was clearly drawn to family involvement with schizophrenia and spawned several hundred studies that attempted to isolate the specific "schizophrenogenic" behavior in the family patterns of interaction. Structure to this research effort was provided by a number of theorists, who based their theories on observations of a small series of families seen in naturalistic and therapeutic settings. The four major early proponents of the family etiology of schizophrenia were Lidz, Bowen, Bateson, and Wynne. Each of these theories will be outlined with the research evidence to support or refute their utility. Although none have survived as a comprehensive explanation for the development of schizophrenia in any individual, they have provided a major contribution to our understanding of stress in families and its association with interpersonal problem-solving functions within the family system.

The Psychoanalytic-Based Theories of Lidz

Theodore Lidz, a student of Sullivan, followed his master's footsteps in examining the role of the family in the development of schizophrenia in their offspring. He worked first at Johns Hopkins and later at Yale. His initial hypothesis was that early failure of personality integration was related to the family environment and resulted in disruption of learning the meaning of language. This developmental disability then contributed to severe regression when the adolescent failed to surmount the developmental tasks of adolescence, became overwhelmed, and suffered emotional and egocentric deterioration. Lidz rejected the genetic findings in favor of his familial theories and attempted to support his arguments with a number of careful, yet uncontrolled, studies of young adult patients and their parents. Each family member was assessed individually on a battery of psychological tests, including the Rorschach, as well as with psychoanalytic interviews.

In his first study at the Phipps Clinic, he compared 50 young patients from very different family backgrounds. He noted that the adverse intrafamilial factors were more prominent in the parents of schizophrenics, but was unable to delineate any specific communication disturbance (Lidz & Lidz, 1949).

A second study followed that involved intensive study of 17 families with a schizophrenic member (Lidz, Fleck, & Cornelison, 1965). Several families in the group were considered to provide good family milieus, but on closer examination these families were found to be as disturbed as the others, but with less overt expression of their marked difficulty. Nine of 15 had at least one parent who was "more or less schizophrenic" and, of 15 same-age siblings, eight had definite or borderline schizophrenia. This high rate of overt disturbance as well as clear interactional peculiarities led Lidz to conclude:

The disturbed families do not in themselves cause schizophrenic states, but we hoped to find something etiologically specific by following the tangible lead that schizophrenic patients came from seriously disturbed families. A major difficulty soon arose. Whatever aspect of these families we examined, we found something seriously amiss. (1973, p. 14)

He observed that the mothers of schizophrenic offspring were almost always highly unstable, strange persons who had difficulties setting boundaries between themselves and their children. Some were very intrusive and others aloof (Lidz, Cornelison, Singer, Schafer, & Fleck, 1965).

Fathers were just as disturbed as the mothers, but again, no clearly defined patterns were evident. Hostility and aggression, passiveness, and overprotective behavior were elicited in response to the child with schizophrenia.

Perhaps the major feature of Lidz's reports was his finding of a high rate of marital discord that led to severe tensions within the family (Lidz, Cornelison, Fleck, & Terry, 1957). As a direct result of persistent parental discord, the children were emotionally abused by the parents, who appeared to use the child as an emotional replacement for their ineffective spouse. The children were presented with faulty role models and were discouraged from attaining independence from their parents. With 60% of the families having at least one parent with severe personality disturbance or schizophrenia, communication in the family seemed seriously disturbed. A high degree of tolerance on the part of the less disorganized spouse reduced the rates of hospital admission, and few of these cases had been formally diagnosed.

Lidz believed that the tendency for parents to insist that other family members perceive the world as they did tended to invalidate the child's perception of the world. He termed this "training in irrationality" (Lidz, Cornelison, Terry, & Fleck, 1958).

No specific pattern of schizophrenogenic interaction was isolated, but parents showed a high rate of personality disturbance and marital discord, and their interactions with their children were characterized by inconsistency and a tendency to involve them inappropriately in the parental difficulties. This parenting disturbance prevented the child from establishing a stable perception of the world and an inability to develop effective adult role behavior. This overwhelming stress led to autistic, schizophrenic regression.

The careful observation of the interaction between parents and their young adult children with schizophrenic disorders led Lidz to conclude that severely disturbed relationships between the parents and the child, and between the parents themselves, contributed to the development of schizophrenia.

Numerous studies have sought to validate Lidz's observational data with controlled, laboratory examination of family interaction. There is abundant evidence that family interaction patterns in families with schizophrenic offspring differ in some respects to the interaction of families with "normal" offspring (Lennard, Bernstein, & Beaulieu, 1965; Mishler & Waxler, 1968; Friedman & Friedman, 1970; Cheek, 1965; Ferreira & Winter, 1968; Stabenau, Tupin, Werner, & Pollin, 1965). However, no consistent patterns of family role structure and parent–child conditions have been identified. Moreover, when families with schizophrenic members have been contrasted with families of persons suffering chronic physical or mental illnesses, these interaction differences have been minimal (Farina & Holzberg, 1970; Becker & Finkel, 1969; Caputo, 1963; Lerner, 1965; Stabenau et al., 1965). This suggests that most of the interaction anomalies may be related to the presence of a chronic illness and not specific to schizophrenia.

On the other hand, consistent evidence of marital disagreement and discord between the parents of schizophrenics has been reported in many studies of family interaction (Caputo, 1963; Cheek, 1965; Farina, 1960; Farina & Holzberg, 1970; Sharan, 1966; Fisher, Boyd, Walker, & Sheer, 1959; Sølvberg & Blakar, 1975). Marital disharmony appears to be more marked in families of chronic schizophrenics than in other psychiatric patients. However, very few studies have focused on the issue of these marital problems and one can only speculate on their origins and their relevance to the course of schizophrenia.

Lidz and his followers have clearly demonstrated that families with members who have developed schizophrenia often have distorted role structures, marital discord, and difficulties communicating clearly with their schizophrenic members. These difficulties may be similar to those found in families of persons who suffer from other chronic illnesses, but are nevertheless major sources of stress and impediments to effective psychosocial rehabilitation.

Bowen and the Development of the Family Systems Approach

Murray Bowen, like Lidz, was a psychoanalyst who sought to study the entire family unit of an adolescent diagnosed as having schizophrenia. He was able to admit several families to an inpatient unit of the National Institute of Mental Health (NIMH) in Bethesda, Maryland, over periods as long as 2 years. During this time, the family lived together on the unit alongside other families. They left the hospital to attend their work, but throughout this period their home was the hospital ward. This provided an unparalleled opportunity to observe the working of a family in detail over a substantial period.

Bowen and his specially trained staff provided support for the families when necessary and combined individual psychoanalysis of all family members with family groups (Bowen, 1961). A total of 14 families were studied in this fashion. Initially, he had sought to focus on the symbiotic relationship between a patient and his or her mother, but soon realized that fathers were an integral part of the family disturbance and began to study the entire nuclear family unit.

His main hypothesis was that schizophrenia is a manifestation of a process that involves the entire family and that the patient is merely the diseased part that displays the psychosis. He observed that the "family, in constant living contact with a psychotic family member, is in a state of intense conflict and emotional turmoil" and that a supportive, concerned therapist readily becomes sucked into the turmoil (Bowen, 1960). He later described this state as an "undifferentiated ego mass."

Bowen claimed that every one of the 11 two-parent families he studied demonstrated serious marital discord. This was frequently covertly expressed—possibly on account of the environmental constraints? He coined the term "emotional divorce" to describe the marked emotional distance between the parents, who were unable to communicate personal feelings, thoughts, and experiences. In some marriages, overt hostility between the parents also contributed to physical distancing. Bowen noted that reciprocity was an important feature of family interaction and that patterns of communication and role functioning were not fixed. At times one family member might exhibit dominant behavior while the other played a submissive role; but at other times individuals might reciprocate their dominance–submission characteristics. This rather obvious observation helped explain the inconsistency of data from many family interaction studies that involve one segment of family behavior at one point in time. This notion that individual family members respond in a systematic way to each other led to Bowen conceptualizing the family as an interactive system in which each component person behaves in conjunction with each other person.

Bowen supported Lidz's contention that the child who developed schizophrenia was intimately involved in stabilizing his parents' marriage. He described this mother–father–child interrelationship as the "interdependent triad." The child became the center of mother's attention. She conveyed her wishes for the child to remain helpless on a nonverbal action level, while verbally saying that she expected him or her to become a gifted and mature person. The intense relationship between mother and child resulted in the father's becoming more distant and aloof—a finding reported for all fathers in the sample. The patient was clearly placed under exceptional stress that he or she was powerless to cope with. The mothers in the sample all appeared to be excessively concerned with their disturbed offspring, but the tension created resulted in the index patients' often perceiving them as rejecting.

Schizophrenia developed as the child reached adolescence and his or her rapid growth toward physical maturity upset the equilibrium of the interdependent triad. The helpless child failed to adapt to the demands of adulthood and became the helpless patient, who at the same time denied his or her incapacity through distorted verbalization and psychotic behavior. However, Bowen does not strongly endorse this etiological scenario in his writing and appears more concerned with family therapy techniques for assisting family members to establish themselves as independent, mature persons separated from the family turmoil.

Bowen presents no data on the outcome of his therapy efforts. He describes a case study of a father who increased his assertiveness. This was accompanied by the mother's relaxing into a less dominant role with subsequent improvement in their daughter's illness. He concludes that reestablishing the primacy of the marital relationship leads to improvement in the children. This is a core concept of the family systems approach to therapy. It is apparent that poor communication between the parents mitigates against effective family problem solving and leads to escalation of family tension.

Bowen's theories have seldom been subjected to experimental validation. They tend to describe complex dynamic processes that are not readily subjected to cross-sectional analysis. However, the notion that families with schizophrenic members are undifferentiated or chaotic in their functioning is supported by many studies that indicate that decision making is disorganized and distorted in many such families (Stabenau et al., 1965; Caputo, 1963; Lerner, 1965; Wild & Shapiro, 1977; Sølvberg & Blakar, 1975; Ferreira & Winter, 1965).

"Emotional divorce" is one extreme pattern of the marital discord that has been reported frequently in experimental studies of schizophrenics and their parents. The distant, uninvolved father has not been evident in studies of brief family discussions, and may become apparent only under the naturalistic long-term studies that Bowen and Lidz have conducted. Such a longitudinal study is fraught with methodological and economic constraints, but should not be underestimated as a resource for enhancing our understanding of complex family factors. Most laboratory studies have examined no more than 30 minutes of family interaction under highly contrived circumstances that have varied substantially from study to study. Their studies have not been supported by longer-term clinical observations to validate the assumption that these interaction samples are typical of family behavior in less restrictive settings. The caged lion in the zoo may bear only faint resemblance to the majestic, powerful, and graceful king of the jungle! Moreover, the measurement of interaction characteristics seldom captures the multifaceted complexity of the dynamic, interactive systems that Bowen and others have described.

The need for bringing order to the chaos of families with schizophrenic members is clearly indicated by Bowen's work. This may be achieved by encouraging fathers to become more assertive and to work together with overburdened mothers to provide a consistent structure to family problem solving. This concept of family relationships as an interactive system, whereby change in the behavior of one member may lead to indirect changes in others, is crucial to the understanding of the therapeutic process in families.

Bateson, Jackson, Haley, Weakland, and the Palo Alto Group

While Lidz and Bowen were clinicians with a psychoanalytic background, a group of investigators in Palo Alto were attempting to study socio-anthropological aspects of schizophrenia. Led by a British expatriate, Gregory Bateson, who was married for a period to the renowned cultural anthropologist Margaret Mead, they employed family discussion groups in the presence of the researcher as their mode of naturalistic observation. These observation sessions were not expected to have a therapeutic effect and the observers aimed to minimize their involvement. However, to their surprise, the sessions did appear to facilitate improvement in the schizophrenia of the index patient, and serendipitously, a family therapy method was born (Jackson & Weakland, 1961).

The observations of Bateson and his colleagues focused on the interpersonal communication patterns of family members. In addition to the verbal messages of *what* was being said, special attention was directed to the nonverbal patterns of *how* it was being expressed. These observations led to the brilliantly conceived "double-bind hypothesis" of the etiology of schizophrenia (Bateson, Jackson, Haley, & Weakland, 1956).

A further theoretical construct propounded by Don Jackson was that of "family homeostasis." The family as a unit engages in negotiating a balance between the resources and needs of the individual family members (Jackson, 1959). This is analogous to the manner in which many of the organ systems of the body are integrated into a steady-state system to maintain the status quo, and react to any change with an effort to restore the physiological balance. This construct had been originally proposed by Richardson (1948) and was elaborated by Jackson with specific reference to attempts to change family transactions through conjoint family therapy. "Homeostasis" did not always imply adjustment to a level where stress and strain were absent. Homeostatic maneuvers were considered at times to result in unsatisfactory and unstable realignments. Stability was often achieved by costly compromises of family members that may have increased an individual's stress and led to physical or mental pathology.

The homeostatic hypothesis has been widely accepted within the field of family therapy, and has established validation from the work of numerous clinicians who have observed the beneficial and detrimental effects of changes in the behavior of one family member affecting the functions of all other family members. Controlled studies have not been reported, but a series of reports on the effects of the behavioral treatment of agoraphobia on the marital relationships of sufferers seems to indicate that rapid symptom removal that alters the social functioning of one spouse necessitates substantial accommodation in the other for improvement to be sustained (Hafner, 1977). It is not always sufficient to treat only the most overtly disturbed member of a family unit. Before any intervention is planned, a careful evaluation of the likely effect on other family members should be conducted to ensure that tensions are reduced for the entire family system. As Jackson (1959) points out, some families are very precariously balanced, so that attempts to change their long-standing patterns of behavior must be approached with caution in a highly supportive manner.

The theoretical concepts of homeostasis that postulated linear cause–effect relationships in which beneficial changes in one family member resulted in reciprocal detrimental changes in another family member have been challenged (Dell, 1982; Hoffman, 1981). The notion that homeostasis prevents families from significant growth and development has similarly been revised. In its place a more sophisticated cybernetics model that considers the way components of family transactional behavior fit together into a coherent system has been proposed (Dell, 1982; Hoffman, 1981). A detailed analysis of all the contingencies surrounding family behavior, particularly behavior considered disordered or deviant, is crucial to any effective family intervention program. This enables the therapist to see how the varied contributions of each family member interlock and often serve to sustain the problem despite the best efforts of the family to achieve resolution.

While homeostasis and its more recent developments have had a major impact on the theoretical constructs of conjoint family therapy, the double-bind hypothesis has been a major influence in the environmental theories concerning the etiology of schizophrenia. The double-bind concept has the apparent beauty of being a precisely operationalized phenemonen of communication between two or more persons. Moreover, its proponents maintain that such a phenomenon occurs frequently in daily conversations between members of families with a member who suffers from a schizophrenic illness.

As defined by Bateson and his colleagues in 1956, double-bind communication is characterized by the following:

1. A repeated, everyday communication sequence between two or more people who are engaged in an intense relationship.
2. One person, the "victim," becomes the recipient of an injunction, usually verbal, either (a) not to do something, or (b) "If you do [something], I will punish you." A punishment mediated through withdrawal of love and abandonment, or expression of hate or anger, characterizes this communication as highly coercive.
3. A second coercive communication, often abstract and nonverbal, that conflicts with the first message at a more abstract level is, for example, "Do not see this as punishment"; "do not submit to my prohibitions"; "do not question my love, of which the primary injunction is [or is not]." When two persons interact with the victim (e.g., parents), one may negate the initial injunctions of the other.
4. A third injunction prohibits the victim from escaping from the field. At times, these are not overtly negative (e.g., promises of love).
5. Discriminatory learning occurs so that any part of the sequence may precipitate reactions in the victim.
6. Because victims are caught attempting to respond to injunctions they cannot fully comprehend, and yet feel duty-bound to respond appropriately, they find themselves constantly "on the spot." Their efforts may appear irrelevant, off the point, delusional, and incoherent, expressed with inappropriate affect. The pattern of conflicting injunctions may be reflected in verbal hallucinations. In other words, responses that are made by the victim are unconventional, yet in some sense appropriate reactions to the confused stimuli presented. The resulting communication disorder is labeled "schizophrenia" (Bateson *et al.*, 1956).

This theory is clearly the work of creative genius. Its greatest theoretical strength, that of defining human communications in terms of simultaneous and often contradictory messages, delivered by nonverbal and verbal modes of expression, is also its greatest pragmatic weakness. The sheer complexity of the operational definition of such a pattern of behavior defies empirical analysis. Even experts in double-bind theories were unable to reliably define examples of double-bind communication occurring in transcribed letters (Ringuette & Kennedy, 1966). Very few studies have been reported to support a specific association between the double bind and schizophrenia (Schuham, 1967).

However, the theory provides a compelling view of the perceptual confusion of schizophrenia. Persons experiencing the thought interference, delusional perceptions, and hallucinations characteristic of this disorder are unable to readily discriminate the injunctions to which they should respond, and their answers may appear to be off the point. Any lack of clarity in the information communicated by family members to the floridly ill patient has the tendency to accentuate his inadequate discriminatory functions and lead to increased tension and further decompensation. The implication for the family members and therapists is to communicate as clearly as possible, particularly when expressing emotional responses.

From the patients' point of view, one wonders what might happen if they were to openly communicate their confusion and simply ask for clarification when they perceive they are being put on the spot? An effective therapeutic strategy may be to teach the patient to ask for clarification of messages that he or she cannot readily discriminate. It is not clear whether these difficulties are prevalent when the patient is less floridly disturbed. The findings that suggest cognitive deficits remain after florid symptoms have remitted lead us to conclude that the person who has suffered schizophrenia is especially vulnerable to misunderstanding complex or unclear communication at all times and that this persists as a potential source of stress. Thus, the family therapist may train all members of the family to make clear, straightforward responses and to develop effective skills in receiving these messages accurately.

Wynne and Singer

Lyman Wynne followed Murray Bowen in the Family Studies Unit of NIMH and brought a more sophisticated research technology to the field. His earlier theoretical papers had outlined characteristic family transactional patterns that focused on the homeostatic mechanisms of the family system. He coined the phrase "pseudomutuality" to describe the bonhomie often displayed by families in public situations to mask their serious underlying conflicts. This same phenomenon was noted by Lidz and by Manfred Bleuler, who noted that families that appeared well adjusted in the clinic setting were observed to be much more disturbed on home visits (Bleuler, 1974). Wynne used a vivid metaphor of the "rubber fence," within which the family set limits on the behavior of its members allowing stretching of the limits until tension propelled the family back to its original constricted boundaries. Difficulties in sustaining long-term, substantive changes in families is well illustrated by this imagery (Wynne, Ryckoff, Day, & Hirsch, 1958).

However, Wynne's subsequent work focused less on family systems than on the identification of communication abnormalities in the parents of established cases of schizophrenia. He was joined by Margaret Singer, a brilliant clinical psychologist, and their long and fruitful association produced a number of well-designed studies.

Their main theoretical base was an assumption that abnormal communication styles of parents induce difficulties in a child's ability to focus his or her attention on what is being said, and to comprehend its meaning. This may impair the child's development of effective reality testing and subsequent perceptual ability. Such faulty perceptual learning may *predispose* the child to schizophrenia (Wynne, 1968). The early work on the projective testing of individual family members, which Lidz had abandoned, was the basis of a series of studies that associated the communication patterns of family members to the specific diagnosis of their offspring. Four types of communication deviance were identified:

1. *Amorphous.* This referred to vagueness of speech, without a readily recognizable unifying goal, and a tendency to drift toward subjective experience. Thought blockage and circumstantiality were included.
2. *Fragmented.* Although the overall coherence and clarity of goals is greater than with "amorphous" speech, communication is frequently disrupted by disturbing ideas, impulses, and affect changes. This makes the communication difficult to follow.
3. *Mixed.* This is a combination of "amorphous" and "fragmented."
4. *Constricted.* Speech is coherent, but aspects of reality are split off.

In most of their studies, Wynne and Singer examined transcripts of the speech of parents while they were performing Rorschach or TAT tests in *individual* sessions with an examiner. The form of the communication, not the content, was the major interest of these investigators.

The first study (Singer & Wynne, 1963) compared matched samples of parents of young adult schizophrenics, childhood schizophrenics (infantile autism), neurotics, and those with conduct disorders. Singer rated the transcripts of the parents' Rorschachs and TATs without knowlege of the diagnoses of their offspring. From her ratings of the parents' communication deviance, she was able to make a remarkably accurate blind prediction of whether their child had childhood schizophrenia or a neurotic disorder. The proportion of parents in each group showing deviant communication patterns varied from 95% with adult schizophrenics to 0% with conduct disorders. This striking ability of communication deviance in the parents to predict the psychiatric disturbance of their children was considered to offer validation for the hypothesis that communication disturbances in parents are closely associated with formal thought disorders in their children.

Subsequent studies have refined these assessment procedures and provided additional support for the theory. Singer continued to exhibit an uncanny skill at predicting diagnostic classification of index patients from the parental Rorschach responses and was able to train reliably other raters to do likewise. Schizophrenia, borderline personality disorders, and neurotic conditions were successfully discriminated (Singer & Wynne, 1965; Wynne, Singer, Bartko, & Toohey, 1977). Furthermore, recent studies have noted a close relationship between the parents' communication deviance scores and the *severity* of psychopathology in their offspring. Correlations were less strong between parents' communication deviance and the communication deviance of their children. They concluded that this suggested it was unlikely that the children simply inherited a communication disorder from their parents, and that communication deviance in the parents may affect the mental state of their offspring independent of genetic factors.

The Wynne and Singer studies offer the strongest support for the clinical observation that parents of children who suffer from schizophrenia themselves show communication disorders in their speech. The strongest criticism of this work has come from a replication study conducted in London by Hirsch and Leff (1975). Although the parents of schizophrenics did show more communication deviance than parents of neurotics (mainly depressives), the difference was less striking than in the U.S. studies. The British investigators concluded that excessive communication deviance resulted merely from greater verbosity of parents of schizophrenics. However, it may be further argued that verbosity may occur as a direct result of an inability to communicate clearly (Woodward & Goldstein, 1977).

Several other studies have supported the communication deviance hypothesis (Behrens, Rosenthal, & Chodoff, 1968; Jones, 1977; Wild, Singer, Rosman, Ricci, & Lidz, 1965). However, the conclusion that communication deviance in the parents *causes* schizophrenia in their children can hardly be inferred from the data. Several alternative explanations cannot be ruled out, these including (1) that the communication disorder is a genetic marker of schizophrenia found in persons who show no symptoms of the illness, but who may carry genes that predispose to the fully developed syndrome, or (2) that communication deviance develops as a result of living with a child with schizophrenia. Some answers to these questions have been provided in longitudinal prospective studies of children at risk for developing schizophrenia and in genetic studies, both of which are described later in this chapter.

A further set of studies that have emanated recently from the Wynne group, now based in Rochester, may have even greater significance to clinical interventions. These studies have examined the beneficial impact of effective or "healthy" communication on the children of mentally impaired parents. This work will be described in the next section of this chapter.

Fragmented, disorganized communication by the parents clearly impairs the family ability to attend to relevant detail in their problem-solving functions. While the double-bind paradigm applies to emotional expression, communication deviance has been obseved in the communication of information that is not emotionally toned. The importance of improving the family's ability to communicate clearly and effectively in many different contexts is evident.

Conclusions

Distorted family interaction has not been found to account for the development of schizophrenia. Furthermore, no pattern of interaction specific to families with schizophrenic members has been isolated. Nevertheless, discordant family communication appears very common in these families, but not substantially more common than that found in other families where a member is suffering a serious, poorly understood condition. The stress generated by poor communication and inadequate problem solving is undoubtedly a contributing factor in sustaining a disorder such as schizophrenia that appears to be stress-related. However, the major question left unanswered by these early studies is whether these difficulties in family interaction preceded the onset of the illness or resulted from the problems of coping with a severely impaired family member. Several prospective studies that seek answers to these issues are now under way and will be discussed in the next section.

Arguments concerning etiology notwithstanding, the clinical implications of this body of work are clear. Families with offspring suffering from schizophrenia show a high prevalence of marital discord, role distortions, confusing verbal and nonverbal communications, and difficulties attending closely to important issues. Such communication difficulties substantially hamper effective resolution of family problems through structured problem-solving discussions. Most of these early researchers were active therapists, with predominantly psychoanalytic training. Their most important observation was that improvement in one family member may be achieved through effecting constructive changes in the behavior of family members other than the index member. The importance of establishing the primacy of the parental relationship to ensure a cooperative base for effective problem solving was clear. Training improved communication behavior, with special reference to the congruence of verbal and nonverbal channels and to the attention provided to the relevant details, is a crucial prerequisite to resolution of family problems. However, an adequate repertory of communication skills is itself not sufficient for a family to achieve competent problem-solving functions. The ability to structure family discussions to deal with important, potentially stressful issues would appear to be critical.

CHILDREN AT RISK FOR SCHIZOPHRENIA

The limitations of the study of families in which a member has already developed schizophrenia prevent a clear statement concerning the role of the family in the etiology of the disorder. For this reason, attempts to unravel the causes of schizophrenia have shifted to an examination of family factors that existed prior to the appearance of florid symptoms of schizophrenia. Because the lifetime risk of schizophrenia in the general population is around 1%, researchers have attempted to define factors that may be associated with a higher risk ratio in order to reduce the population studied to a manageable size. Once a population has been defined and assessed at baseline, serial assessments are conducted in a longitudinal fashion until subjects develop schizophrenia. The subjects who develop the disorder are compared with those who do not in an attempt to identify features associated with high vulnerability to schizophrenia. For the family therapist, a knowledge of such warning signs may aid in early detection of vulnerable persons, and possibly lead to methods to counter this vulnerability.

Several studies have been launched in the United States and Scandinavia, most of which employ similar methodology. Their major differences concern the selection of the "high-risk" population, and the parameters that have been chosen for baseline and subsequent assessment. High-risk populations have been identified either through parental attributes or through features associated with children.

High-Risk Attributes Associated with Parents

The increased association between parents who suffer from schizophrenia and its development in their offspring has been well documented in familial incidence studies (Gottesman & Shields, 1976). A single parent with schizophrenia increases the risk to about 10%; both parents diagnosed as schizophrenic increases the risk of schizophrenia occurring in their children to 20–40%. Despite difficulties in establishing reliable diagnosis, many studies have employed this parental marker in defining their populations.

The offspring of mothers with a diagnosis of schizophrenia have been the most commonly studied group (Erlenmeyer-Kimling, 1968; Garmezy, 1972; McNeil & Kaij, 1973; Mednick & Schulsinger, 1964; Sameroff & Zax, 1973; Wynne, 1968). Having a mother or father with schizophrenia (Anthony, 1968; Neale, 1969), a father with schizophrenia, or both parents concordant for schizophrenia (Erlenmeyer-Kimling, 1968) are other ways in which the risk for schizophrenia in children has been defined.

Many of these studies have been following children for 10 years or more, and high-risk subjects are beginning to enter the period of maximum incidence of the schizophrenic illness. Comparisons between the children of schizophrenic parents and matched nonschizophrenic parents have suggested that environmental factors that increase a child's vulnerability to schizophrenia may include perinatal complications (Sameroff & Zax, 1973) and the child's involvement in the sick parent's psychotic behavior (Anthony, 1968). Both these studies examined the parent–child interaction where the mother was disabled by a serious mental illness.

The importance of comparing the offspring of parents with psychiatric impairment other than schizophrenia is highlighted by the Sameroff and Zax project. These investigators are studying children of mothers who have schizophrenia, neurotic depression, personality disorders, or no psychiatric diagnosis. While many of their measures have distinguished differences between the children of schizophrenic and normal mothers, most of these features have been indistinguishable from those found in the children of mothers with other psychiatric diagnoses. The quality of mother–child interaction has been noted to deteriorate in the most severely ill mothers, both depressed and schizophrenic. Physical contact and communication with the young child have been particularly deficient and are associated with disturbances in the child's behavior. This cohort was studied before the birth of the index children and hopefully will continue until they all pass through the crucial period for the development of schizophrenia (i.e., 40–45 years). The promise of associating specific features of early development with subsequent development of schizophrenia is an exciting one that may take the lifetime of the investigators to fulfill (Sameroff, 1974).

The Copenhagen project of Sarnoff Mednick and Fini Schulsinger (1968) is the most comprehensive study of genetically predisposed children. In 1962, Mednick and Schulsinger scoured the psychiatric hospitals on the island of Zealand in Denmark for chronic, process schizophrenic women who had children between 10 and 20 years of age. Two hundred and seven offspring of these severely ill mothers were matched with 104 low-risk children of parents who did not have mental illnesses. This cohort has been studied intensively at the time of intake, and 5, 10, and 15 years later. In 1972–1974, an intensive diagnostic assessment was conducted with the Present State Examination (PSE) and Current and Past Psychopathology Scales (CAPPS) diagnostic interviews (H. Schulsinger, 1976). At that time the average age of the high-risk subjects was 24 years (18–30 years), and 173 completed the assessment. Fifteen subjects had diagnoses of schizophrenia in a consensus between the examiner's clinical judgment, the PSE, and the CAPPS criteria, and only one case was identified in the low-risk group (Table 1-1). Using the CAPPS system alone, 30 high-risk and six low-risk subjects were also diagnosed. When borderline schizophrenia and schizoid personality disorders were included, 55 subjects were included under the concept of "schizophrenic spectrum disorder." A mere 25 high-risk subjects were not given any consensus psychiatric diagnosis. Furthermore, only one-quarter of the low-risk subjects escaped a consensus psychiatric diagnosis—although most were mild disturbances not requiring clinical attention. The importance of a reliable, standardized diagnostic system is illustrated by these rather confusing findings—a problem that pervades both research and clinical work in psychiatry.

TABLE 1-1. *Diagnosis of Schizophrenia in High-Risk Children*

Diagnostic system	High risk (*n* = 173)	Low risk (*n* = 104)
Schizophrenia		
PSE/CATEGO	10 (6%)	1 (1%)
CAPPS/DIAGNO II	30 (17%)	6 (6%)
"Consensus"[a]	15 (9%)	1 (1%)
"Schizophrenic spectrum"	55 (32%)	4 (4%)
Any psychiatric disorder	148 (86%)	77 (74%)

Note. Diagnoses of schizophrenia in 173 children of schizophrenic mothers after 10-year follow-up compared with 104 matched controls (based on Schulsinger, 1976).

[a]Agreement on two out of three diagnostic systems—PSE, CAPPS, or interviewer's clinical determination.

Mednick and Schulsinger (1968) did not collect direct measures of the family milieu provided for the high-risk cohort. However, some data were available that allowed speculation about the potential role of family relationships in the development of schizophrenia. It was noted that the mothers of children who developed schizophrenia often had their own schizophrenia precipitated by childbirth, that they developed schizophrenia at an earlier age, and that most were separated from their children when the index child was quite young. These mothers tended to exhibit aggressive, temperamental traits and to associate in unstable relationships with sociopathic men. This suggests that the children who developed schizophrenia may have suffered inadequate parental nurturance, bordering on abuse, at least in their formative years (B. Mednick, 1973; Talovic, Mednick, Schulsinger, & Falloon, 1980). This suggestive evidence is tantalizing, but as Mednick laments, one cannot measure all the variables that might be considered relevant to the development of schizophrenia. Fortunately, several more recent studies of high-risk children have sought to examine specific family factors in detail, so that eventually our understanding of the nurture–nature components of the etiology of schizophrenia may be improved.

The impaired parent is a major issue for family therapy. Where parenting functions are shared with a well-adjusted parent, this may be less of a problem than with an impaired single parent, or where the second parent is also disturbed. Family structure may play an important role in determining the adequacy of parenting. Although almost all the family studies of schizophrenia have examined the classic two-parent family, the structure of families varies considerably (Kellam, Ensminger, & Turner, 1977). Family therapy methods may need to be adapted to the single parent, grandparents, adult siblings, and other individuals who may assume primary parenting responsibility or who may assist the parents in this role.

However, not all parents who suffer from a mental illness such as schizophrenia lack parenting skills. In some cases, their behavior may make a positive contribution to the psychosocial development of their children. Recently, Wynne and his colleagues in Rochester have extended their studies to include an investigation of resources present in impaired parents that can help promote healthy functioning in their children (Wynne, Jones, & Al-Khayyal, 1982). The relatively low incidence of schizophrenia in the children of families in which one parent has the disorder prompted this search for health-promoting factors. Al-Khayyal (1980) developed a method of measuring effective problem-solving behavior in families engaged in reaching a consensus about the objects they perceived on a Rorschach card. She found a significant association between the degree of healthy problem-solving communication by the parents and a measure of the child's functioning made by teachers and peers. Children showed higher academic and social competence when they came from families in which parents communicated clearly and provided structure for the problem-solving task in an organized, systematic fashion. This study suggests that the ability of family members to apply effective problem-solving strategies in coping with the stresses of daily living, particularly where one family member is mentally ill, may be crucial not only in preventing the breakdown of family members, but also in promoting the psychosocial functioning of all family members.

High-Risk Attributes Associated with the Child

While most high-risk studies have chosen tainted parentage to define predisposition to schizophrenia, another route has been to define vulnerability characteristics of the child that are associated with the subsequent development of schizophrenia. It may be possible to select children who show specific forms of behavioral disturbance that might be associated with the subsequent development of schizophrenia or other major mental illnesses.

A group of researchers at UCLA, headed by Michael Goldstein and Eliot Rodnick, have been conducting a study of high-risk adolescents who were receiving treatment for severely disturbed behavior. At the time they were selected for the study, no evidence of florid schizophrenic phenomenology was noted. Behavior disturbance was classified into four groups: (1) Aggressive, Antisocial; (2) Active Family Conflict; (3) Passive, Negative; and (4) Withdrawn, Socially Isolated. It was hypothesized on the basis of Lee Robins's study of psychopathology associated with prior adolescent behavior disturbance that groups 2 and 4 (Active Family Conflict and Withdrawn, Socially Isolated) would be at high risk for developing schizophrenia as adults.

A second risk factor examined by Goldstein and Rodnick was the communication deviance of the parents. This was derived directly from the work of Singer and Wynne, who were able to discriminate between parents of established cases of schizophrenia and other psychiatric conditions. Jones and his colleagues (1977) used their scoring methods to assign adolescents into three risk categories—high, intermediate, and low—on the basis of their parental communication deviance on a TAT report. No genetic risk factors were invoked.

Finally, a measure of observed communication behavior was examined. This involved coding the communication of feelings expressed by both parents toward the child in a discussion about a significant family problem. A series of reliable codes of statements of support, criticism, guilt induction, and intrusiveness were employed and used to categorize parental communication styles into three groups—benign, intermediate, or poor (Doane, West, Goldstein, Rodnick, & Jones, 1981).

Five years later, 52 children were reexamined. The severity of adolescent disturbance predicted the severity of adult psychopathology. Two-thirds of the subjects who subsequently developed disorders resembling schizophrenia had shown family conflict or social isolation 5 years earlier. Communication deviance was present in almost all the "schizophrenic spectrum" cases, but also occurred in a large number of good-outcome cases. But where communication deviance in the parents was combined with poor emotional communication to the child, a significant prediction of severe adult psychopathology could be made (Goldstein, 1978; Doane et al., 1981).

It is not clear whether the parental communication difficulties are merely a response to the adolescent's behavior disturbance, and the diagnostic evaluation cannot be readily compared with DSM-III schizophrenic disorders. However, the link between family communication and problem-solving effectiveness and subsequent mental illness is strengthened by this study. Parents with high communication deviance have difficulties structuring family problem-solving discussions and have deficient listening skills (Herman & Jones, 1976; Lieber, 1977). These features, combined with hostile criticism and intrusive communication, severely limit the problem-solving capacity of the family unit. On the other hand, it is also apparent that the family may assist in averting ongoing and potentially more severe psychiatric disturbance through clear communication and efficient problem solving of family difficulties.

GENETIC STUDIES

If the manner in which families interact is not sufficient to account for the development of schizophrenia, then it may be possible that the answer lies in genetic predisposition. The search for a unitary biological factor has been pursued with similar ardor to that of the family theorists. This separation of thinking has been unfortunate and has often led to confusion in clinicians and patients who have been given contradictory information about the illness, often by experts at the same clinic. The issues are undoubtedly complex, but it is important that clinicians working in mental health clinics have a rudimentary understanding of them so that they may provide correct counseling to their patients.

Early Studies

Eugen Bleuler (1911) recognized that "hereditary predisposition certainly plays an important role among the causes of schizophrenia" (p. 340). He considered that "90 percent show hereditary tainting" and found "mental disease in 65 percent of families of schizophrenics" (p. 338). It is not clear what Bleuler meant by "hereditary tainting," but his report of a very high incidence of mental illness of all sorts in the families has been borne out by recent reports.

Franz Kallmann began a series of remarkable pioneering studies at the Herzberge Hospital in Berlin in the 1930s when he undertook to review all cases admitted to the hospital with a diagnosis of schizophrenia between 1893 and 1902—the first 10 years the hospital was in existence. He found 1087 definite severe cases and proceeded to study their descendants. He is said to have collected information on as many as 14,000 persons, including great-great-grandchildren, nephews, and nieces, and non-blood relatives who married into these families. He obtained almost complete data on all the first-degree relatives of the index cases. He found that 11% of the offspring had definite or doubtful schizophrenia at the time of interview as well as a substantial percentage with schizoid traits, giving 44% with psychiatric disturbance (equivalent to the "schizophrenic spectrum disorder" concept employed in recent high-risk studies). Fewer (9%) of the patients' siblings had schizophrenia. Nephews and nieces (second-degree relatives) had concordance rates similar to those of the general population, unless they had parents with schizophrenia. At the time of follow-up, many of the subjects were still at risk for schizophrenia; and when corrections were applied, the expected concordance rates for children and siblings were increased to 16% and 12%, respectively (Kallmann, 1938).

Kallmann's work has been challenged on several points. A major criticism was his choice of severe, hospitalized cases that might have represented a heavily genetically loaded population. However, Böök (1953) found very similar familial incidence in an epidemiological study in an isolated region of Northern Sweden. Böök found there was a slight excess of male schizophrenics, but that the women cases were three times more likely to marry. A further finding of interest was an extremely low incidence of manic–depressive illness—two cases compared to 93 schizophrenics. This finding is in stark contrast to a U.S. study of an isolated subcultural group of Hutterites who showed an excess of manic–depressive psychoses and very few cases of schizophrenia (Eaton & Weil, 1953). The lack of standardized diagnosis may account for such biases.

There is a tendency in genetic research to make the diagnosis fit the hypothesis. If diagnosis of relatives is made with knowledge of the diagnosis of the index case, this bias is intensified. In a blind assessment of diagnosis by Elliott Slater in pairs of siblings who were both hospitalized for mental disorder, only 41% of siblings were given the same diagnosis, compared to a chance expectation of similarity of 36% (Tsuang, 1967). A substantial overlap between manic–depression and schizophrenia has been observed in several studies. It has been suggested that this may be due to the similarity between good prognosis schizophrenia and affective disorders (McCabe, Fowler, Cadoret, & Winokur, 1972). In recent years, standardized psychiatric examination and classification criteria have assisted in establishing a greater degree of rigor in diagnosis (Spitzer, Endicott, & Robins, 1975; Wing, Cooper, & Sartorius, 1974). Such precision is vital to the field and subsequently assists the clinician in making more specific choices for treatment and prognosis.

Twin Studies

Another approach to understanding the role of genetics in schizophrenia has employed the study of monozygotic (MZ) and dizygotic (DZ) twins when one sibling of each pair of twins has been diagnosed as having schizophrenia. While MZ twins develop from a single fertilized ovum and are thus genetically identical, DZ twins share a genetic similarity no greater than that of ordinary siblings. If schizophrenia has a genetic component, then it would be expected that MZ twins would show a higher concordance rate for the illness than DZ twins. This has indeed been the case. The pooled results of several studies reported in a recent review revealed a probandwise concordance for MZ to average 45% whereas the concordance rate in DZ twins was around 15% (Gottesman & Shields, 1976).

In a study of 1232 psychotic index twins in New York State, Kallmann found concordance rates of 86% and 97% for co-twins of schizophrenic and manic–depressive diagnoses. There was a striking lack of discordant twins—not one manic–depressive member was found in a schizophrenic's family! Diagnostic methods are clearly implicated in such data. Kallmann included simple, atypical, pseudo-neurotic, acute confusional, and schizo-affective schizophrenia in the study—a broad "schizophrenic spectrum."

Perhaps the most carefully conducted twin study was conducted by Irwin Gottesman and James Shields (1974) at the Maudsley Hospital. The foresight of Elliot Slater to establish a twin register in 1948 enabled a sample of consecutive acute admissions to be studied. Only same-sex twins were sampled and zygosity was established carefully through blood groups, fingerprints, and appearance. They found 42% of MZ twins and 9% of DZ twins who had a diagnosis of schizophrenia, reached through a consensus of a group of eminent psychiatrists. It was of interest to note that the difference in concordance diminished when broader diagnostic classification was used. In addition, whereas more than half DZ cotwins showed no evidence of psychiatric disorder, only one-fifth of the MZ cotwins were similarly unimpaired. Gottesman and Shields concluded that inheritance was probably polygenic, and the schizophrenia genotype required additional interaction with stress to break down into a phenotypic case of schizophrenia. A poor premorbid personality reduces the individual's ability to cope effectively with overwhelming stress and thereby predisposes to subsequent decompensation.

This hypothesized gene–environment interaction was noted in the celebrated reports of the Genain quadruplets, who were studied extensively by Rosenthal (1963) at NIMH. All four girls showed poor premorbid personalities and suffered from poor parenting, with a very disturbed, paranoid, alcoholic father, who although himself not schizophrenic, had a family history of the condition. All four developed schizophrenia with differing features and severity. While family environment is undoubtedly a factor in determining whether a genetically vulnerable individual may or may not develop florid schizophrenia, the twin studies data offer compelling evidence to suggest that environmental factors alone are probably an insufficient cause of schizophrenia. However, it has been argued that being an identical twin is a major environmental stressor in itself, especially when the co-twin develops schizophrenia (Jackson, 1960). Thus, twins living together may suffer excess environmental stress that impairs development and increases vulnerability to mental illness. In an attempt to tease out the relative genetic and environmental contributions, a series of studies of adopted children of schizophrenic parents has been conducted.

Adoption Studies

The most definitive evidence that implicates genetic factors in the etiology of schizophrenia comes from studies of families in which the offspring have been raised apart from their biological parents. These adoption and cross-fostering studies range from investigations of children born to schizophrenic parents and reared in foster homes (Heston, 1966; Rosenthal, 1968; Karlsson, 1966), to studies of families in which children were adopted by a parent with a "schizophrenic spectrum disorder" (Wender, Rosenthal, Rainer, Greenhill, & Sarlin, 1974), to a study of the incidence of schizophrenia in the first-degree relatives of adoptees who were diagnosed as having schizophrenia (Kety, Rosenthal, Wender, & Schulsinger, 1968).

Heston (1966, 1967) examined 74 children of schizophrenic mothers who were born in an Oregon state mental hospital between 1915 and 1945, and appeared normal at birth. They were separated from their mothers at birth and were established in foster homes within 3 days. None went to the mother's relatives or to homes suspected of having characteristics that might predispose to schizophrenia. Twenty percent of the children died before school age—a disturbing mortality rate. A cohort of 42 were traced and completed follow-up examination. Five (10.6%) developed definite schizophrenia and four manic–depression. Several others showed sociopathic personality traits, leaving 21 (50%) without psychiatric disorders. Although the numbers are small, these data are remarkably similar to those found in the previous studies where the offspring of parents with schizophrenia were raised by their biological parents. In a matched control group from the same foster homes, no cases of schizophrenia or manic–depression were observed.

Kety and his colleagues (1968) conducted an interesting study in Copenhagen. He examined over 5000 adoptees and discovered 33 with definite diagnoses of schizophrenia. He then looked for schizophrenia in their biological relatives. He found 5–6 times more schizophrenia in these blood relatives than in the relatives who had adopted the children. A further comparison of a cohort of schizophrenics who were carefully matched but were not adopted showed a similar prevalence of schizophrenia in their biological relatives. However, these relatives were more severely ill than the relatives of the adopted group. Thus, it has been concluded from these adoption studies that the genetic predisposition to schizophrenia is relatively unaffected by the family environment in which a child is raised. But a disturbed family environment may contribute to the *severity* of the disorder—a highly relevant finding for the clinician.

Gene versus Environment: Clinical Implications

The complexity of the genetics of schizophrenia may lead the clinician to conclude that this issue has little relevance, especially when genotypes cannot be readily modified by psychosocial interventions. However, family therapists have shown considerable interest in the inheritance of character traits and behavior patterns. Genograms have been considered important, and theories that schizophrenia and other mental illnesses develop over several generations of assortative mating have been proposed (Bowen, 1960). Much of this clinical work has been conducted in the absence of a sound knowledge of the genetic research. Clearly, the biochemical makeup of an individual can be inherited, but familial transmission of behavioral patterns, cultural variables, expectations, and moral values may play an equally powerful part in molding each member of a family unit. Knowledge of the interaction between genes and environment is crucial to understanding how the clinician may be able to intervene to prevent the occurrence or reduce the severity of genetically determined conditions. This collaboration between behavioral science and clinical practice is essential for major advances in the treatment of mental illness.

It has been demonstrated convincingly that the offspring of parents who have suffered schizophrenia are more likely to develop schizophrenia. This risk appears the same even when the children are not raised by their biological parents. The incidence of schizophrenia increases substantially when both parents have schizophrenia, or when an identical twin develops the disorder. The collective weight of these studies strongly suggests the involvement of genetic factors in the etiology of schizophrenia. However, the exact mode of this genetic transmission remains a mystery. None of the existing theories adequately account for the low familial incidence of around 10% (see Figure 1-1). Nine of ten persons with first-degree relatives who have schizophrenia do not develop the disorder, and no more than half the identical twins are concordant.

It has been argued that it is not the disorder of schizophrenia that is inherited, but a *vulnerability* to develop this disorder. The high incidence of schizoid and antisocial traits in parents and siblings, as well as psychoses other than schizophrenia, has been postulated as evidence for this. Some investigators have broadened the concept of schizophrenia to include all these conditions under the rubric of "schizophrenic spectrum disorder." This classification tends to view mental illness along a spectrum of severity of psychopathology. Schizophrenia is at the severe end of the spectrum and neurotic disorders at the mild end. Such a classification ignores qualitative distinctions of phenomenology and is not compatible with the American Psychiatric Association's DSM-III classification system. The need for reliable and valid diagnosis has been mentioned earlier, but few etiological studies have addressed this issue effectively. A notable exception was the Gottesman and Shields study (1974). In this study, a panel of eminent international psychiatrists showed considerable variation in their diagnostic opinions. A consensus approach was employed that gave a more solid foundation to their data.

If a vulnerability (or biological weakness) to schizophrenia is inherited, not the disorder itself, then that vulnerability can be expected to prove pathogenic only when accompanied by other environmental factors

A. ONE PARENT HAD SCHIZOPHRENIA: 10% RISK

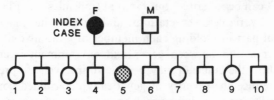

B. ONE SIBLING HAD SCHIZOPHRENIA: 10% RISK
(OR NON-IDENTICAL TWIN)

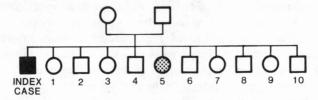

C: BOTH PARENTS HAD SCHIZOPHRENIA: 20%–40% RISK

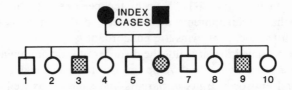

D: IDENTICAL TWIN HAD SCHIZOPHRENIA: 50% RISK

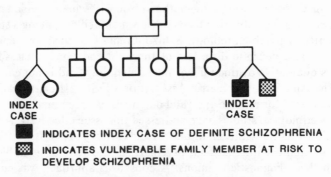

■ INDICATES INDEX CASE OF DEFINITE SCHIZOPHRENIA

▨ INDICATES VULNERABLE FAMILY MEMBER AT RISK TO DEVELOP SCHIZOPHRENIA

FIGURE 1-1. *Familial risks of schizophrenia.*

that provoke the appearance of the illness. These postnatal factors may be influenced by therapeutic interventions that enable the individual to overcome his biological vulnerability. Postnatal brain damage, season of birth (? viral factors; ? increased obstetric risks), and family environment appeared to play a greater role in the etiology of schizophrenia in the adopted children of parents with a low genetic risk ("normal" biological relatives) when compared with those with a high genetic risk (schizophrenia in biological relatives) (Kinney & Jacobsen, 1978). Thus, a detrimental family environment may contribute in a major way to pathogenesis in the absence of pathogenic genes, but may have less impact where pathogenic genes are present.

A further intriguing finding of potential gene–environment interaction was uncovered in a study of parental Rorschachs in the Maryland adoption study (Wynne, Singer, & Toohey, 1976). High levels of communication deviance were found in both the biological and adoptive parents of children who developed schizophrenia. However, psychopathology was greater in the biological parents. Thus, parental communication disorder was a better predictor of the development of schizophrenia in a child reared in a household than the severity of the house parents' psychopathology. Further studies of the quality of the family atmosphere provided by adoptive parents are required before it can be assumed that they provide a more nurturant environment than biological families in which one spouse has had schizophrenia. Undoubtedly, the child-rearing capacities of some parents are more seriously impaired than others. Furthermore, the effectiveness of the *unimpaired* parent may reduce the stress on the developing child. Careful studies that look closely at genetic and environmental factors are currently under way to explore many of these issues (Tiernari, Sorri, Naarala, Lahti, Boström, & Wahlberg, 1981). At this stage of our knowledge, it appears best to conclude that a supportive, nurturant, problem-solving family environment may be the most effective weapon to reduce the risk of schizophrenia in those genetically predisposed to the disorder. Such a family support system may not be able to negate the risk, especially in cases with a high genetic loading. However, in the next chapter, we will examine evidence that suggests that in established cases of schizophrenia, the family environment may determine the course of the condition.

A further issue for the clinician is the obligation to educate the patient about the inheritability of his or her condition. Genetic counseling should be provided to all persons with schizophrenia and their families, despite the relatively low familial incidence. Therefore, a clear understanding of the genetic research is essential for every therapist who treats persons with schizophrenia.

CONCLUSIONS

The familial studies on the causes of schizophrenia have not succeeded in finding a unitary cause for this condition. At best, a combination of factors including genetic inheritance and disturbed family environments may contribute to the development of schizophrenia. However, nonfamilial factors such as biochemical, viral disorders, extrafamilial life stressors, and neuropathological conditions have strong support in the search for etiological variables. These factors have been excluded from the present discussion, which focuses on the family. The evidence reviewed indicates that there is no adequate research to support the theory that schizophrenia is caused by disturbed family relationships in the absence of any other predisposing feature. Undoubtedly, some very disturbed individuals emerge from disturbed families, many of whom were, until the recent advent of more effective diagnostic criteria, considered to suffer from schizophrenia. With revision of the diagnosis (DSM-III), many earlier studies must be revised accordingly.

Before casting aside the pioneering work that sought to find schizogenic family interaction patterns, it is important to recognize the major clinical contributions of these early studies. One of the most important was the advent of conjoint family therapy. No longer was the patient viewed as an isolated person with a mental illness, but he or she was seen as a functional part of a dynamic family system, and effective treatment almost always entailed interventions directed at minimizing stress and maximizing the problem-solving potential of the entire family unit. This notion, clearly understood in general medical practice, was alien to psychiatry until quite recently; the current functioning of the patient's family was given relatively little attention compared to early childhood experience. While both are important, family therapists drew attention to the more readily transmutable here-and-now interactions that produce current stressors and sustain nonadaptive patterns of behavior. A further heritage of early family research is the greater attention given to the form and patterns of communication, including the nonverbal components of interaction tasks. Recent developments have tended to focus more specifically on the strengths and weaknesses of family communication when attempting to solve problems. The tendency to develop alternative theories of schizophrenia based solely upon environmental stress have been superseded by attempts to examine the interactions between biological and psychosocial factors. This collaboration has been important in the development of the behavioral family management approach that we have employed. Empirically valid concepts from family interaction, high-risk, and genetic studies have been seminal in the formulation of this approach.

CHAPTER 2

FAMILY COPING METHODS
AND THEIR EFFECTS
ON THE COURSE OF SCHIZOPHRENIA

The familial nature of schizophrenia is indisputable, although the precise nature of genetic and environmental factors in its pathogenesis will undoubtedly be debated for many years to come. Research on the etiology of schizophrenia has not led to any effective methods of preventing the development of this disorder nor to date has it been productive in developing more effective treatment approaches once a person has succumbed to the illness. A negative feature of the familial search for etiology has been the stigmatism of the family. Their efforts at support and coping with their schizophrenic family members have been characterized by such epithets as "schizophrenogenic," "transmission of irrationality," and "driving [their relatives] crazy." Despite the finding of genetic researchers that predisposed children are at equal risk of developing schizophrenia when removed from the care of their biological parents, family environments have been considered universally detrimental to the person with schizophrenia. Yet despite this, social policy has demanded that families become increasingly responsible for the primary care of their often severely disabled relatives, with minimal provision of community support systems.

Despite this abuse the vast majority of families continue to play an heroic part in the mental health care system and show eagerness to become increasingly involved in the process. A series of studies published in recent years give encouragement that family support may indeed play a major role in the treatment of schizophrenia, and that families may indeed become highly esteemed collaborators in the community management team. This chapter will review these studies in an attempt to define some of the parameters to be considered in the development of a comprehensive family management program that aims to enhance the quality of life of the *entire family*.

THE BURDEN OF CARING FOR THE CHRONIC PATIENT

Although the advent of neuroleptic drug therapy and social rehabilitation programs has reduced the proportion of individuals who are severely handicapped from schizophrenia, they remain a substantial population (25–35%). In addition, many patients make good social recoveries from an acute episode but periodic relapses are likely. The common onset of schizophrenia in late adolescence or early adulthood in men mediates against their having attained independence from their families, and if not living at home at the time they become ill, they are likely to return to the parental home thereafter. Women, on the other hand, tend to experience a later onset, and are more frequently married with children. However, the risk of subsequent divorce or separation is high (Rutter, 1966) and they, too, frequently return to live with their parents. As a result, much of the literature focuses on parental rather than spousal relationships.

The burden of living with a person with a chronic illness can be examined from two perspectives. First, the "objective" burden of the economic and social impact on family members can be assessed in terms of loss of potential earnings, additional costs of providing special care, disruption of the household routine, restriction of social and leisure activities, and physical and mental health problems. Such stressors may or may not have a direct effect on the quality of life of the patient and affect the quality of supportive care provided. However, the direct impact of such burden on family members and the disabled patient may be more closely associated with the subjective perception of the burden and the ability of the family to minimize the impact of such stressors through effective problem solving or coping strategies. Before examining family members' perceptions and attitudes toward the patient and his or her illness, it is important to obtain a picture of the characteristic behavioral anomalies that are observed in persons with schizophrenia who are living at home.

The most detailed survey of the problems of schizophrenia that are observed by family members was conducted by Clare Creer, a social worker, in England (Creer & Wing, 1974). She conducted in-depth interviews with 80 relatives, the majority of whom were members of an advocate group, the National Schizophrenia Fellowship.

Two major behavioral problems were severe social withdrawal and disturbed, socially embarrassing behavior. A lack of interpersonal skills often accompanied by social anxiety led to avoidance of social interaction in many patients. Few of these individuals were schizoid but most craved companionship. As a result they made excessive demands for social contact with their relatives, with whom the demand for competent performance of social interaction skills was less than for social contact outside the home. Mothers, in particular, were often the targets of these overly dependent relationships in which the patients often strongly resented being left alone or sharing the parent with any other person. Thus parents found their social lives becoming increasingly restricted. Their attempts to encourage increased socializing by their disabled sons and daughters were usually unsuccessful. In some cases, patients showed considerable difficulties communicating with their parents, especially in disclosing their feelings and concerns. This militated against effective problem-solving discussions.

The more active, disturbed behaviors tended to result in social embarrassment for patients and family members. The most common form was uncontrollable pacing and restlessness which occurred, not infrequently, at night, sometimes accompanied by playing loud music that prevented family members, and occasionally neighbors, from sleeping. A wide variety of socially inappropriate behavior was associated with the presence of persistent delusions and hallucinations. Relatives had little understanding of how best to respond to such behavior and received minimal guidance from the mental health services. Violent and suicidal behavior was relatively infrequent, but was associated with considerable apprehension in the relatives, even when these incidents had occurred a long time ago. Problems with sexual behavior were very infrequent. Overall 80% of the patients surveyed were reported to have moderate or severe behavior disturbance.

The effects of the patients' behavior on the relatives were minimal in one-fifth of families, and one-half reported serious effects on their health and general well-being. Apprehension and worrying about the future or the unpredictability of the patients' behavior were common. Some relatives reacted with feelings of frustration, helplessness, and anger at the more passive patient behaviors. Depression with guilt and worthlessness was not infrequent—a state many relatives reported to increase *after* the index patient had met with mental health professionals. Considerable family friction was reported in families in which the patient was living with siblings. The disruption in family social activities and household routine was often severe. In one-sixth of the households another sibling was reportedly disturbed, thereby compounding the family burden.

In the few spousal households, problems usually centered around difficulties in child care. When the patient was a mother of small children, the husband had to assume a greater than usual role as homemaker.

Creer and Wing found the resources and support provided for families inadequate, especially at the level of providing a basic understanding of the nature of the illness, guidance in the everyday management of behavior disturbance, and in methods of psychosocial rehabilitation. It could be argued that the families contributed to the handicaps of their relatives, but many of those surveyed were eager to learn more effective ways of interacting with their disabled sons and daughters, and freely acknowledged their lack of understanding. Their pleas were seldom viewed in a constructive manner by professionals, and their potential resourcefulness largely went untapped.

In an earlier study of family burden, Grad and Sainsbury (1963) conducted a community survey of mentally ill patients, including a substantial cohort of schizophrenics. Two-thirds of the families surveyed suffered some form of hardship, with one-fifth experiencing severe burden, even in a region of southeast England where excellent community services were provided. The family difficulties reported were very similar to the Creer study. The behaviors that most irritated family members were patients' going on and on about bodily complaints, fear of suicide, and excessive importunate demands. Social embarrassment was mentioned least often. Patients with organic brain syndromes and personality disorders were an even greater burden than those with schizophrenia.

It was of interest to note that patients who had moved away from home but were living alone continued to be a burden on their families, whereas those who lived in hostels or supervised lodgings presented no problems for the family. Furthermore, negative, rejecting, or excessively close relationships were associated with great problems for the family compared to families where positive, accepting attitudes prevailed.

Overall the level of family burden was substantially greater in a well-organized, community-based program than where hospital care was the focus of community intervention. The importance of family support and attitudes in community mental health programs was strongly advocated.

Several other studies have described the objective burden of family care. Hoenig (1974) found objective evidence of burden in 84% of 102 families caring for chronic mentally ill relatives in Manchester, England. However, only one-quarter complained of the burden as being severe, and a further quarter had no complaints at all. Less burden was evident in the families of patients receiving care from general hospitals rather than mental hospital clinics. Hoenig concluded that since the quality of care was similar in both settings the excessive burden perceived may have been related to the "stigma" of mental illness.

Agnes Hatfield (1979) drew attention to the unrelieved tension that relatives feel when they have to keep on constant guard, not being able to predict the behavior of the schizophrenic member. Yet despite these intolerable burdens, most families chose to have the patient live with them.

A special case of family burden is that of the patient living with elderly parents. Barbara Stevens (1972) undertook a systematic study of this problem and found that a substantial number of schizophrenics were living with aging family members in a very dependent manner. While this presented problems when the relatives died, the patients did provide companionship for their often widowed parents.

Thus, it may be concluded that families caring for a mentally ill individual suffer excessive hardships in the vast majority of cases. However, for the most part these burdens are not severe, and in some instances the presence of the patient in the household may provide some tangible benefits (e.g., help with chores, companionship). The emphasis on community care for the mentally ill has resulted in more stress on family members who stoically continue to care for their handicapped members with very few overt complaints. In recent years the discontent of family members with the woefully inadequate support services provided them has led to the formation of numerous self-help groups (Lamb & Oliphant, 1978).

None of the studies of family burden have examined the relationship between burden and the severity of the patient's symptoms. Undoubtedly the care for a severely disabled, persistently psychotic person is substantially greater than for a person with symptoms in remission. With the very severe chronic patients, parents are often asked to provide skilled nursing care with minimal guidance from professionals. This expectation appears to be an inappropriate utilization of the family resource. The use of the hospital as a means of providing a week or two respite for parents, although often employed in other chronic illnesses, has seldom been employed in community mental health programs, although many families members have requested such a service (Creer, 1974; Hemmings, 1981).

"Burnout" of professional staff employed in community mental health clinics has received considerable attention in recent years. The same phenomenon undoubtedly occurs in relatives who have 24-hour-a-day responsibility for the care of their disturbed relatives. Hatfield (1979) has noted that family system changes were reported contingent upon this stress, with one parent, usually the mother, accepting the major responsibility for care while the other family members (siblings, father) become increasingly removed from this arduous task. This pattern was considered by early family investigators (Lidz et al., 1965) to be of etiological significance, but is probably a pattern of coping with a persistently disturbed relative, and may well occur as a result of the unrelieved stress experienced by families that were well adjusted prior to the onset of schizophrenia in one of their members.

This body of research leads to the conclusion that from a family perspective the support provided for the majority of persons with schizophrenia who are living at home is considerable, but that few families are able to cope adequately with the daily tension of living with a mentally disabled person, and that professional support is frequently lacking or, unfortunately at times, appears to be detrimental. The need for preparation of the patient and his or her relatives for community care is clear. Clinical strategies might include the provision of specific information about the nature, causes, courses, and basic management strategies for dealing with mental illness to enable families to function with a greater degree of competence in their roles as primary care givers. In addition, the provision of specific supportive services for both the patient and his or her family may need to include home visits, crisis intervention, counseling for family members (as well as patients), and the provision of temporary care for patients to enable their families to have a break from their caring roles at regular intervals. Nurturance of patients' support systems appears to be an essential, yet often overlooked, ingredient in effective community care programs.

TOLERANCE AND COPING

Family burden studies have tended to focus on measurable disruption of family activities and the economic and social costs to the family when the patient has returned to the household after a period (often prolonged) of hospital care. They have been predicated on the deinstitutionalization policies of the past 25 years. A further line of study has examined the process by which patients, including acute cases, return to the hospital or suffer major exacerbations of their symptoms. These studies have examined the nature of the social crises that result in hospital admission of the schizophrenic patient and the effects of the family's tolerance and coping on the course of schizophrenia.

Tolerance of Social Deviance

The Boston Study of Freeman and Simmons (1963) was one of the earliest to examine the subjective sense of burden expressed by relatives toward their chronically ill family members. They examined a massive list of variables that might predict community tenure in patients returning to live at home. They hypothesized that where levels of a patient's performance in social roles fell short of the expectations of household members, rejection would occur and result in early return to hospital. However, neither inadequate social performance nor discrepant family expectations were clearly associated with rehospitalization. The level of social functioning of the patient and characteristics of the family were closely associated, but did not predict the duration of community tenure. Relatives reported that most often they sought readmission to a hospital for severe bizarre behavior that the family could no longer tolerate (Angrist, Dinitz, & Pasamanick, 1968; Pasamanick, Scarpitti, & Dinitz, 1967; Myers & Bean, 1968). These studies suggest that families do not effectively discriminate symptom behavior from social deviance that derives from other sources. Because bizarre behavior cannot be equated with symptoms, psychiatrists' ratings of psychopathology have not been good predictors of hospital admission (Wing, 1968). Nevertheless, the family's ability to cope with behavior disturbance whatever its origin appears to be crucial to maintaining the patient in the community.

Tolerance of Symptom Behavior

Greenley (1979) conducted a detailed study of the nature of family tolerance in relationship to various behaviors. He postulated that the level of family concern about their ability to cope with certain patient behaviors was a critical factor. He conducted a 4-year follow-up study of 31 mentally ill individuals and their relatives, two-thirds of whom had schizophrenia. He found that family fear about a patient's behavior and their perceived inability to cope with it correlated with more rapid rehospitalization. Rehospitalization was not related to psychiatric impairment, but was related to a previous history of multiple hospitalizations. Patient's role functioning, family stigma about having the patient at home, family friction, family burden, and a history of violence were not associated with hospital admission. Family fears remained significantly associated even after taking into account the severity of the patient's symptoms.

The possible sources of these family fears included previous episodes of violence toward family members and incomprehensible bizarre behaviors, but not suicide attempts. The family's coping skills in dealing with the feared symptoms was important. It was evident that families that developed negative attitudes toward the patient and which infantilized him or her provided the least effective environment. Rejecting and ambivalent attitudes were more common in the families of readmitted patients. Such attitudes militate against effective coping with a person's uncontrollable behavior, and readily lead to involvement of professionals to assist in the crises.

Cultural Acceptance

The acceptance of behavior disturbance associated with symptoms of schizophrenia and the course of the illness has been explored in several studies of the prognosis of schizophrenia in different cultures. It has been observed that in cultures where the prognosis of schizophrenia tends to be more benign, attitudes toward mental illness are more accepting.

Murphy and Raman (1971) examined all first admissions to the Brown–Séquard Hospital on the island of Mauritius in 1956. A 12-year follow-up of 90 persons with an initial diagnosis of schizophrenia was conducted and the outcome compared with a similar follow-up study conducted in England (Brown, Bone, Dalison, & Wing, 1966). Although the incidence of schizophrenia appeared similar, the percentage of those who were functioning normally and were symptom-free at follow-up was higher in the Mauritius sample, and they showed fewer relapses during the follow-up period. The better outcome could not be attributed to differences in phenomenology or treatment factors.

This finding has been replicated in the 5-year outcome study of the World Health Organization sponsored International Pilot Study of Schizophrenia (IPSS). Schizophrenia appears to run a more benign course in the less industrialized countries despite the inadequacy of effective community aftercare programs (Day, 1982). However, a study conducted in an urban area of India did not support these findings (Kulhara & Wig, 1978). These investigators found that outcome for schizophrenia in this setting was similar to that in England (Brown et al., 1966). They noted that the proportion of patients who were continuously ill throughout follow-up was similar to that in the Mauritius study; the major difference was found in the proportion of those who were considered to have recovered. They concluded that the high levels of acceptance of relatives may have confounded reporting, with underreporting of relapses and exacerbations in the Mauritius study. A similarly high degree of tolerance and support for the mentally ill was observed in the Hutterite community of the northern United States (Eaton & Weil, 1955). The onset of mental illness was a signal for the whole community to demonstrate support and love for the afflicted person, who was considered "ill" rather than "crazy." Despite this massive support, the prognosis did not seem remarkably different.

Thus, it seems of crucial importance to separate the underlying symptoms and illness from the social response and social crises that may determine the level of instrumental functioning of the impaired individual, and may minimize but not necessarily abolish symptomatology. Symptoms may be tolerated differently in different cultures. For example, auditory hallucinations such as hearing voices are considered a positive, creative, spiritual phenomenon in many societies and are unlikely to result in hospitalization of the fortunate person who has this experience (Al-Issa, 1976). Several studies have found that very few mentally ill persons or their families seek professional advice at the onset of the disorder because they recognize the features of mental illness and believe there is no effective treatment. Referral is initiated when the families find they are no longer able to cope with disturbed behavior (Myers & Roberts, 1959; Whitmer & Conover, 1959; Wood, Rakusin, & Morse, 1960).

While the issue of whether the severity of the actual symptoms of the illness are modified by the social response of people in the patient's environment is not clear, it is evident that in a good family milieu the *social* outcome is improved and a higher level of functioning with fewer social crises may result. It seems probable that a greater degree of acceptance of the patient's illness with more supportive, understanding relationships may mediate this effect, whereas rejecting, ambivalent, and fearful responses may tend to exacerbate socially deviant behavior. Supportive family systems appear to be more readily found in non-Western cultures. One study in the United States found that although the majority of chronic, handicapped patients are tolerated by the family, relatively few are integrated into the family's social activities. The level of acceptance of the patient is restricted and undoubtedly detracts from the rehabilitative capacity of the family system (Evans, Bullard, & Solomon, 1960).

It is evident that such restrictive attitudes also limit the social functioning of all family members, who often withdraw from their network of friends and acquaintances. This may account for the finding that persons with schizophrenia and their families have sparse social networks (Cohen & Sokolovsky, 1978). Patients may become the center of family life, with parents wishing they would enlarge their repertoire of social contacts, but becoming very anxious for their welfare when they venture out to seek potential friends. Scott (1974) describes this dilemma and maintains that hospitalization does not generally reduce the family burden. In the same review of his studies of the roles of hospital and family in the long-term management of schizophrenia Scott describes a method of predicting the outcome of family care from a survey of the attitudes of the patient and family members. He employed a checklist to obtain interpersonal perceptions of how patients and parents (1) see themselves, (2) see each other, and (3) *expect* others to see them. In cases where the patient's view of his or her parents conflicts with how the parents view themselves, the patient tends to have a poor outcome in the family setting and to spend more time in the hospital. This group of patients usually see their parents as "ill," a view not validated by the parents' self-concepts. The patient's view threatens the identity of often vulnerable parents and leads to his or her rejection. This transactional assessment of family atittudes is a fascinating one that considers both the patient and his or her family members in determining the social outcome of schizophrenia.

Effective social rehabilitation of patients who have suffered from schizophrenia requires the close collaboration of their families. Some family members display long-standing attitudes of intolerance and rejection that are unlikely to be modified and which make the family living situation untenable. However, many others appear fearful on account of their lack of understanding of schizophrenia. Much of this anxiety might be relieved by appropriate education of the family about the illness and its management.

EXPRESSED EMOTION

The relationship between the quality of the family milieu and the outcome of schizophrenia has been considered in terms of community tenure. Studies have concluded that readmission to the hospital may be associated with feeling of intolerable burden experienced by family members, often associated with bizarre behavior disturbance, and possibly related to incongruent interpersonal perceptions of patients and their parents. Rejecting, ambivalent, and infantilizing attitudes toward the patient may have contributed to a more extensive hospital stay, whereas supportive and accepting attitudes may foster improved social functioning. However, few of these studies have examined the relationship between family variables and the severity of symptoms—that is, whether family factors influence the psychopathology of the illness or merely modify its *social morbidity*. A series of studies begun in the 1950s by George Brown and his colleagues at the MRC Social Psychiatry Research Unit of the Institute of Psychiatry in London have sought to address this issue.

This work derived from studies of the impact of the deinstitutionalization policies. It was noted that schizophrenic patients' community tenure appeared to be associated with the type of living situation they returned to upon discharge from the hospital and whether they were employed. Patients who were discharged to the care of parents or spouses or to hostels were less able to sustain a community life-style than those who returned to live with their siblings or other kin or to lodgings. Rehospitalization was more likely when contact with people in the living groups was prolonged (Brown, Carstairs, & Topping, 1958). More severely ill patients went to hostels or parental households, but the results remained when this bias was accounted for. Overly dependent relationships were noted in many unemployed schizophrenics living with their parents, whereas few patients with a good employment record had overinvolved relationships. It was suggested that it was not beneficial for a person with schizophrenia to return to a household where close emotional ties were prevalent, but it is not clear whether the close emotional ties were a response to social handicaps, such as an inability to work, associated with more severe cases of schizophrenia, or the emotional response in some way *caused* the social and clinical deterioration.

In their second study Brown, Monck, Carstairs, and Wing (1962) examined in greater detail the features of the living situation that were considered potentially relevant to this finding. Only patients with a diagnosis of schizophrenia were included in this study. Interviews with the key relatives were conducted prior to discharge and 1 year later. A joint interview with the patient and his or her relatives was conducted 2 weeks after discharge. These interviews focused on the emotion expressed by the patient and his or her relatives. An index of "emotional involvement" was derived from these interviews. Patients who returned to live with relatives who were highly emotionally involved were more likely to suffer a relapse of schizophrenia than those who showed less "hostility" or "expressed emotion"—the two components of the index. A measure of "dominance" did not contribute to this outcome. The relationship between emotional involvement and relapse was independent of the severity of symptoms at discharge. Where a partially recovered patient had limited contact with an emotionally involved relative, relapse was less likely. A discrepant finding was that in this study patients who lived in lodgings fared no better than those returning to parental households. It was suggested that a *lack of supportive relationships* may be as detrimental as excessively involved, hostile relationships. Unfortunately this finding has not been followed up in the later studies, although evidence for the importance of a supportive relationship has been reported by other researchers (Kayton, Beck, & Koh, 1976).

This study left many questions unanswered. In particular, the components of "emotional involvement" were not clear; nor was the relationship between the patient's behavior disturbance and the level of relatives' emotionality. The nature of contacts between the patient and relatives and its effect on relapse risk was not evaluated, nor were the effects of medication. The measures that had been employed were crude, global ratings based on commonsense notions rather than theories of family stress.

Another study was planned to answer some of these questions and to refine the measurement techniques (Brown, Birley, & Wing, 1972). An extensive family interview had been developed to measure the emotional expression and attitudes of family members (Brown & Rutter, 1966). This semistructured interview became known as the Camberwell Family Interview (CFI). The interview was standardized and showed acceptable levels of interrater reliability on most of the scales. The major task of the interview was to measure the feelings expressed toward a spouse or child (e.g., warmth or criticism). Other ratings included reports of activities and events in the home (e.g., leisure activity, arguments), and overall ratings of relationships (e.g., marital tension).

The CFI was used to elicit responses from a relative that dealt with the impact of the patient's illness on various aspects of family life, such as the participation of family members in household tasks, the frequency of irritability and quarreling, and the amount of contact between the patient and the rest of the family. The relative's behavior in the interview situation was observed and the spontaneous feelings he or she expressed about family members was noted, especially about the patient's actions during the 3 months preceding the interview. Emphasis was placed on the vocal aspects of speech in the measurement of expressed emotion. Tone, pitch, rhythm, and intensity of the emotion with which a comment was made was considered in the ratings in addition to the specific emotional content. Raters listened carefully to audio-taped recordings before making their ratings. The training of raters was extensive and guidelines were provided so that high levels of interrater agreement were achieved. However, apart from the consistency of reports of two family members, no attempt was made to validate these scales in terms of observable characteristics of interactive behavior between family members or of actual performance in the home.

In the 1972 study the CFI was administered to the relatives of patients diagnosed as having schizophrenia. They were conducted with each household member separately prior to the patient's discharge and 9 months after discharge; a briefer, joint interview with the patient and his or her family was conducted soon after discharge. The ratings of emotional response are summarized in Table 2-1. The index of expressed emotion (EE) made at the initial relative interview proved to be the best single predictor of symptomatic outcome during the 9-month follow-up period. Relapse of florid symptoms of schizophrenia occurred in 58% of patients who returned to households where one or more members were rated as "high EE" compared to a 16% relapse rate in patients living in "low-EE" households.

The EE index was made up predominantly of relatives who made frequent critical comments. No overall association between dissatisfaction or warmth and relapse was noted, although warmth appeared to be an added protection for persons living in low-EE households and dissatis-

TABLE 2-1. *Summary of Expressed-Emotion Rating Criteria from the Camberwell Family Interview*

---

1. *Critical comments about family members.* These are statements of resentment, disapproval, or dislike. In addition, any comment adjudged expressed with critical intonation may be included irrespective of content.

2. *Hostility.* Hostility is adjudged to be present if a remark is made that indicates personal criticism. This is criticism for what a person *is* rather than for what he or she *does.* Excessive, generalized criticism of the kind "He's the worst in the world!" is likewise rated as hostility.

3. *Dissatisfaction.* These are ratings of dissatisfaction with a person's instrumental role behavior. They may be based on critical or hostile remarks, but it is possible for subjects to be highly dissatisfied without expressing this in a critical or hostile manner.

4. *Warmth.* This is based on the expression of warmth in terms of positive comments and voice tone regardless of negative feelings that may be expressed during the interview.

5. *Emotional overinvolvement.* This measures unusually marked concern about a person. It is based on feelings expressed during the interview and reported behavior outside it. Expression of constant worrying about minor matters; overprotective attitudes and intrusive behavior are major components of this scale.

6. *Index of relatives' expressed emotion (EE).* An overall rating of *high* expressed emotion is based on the presence of one or more of the following features:
    a. Seven or more critical comments[a]
    b. Marked emotional overinvolvement
    c. Presence of hostility
    The absence of these features constitutes *low* expressed emotion.

Note. See Brown, Birley, and Wing (1972, pp. 243–244).

[a]The frequency of critical comments employed as a criterion has varied in subsequent studies.

faction appeared to increase the relapse risk in high-EE households. Work impairment and behavior disturbance appeared to predispose to EE in the household, but they were not strongly associated with relapse themselves. Thus, it was concluded that the EE index was the best single predictor of relapse.

Other variables that increased the risk of relapse were being male, being single, and having first-rank symptoms of schizophrenia. A lower relapse rate was found in patients who spent less than 35 hours a week in contact with their relatives, who took regular neuroleptic medication, and who had previously rejected admission to the hospital. No adequate explanation was offered for the high relapse rate of single, male patients. Drug therapy appeared to offer partial protection for relapse in the high-

EE group but appeared to be of little value in the low-EE patients—more than half the sample. However, the "no drugs" classification is a misnomer for "irregular" drug taking—a very different contingency. Subsequent studies have suggested that *irregular* drug taking may be a predictor of outcome independent of its pharmacological component. Two studies have found that irregular ingestion of placebos was as predictive of relapse as irregular ingestion of active drugs (Falloon, Watt, & Shepherd, 1978a; Schooler, Levine, Severe, Brauzer, DiMascio, Klerman, & Tuason, 1980). The ability to adhere rigidly to a daily tablet-taking regimen may be a marker of cognitive vulnerability that predicts relapses of florid symptoms.

The major criticism of this study is the manner in which "relapse" was rated. In most instances this was associated with admission to hospital when it was assumed that an increase in florid symptoms of schizophrenia had occurred. A PSE interview was conducted to confirm the presence of these symptoms. However, PSE interviews were not conducted at discharge from hospital to establish the baseline level of symptoms. Half the patients are reported as having "no schizophrenic symptoms" throughout the 9-month follow-up period. This is a very high proportion, despite a rather broad diagnosis that included patients with probable affective disorder diagnoses (DSM-III). The lack of serial assessment of mental status by research staff leads one to suspect that many more patients may have displayed florid symptoms that, owing to their social withdrawal or lack of associated behavioral disturbance, did not lead to major social crises. The finding that a reluctance to be hospitalized was associated with fewer "relapses" may indicate that symptomatic patients who successfully avoided hospitalization through denial of their symptoms and/or social withdrawal were not reported as relapses. Successful avoidance and denial behavior may characterize low-EE patients and their relatives and contribute to a reduction in morbidity without necessarily modifying the psychopathology.

Further support for this notion is provided in the discussion about the benefits of social withdrawal. A high level of involvement of the patient in family social and leisure activities appeared to be associated with relapse in single patients. Many patients characteristically withdraw when florid symptoms reappear and are much less likely to be considered to have relapsed than those who display their florid psychopathology in a more public and embarrassing manner. In research that explores interactions between social and illness variables, it is crucial to avoid any possible confounds between measures of the dependent variables. Frequent independent assessment of symptom severity is essential to avoid excessive focus on episodes of *social* crises—for example, hospital admission (Falloon, Marshall, Boyd, Razani, & Wood-Siverio, 1983). A further weakness of the study was a lack of data on the social outcome of the patients. Relapse of florid schizophrenia is often a relatively minor feature in the course of the illness. A more important measure is the social functioning of the individual. High EE might be a positive factor in sustaining a high level of social rehabilitation; low EE may foster withdrawal and apathy. Brief relapses may be a small price to pay for increased quality of life.

Brown and his colleagues explored other determinants of the relatives' expressed emotion. In addition to a poor work history and previous behavior disturbance, they found that parents who were socially isolated and who depended on the patient for much of their social interaction showed higher expressed emotion than those with greater contact with other relatives, friends, and acquaintances. This was not true for married patients in whom EE was highest where their spouses had more social contacts. Thus, although social networks may play an important part, a large network is not necessarily optimal. The quality of social contacts for the patient and his or her relatives, including the ratio of support provided to stress involved in the 'supportive' relationship, may be the crucial determinant.

Expressed emotion levels at the follow-up assessment (either at readmission to hospital or at 9 months) were substantially reduced. Critical remarks were much less frequent, particularly where the clinical status of the patient had improved. This lack of stability suggested that the criticism component was situation-specific, rather than an enduring characteristic. In addition, a low rate of criticism was evident in the joint family interview shortly after discharge. Questions of how high EE was transacted in the family setting and the process through which the risk of relapse was enhanced remained unanswered. Brown concluded that high EE is an index of family tension that leads to increased arousal and subsequent appearance of symptoms. Recent studies of physiological changes in the presence of a high-EE relative support this hypothesis. High arousal levels are maintained in the presence of high-EE relatives but dissipate after relatively brief contact with low-EE relatives (Tarrier, Vaughn, Lader, & Leff, 1979; Sturgeon, Kuipers, Berkowitz, Turpin, & Leff, 1981). The *absence* of high-EE attitudes appears to exert a calming effect upon the overaroused individual. However, it is not clear what attributes of the low-EE family members contribute to this calming effect and whether relatives and other caregivers can be taught to exhibit these apparently beneficial behaviors. The exquisite sensitivity of persons suffering from schizophrenia to individuals in their social environment illustrates the extraordinary difficulties faced by these individuals and their families in coping with everyday social intercourse.

Despite the complexity of this issue, research interest has remained high. Christine Vaughn and Julian Leff further refined the measurement of expressed emotion and reduced the interviewing time from 3–4 hours to a more manageable 1–2 (Vaughn & Leff, 1976a). They examined the relapse rates of definite schizophrenics over a 9-month postdischarge period. The CFI was conducted only after patients were hospitalized. To test Brown's suggestion that the EE index might not be specific to schizophrenia and might effectively predict the outcome of other psychiatric conditions, a cohort of hospitalized neurotic depressives was followed in an identical fashion. The results were very similar to the 1972 study and confirmed the association between EE and florid relapse (see Figure 2-1). Depressives appeared even more sensitive to the criticism component, which was highly predictive of relapse of depression when two or more critical remarks were made by a relative (Vaughn & Leff, 1976b).

The "protection" against schizophrenic relapse afforded by regular medication and reduced contact with the high-EE relatives was again evident (see Figure 2-2). When data from the 1972 study were combined, an additive benefit was noted for low-contact and *regular* drug-taking patients who had a relapse rate of 15%—comparable to that of the low-EE group, who again did not appear to benefit from *regular* medication (compared to irregular or "intermittent" drug taking). A 2-year follow-up of the patients with schizophrenia indicated that low-EE patients did derive benefit from regular medication in the second year after discharge whereas the benefits for high-EE patients appeared to dissipate with time (Leff & Vaughn, 1981). It is clearly premature to draw conclusions about

FIGURE 2-1. *Family "expressed emotion."*

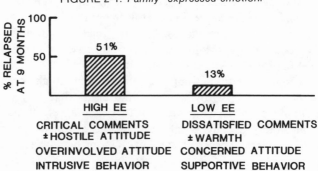

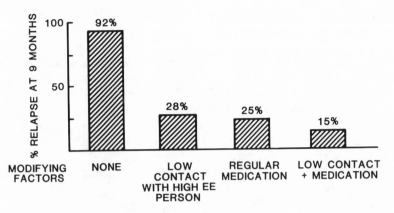

FIGURE 2-2. *Modifying factors.*

the significance of long-term drug treatment in these patients, and further prospective studies are necessary to clarify these issues.

Unfortunately, in an effort to closely replicate the earlier study, Vaughn and Leff (1976b) neglected to correct any of the criticisms associated with that work. The causal link between relatives' experienced emotion and relapse of schizophrenia is strongly emphasized despite the correlational nature of the study. Again a strong *association* is evident, but in the absence of experimental design a conclusion of causality is not justified.

The nature of these emotional responses was examined through a detailed content analysis of the audio-taped interviews of the relatives of schizophrenic patients (Vaughn, 1977). Vaughn noted the same tendency for social withdrawal reported by parents in the earlier studies of Brown. Difficulties in everyday conversations as well as discussion of more intimate thoughts and feelings were reported in patients regardless of the household tension. While low-EE relatives accepted this lack of conversation behavior, and detached relationships, high-EE parents tended to express their frustration with this behavior and their desire to change it. Often these social inadequacies were lifelong and did not appear related to symptoms of the illness, although withdrawal tended to be exacerbated during episodes.

Overall, low-EE relatives tended to remain strikingly calm, even in the face of extremely bizarre behavior including overt threats of personal violence. They tended to view the patient as having an illness that he or she could not help. They showed understanding and support, but were accepting of the situation. They were seldom intrusive in attempts to hasten change in the patient's behavior.

On the other hand, high-EE relatives tended to respond to behavioral deviance in the patient in a more expected fashion. In some cases, parents (especially mothers) were excessively indulgent and self-sacrificing in a noncontingent, overinvolved manner. Despite gross antisocial behavior, these parents tended to be accepting, sometimes in the face of conflict with their spouse, who took a more critical stance. Despite the apparent concern and caring expressed, patients tended to resent the patronizing behavior of their overinvolved parents. Patients often showed an extreme dependence on the overinvolved parent with few outside interests. Parents tended to lack objectivity in viewing the patient and his or her illness. They appeared bewildered and distressed, and tended to worry endlessly about the patient. Such parents tended to search for explanations for the patient's condition, and often blamed themselves for the illness.

The critical response tended to be more commonly expressed toward a son than a daughter and tended to focus on long-standing faults rather than features of the illness. Exacerbations of these irritating behaviors were seen as "bad behavior" rather than "symptoms." The patient was blamed for his or her faults with little allowance made for having a handicapping condition. Criticism and overinvolvement tended to be worse at times of crisis, when tension rose rapidly. Low-EE families tended to cope in a more matter-of-fact way with effective problem solving among family members.

These ineffective coping mechanisms were not found in all families. In one-third no critical remarks were expressed, and two-thirds of the mothers were not emotionally overinvolved. Mothers tended to be over-involved more often than fathers, but this pattern was not universal. Thus, patterns of family emotional expression tended to vary substantially with no one pattern predominating. Moreover, half the families showed the remarkably tolerant low-EE patterns. With excessive attention paid to the "noxious" family environment, researchers have neglected to examine those families that provide a benign, supportive milieu. Much may be learned from their experiences and coping techniques that could be of value to the therapist.

All these studies reported to this point have been conducted in the London suburb of Camberwell with an Anglo-Saxon lower- and middle-class population. It could be argued that this phenomenon is biased to that subculture. However, a replication study conducted with Caucasians in southern California has again confirmed the strong association be-tween EE and florid relapse. In this study an attempt was made to refine the measurement of relapse through the use of specific rating scale criteria based on changes from the severity of symptoms at discharge (Vaughn, Snyder, Jones, Freeman, & Falloon, 1984). Of note was the finding that the expressed emotion index was predictive of relapse even when the relative was not living with the relatives after discharge from the hospital. This result is not readily explained, and suggests that the expressed-emotion measure remains a crude tool that may reflect more than one variable that is predictive of relapse. Further transcultural replication studies with mixed ethnic populations are being conducted in Pittsburgh, Rochester, Denmark, and India. The results to date show less consistent patterns of emotional response and relapse than in the studies emanating directly from the London group.

Replication studies provide an indication of the robust relationship between emotional responses of family members and relapse of schizophrenia. But what exactly do these attitudes expressed in an interview reflect in everyday family living? It is presumed that emotional responses expressed to the interviewer in the Camberwell Family Interview are a reflection of how the family member responds to the patient in the interpersonal transactions of daily life. A pilot study of 15 high-EE and five low-EE families indicated that emotional responses in observed discussions of family problems appeared to correspond with attitudes expressed in the CFI (Doane, Miklowitz, Goldstein, & Falloon, 1981). Families characterized by highly critical attitudes were observed to make more critical remarks in the discussion of family problems than low-EE or highly overinvolved families. Families that were high on the emotional overinvolvement scale and low on criticism made significantly more intrusive remarks, such as telling the patient what he or she thinks or feels (Figure 2-3). More definitive studies of the relationship between expressed-emotion attitudes and critical and intrusive behavior are currently in progress at the Family Laboratory of Doane and Goldstein at UCLA. These studies appear to show more complex relationships between family attitudes and observed behavior. However, the observed patterns of critical and intrusive interaction appear to be stable over time in the absence of any specific family intervention. This contrasts with the findings of the earlier interview studies that found a tendency for the attitudes expressed, particularly criticism, to moderate with time.

CONCLUSIONS

The onset of a chronic, relapsing illness in a family is a major source of unremitting stress for every member of the family. This is engendered not merely by concern about current symptoms and handicaps, but also by

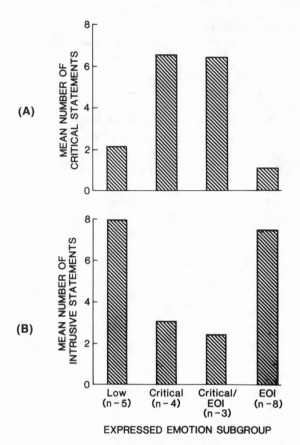

FIGURE 2-3. *Critical comments (A) and intrusive statements (B) expressed in direct interaction by mothers in different EE subgroups.*

the fear of future exacerbations throughout the symptom-free state. When these symptoms include bizarre, incomprehensible patterns of behavior, these concerns are heightened and at times become an intolerable burden to family members. It is evident that the mental health services focus on the patient's condition but generally provide relatively little functional support to other family members to assist them in coping with the day-to-day management of the illness. The resources of the family in terms of providing support for effective treatment and social rehabilitation are seldom utilized. Such neglect leads to "burn out" in the families, and in some cases to rejection of the patient.

Where tolerance for the patient's behavior is low and family stress is high, the rate of rehospitalization is high. Such families have little potential to cope with even minor behavior disturbance in the patient. On the other hand, where a high degree of tolerance and a more matter-of-fact attitude toward the patient's social deviance is evident, the frequency of major symptomatic exacerbations appears to be diminished. However, it is not clear how these reported overburdened and rejecting feelings are translated into actual family interaction. It is probable that at times of social crisis, the index patient becomes the family scapegoat, especially when his or her behavior is overtly disturbed. Overemotional responses at this time would seem to mediate against effective problem solving and stress reduction. Hospital admission for the patient is an obvious, short-term solution to reducing family tension, but seldom accomplishes long-term stress reduction. The latter seems feasible when the resolution of ambient family stress can be achieved. Training patients and their families in the management of schizophrenia, including not only the handling of symptomatic exacerbations but also the promotion of healthy social functioning and coping ability of all family members, is the objective of a comprehensive family management program.

CHAPTER 3

STRESS, COPING, AND SCHIZOPHRENIA

OVERVIEW

The psychosocial study of the role of the family in schizophrenia has emphasized the negative aspects of the family support system. The focus has rested on the genetic transmission of vulnerability to schizophrenia, pathogenesis resulting from patterns of "deviant" communication or suboptimal child rearing, complaints about the burden of caring for a disabled person, or critical and overinvolved attitudes of relatives associated with increased florid symptoms. The overall message concerning family involvement with schizophrenia has been overwhelmingly negative—so much so that family support systems have been universally considered untenable and patients have been removed and placed in often grossly inadequate residential care programs (Lamb & Goertzel, 1971; Lamb, 1979). A reassessment of the literature reveals that these detrimental features are present (at least to a severe degree) in no more than half the families studied. Most families of the mentally ill provide excellent support systems with minimal assistance from mental health services. It would appear that one of the greatest natural resources for the care of the mentally ill in our society has been unappreciated, maligned, and poorly utilized by mental health programs. The economic and social cost of this mismanagement has been enormous.

In this chapter we will attempt to redefine the role of the family as a major potential support system upon which the rehabilitation of schizophrenia can be readily shaped. This idea is not new. Kraepelin (1913) advocated early discharge of patients to their families once the most disturbing features of schizophrenia had diminished. He expressed his surprise that "more difficult patients behave themselves at home surprisingly well" (p. 281). He considered that prolonged institutional care blunted the intellect and sapped motivation, and he advocated work programs to prevent such deterioration. His observation about the good

behavior of disturbed patients in the home environment has been noted in
the more recent expressed-emotion studies in which researchers have
wondered at the tolerant attitudes of many family members even in the
face of severe symptoms of the illness. The capacity of family members for
compassionate care and assistance in the rehabilitation of their less fortunate members remains largely unexploited in the mental health field.
This potential is further explored in this chapter as we move from
consideration of the deficits of the families of persons who succumb to
schizophrenic illnesses to the positive assets of the family support system.

Our major assumption is that schizophrenia is a stress-induced,
neurophysiological abnormality that can be effectively managed, with
minimal morbidity, through application of well-established treatment
methods. These usually involve psychosocial and pharmacological interventions in various combinations, including, on occasion, the exclusive
use of psychosocial approaches. The heterogeneity of management is a
feature of all medical practice, with less invasive psychosocial interventions taking priority over drug and surgical methods as the first level of
treatment. Bed rest and dietary support remain the primary treatment for
acute tuberculosis or coronary thrombosis, and regulation of blood glu-
cose through diet and exercise is the basis for the treatment of diabetes.
Congenital disorders such as phenylketonuria can be corrected by adherence to a specific diet, enabling profound mental retardation to be
prevented. Drugs provide secondary support in certain instances and may
enhance the body's attempts to reconstitute. The development of new
drugs and their promotion by the manufacturers tend to obscure these
basic tenets of medical practice and at least temporarily diminish the
stature of the less profitable and less dramatic psychosocial procedures.
Schizophrenia has not been immune to these phenomena. Indeed, much
of the improved prognosis of schizophrenia that has been attributed to
the development of the neuroleptic drugs appeared to precede the use of
these drugs and to be associated with the social rehabilitation strategies
that accompanied deinstitutionalization.

THE STRESS–DIATHESIS MODEL OF SCHIZOPHRENIA

Psychosocial interventions in schizophrenia are predicated upon the
stress–diathesis paradigm. What evidence do we have to support the
stress–diathesis model of schizophrenia? To date there is only suggestive
evidence to indicate that stress *causes* schizophrenia. However, two
sources of stress have been examined for their effects on the course of
schizophrenia: family tension, and life events. The former has been dis-

cussed at length in the previous chapter. Consistent findings of poorer prognosis for patients who return to a family environment characterized by a lack of functionally supportive attitudes after treatment of a florid episode has suggested that intrafamilial stress may be implicated in the course of the illness. Unfortunately the focus of much of this research has been upon major crises in the long-term management. Regrettably, the relationship between day-to-day levels of family tension and the severity of symptoms has not been demonstrated. It may be a reasonable assumption that the fluctuations in family tension common to most family milieus are associated with parallel fluctuations of symptoms. However, while this may be the case for persons with persistent florid symptoms (delusions, hallucinations, thought interference), many patients are symptom-free for long periods. In such cases a threshold model has been hypothesized (Zubin & Spring, 1977). In this model symptoms appear when a specific level of stress is attained. In low-tension families this threshold is seldom exceeded by intrafamilial stressors. In high-tension households the everyday ups and downs of family stress may at times exceed the symptom threshold and result in florid symptoms.

While family tension levels undoubtedly contribute to a person's baseline of ambient stress, other stressors that arise from extrafamilial sources may be equally potent contributors. The impact of life events on the course of schizophrenia has been explored in several studies. Kraepelin (1913) observed that many cases of spontaneous remission were terminated by major incidents in a person's life. However, E. Bleuler (1911) adopted a less sanguine view of "psychic etiology." Although he acknowledged the association between episodes of schizophrenia and unpleasant events, he believed that the illness probably preceded the psychic trauma. This issue remains to be clarified to this day.

Two case-control studies have found an excess of life events reported by persons in the period preceding the onset of an episode of florid schizophrenia that resulted in hospital admission. One study was conducted in London by Brown and Birley (1968) and the other by Jacobs and Myers (1976) in New Haven, Connecticut. In the London study, newly admitted cases of acute schizophrenia were interviewed with the PSE to confirm their diagnosis and subsequently were questioned in detail about life changes in the 3 months prior to the onset of their current episode. Only patients who could date the onset of florid symptoms accurately and within 3 months of their hospital admission were included. This excluded more than half of the potential candidates who met the diagnostic criteria. Half the patients were experiencing their first admission to the hospital, and a third were experiencing their first episode of schizophrenia. A control group of local employees were given the same interview concerning life events. A life event was considered to be any incident that would be likely to produce emotional reaction in most people in the community. Desirable as well as undesirable events were sampled on the basis that both often required considerable readjustment (e.g., marriage, divorce, job promotions and demotions). There was a significantly higher incidence of life events in the 3-month period prior to onset of florid episode of schizophrenia than in a comparable period in the controls. Furthermore most of this excess was concentrated in the 3-week period immediately preceding the onset of the episode. This finding remained after events that could have been brought about as a direct or indirect result of disturbance in the person's behavior had been excluded.

This finding of an independent life event closely preceding the onset of an episode of schizophrenia was replicated by Leff and his colleagues (1973) in a study of long-acting neuroleptic drugs in the prevention of relapse. Patients who were taking placebo medication were less likely to experience a major independent event in the 5 weeks before onset of a relapse, whereas those on active drugs almost without exception experienced a life event preceding relapse. It was concluded that relapse was precipitated by day-to-day problems in the placebo group, but required a greater level of provocation in those taking regular medication. A similar protective effect for medication had been noted in the earlier London study (Birley & Brown, 1970). Leff's study was conducted with outpatients who were surveyed for life events at the point of relapse. The argument that life events predict hospitalization, but not symptom exacerbation per se, can be somewhat countered by this study where many patients who relapsed were not admitted.

The New Haven study consisted of sampling persons at their first admission for schizophrenia. Sixty-two patients, diagnosed using a much broader definition of schizophrenia than Brown and Birley, completed an interview concerning their experience of any of 58 life events during the 1 year prior to the onset of their illness. Onset was defined as a combination of occurrence of symptoms and change in social functioning. Unlike the London study, cases with insidious onset were included, making the pinpointing of the beginning of the illness extremely difficult. The schizophrenics showed a higher total of life events over the 1 year than a matched, normal, control group. However, there was no significant difference between schizophrenics and controls when events that could have been caused by a person's own behavior were excluded. Events associated with the families of cases occurred more often in the schizophrenic group, supporting the view that family stress may be associated with the onset of schizophrenia. The only independent event found more often in the schizophrenic cohort was the death of a pet. The dating of events was stratified into two 6-month periods. Events were more frequently reported in the 6 months nearest the onset. However, this may have been due to more complete recall of recent events. The equivalent time stratification in the control group was not reported. Thus, the London studies were not substantially supported by these data. Jacobs and Myers concluded that life events probably play only a marginal role in the onset of schizophrenia, but may contribute in precipitating the onset. This view was expressed earlier by Brown and his colleagues (1973), who suggested that life events served merely to trigger the onset of an episode of schizophrenia that would have occurred eventually in the absence of a precipitating life event.

In a study of chronic schizophrenic patients in the community, Schwartz and Myers (1977) suggested that life events may have a more substantial role on the neurotic symptoms frequently associated with schizophrenia than on the schizophrenic phenomenology. Anxiety, depression, and somatic preoccupation appeared to be associated with life events. They concluded that life events may contribute to the development of episodes of schizophrenia, or to increased morbidity, through increasing the vulnerability or ambient stress level as a consequence of increasing the severity of neurotic symptoms.

All these studies have suffered from major methodological weaknesses inherent in retrospective designs. Until prospective studies have been conducted, the relationship between life events and exacerbation of schizophrenic symptoms must remain tentative. Support for the relationship between life changes and schizophrenic episodes is provided by the observations of clinicians. Early attempts at social and vocational rehabilitation of institutionalized chronic schizophrenics led to relapse of florid symptoms in patients who had been reported in remission for years (Wing, Bennett, & Denham, 1964). This phenomenon was less evident when changes were introduced more gradually with careful preparation at each stage. High levels of physiological arousal tended to be a marker of vulnerability in these often withdrawn patients (Venables, 1964). Additional environmental stimulation tended to increase arousal further and was associated with cognitive decompensation.

Another series of studies has noted the high incidence of schizophreniform conditions associated with immigration. As early as 1932, Ødegaard noted this phenomenon in Norwegian immigrants to the United States (Ødegaard, 1932). However, the issue of whether immigrants' groups tended to include many persons predisposed to mental illness has not yet been clarified. A wide range of stresses may be associated with immigration. As with the overstimulating rehabilitation stresses, the contingencies surrounding this social upheaval, such as the quality of planning, preparation, and reception in new culture, may determine the level of stress for each individual.

Common sense dictates that the association between potentially stressful event and the resulting stress it causes a person is variable. The same event may affect different persons in quite distinctive ways. This will include the person's previous experience at handling the situation, as well as his or her cognitive appraisal of its threatening qualities. For example, a person who has never lost a job before, and believes that he or she will never find another, will experience greater stress than a person who has lost many jobs and cheerfully anticipates finding a better one next time. In addition, the coping resources of the individual and his or her social environment may serve to mediate the effects of any potential stress. While clinicians seldom doubt the effects of stressful events on the course of the major mental illnesses, they are mindful of the relatively poor correlation between such events and major exacerbations. Life events cannot be considered independent from other sources of stress in the patient's environment including schizophrenic illness. Clearly a multifactorial model is required to examine the relationships between stress, and symptoms and social functioning.

It can be hypothesized that stressors are compounded in an additive fashion. The overall level of stress that a person experiences from *all sources* provides a more reliable indicator of his or her vulnerability to an exacerbation of schizophrenia than a mere sampling of major life events. In some cases, the everyday stress of living in an overly tense family relationship or coping with a particularly unpleasant work situation may be more stressful than dealing with a major life event. A high level of family tension may require a much smaller increment in stress from extrafamilial sources to precipitate an exacerbation, whereas a low level of family tension may protect the individual from being overwhelmed by substantial life events (see Figures 3-1 and 3-2). In families where a high level of ambient stress persists, everyday stresses such as a minor illness or an argument with a friend may precipitate an exacerbation of symptoms; whereas when ambient stress is low only a major event such as a death of a family member or breakup of an important relationship will overwhelm the individual. This proposition was supported in an examination of the impact of life events on high- and low-tension households. Leff and Vaughn (1980) found that patients living in high-tension households were less likely to have their episodes of schizophrenia precipitated by *major* life events than patients who lived in low-tension families. In high-tension households everyday stresses were sufficient triggers of symptom episodes. More than two-thirds of the episodes of schizophrenia in low-tension

FAMILIES AND SCHIZOPHRENIA

families were preceded by major life events in the 3 months before onset. As in the earlier Brown and Birley study these events tended to be clustered in the 3 weeks immediately before onset. This study suggests the need to account for ambient stressors when examining the impact of life events. Further studies are necessary to define this interaction more precisely.

Serban (1975) attempted to measure ambient stress in acute and chronic schizophrenics and normals living in New York City. He defined stress in terms of "an imbalance between environmental demands and the respondent's ability to meet that demand successfully" (p. 397). He measured the stress experienced by each individual in relation to 21 dimensions of social functioning, independent of the level of performance in these areas. He found that stress was higher in chronic schizophrenics than in those with acute conditions, and that the schizophrenic group as a whole suffered significantly greater total stress than matched normals. Chronic schizophrenics had significantly higher stress than normals in almost all categories of family, social, and interpersonal functioning. These differences were less prominent for the acute patients, who showed significantly less stress than their chronic counterparts on most areas examined. The question of whether these stress levels contribute to the

FIGURE 3-1. *Psychosocial factors in relapse: I.*

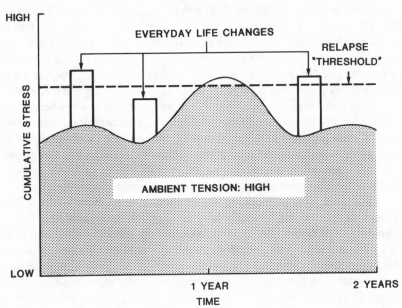

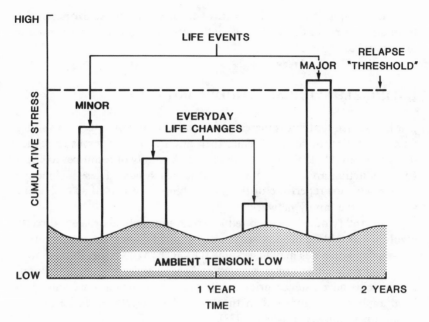

FIGURE 3-2. *Psychosocial factors in relapse: II.*

chronicity of the disorder or *vice versa* was not addressed in this study. However, the implications for community treatment are clear. In order to improve the quality of life of persons with chronic schizophrenia, re-habilitation programs that are effective in reducing ambient stress levels and which enable these individuals to cope with everyday living are essential.

A second part of this study examined the significance of factors that appeared to precipitate readmission to hospital. One-third of both chronic and acute patients reported clear precipitating factors for hospital ad-mission. Acute patients reported more stress associated with family inter-action, sexual difficulties, friends, and work. Chronic patients ascribed stressors from welfare and finances, parents, friends, and sex as precipi-tants of readmission. Serban concluded that these data raised doubts about the oft-cited association between precipitating events and a good prognosis. However, the study was not related to the onset of an exacer-bation, but to the phenomenon of hospital admission. Stress in the home environment appeared to contribute to more frequent hospital admission. As we have previously noted, a family already overburdened may experi-ence any added stress, even when minor, as overwhelming, and seek to extrude a major source of their stress—the relative with schizophrenia—from the household through the socially acceptable and available strategy of hospital admission.

COPING BEHAVIOR AS A MODIFYING FACTOR

If it is assumed that stress increases the vulnerability of a person to suffer an exacerbation of schizophrenia, then any factor that serves to reduce this stress should likewise prevent relapses. A variety of resources to effect stress reduction are available within the family system. These include the coping behavior repertoire of the patient himself or herself as well as the support of the family network.

The ability of a patient to reduce stress in which he or she is directly involved has seldom been systematically studied. Research on premorbid personality attributes may have some relevance to this issue. Persons who possessed only limited interpersonal and social skills and led a predominantly schizoid existence prior to the onset of schizophrenia tended to have a poorer prognosis than those who had developed more mature social functioning (Goldstein, 1978).

The attainment of higher levels of social competence as indicated by variables such as educational and work attainment and marital status similarly predicted a better outcome (Zigler & Phillips, 1961). This latter finding may help explain the better prognosis found in women patients, who generally experience the onset of schizophrenia when they have reached adult maturity in contrast to the onset in early adulthood that is characteristic of male sufferers. Efforts to enhance interpersonal and social functioning through social-skills training (Wallace, Nelson, Liberman, Aitchison, Lukoff, Elder, & Ferris, 1980; Hersen & Bellack, 1976; Falloon, 1978) and vocational rehabilitation (Anthony, Buell, Sharratt, & Althoff, 1972) have sought to build skills that may serve to bolster an individual's ability to cope with major stressors. In some cases this may reduce overdependence on intrusive family relationships.

Another factor that may modify the impact of stress on the symptoms of schizophrenia is the degree of understanding or insight the patient possesses about the nature of the disorder. Many patients learn slowly, through a trial-and-error process, that their symptoms reappear or get worse when they experience excessive stress. Patients who appear to comprehend the nature of their condition and its possible relationship to stress more readily employ self-control strategies to ensure that they are not overwhelmed by stress. Social withdrawal, a coping technique emphasized by Wing and his colleagues (Wing, 1978), is one self-control method that patients employ. To develop effective self-control procedures, it is helpful to be able to recognize prodromal "warning" signals of an impending relapse. Recent studies suggest that a relapse of florid symptoms of schizophrenia is not usually a sudden occurrence, but is usually preceded by a range of neurotic symptoms with characteristic patterns for each patient (Herz & Melville, 1980). Some complain of sleep disturbance, others feel despair and depression, still others become tense, anxious, and confused, or have somatic aches and pains. These symptoms are remarkably similar to those reported by most individuals under stress. It is apparent that if the patient heeds these warning signals and is able to modify his or her current stress that relapse can be averted. Such symptoms may indicate a high level of physiological arousal. Measures of physiological responses after a major life event have shown a hyperaroused state (Tarrier, Vaughn, Lader, & Leff, 1979). In addition to psychosocial coping strategies, this arousal may be dampened by the administration of neuroleptic drugs, or, if drugs are already being taken, by increasing the dosage temporarily as prophylaxis against symptom exacerbation.

Not all sufferers of schizophrenia experience a relapsing course. A substantial proportion have persisting florid symptoms that may diminish but seldom dissipate. In such cases recurrence of symptoms is more rapid. Nevertheless, similar warning signals may be detected and serve as cues for stress-reduction strategies. The prognosis for these persons with persisting symptoms may be appreciably modified by their ability not only to cope with external stressors, but also to cope more effectively with the disruption and stress associated with the symptoms themselves. It seems probable that the manner in which a person copes with a symptom such as auditory hallucinations may determine the disruption and resulting stress that this phenomenon may engender (Falloon & Talbot, 1981). For the patient and the clinician, it matters little whence the stressors arise. Their concern is to modify the impact of all stress. However, that is not to imply that stress should be avoided at all cost. The effects of an understimulating environment on schizophrenia produces even more devastating deterioration of social functioning than an overly stimulating milieu. The chronic defect state characterized by apathy, lack of goals and motivation, and atrophy of social skills and emotional expressiveness is a well-known phenomenon of the long-term institutionalized patient (Wing & Brown, 1970). Similar protection from the stressors of the real world results in similar presentations of "negative" symptoms for understimulating living environments in the community (Lamb & Goertzel, 1971). In terms of quality of life, the risk of occasional relapses may be a small price to pay for rehabilitation that aims to maximize an individual's social functioning. However, the ability to cope with the myriad stresses that may befall any active participant in society is the major challenge not only for those who have already succumbed to mental illness, but also for the remainder, who seek to avoid developing such disorders. Undoubtedly the risk is substantially higher for the victims of schizophrenia, but the principles involved are similar. Those persons with higher levels of social competence have a greater capacity for managing stress, and are therefore less likely to succumb to these effects when they seek to attain their expected levels of social functioning.

FAMILY AND COMMUNITY SUPPORT

The final component of this stress–diathesis model is the support available for the patient from his or her family and community support network. The level of family tolerance has been observed to be a crucial component of the expressed emotion index, with low-EE family members showing exceedingly tolerant attitudes. Similar evidence that a high degree of tolerance for the patient's social deviance tends to reduce the risk of subsequent hospital admission has been reviewed in the previous chapter. However, the focus of most of these studies has been on the more passive coping functions derived from reports of highly accepting attitudes toward the index patient's idiosyncracies. Few studies have examined the *behavior* contingent upon such attitudes.

One uncontrolled study by Tolsdorf (1976) revealed that a lack of problem-solving interaction between family members and the relative with schizophrenia or among other family members resulted in a lack of any intervention until the patient's mental status was severely impaired and a major management crisis, usually involving hospital admission, was inevitable.

There is further evidence that persons with schizophrenia tend to have fewer social contacts than persons with other psychiatric conditions (Hammer, 1964; Cohen & Sokolvsky, 1978; Pattison, de Francisio, & Wood, 1975). Furthermore, much of their social network participation results from contact with close family members. This may be partly explained by the lack of social functioning of many schizophrenics, particularly in work and related activities where many extrafamilial contacts may be a less relevant factor than the quality of such contact in the mediation of stress. On the other hand, social contacts can prove stressful, particularly for persons with poorly developed social skills.

Brown and Harris (1978) found that having one person to confide in on a regular basis was a substantial protection from depression associated with major life events. Nuckolls and her colleagues (1972) found that a high level of psychosocial support moderated the effects of life events on the outcome of pregnancy. Women experienced less complicated pregnancies when they showed positive personality attributes and attitudes toward the pregnancy and when they reported supportive marital, family, and friendship relationships. Andrews, Tennant, Hewson, and Vaillant (1978) found that coping style and support with crises reduced the risk for psychological impairment from 43.3% to 12.8% following a major life event. Coping style was measured in terms of the maturity of ego defense mechanisms reported as the most likely responses to a series of novel interpersonal stressors presented in a multiple-choice questionnaire. Social support was measured in terms of the availability of persons who could assist in a crisis, the quality of neighborhood interaction, and participation in community groups. However, only the measure of crisis support appeared to have an impact on the effects of life stressors. This suggested that the ability to seek appropriate social support at times of crisis may be more crucial than the mere availability of potential supporters. This help-seeking behavior was previously pinpointed by Tolsdorf (1976) in schizophrenics living with their families. The ability to acquire assistance appropriately from the social network may determine admission to hospital of psychiatric patients (Fontana, Marcus, Noel, & Rakusin, 1972). Fontana and his colleagues found evidence that most of the life events occurring in the few months prior to hospital admission appeared to result from inappropriate attempts to seek assistance for life problems, although the events superficially appeared independent of the patient's mental illness.

Research into the nature of the coping behavior of the person with schizophrenia and his or her family and community supports is at an early stage of development. It is too early to draw definitive conclusions about the precise mechanisms that operate to reduce the impact of life stressors. However, it is probable that the presence of potentially supportive individuals in the patient's everyday environment, coupled with an ability for the patient and supporters to communicate their concerns at an early stage, and subsequently to perform effective problem solving to seek out and implement strategies that moderate the stress, may serve to prevent severe exacerbations of the florid symptoms of schizophrenia. Better still, wherever stressors can be predicted prior to their occurrence (e.g., starting work, getting married, moving house) and contingency plans made in anticipation, the stressful impact of life events may be minimized. When patients are living at home and have few intimate contacts in the community, the family appears the most readily available source of such problem-solving potential. Highly critical or intrusively overinvolved attitudes may militate against open communication, and family interventions that promote mutual empathy and nonpossessive warmth may be essential to the problem-solving process in the same manner as it is a prerequisite of a psychotherapeutic relationship (Truax & Carkhuff, 1967). In the absence of a family support system, a therapist who is readily available and possesses the same open communication characteristics of a "close friend" may serve a similar problem-solving function.

In many studies of life events, the major source of stress is the family itself. While we have reviewed stress in terms of events directly affecting the persons most vulnerable to schizophrenia, it is evident that stressful events affecting any member or members of the family may result in stress for other members. Thus, it is important to sample not only the events directly confronting the person with schizophrenia, but also those events impinging on every other household member. While the impact on that person's self-image may be somewhat less when his or her father loses his job than when the patient himself or herself is fired, substantial adaptation may be required, particularly if the father is providing the sole source of family income. The context in which such events occur is an important consideration that has been addressed by George Brown in his life events studies. Other researchers have avoided such idiographic sampling methods and have employed checklists of events that, while adequate for large scale epidemiological studies, are less appropriate in smaller clinical studies where greater precision for measuring stressors is needed.

SUMMARY OF THE STRESS–DIATHESIS MODEL

The simple cause–effect hypothesis offers an oversimplified explanation for the association noted between the occurrence of life stressors and the exacerbation of symptoms of schizophrenia (see Figure 3-3). This effect is not well understood, but our present level of understanding suggests the following:

1. A life event is perceived as stressful by an individual who detects a discrepancy between his or her personal and environmental resources and the amount of adaptation required. Where the ambient life stress is already high, resources for effective coping are limited and a relatively minor stressor may upset the applecart. But where ambient stress is low, a more substantial event may be required to produce the same overall level of stress.

2. Stress is associated with physiological changes in many bodily systems which, when moderately severe, may lead to symptoms such as muscle tension, agitation, and appetite and sleep disturbance. Such non-

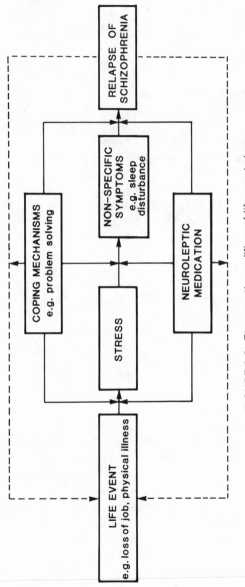

FIGURE 3-3. *Therapeutic modifiers of life-event stress.*

specific "stress" symptoms may serve as "warning signals" to the patient and his or her relatives that an exacerbation of schizophrenia may be imminent.

3. The next step if the stress persists is the recrudescence of schizophrenia.

4. If the stress persists, or is increased by the symptoms of schizophrenia, a vicious cycle may develop and the patient may be at risk of sustaining a chronic course.

5. At each step the combined effectiveness of the individual's coping efforts, including the supportive assistance of his or her family and friends, may lead to effective problem solving with moderation of the effects of the stressor. In addition, preparation prior to the occurrence of any anticipated stressful situation may be undertaken.

6. The physiological changes associated with stress may be moderated by the administration of neuroleptic drugs. Although the precise nature of the drugs in countering stress are not understood, they appear both to act on the autonomic features associated with arousal of the peripheral nervous system and to have a central tranquilizing effect that reduces the cognitive disturbance associated with schizophrenia. The prophylactic effect of taking small doses of neuroleptics in the absence of symptoms of schizophrenia appears to slow down the impact of a life stressor upon the individual, allowing more time for the individual to muster his or her coping resources, including possibly increasing the dosage of his neuroleptic medication.

CONCLUSIONS

It is concluded that stress plays a major role in determining the course of schizophrenia. Stress may arise from both intrafamilial and extrafamilial sources. At times the stressors may be expected (e.g., death of a person who has been seriously ill) or unexpected (e.g., accidental death). Stress may also result from the index patient's persistent symptoms or behavioral disturbance. All these sources of stress contribute to the vulnerability of an individual at any point in time, and if they reach a high level may trigger a symptomatic exacerbation of the illness.

Two factors are considered potential modifiers of this stress. The first is the physiological action of neuroleptic drugs in countering the peripheral arousal and central cognitive disturbance associated with stress. The second is the problem-solving or coping capacity of the index patient and his or her social environment that enables the source of stress to be effectively resolved. This latter method of modifying stress can be achieved through a family intervention method that aims to reduce ambient stressors associated with day-to-day living in the family and community, and in addition, to anticipate and intervene at the earliest possible time to resolve the stress associated with life events. The major component of this intervention is the enhancement of problem-solving effectiveness of the index patient and his or her household members through behavioral family therapy. The family intervention is conducted within a framework of community management of schizophrenia that includes optimal neuroleptic drug therapy and psychosocial rehabilitation methods where these are indicated as the best solutions for specific problems. In the next chapter, we will review these basic components of community care that provide the structure upon which family management has been developed.

CHAPTER 4

THE COMMUNITY MANAGEMENT
OF SCHIZOPHRENIA

The goals for community management of schizophrenia have evolved
from those of the 1950s and 1960s, when the majority of persons suffering
from this disorder spent much of their lives warehoused in suburban or
rural asylums where they were provided with custodial care and institution-
based work therapy. Since that time the locus of treatment has shifted
dramatically to community settings. This move has been accompanied by
vigorous attempts to minimize the florid symptoms of schizophrenia, and
to rehabilitate afflicted individuals to normal social functioning. The
importance of effective control of life stress is the basis for the psychosocial interventions that have assisted this process, and the advent of drug
treatment that not only promotes symptom reduction in acute exacerbations, but also appears to have a prophylactic effect in preventing subsequent exacerbations, has contributed to the substantial improvement in
the outlook for persons who have developed schizophrenia in the last
quarter-century. Nonetheless, schizophrenia remains a crippling disorder
with a "cure" rate that has not changed substantially since the beginning
of the century. Community management is usually long-term and makes
high demands on treatment services and community care givers. In this
chapter we will discuss some of the important components of a community care model for the treatment of schizophrenia. The discussion will
be restricted to components that do not include specific family intervention, which will be discussed in the next chapter. These nonfamilial
components include specific treatment of the illness factor through neuroleptic medication, including the prevention of exacerbations; social rehabilitation to restore social functioning and strengthen social competence; and psychosocial treatment that aims to enhance problem solving
and reduce the impact of stress upon the patient and his or her family
support system.

SPECIFIC TREATMENTS
OF THE SCHIZOPHRENIC ILLNESS

Neuroleptic Medication

Evidence for a *specific* effect of neuroleptic medication on the symptoms of schizophrenia is lacking. While the precise basis for the effectiveness of these drugs in ameliorating the florid delusions, hallucinations, and thought interference of schizophrenia is unknown, their impact in reducing the intensity of the illness is clear (Davis, Schaffer, Killian, Kinard, & Chan, 1980). For many years these drugs, derived from the phenothiazine and butyrophenone molecules, were known as tranquilizers. Their remarkable ability to induce a calming effect on patients in excited psychotic states was readily observed. This resulted in a dramatic change in the milieu of the psychiatric hospital ward. No longer were physical restraints, padded cells, or even locked doors necessary to control hyperactive schizophrenia victims. A similar response was noted in patients with mania.

This calming effect appeared to be somewhat independent of sedation and could be achieved at doses allowing the patient to remain relatively alert and able to participate in social activities. In addition, when administered to socially withdrawn, catatonic patients, a paradoxical activating effect was noted resulting in improved social functioning of these individuals. These apparent contrasts in action appeared to result from a selective effect on the characteristic cognitive disturbances of schizophrenia, including the florid delusions, hallucinations, and thought interference (insertion, withdrawal, and broadcast). Physiological studies have indicated that high levels of arousal may be found in both active and withdrawn cases of schizophrenia and that a reduction to normal levels is contingent upon administration of neuroleptic drugs.

The precise mechanism for the antipsychotic action of these drugs has been difficult to determine because of their large range of actions upon biochemical systems. Chlorpromazine, one of the earliest of these drugs, was developed for use as a hypothermic agent in early open-heart surgery. It is marketed in Europe under the trade name Largactil—a reference to its *large* range of *actions*, which include changes in the central and peripheral nervous system, as well as cardiovascular, gastrointestinal, endocrinological, genitourinary, and dermatological effects.

Thus, while the focus of most biochemical studies has been upon the effects of drugs on neurotransmission in the brain, it is conceivable that the beneficial effects may be at least partially mediated by changes in other systems. Current consensus proposes that the antipsychotic action of neuroleptics is associated with the changes they appear to induce in the neurotransmitter actions of dopamine. Dopamine and noradrenaline are the two principal catecholamines found in the brain. Dopamine is converted into noradrenaline, and it appears to have independent functions in regulating endocrine effects and emotional behavior. An excess of dopamine activity has been postulated in schizophrenia (Snyder, Banerjee, Yamamuro, & Greenberg, 1974). This activity is thought to be reduced by blocking the dopamine receptors by neuroleptic agents. However, it is important to note that the evidence supporting this hypothesis remains speculative and is far from proven. As with many medical treatments, the clinical effectiveness of neuroleptic drugs has been attested long before their precise mode of action has been determined.

Not all symptoms of schizophrenia respond well to neuroleptics. While the florid symptoms of delusions, hallucinations, thought interference, and overactivity respond very well, blunted affect, poverty of thought, and social withdrawal improve to a lesser degree (Goldberg, Klerman, & Cole, 1965). Despite optimal drug therapy, with evidence of compliance and adequate plasma levels, a proportion of patients remain refractory to drug treatment and continue to suffer from florid symptoms of schizophrenia such as auditory hallucinations and persistent delusional beliefs (Simpson & Pi, 1981). However, it is unusual that over a trial of 6 months or more some reduction in the intensity of such symptoms is evident with continued optimal medication. Thus, most patients are able to leave the hospital and return home in at least a partially remitted state.

Continued Medication for Schizophrenia: Prophylaxis

Continuation of neuroleptic drugs after improvement of a florid episode of schizophrenia has been demonstrated to reduce significantly the risk of further hospital admissions and major exacerbations of florid symptoms. A series of double-blind, placebo-controlled studies has provided convincing confirmation of this effect (Davis et al., 1978).

Further evidence has supported the efficacy of neuroleptic drugs in moderating the impact of family and life event stressors (Vaughn & Leff, 1976; Birley & Brown, 1970; Leff et al., 1973). The most parsimonious therapeutic strategy for preventing relapse of schizophrenia would appear to be the provision of adequate continuation of medication, with methods that enhance compliance—for example, minimally effective dosage to minimize side effects, ensuring rapid follow-up of missed clinic appointments with home visiting when necessary; the use of long-acting intramuscular neuroleptics for persistent noncompliance; and the education of the patient and his or her support system about the illness and the rationale for the continuation of medication as prophylaxis.

However, despite evidence of adequate compliance, a substantial proportion of patients relapse while taking medication. A series of recent studies where medication was ensured through intramuscular administration of long-acting neuroleptics has demonstrated that relapse occurs in 30% to 50% of patients in their first year after hospital discharge (Falloon et al., 1978a; Hogarty et al., 1979; Schooler et al., 1980). In addition, the social performance of those who remain symptom-controlled is less than adequate, particularly when receiving the intramuscular preparations (Falloon, Watt, & Shepherd, 1978b). A further limitation of long-term continuation of medication is the occurrence of bothersome and often persistent side effects. These unpleasant effects include a variety of movement disorders, such as slowed, stiff motor behavior, involving gross limb and body movement as well as facial and gestural expression; dystonic muscle spasms; irregular dyskinetic movements of limbs; trunk and orofacial muscle groups; gait disturbances and tremor resembling Parkinson's disease; and general restlessness. Drowsiness, hypotensive episodes, loss of vision, weight gain, skin sensitivity, and feelings of apathy have all been associated frequently with neuroleptics. Some of the neuromuscular disturbances, such as the dyskinesias, have occasionally persisted even when the drug has been discontinued. This has led some researchers to postulate that the long-term use of these drugs, at high doses, may contribute to permanent damage of the basal ganglia of the brain.

It may be concluded that the continuation of neuroleptic drug therapy during the community aftercare of patients who have recovered from acute exacerbations of schizophrenia substantially reduces the risk of subsequent decompensation. However, the protection afforded is only partial, and at least one-third of drug-taking patients relapse over the course of a year. This proportion is not significantly changed by ensuring medication compliance through the intramuscular administration of the drugs. There is evidence to suggest that environmental stressors (both ambient stressors and discrete events) may play a role in precipitating episodes even when the patient is taking optimal doses of medication. The impact of stress is dampened, but not removed entirely. Serious side effects further detract from the benefits of continued therapy, but are usually dose-related. Those that persist while patients are maintained on low doses of the drugs tend to be mild and seldom necessitate complete withdrawal of the drugs. Careful administration of the lowest effective dosage of neuroleptic drugs, accompanied by efforts to maintain compliance, remains the basis of most community treatment approaches for schizophrenia. To date efforts to withdraw the drugs after a year or two of stability of the illness have proved unsuccessful (Hirsch, Gaind, Rohde, Stevens, & Wing, 1973; Falloon, *et al.*, 1978a). Preliminary attempts to use neuroleptic therapy on an intermittent basis in remitted patients appear promising, but definitive studies have not been completed (Herz & Melville, 1980).

PSYCHOSOCIAL INTERVENTIONS
FOR THE TREATMENT OF FLORID SYMPTOMS

Milieu and Psychodynamic Therapy

Neuroleptic drug therapy is the mainstay of treatment of florid symptoms of schizophrenia. However, the social intervention of admission to a hospital has frequently accompanied, and often preceded, drug therapy in the management of acute episodes. In a recent study, Carroll and his colleagues (1980) found that many carefully diagnosed cases of schizophrenia did not require drug therapy to induce definite improvement in the severity of their symptoms. The milieu of the ward combined with well-organized occupational therapy appeared to provide a major therapeutic effect. Removal of the patient from an overburdened home environment at times of exacerbation may help explain this effect. It is important to note that when the patient returns to the same environment upon improvement, a further exacerbation may result unless interventions to reduce the environmental stressors or bolster the patient's coping mechanisms are undertaken prior to his or her return.

Psychodynamic psychotherapy has been employed in the treatment of schizophrenia for over half a century. Sullivan (1962) and Meyer (1948–1952) and their followers (e.g., Fromm-Reichmann, 1948) demonstrated the clinical benefits of long-term psychotherapeutic relationships with chronic schizophrenic patients in mental hospitals. The need for a more flexible approach that emphasized interpersonal relationships rather than early childhood conflicts necessitated substantial changes from traditional psychoanalysis. The focus of therapy became much more problem-oriented, with the therapist and the ward staff becoming a surrogate family for the immature "child" (Sullivan, 1962). The therapeutic community model was developed as a somewhat different method of providing an environment in which the patient could develop more mature coping methods and enhance his or her interpersonal skills (Cumming & Cumming, 1962). The entire inpatient unit functioned in a manner that resembled a large, democratic family system. The distinction between staff and patients was similar to that between parents and children, with increased responsibility and a greater degree of everyday social interaction with the staff being accorded the patients. An extension of the therapeutic community approach was developed by R. D. Laing in London. He viewed the disordered cognitions of schizophrenia as a normal coping response of individuals to an intolerable and abnormal family situation. He provided a crisis unit where the patient and at times the entire family could be supported through acute episodes of schizophrenia. Existential psychotherapists sought to enhance understanding about the meaning of the delusions and hallucinations of the scapegoated relative in a supportive family-like environment (Laing, 1967).

Attempts to validate the effectiveness of these psychotherapeutic approaches have been disappointing. Case reports indicate that they are highly effective in at least some circumstances. However, group design studies necessitate substantial compromises and have not supported their efficacy (Falloon & Liberman, 1983). Methodologically, the soundest study was conducted at Camarillo State Hospital in California by Phillip May (1968). Two hundred and twenty-eight first-admission inpatients were randomly assigned to one of five treatment conditions: (1) individual psychotherapy, (2) individual psychotherapy plus neuroleptic drugs, (3) neuroleptic drugs only, (4) electroconvulsive therapy (ECT), and (5) ward milieu only. Psychotherapy for up to 1 year was found to be no more effective than standard ward milieu on measures of psychopathology, psychological functioning, and length of hospital stay. The two groups of patients receiving drug treatments achieved significantly greater improvements than those receiving only psychotherapeutic treatments; the ECT condition showed an intermediate response. A small, nonsignificant advantage for the addition of psychotherapy to drug treatment was reported. However, although they received expert supervision, the psychotherapists employed were psychiatric residents who had spent a minimum of 6 months in their residency training. It is evident that the psychotherapy of schizophrenia requires substantial expertise, and such inexperienced therapists are unlikely to prove highly effective practitioners of this craft. The precise nature of the psychotherapy varied as did the duration of treatment, with a range of 7 to 87 hours. Under such circumstances individual psychotherapy proved relatively ineffective.

Similar lack of effect for individual psychoanalytic psychotherapy was found in a study that employed experienced therapists over a 2-year period (Grinspoon, Ewalt, & Shader, 1972). Once again, psychotherapy proved effective only when accompanied by neuroleptic drugs. However, chronic hospitalized male patients were employed in this study—a population that could not be considered ideal candidates for a psychodynamic intervention. Although it is possible that a small percentage of persons hospitalized for treatment of schizophrenia may derive worthwhile benefits from psychodynamic therapy, it is evident that such approaches are unlikely to benefit all subjects. Improved social functioning rather than reduction of psychopathology may be more appropriate goals for such interventions. It is also evident that concomitant neuroleptic drugs do not appear to interfere with the process of psychotherapy, but may indeed interact in a potentiating fashion.

Behavioral Psychotherapy

The treatment of persistent florid symptoms with behavioral psychotherapy methods has been reported. Several treatment strategies have shown limited effectiveness in reducing the intensity of hallucinations. The methods employed have been selected after careful pinpointing of the contingencies that appear to trigger and maintain hallucinatory phenomena in individual cases. Techniques have included self-administered aversive stimuli, cognitive restructuring, assertiveness training, and relaxation (Falloon & Talbot, 1981). Despite showing promise that monitoring of hallucinatory experiences and training in a variety of self-control methods may assist the patient to cope more effectively with abnormal perceptions, there are no adequately controlled studies that show how widely these methods can be applied and whether they offer any significant long-term benefits.

Few attempts have been made to modify persistent delusions. A problem-solving approach was employed in one study that attempted to reduce the intensity of fixed beliefs in chronic schizophrenics (Milton, Patwa, & Hafner, 1978). This method produced modest improvements, but was no more effective than merely confronting the patient with the irrationality of his or her beliefs. Other cognitive restructuring approaches have been described, but lack experimental validation for their efficacy (Jacobs, 1980). Operant approaches have proved effective in reducing the time patients spend talking about their delusions (Liberman, 1976). Whether such overt suppression of behavior is accompanied by changes in delusional cognitions is difficult to assess. However, improved interpersonal functioning may lead to significant benefits for the patient regardless of the persistence of delusions or hallucinations. It should be remembered that the aim of treatment is to maximize the *functional capacities* of our patients, not merely to remove symptoms. Psychotherapeutic interventions in the management of florid episodes of schizophrenia may be invaluable in preserving the interpersonal functioning of the individual and expediting the rehabilitation process once the florid symptoms have abated.

PSYCHOSOCIAL INTERVENTIONS
IN COMMUNITY REHABILITATION

It is evident that neuroleptic medication is the most effective specific treatment for the acute symptoms of schizophrenia, and that in low doses it is a highly effective prophylactic against subsequent exacerbations once the florid symptoms have become quiescent. However, psychosocial methods are crucial in the community rehabilitation process. Once freed from the cognitive interference of delusions, hallucinations, or thought interference, persons recovering from an acute episode of schizophrenia may encounter considerable difficulty retracing their steps into their former life roles. As well as the difficulty of performing job or social skills at their premorbid level, they may suffer the negative set accorded those who have suffered a mental illness. Unlike severe physical illness such as heart disease or stroke, schizophrenia is a diagnostic label that seldom engenders sympathy and support among the lay public, or even, regrettably, among the medical profession. This undoubtedly increases the burden individuals carry in their efforts to restore their social status. Psychosocial rehabilitation has focused predominantly upon two areas—(1) work, and (2) interpersonal skills. In this section, we will review interventions in these two areas and examine efforts to develop comprehensive psychosocial intervention programs.

Work Rehabilitation

The belief that work has an important role in recovery from schizophrenia stems not merely from a puritanical work ethic, but from evidence of the predictive value of premorbid occupational attainment in determining the community outcome of patients (Brown et al., 1966; Strauss & Carpenter, 1977) and from clinical evidence that structured daily activities appear to prevent social deterioration and possibly lead to a reduction in some persistent symptoms (Wing & Freudenberg, 1961).

Patients who worked effectively in a stable occupation prior to the onset of schizophrenia frequently have a successful return to work after the acute symptoms have subsided. Those who have not developed competence in an occupation appear less likely to adjust after the onset of the disorder. There is some evidence that good premorbid work status predicts a similarly good prognosis for the recurrence of florid episodes. Everyday work stress as well as major life events associated with the workplace may account in part for this predictive power. Patients living in high-tension households also appear to benefit from the separation from unsupportive family members through escape to a comfortable work environment (Vaughn & Leff, 1976). Thus, it might be hypothesized that interventions that enhance vocational functioning in persons recovering from schizophrenia might serve a therapeutic function. Disappointingly, there is scant evidence to support this proposition. Indeed, there is very little evidence that vocational rehabilitation interventions have any measurable impact on the probability of patients' obtaining employment in the community (Anthony et al., 1972; Griffiths, 1974).

A series of studies with chronic hospitalized schizophrenics in industrial rehabilitation workshops offer a possible explanation for the disappointing impact of many work-therapy programs (O'Connor, Heron, & Carstairs, 1956; O'Connor & Rawnsley, 1959). It was found that individuals with schizophrenia showed gradual but steady increments in their level of production in simple factory-style work tasks. They did not appear responsive to the work incentives generally provided in such work settings, but appeared to improve solely as a function of practice. However, they were highly sensitive to criticism, which led to a falloff in production. A supportive work environment did enhance performance while it was sustained. Nonschizophrenic patients showed more rapid learning of tasks, and responded with enhanced performance to both positive reinforcement and criticism. A further observation was that exhortations to work harder tended to result in an increase of florid symptoms. This may explain the lack of success of "total push" programs for schizophrenia.

These features of schizophrenia that have been observed in sheltered workshop programs would appear to mediate against the success of such individuals in the community job market, where the environment for their optimal performance is seldom met. Attempts to intervene in this process may need either (1) to train the patient to cope with vagaries of the work place, or (2) to restructure the work place to accommodate the idiosyncrasies of the patient. To date we are unaware of programs that have specifically addressed these issues.

In times of economic hardship when unemployment in the general population approaches or exceeds 10%, the prospects for employment of persons who have suffered a major mental illness are reduced. Sheltered workshops in the community offer an important support system for patients and their families. Vocational training programs that specialize in assisting persons with schizophrenia to acquire marketable skills are a much needed resource. Unfortunately, relatively few such services are available, and patients are often faced with the choice between staying at home or attempting unrealistically to enter the competitive job market or high-pressure vocational training courses. Both these alternatives are likely to increase stress and thereby enhance the risk of exacerbation of the illness.

Day Treatment

Day treatment is an important resource for patients with schizophrenia. For patients whose recovery from the acute episode is prolonged, with florid symptoms or cognitive impairments that persist for several months after discharge from the hospital, the day hospital offers a structured program that promotes reconstitution. Patients who are unable to enter employment or training programs, but who benefit from a daily routine of constructive activity, may derive similar benefits. It has been suggested that day treatment programs may benefit any patient who spends a large portion of his or her time in contact with family members who display high "expressed emotion" (Vaughn & Leff, 1976). The day hospital may offer refuge from this family tension—assuming, of course, that the milieu is supportive and not itself a further source of environmental stress. The goals of day treatment are seldom clearly defined, although most provide a program of structured occupational and recreational activities directed toward normalization of community functioning. Treatment programs vary substantially, and empirical evidence suggests that most are not particularly effective in assisting individuals suffering from schizophrenia (Beigel & Feder, 1970; Hogarty, Guy, Gross, & Gross, 1969; Michaux, Chelst, & Foster, 1973).

Margaret Linn conducted a collaborative study of day treatment programs in ten Veterans Administration hospitals (Linn, Caffey, Klett, Hogarty, & Lamb, 1979), and found that some centers treated schizophrenia more effectively than others. The more effective centers were characterized by structured programs that focused more on the community functioning of the patients. Occupational therapy and recreational activities were emphasized more than group and individual psychotherapy. It was concluded that psychotherapeutic relationships proved too intense and were akin to the high emotional relationships found in some families. Centers with poorer outcome, somewhat surprisingly, tended to offer more family counseling, but it was not clear which of these negative features accounted for the detrimental effects. The psychodynamic milieu, with its emphasis on intrapersonal exploration, appears to be too stressful for the majority of sufferers of schizophrenia.

The behavioral approach to day treatment emphasizes well-defined, functional goals in the rehabilitation of patients with schizophrenia (Falloon & Talbot, 1982; Liberman & Bryan, 1977). Goals are carefully negotiated with individual patients concerning their social and vocational functions, such as conversational skills, handling criticism from supervisors, joining a social club. A wide range of behavioral treatment strategies are then individually tailored to assist the patient in achieving his or her goals. The patient's family was involved throughout the assessment and treatment process to help ensure that the newly acquired behaviors learned in the center are transferred to the natural environment.

A controlled comparison with a less structured, dynamically oriented day treatment program suggested that the behavioral approach was somewhat superior in achieving the patient's goals (Austin, Liberman, King, & DeRisi, 1976). However, this study did not employ random assignment, the therapy was not carefully monitored, and the assessment procedures were not independent of the treatment. The lack of significant differences may have been partly explained by these deficiencies, and further carefully controlled studies are essential to evaluate the effective components of the day treatment approach. Another behavioral day treatment program showed that patients who had schizophrenia were among the highest achievers (Falloon & Talbot, 1982). This contradicts earlier findings, which suggested that schizophrenics benefit little from day treatment approaches. The same study found that goal achievement was greater where patients were involved in defining their goals and where social and vocational functioning rather than intrapersonal goals was targeted. It may be concluded that day treatment is most effective as a psychosocial rehabilitation modality, and not as an intensive psychotherapy resource. There is little evidence that day treatment substantially reduces the risk of exacerbation of schizophrenia beyond that achieved by outpatient continuation of neuroleptic drugs (Linn *et al.*, 1979).

Social-Skills Training

A common deficit noted in patients who have suffered from schizophrenia is an inability to function effectively in a wide range of interpersonal contexts. Difficulties exist even within the family. Brown and his colleagues noted the inability of many patients to communicate their needs and feelings to other family members, thereby mediating against effective problem solving prior to relapse crises (Brown *et al.*, 1972). These difficulties of expression are often more pronounced in the community settings and militate against the development of friendships outside the family, participation in day treatment, vocational programs, and work; they may even lead to an avoidance of attending clinics where patients are expected to sit in waiting rooms, to converse with nurses, and to assert themselves with physicians.

While often labeled a "schizoid" disposition, a closer assessment of these socially inadequate patients seldom concurs with this concept of an *active* preference for solitude and contentment in one's own company. More often the patient describes his or her lack of social contact as withdrawal from the anxiety of social performance, an inability to function adequately in social situations, and an inability to cope with intimacy in relationships. The patient's motivation to function in these roles is strong, but his or her coping ability is low. A behavioral psychotherapy framework for enhancing the social performance and reducing the discomfort is known as social-skills training. (Assertiveness training, structured learning therapy, and personal effectiveness training are other labels used to describe this modality.)

Essential ingredients of this approach are a behavioral assessment of the specific social and interpersonal situations that the patient finds difficult to handle, and repeated rehearsal of alternative methods of performing in these situations with coaching of more effective responses (Falloon, 1978). Considerable attention is focused on the nonverbal components of expression, such as eye contact, posture, and voice tone. Feedback is provided by the therapist, sometimes assisted by video tapes. Praise and encouragement are given for small improvements. In the therapy sessions the rehearsals are usually conducted in role-played sequences with the therapist or group members (when the therapy is administered in a small group) acting in a variety of social roles relevant to each patient's targeted difficulties—for example, initiating a conversation with a neighbor. However, emphasis is on transferring acquired skills to the natural setting through setting realistic homework tasks and sometimes *in vivo* therapy sessions. The aim is not to program the patient to perform skilled social behavior on cue, but to integrate a more effective set of responses into his or her existing social repertoire. This approach uses modeling from the therapist and group members and can be conceptualized as akin to the process of development of social skills in a supportive family and peer group during adolescence—a phase in the development of schizophrenics often seriously disrupted by the onset of their illness.

A crucial component of social competence is the ability to perceive and accurately process relevant social cues that guide an individual in selecting the appropriate response to any situation—for example, deciding which person is most likely to respond positively to an attempt to engage him or her in a conversation. This cognitive-processing function appears to be deficient in many patients with schizophrenia and forms the basis for the comprehensive training in social skills that has been derived by Charles Wallace and his collaborators at Camarillo, California (Wallace, *et al.*, 1980). This method has been evaluated in a controlled outcome study with 28 male patients who were diagnosed as having schizophrenia on the Present State Examination, and were living with parents showing high "expressed emotion" attitudes. Half the patients were randomly assigned to 10 weeks of intensive (3–6 hours daily) social-skills training in small groups, while the other half received a control therapy of similar intensity. All patients were maintained on neuroleptic drugs and remained on a token economy ward throughout the 10 weeks. At the end of treatment, the social performance of the social-skills training group had improved, but there was no difference in ratings of psychopathology. Fewer patients who received social-skills training relapsed or were rehospitalized in the 9 months after discharge, and their social functioning appeared somewhat better than the control patients' (Liberman, Wallace, Falloon, & Vaughn, 1981).

The results after discharge were somewhat disappointing, with few significant differences. It is apparent that long-term support for competent social functioning is essential in the community. The modest gains achieved by the patients in this study may well have resulted from the weekly sessions of behavioral family therapy provided for the experimental group. The family or an adequate substitute appears to be an essential ingredient in sustaining and extending changes in social competence (Falloon, 1978). It is conceivable that family members might be taught to carry out a simplified version of social-skills training to assist the patients as well as other family members with their interpersonal difficulties. Similar support from family members was found beneficial in a study of socially deficient outpatients (Falloon, Lindley, McDonald, & Marks, 1977).

This approach to enhancing social functioning and reducing associated stress and anxiety is a promising innovation. Further development is in progress that may lead to wider and more successful application of these methods.

COMPREHENSIVE AFTERCARE PROGRAMS: CASE MANAGEMENT

It is evident that a range of treatment interventions are available that appear to be effective for individuals who are living in the community after a florid episode of schizophrenia. Continued neuroleptic medication, structured day treatment, and social-skills training have demonstrated effectiveness in reducing rehospitalization and severe exacerbations of florid symptoms. Work therapy and individual psychodynamic psychotherapy have shown more selective benefits. Group studies obscure the changes in individuals, and some patients derive considerable benefits from these latter approaches. A vital ingredient in aftercare is the comprehensive management of the case so that each individual is carefully evaluated and the most effective treatment modalities provided for all his or her needs. Several studies that examine the mode of provision of aftercare services have been conducted. These include (1) home care programs; (2) residential care; and (3) outpatient psychosocial programs.

Home Care Programs

The management of the psychotic patient in the home environment during acute and maintenance phases of treatment has been advocated as an alternative to hospital treatment (Pasamanick, Scarpitti, & Dinitz, 1967; Polak, Deever, & Kirkby, 1977; Stein & Test, 1980). These programs have varied from having a nurse visit the patients' homes (Pasamanick et al., 1967), to provision of acute care in the private homes of supportive foster families (Polak et al., 1977), to removal of patients from family care to independent living settings with extensive nursing support (Stein & Test, 1980). These programs are predicated on the assumption that hospital care, even when brief and crisis-oriented, is detrimental to the individual as well as expensive. The aim has been to eliminate hospital care entirely for the management of the severely mentally ill.

In the Pasamanick study, public health nurses with limited psychiatric backgrounds and training visited patients at home to provide supplies of neuroleptic drugs and to assist the patient and family members in the practical management of schizophrenia. Visits were made at weekly intervals, or less frequently as indicated. The psychiatrist saw the patients at 6-month intervals to reevaluate medications. A controlled comparison was made with patients randomly assigned to home or hospital care. A proportion of the home care patients were also assigned to placebo medication under double-blind conditions.

The results over a 30-month period indicated that 77% of the home care patients who were receiving the active drugs were successfully maintained at home, whereas only 34% of the patients on placebo remained at home throughout their time in the study. The importance of neuroleptic drugs in stabilizing symptoms is evident. Social support alone appeared of limited value. Five years later the advantages for the home care group were lost and the time spent in hospital was similar for hospital-based and home-based treatments. Presumably few patients continued to receive optimal drug treatment throughout this follow-up period.

The Southwest Denver program (Polak et al., 1977) attempted to harness the community resources in a home-based program. Mental health professionals were trained to evaluate and treat patients in their own homes. Where social supports were lacking at times of crisis, patients were "admitted" to short-term (a few days to a few weeks) foster homes run by lay persons who provided a supportive, structured milieu. Each patient's care was supervised by a professional who continued to manage the case throughout all phases of treatment. Hospital care was available when essential for medical evaluation or unmanageable behavior disturbance. Eighty-five patients were randomly assigned to either home-based or hospital-based treatment at the time of a social crisis. A third were diagnosed schizophrenic. One-fifth of the patients assigned to the home program could not be managed at home and were subsequently admitted to hospital. Those treated at home reported greater satisfaction with their treatment, and rated themselves as having achieved a higher level of goals and as being more open in discussions with their significant others. The quality of this research design and the largely self-report data gathered leave much to be desired, but they do support the claim that home-based care is feasible for a large proportion of patients who are admitted to hospitals.

The third study of alternatives to the mental hospital provides the most comprehensive conceptual model, treatment program, and evaluation. Stein and Test (1980) developed the Training in Community Living (TLC) project from a study of the needs of patients living in the community. These included the following:

1. Material resources: food, shelter, clothing, medical care.
2. Basic coping skills to meet the demands of community life: use of public transportation, meal preparation, budgeting money, and so on.
3. Motivation to persevere and remain involved with life. This included readily available support for problem solving to cope with stress.
4. Freedom from pathologically dependent family relationships.
5. Support and education of community members who were involved with patients. This included family, police, landlords, and others.
6. An *assertive* support system to help the patient with the above five needs. This involved home visits and assistance to ensure continuity of care.

The TLC program treated patients who had been assigned for admission to the local mental hospital and immediately returned them to the community where staff coverage was provided 24 hours a day, 7 days a week. Independent living situations were preferred to living with families, and patients were actively removed from the family. Support to the families and other community members was provided. The program was tailored to the deficits of the individual and took the form of assisting the patient in coping with his or her daily activities such as cooking, cleaning, grooming, and shopping. Patients were helped to find themselves jobs or sheltered workshops, and staff continued to provide problem solving on the job. The focus was on developing the patient's strengths. Assertive outreach was provided for nonattendance at work or other appointments. Medication was prescribed throughout for all patients with schizophrenia.

An evaluation of 65 patients (approximately 50% with schizophrenia) receiving TLC over a 14-month period indicated that hospital care was minimal and that symptoms, noncompliance with medication, and unemployment were less than among a group of 65 subjects who were randomly assigned to hospital care. The burden on relatives and significant others was no greater in the community-treated group (Stein & Test, 1980). The cost of the community approach was similar to that of the hospital-based method, giving lie to the assumption that effective community programs are cheaper (Weisbrod, Test, & Stein, 1980). Unfortunately it was salutary to note again that once the experimental program was completed and patients returned to community aftercare programs the gains achieved were rapidly eroded (Stein, 1978).

It can be concluded that home-based alternatives to hospital admission are feasible and provide satisfactory treatment of acute episodes of mental illness. Continued drug therapy appears essential for patients with schizophrenia. However, many of these programs are very complex and provide little more than good traditional community mental health programs. Their effectiveness as aftercare programs is less clear and deserves further study. Professional support is not clearly defined, but the emphasis on treating the patient in his or her natural environment, dealing with everyday stress with pragmatic training in the necessary coping skills, and using a problem-solving model seems indicative of a potential for effective reduction of stress. The lack of support for the natural family as a viable resource is a potential disadvantage of the Stein and Test model. This appears to be based on earlier notions of "pathological dependence" that have not been well validated (see Chapter 1). Moreover, decisions to remove patients from the household were not preceded by extensive assessments of the strengths and weaknesses of each family system. In particular, the healthy supportive and problem-solving functions of the family are often ignored. Finally, the effects of such programs do not appear to extend beyond the duration of the project. Once the special resources are withdrawn, patients rapidly regress to the levels of functioning achieved by standard community care programs. It is apparent that long-term continuation of such psychosocial interventions are as important as continued drug therapy.

Residential Care

The movement of patients with chronic schizophrenia out of the long-stay hospital wards into the community was proposed as a means of reducing the incidence of the social withdrawal, apathy, and other effects of institutionalization. Many patients did return to environments that provided support for their psychosocial rehabilitation and returned to competent functioning in the community, but many others showed little change in their functioning and were warehoused in substandard boarding homes where their passive withdrawal was reinforced and little encouragement was provided for seeking active roles in the community (Lamb & Goertzel, 1971). Patients who were discharged to concerned family members, and who showed high expectations for social competence, may have shown better role functioning, but this was at the expense of more frequent episodes of florid symptoms (Brown et al., 1958). The ideal social environment appears to lie somewhere between the low expectancy of many boarding homes and the unrealistic aims of many family households.

Unfortunately, much attention has been given to the findings of the detrimental impact of family emotional responses that were associated with a return to hospital—albeit for brief admissions—and much less to the replication of institutionalism in the community setting. The negative view of family care has been supported by the early family studies implicating family communication in the etiology of schizophrenia. The result: a firm notion that family care was incompatible with rehabilitation of schizophrenia. Since that time numerous attempts to create adequate alternatives to family care have been launched. Most have failed to replicate the warmth, concern, and tolerance afforded by the majority of families with disabled schizophrenic members, but there are some exceptions that merit our attention.

In the United States most of the programs have been demonstration projects, but several charitable organizations have been responsible for managing residential homes for the care of the mentally ill. In Britain the Richmond Fellowship, Cheshire Homes, and the Mental Health Aftercare Association have been the most prominent contributors. Prominent U.S. projects have included Fairweather's Lodges and Soteria House. These projects have aimed to provide a comprehensive rehabilitation service based on the patient's residence.

Fairweather's influential work (Fairweather, Sanders, Maynard, & Cressler, 1969) was based on the premise that if a cohesive, problem-solving group of patients could be developed and then moved into a codependent-living arrangement that the mutual support of the group members might assist in developing effective community functioning. When an initial experiment with hospital-based groups failed after the patients were discharged into the community, Fairweather employed the same methods in a halfway house ("lodge"), in which patients eventually developed their own janitorial and gardening business. A controlled comparison of patients randomly assigned to either the lodge program or to traditional aftercare indicated that the lodge group spent significantly more time in the community, although a similar proportion of patients were readmitted to hospital. Although most of the patients were described as "psychotic," it is not clear how many were diagnosed as having schizophrenia. Because employment was provided, it was not surprising to find a much higher employment record for the experimental subjects, but this advantage was lost when patients left the lodge to seek competitive employment. This is another example of the lack of maintenance of gains once patients leave demonstration projects and return to the "real" world.

Soteria House in Palo Alto, California, was developed as an alternative to traditional hospital treatment of schizophrenia (Mosher, Menn, & Matthews, 1975). This approach was derived from the existential concepts of Laing (1967). In contrast with the emphasis on neuroleptic drug treatment prevalent in most hospital wards, schizophrenia was viewed as an existential crisis in a young person's life that had the potential for positive personality development. Staff were instructed to accompany the patient through his or her altered state of consciousness, to view the psychosis as a valid experience, and to show tolerance for inappropriate behavior. Most of the staff were young people untrained in the mental health field and lived together with the patients in the residence. Drug therapy was eschewed, but used occasionally for cases unremitted after 6 weeks. Discharge was made through an informal agreement between residents. Six patients and at least two staff shared the residence at any time.

A comparative study was conducted with consecutive assignment to the Soteria program and to standard hospital treatment at a community mental health center. The two groups were well matched at entry to the study. At discharge the experimental patients scored significantly lower than controls on the global psychopathology scale, whereas the controls were less excited and showed more perceptual distortion. During the first year after discharge, more Soteria graduates were living independently and had been working. However, there were no differences in numbers of readmission to hospital or in overall social adjustment between the groups. The number of patients assessed at the assessment points seems to vary substantially, and this, together with the lack of random assignment, considerably reduces the validity of the study.

A larger sample was followed up for 2 years after discharge. In this sample the Soteria patients stayed in the residence for a mean of 166 days compared to 28 days in hospital for control subjects. Only 8% of Soteria patients received neuroleptics. At 2-year follow-up there were no significant differences in the number of readmissions or on psychopathology ratings, but Soteria patients again were substantially more likely to be living independently and used outpatient and other treatment facilities less frequently. Only one ex-resident was prescribed neuroleptics. The same criticisms apply to this later study, but in addition, the much longer stay in Soteria House seriously distorts the postdischarge comparison data. Tentative conclusions suggest that it is feasible to treat recent-onset, young patients with schizophrenia with a supportive milieu and minimal drugs, although the process appears attenuated. Other potential benefits are an enhanced ability to live independently and less utilization of community aftercare facilities.

The promise of residential care as a substantially superior alternative to family care has not been tested. Family-type groups in Fairweather's lodges or Soteria have not produced any major changes in the course of the illness and have not appeared to have many substantive advantages over standard procedures. The benefits of long-term residential care have not been carefully evaluated, but uncontrolled surveys are not encouraging (Lamb, 1979; Ryan, 1979; Segal & Aviram, 1976). Of course not all persons who succumb to schizophrenia are living with their families, and for these individuals residential care may be superior to independent living or lodgings. But with very few residential programs offering the support and concern shown by the majority of family members there appears little rationale for the removal of patients from their homes before adequate efforts have been made to evaluate the potential support of the family. Methods to educate family members about the management of mental illness and its community rehabilitation that are combined with assertive outreach support may prove highly effective for families eager to continue caring for a disabled relative.

Outpatient Psychosocial Programs

The continuation of neuroleptic drug therapy after the florid symptoms of schizophrenia have abated has been the mainstay of outpatient care for schizophrenia. As we have discussed earlier, the drugs appear to have a prophylactic effect on preventing severe exacerbations of symptoms and to assist in reducing the amount of hospital care required in the long-term management of this disorder. The precise mechanisms of the drug effect are poorly understood, but it is apparent that they may reduce the impact of stress from life events and ongoing family tensions. However, it is clear that this effect is only partially successful in blocking the impact of stress and that a substantial proportion of patients on optimal drugs suffer stress-induced recurrences of the condition. Still others, while not suffering florid delusions, hallucinations, or thought interference, appear to cope with stress by withdrawal from social functioning and avoidance of the stress endemic in active participation in friendships, family relationships, work, and community activities. Further problems related to long-term prophylactic medication are lack of compliance and unpleasant side effects, more prevalent with high doses.

Drug therapy alone is insufficient to improve the clinical and social outcome of schizophrenia. Patients who are severely disabled by persistent symptoms, lack of premorbid coping skills, or inadequate social support systems may benefit from intensive day treatment, residential programs, or vocational and social rehabilitation. The majority of persons who suffer an episode of schizophrenia can be managed with less intensive aftercare. While all these rehabilitation services may provide valuable resources from time to time, less intensive psychosocial treatment may produce equally good results over the long haul. Several methods of providing this ongoing psychosocial treatment have been employed. Some have evolved from psychoanalytic theory and others from a sociological background.

Psychoanalytic psychotherapy is still widely practiced in the private treatment of schizophrenia in outpatient settings. However, although it appears ineffective in treatment of the acute phase of the illness, there have been no studies to demonstrate its effectiveness with an unselected population of persons receiving aftercare for remitted schizophrenia. The psychosocial therapies that have been employed in most outpatient clinics have tended to minimize intrapsychic exploration and to emphasize problem solving concerning current and anticipated life stresses. A series of studies have demonstrated similar outcome whether this supportive intervention is provided in a group or individual setting (Herz, Spitzer, Gibbon, Greenspan, & Reibal, 1974; Levene, Patterson, Murphey, Overbeck, & Veach, 1970; O'Brien, Hamm, Ray, Pierce, Luborsky, & Mintz, 1972). One study compared the effects of adding group therapy to drug treatment over a 6-month period (Claghorn, Johnston, Cook, & Itschner, 1974). The group therapy did not show an effect on measures of psychopathology, but some significant changes on projective tests suggested that patients were more insightful and aware of their disabilities, and may have developed a better orientation toward their relationships with others. No measures of social functioning were included, so it was not clear whether any functional gains had accrued.

The most comprehensive studies of psychosocial aftercare treatment of schizophrenia have been undertaken by Gerard Hogarty and his colleagues at NIMH in Maryland and more recently at Pittsburgh. The approach used was called major role therapy (MRT), and as the name suggests, emphasized social casework to encourage the patient to participate more actively in the major community roles of work and social activity (Hogarty, Goldberg, Schooler, & Ulrich, 1974). Intensive MRT was compared with less intensive MRT over a 2-year aftercare period in 374 recently discharged cases of schizophrenia. Random assignment to continued drug treatment or placebo enabled further comparisons with this variable. The major effect was that after 1 year twice as many patients given placebo had relapsed (most were admitted to hospital) as those prescribed the active drug. However, patients who received the intensive psychosocial treatment showed a somewhat reduced rate of relapse that was significant after the first 6 months. Almost three-quarters of the patients in the placebo group with minimal MRT relapsed, compared to one-quarter of the drug group with intensive MRT.

A 2-year follow-up confirmed the earlier findings which showed drug therapy to be the major factor in preventing relapse, but with the contribution of the psychosocial intervention becoming more prominent with time. The social adjustment of patients who did not relapse after 2 years was best in those receiving combined drug and MRT, but poorest in the placebo and MRT group. Thus, it is probable that psychosocial treatments are effective in improving social functioning only when optimal drug therapy is provided concurrently.

In a more recent controlled study the additive effects of psychosocial treatment and drugs were replicated (Hogarty, Schooler, Ulrich, Mussare, Ferro, & Herron, 1979). In this study family stress was the best predictor of relapse in patients whose drug therapy was ensured by intramuscular administration. It was not clear whether the psychosocial intervention induced any changes in family conflicts that may have contributed to its effectiveness when combined with drug therapy. Paradoxically, the group receiving psychosocial treatment and orally administered drugs had the highest risk of relapse. No satisfactory explanation was offered for this. The researchers contend that noncompliance with the oral drug may have been a factor, but this is inconsistent with the findings of the earlier study where similar levels of noncompliance might have been expected, but the combined drug and psychosocial condition was superior.

The mechanisms of action of psychosocial treatment in the outpatient aftercare of schizophrenia are not clearly delineated in these controlled studies. In some situations, seemingly with suboptimal drug therapy, they appeared to be detrimental. In combination with optimal drug therapy they contributed to lowering the risk of relapse, presumably by effecting a reduction in environmental stress. Continued research in this area will need to address the process through which these effects are achieved so that more effective interventions are developed. There are pointers to suggest that resolution of family conflicts may be one worthwhile avenue to explore. Insufficient attention has been devoted to the most important outcome measure—the quality of social functioning. Brief relapses and hospital admissions are less relevant than the ability to live an otherwise productive and satisfying life.

CONCLUSIONS

Despite the rather primitive stage of our understanding of psychosocial interventions in schizophrenia, one observation appears to emerge from research studies and clinical practice: the importance of long-term continuity of a supportive relationship. Such support can be provided in group or individual therapy, group living situations, day treatment, or even perhaps by the physician prescribing medication. When this support is withdrawn it is apparent that many patients readily succumb to the vicissitudes of life. The qualities of this relationship are not well elucidated and may vary, but it is suggested that it may include nonintrusive emotional support with clear recognition of the existential burden carried by the patient and nondemanding problem solving of current and future life stresses and goals, with unconditional reinforcement of all attempts to achieve these aims. Censure should be minimal, but firm limits on unacceptable behavior are encouraged. Such an environment should not be restricted to the psychotherapy setting, but actively promoted in the home environment. Such qualities are often found in the care givers of the physically impaired. Not all mental health professionals or family members are capable of responding to the handicapped in this manner, but many are willing to learn. Mental illness has been conditioned to evoke fear in our Western society, a response not compatible with unconditional rehabilitative support. For community rehabilitation to prove effective, professionals, families, and the community at large may need to be reeducated to view persons who have the misfortune to suffer schizophrenia as potentially productive, creative individuals, not as dangerous, unpredictable threats to society. Until then few of the victims of this condition will achieve full independence from the supportive therapist.

CHAPTER 5

FAMILY TREATMENT FOR SCHIZOPHRENIA: RATIONALE AND METHODS

RATIONALE

There are a multitude of compelling reasons for involving the family members in the community management of schizophrenia. However, as the President's Commission on Mental Health (1978) concluded:

> It is still the rule rather than the exception that most treatment plans for schizophrenics are focused almost entirely on the patient. Either because of treatment philosophy or limited resources, family members are often dealt with only minimally. Clearly, even now, there is enough information to show that there are many reasons to attend to the needs of the families of schizophrenic patients, including providing them with social and community supports to help ease their burden in caring for their impaired family member. (Vol. II, p. 20)

Indeed, perhaps the most compelling reason for providing family treatment is that the family support system remains unrivaled in the care of its disabled members, yet the costs of that care, in both monetary and personal burden, are borne almost entirely by the care-giving family. In many cases of schizophrenia, patients formerly cared for in the long-stay wards of publicly funded hospitals, with expert nursing and medical supervision, are now cared for by relatives, who not only are untrained and ill-informed about the nature of the illness and its optimal management, but also are often denied access to this information and criticized by professionals for the harm they have done the patient. The minimal intervention provided for family members and patients should entail dissemination of information about schizophrenia with guidelines on its management. The genetic implications of this condition, though relatively minor (with the exception of identical twins or marriages between two persons with schizophrenia), should be discussed. The omission of such genetic counseling might be considered negligent practice.

Educating families about schizophrenia appears an important first step in providing support. A second component is the provision of basic social supports such as economic aid, housing, and the provision of supportive services for both the patient and his or her family. For the more disabled patients, day care and brief periods of residential care to provide family members with relief from arduous care giving may provide substantial assistance. For most patients the availability of rehabilitation services, both vocational and social, to assist in their return to active community functioning is crucial.

The provision of support to patients and families is an unglamorous, often overlooked family intervention in the management of schizophrenia, yet is arguably one of the most efficient means of reducing family tension and resentment directed toward the patient. The research on family factors associated with exacerbations of schizophrenia reveals that the level of support provided severely disturbed patients is surprisingly high in more than half the families, and that most appear willing to continue to provide assistance for their disabled relatives (Evans *et al.*, 1960; Leff, 1979). However, a substantial proportion appear unable to cope with recurrent episodes of behavioral disturbance and tend to provide a less optimal milieu that is associated with more frequent exacerbations and admissions to hospital. These families often show deficits in communication and problem-solving skills and tend to cope in a more emotional manner. For this group of families social support alone is insufficient, and family therapy interventions that seek to improve the coping capacity of family members and to reduce family tension are usually indicated. The remainder of this chapter will focus on the intervention strategies that have been employed to achieve a mutually supportive family environment in families with members who have suffered from schizophrenia.

EDUCATING FAMILIES ABOUT SCHIZOPHRENIA

Traditionally, mental health professionals have eschewed direct discussion of diagnosis, symptoms, and prognosis of schizophrenia. This lack of mental health education—a mainstay of prevention—can be partly attributed to a lack of diagnostic clarity or certainty, concern about labeling and stigmatization, and clinical discomfort with imparting such information in a readily comprehensible fashion. When a patient is treated for an episode of schizophrenia, the chances are high that neither the patient nor his or her family will be told much about the illness. No clear rationale will be presented either for the treatment he or she receives for the acute condition or for the need for continued medication and support to prevent further episodes (Soskis, 1978). This undoubtedly is a major factor in the limited long-term compliance with medication noted in community aftercare (Van Putten, 1978). Frequently family members unwittingly discourage long-term "dependence" on medication in the belief that it is better to be self-sufficient and that dependence on drugs is harmful.

In recent years a trend has emerged to correct this deficiency, with educational seminars about schizophrenia and its drug treatment being conducted on hospital wards (Pilsecker, 1981; Patterson, 1980). In an effort to improve compliance with aftercare treatment, family members have been invited to attend medication groups with their index patients where they have been encouraged to become better informed about all aspects of drug treatment (Malhotra & Olgiati, 1977; Powell, Othmer, & Sinkhorn, 1977).

It is not clear how effective these efforts have been in enhancing the understanding of patients and families about schizophrenia, or whether these interventions improve treatment compliance and reduce relapse and readmission to hospital. However, anecdotal reports suggest that patients and family members welcome this approach and that they derive considerable relief from having many of their misconceptions and confusions about the illness alleviated. There are no reports of any untoward effects from this enhancement of knowledge, which, rather than reinforce the patient's illness role, appears to assist him or her to find ways to cope more effectively with the disability. However, controlled data to support these enthusiastic reports are lacking.

Although overall inheritance of schizophrenia is a relatively small component, certain groups can be identified among whom the risk is substantial. These include the offspring of two schizophrenic parents, and identical twins where one twin has developed schizophrenia. Half these individuals are at risk to develop schizophrenia. Although no specific preventive measures have been developed, early detection and treatment appears to improve the clinical course of the condition. Such individuals and their families may benefit from counseling and support. It is debatable whether couples where both partners suffer from definite schizophrenia should be advised against procreation, but the high risks of the disorder in their offspring should be clearly discussed.

The risk of first-degree relatives of a diagnosed case of schizophrenia are relatively low (10%), and while genetic counseling may reassure relatives or prospective parents it may be considered somewhat less important. Fortunately the horrifying castration "treatments" meted out to persons suffering from this condition in the past are no longer advocated. The multifactorial etiology of schizophrenia mediates against a reduction in the procreation rates of established cases having a significant impact on the prevalence of the disorder. Indeed the birthrate of persons with schizophrenia is already lower than that of the normal population, but no reduction in prevalence rates has been recorded. Genetic counseling is an important component of patient and family education that is frequently overlooked but which undoubtedly reduces apprehension and promotes early diagnosis and treatment.

FAMILY SUPPORT

The social casework model has been the prototype for support to families caring for chronically impaired patients, including persons suffering from chronic schizophrenia. These methods aim to assist the patient and his or her family to maximize the use of resources within the family, as well as those available in the community, to overcome their everyday living problems. Referral to specialized treatment resources, such as day treatment, vocational counseling, and sheltered workshops, as well as assistance in obtaining financial support, are some of the tangible interventions. Crisis intervention and 24-hour on-call counseling are provided to both the patient and his or her family. Home visits, at least initially, are advocated to obtain a thorough assessment of the family milieu. Continued home counseling has been used by some caseworkers (Fenton, Tessier, & Struening, 1979; Golner, 1971), and outreach to ensure compliance with clinic visits and medication has been available when necessary. Although this model stresses the practical management of the patient's illness, supportive counseling of family members, including marital therapy for the parents or advice and assistance in dealing with household problems not directly related to the patient, is frequently provided.

When the patient's illness or behavior appears to exceed the coping capacity of the family, separation from the family to alternative living arrangements has been advocated. Separation from "noxious" family environments has been widely prescribed by professionals who have noted the emphasis on the "schizophrenogenic" qualities of family members as in the reports of Fromm-Reichmann (1949) and Laing and Esterson (1964), and the research on the detrimental effects of relatives' emotional responses by Brown and his successors (Brown et al., 1972; Vaughn & Leff, 1976). However, most of these students of families have advocated family interventions that aimed to reduce family tensions or merely reduce *excessive* family contact. But family interventions such as the "constructive separation" of Stein and Test (1980) have considered all family relationships of psychiatric patients to be "pathological" and have insisted that all patients seek alternative living arrangements. They have provided substantial support for family members and patients during this separation process, which has usually resulted in the patients achieving an independent living status.

More extensive review of Brown's studies reveals that a high relapse rate was also associated with nonfamily living arrangements (Brown et al., 1958, 1962). The extraordinary strength of many family ties has been noted (Evans, 1971), and in cases where physical separation is recommended the need for careful support not only for the patient but also for his or her relatives is essential to sustain a successful separation. Without thorough preparation relatives may perceive this separation as implicating them as ineffective parents and care givers. Before advocating such separations, it is important that such interventions be proved effective, and that the quality of life of both the patient and the family be enhanced. There is little direct evidence to support the superiority of extrafamilial living environments, and abundant evidence of their serious limitations (Lamb & Goertzel, 1971). Separation from the family is undoubtedly beneficial in some cases, but should probably be reserved for cases in which family interventions have been applied and shown to be ineffective in reducing intolerable family burden or high family tension. Family care is the mainstay of community management of schizophrenia. It is in the interest of the community to support the family care givers wholeheartedly. It is the duty of mental health professionals to monitor the stresses inherent in this arrangement and to intervene appropriately to maximize family coping and reduce excessive burden.

MULTIPLE FAMILY GROUPS

A variant of the supportive model is multiple family group therapy. Several families (usually three to five) including the patients meet together with one or more therapists to discuss wide-ranging problems such as practical issues of living, family rules, management of schizophrenia, and expanding social networks. Therapists tend to facilitate problem-solving discussion among families, while providing suggestions and professional advice from time to time. Family members and patients are able to share their past experiences and their present difficulties. Psychodynamic interventions are minimized, but the commonality of group themes and the reinforcement of a cohesive group milieu are considered useful vehicles to enhance the problem-solving potential of the group format.

Laqueur (1972) outlined several mechanisms of change in hospitalized patients and their families. These included using families as cotherapists to assist other families in crisis, modeling of effective problem resolution by other families, and learning through identification with family roles and situations. He considered that learning that there are a range of options for behavior, and that long-standing behavior patterns can be changed is an important component of the therapeutic process. He maintained that in multifamily group therapy, change in behavior often precedes insight.

Advocates of this approach have suggested that working with groups of families is superior to working with one family alone (Laqueur, 1972; Norton, Detre, & Jarecke, 1963; Lansky, Bley, McVey, & Brotman, 1978). These claims of clinical effectiveness have not yet been supported by comparative studies.

There are no controlled outcome studies of multiple family group therapy with schizophrenia, but a number of uncontrolled reports support claims for their beneficial effects (Strelnick, 1977).

Laqueur and his colleagues (1964) found that two-thirds of 80 families of hospitalized patients reported definite improvement in their mutual understanding of the patient and his or her illness after 8 months of weekly multiple family therapy in groups of four to six families. Therapists reported improvement in three-quarters and only 10% required rehospitalization in the year after discharge, compared to 40% of patients who received standard treatment at the same hospital. However, no diagnostic data were provided, and this treatment was provided along with the usual range of somatic therapies in a therapeutic community ward. Thus, it was not clear whether the family treatment was the therapeutic component responsible for these benefits.

In a later study (Laqueur & Lebovic, 1968) Laqueur attempted to tease out effects of multiple family therapy upon the levels of prescribed drugs. The methodology and data analysis were confusing and did not show the expected trend for reduced drug dosage with family therapy. Indeed, there was some evidence that paranoid patients may be made worse by this family confrontation.

A decrease in the need for neuroleptic drugs was reported in seven long-stay male schizophrenics when a multiple family group was instituted (Lassner & Brassea, 1968). At 5-year follow-up all but one of the patients were living in halfway houses and foster homes and attending rehabilitation programs. The authors concluded that the family group facilitated the rehabilitation process, but no clear evidence of this was provided.

The effectiveness of this approach in preventing rehospitalization was demonstrated in the treatment of 17 poorly adjusted, young adult schizophrenic patients who were treated in three multifamily groups for 1 year, during which none were admitted to a hospital (Lurie & Ron, 1971). In addition, the patients and their families were involved in an active social club network provided at the rehabilitation center. It was not clear whether these patients were also receiving medication throughout the follow-up period.

Multiple family groups that include patients have been used for many years in the hospital setting to provide a convenient focus of family concern for their mentally ill offspring. Although Lansky *et al.* (1978) strongly advocated homogeneity of diagnosis in these groups, most have included a wide range of young patients. The effectiveness of this family treatment in the outpatient setting is suggested by one study that encouraged the development of a family social support network. While this approach appears promising, further controlled research is needed to establish its efficacy both as a supportive intervention for the families and as a means of enhancing patient rehabilitation and preventing further episodes of schizophrenia.

PARENTS' GROUPS

Support groups for the parents of persons disabled with schizophrenia developed largely in response to pleas from parents who felt they had been wrongfully treated by mental health professionals. Many of these groups have assumed an active advocacy role for improving the services to the severely mentally ill. Spearheading these efforts in the United States has been the National Alliance for the Mentally Ill and Mental Health Association, and in Britain, the National Schizophrenia Fellowship. These organizations have sponsored support groups and symposia to assist their members. Patients have not been involved prominently in these groups, and it is not clear whether they have derived immediate benefits from their relatives' efforts. A wide range of untested treatments that offer hope for cures have been promoted by these groups of concerned parents, despite the lack of data to support their effectiveness. These unrealistic expectations stem largely from unrewarding experiences with traditional community aftercare programs, but often result in disappointment and disillusionment toward all forms of treatment and anger and frustration directed toward all mental health programs. It is apparent that close collaboration between mental health professionals, families, and patients may produce more effective services for the mentally ill.

The "forgotten" needs of families have been addressed in a few community programs where professionals or volunteers have conducted weekly support groups for the family members of patients (Dincin, Selleck, & Streicker, 1978; Thompson & Wiley, 1970; Thornton, Plummer, Seeman, & Littmann, 1981; Zolik, DesLauriers, & Graybill, 1962). These groups have provided a forum for family members to obtain practical advice about rehabilitation, to unburden themselves of their guilt and fears about the illness, and to share mutual experiences and effective methods of coping with patients and their illness. An evaluation of a parents' group at the Thresholds community aftercare program in Chicago suggested that two-thirds benefited from attending the parents' group, but that for one-sixth of the group the experience was considered detrimental (Dincin et al., 1978). Benefits included improved understanding and handling of their relative, acceptance of the importance of medication, reduction of guilt concerning their role in the illness, more realistic goals and expectations of their relative, and improvement in their own social lives. A major thrust of this program was to encourage parents to separate themselves from their mentally ill children who were concomitantly being trained in independent living skills. The nature of the detrimental effects of this parents' group are not described, but may have been associated with a refusal to comply with this emancipation process.

CRISIS MANAGEMENT

The provision of support for the patient and his or her family at times of exacerbation of schizophrenia is a major component of the community management of this condition. At these times alternative options to hospital admission need to be carefully considered. It is clear that many hospital admissions are instigated by the patient or his or her family in an attempt to escape from a family crisis. The recrudescence of symptoms of schizophrenia commonly related to such acute stress serves as an entry ticket to the hospital ward. The importance of expert evaluation of the family situation has been emphasized in a recent report that advocates that all admissions to hospital be preceded by a home visit (Parkes, 1978). Crisis intervention that attempts to maximize the provision of relevant community resources to the patient and his or her family may prove more effective in the long run than hospital admission. In many instances the patient is the least distressed family member, and the question to whom the tranquilizers should be given is not altogether facetious.

Langsley and his colleagues at the University of Colorado developed a program of family crisis therapy that aimed to minimize admission to hospital (Langsley, Kaplan, Pittman, Machotka, & Flomenhaft, 1968). They assumed that the request for hospitalization of one member of the family was often precipitated by a crisis in the family, and that removal of an individual from the family at that point was likely to complicate the resolution of the crisis by distracting effective problem solving of the family crisis. Family crisis therapy employed a crisis intervention model with pragmatic problem solving of the current crisis and efforts to aid the recompensation of the patient. The duration of treatment averaged 3 weeks with about five office visits, a home visit, and 24-hour telephone contact. Treatment was begun at the time of emergency room contact when all members of the family were called together for an emergency family meeting. The sequence of events leading to the crisis was defined, and scapegoating of the patient was prevented. Support, advice, and reassurance were provided to alleviate tension, and drugs were given to *any member of the family* to assist in symptom relief. A plan was developed to resolve the situation and to restore the functional capacity of each family member. Conflict resolution and symptom relief were usually rapid, but referral to long-term individual or family therapy was instigated where long-standing conflicts remained. The crisis unit then provided ongoing contact to assist in subsequent crisis episodes.

In a controlled evaluation of family crisis therapy, Langsley and his colleagues (1971) treated 150 randomly selected families of patients who requested admission to the University of Colorado Medical Center. A matched control group of 150 similar cases where the identified patient had been admitted to hospital for conventional treatment was used for comparison. An 18-month follow up of 80% of the original sample indicated not only that hospital admission could be avoided in the crisis management phase, but that in many cases the rate of hospitalization could be reduced over a much longer period. In an earlier report, it was suggested that the family approach may greatly reduce the costs associated with hospital care, although no detailed cost-effectiveness data were reported (Langsley et al., 1968). Despite avoiding the much vaunted hazards of hospital care, there was no evidence that the social functioning of the family-treated patients was superior to that of the conventionally treated group. A measure of clinical status did suggest that the family group had less symptomatic impairment at follow-up. However, it is not clear what aftercare was provided for either group of patients after the acute episode. In particular, details of drug therapy and subsequent crisis intervention are lacking. This serious omission limits the conclusions that can be drawn from the long-term follow-up study. At best we can conclude that family crisis therapy is a feasible alternative to hospital admission in the treatment of many psychiatric emergencies.

This study included a proportion of patients with schizophrenia, but the outcomes of the various diagnostic groups was not reported. A subgroup of 25 families of schizophrenic patients that participated in the family treatment was compared with an unmatched group of 25 schizophrenics who received conventional treatment. Ratings of life stressors and coping behavior indicated that the family crisis therapy may have reduced the risk of subsequent crises, but did not enhance the family's ability to cope more effectively with life stressors (Langsley, Pittman, & Swank, 1969). Severe deficits in the problem-solving capacity of families with schizophrenic members were noted. It was not surprising that very brief crisis intervention did not bring about lasting changes in the problem-solving methods such families employ. Families of patients with diagnoses other than schizophrenia appeared more self-sufficient in their problem solving after family crisis therapy. This differential outcome was considered to result from more open discussion of conflict by the non-schizophrenic patients that led more readily to problem specification and subsequent resolution. The difficulties communicating with the psychotic patient were considered to mediate against straightforward problem-solving attempts.

Thus, it is apparent that family treatment of schizophrenia may need to focus initially on enhancing the communication process between the patient and his or her family members. This is essential to the vitally important first step of identifying the exact nature of a problem, which must be accomplished effectively before problem-solving options and plans can be developed. A limited repertory of interpersonal communication skills has been observed frequently in famlies of psychiatric patients (see Chapter 1). There can be few situations that demand highly effective interpersonal communication more than dealing with a person who is experiencing a florid episode of schizophrenia. It might be argued that the best time to learn such communication skills is during such a crisis. However, the anxiety engendered in family members is usually extremely high and mediates against the learning process (Guttman, 1973). An alternate method involves improving family communication when the patient and family members are not experiencing a major crisis, in the hope that better communication can be maintained during subsequent family crises and perhaps avert the development of major episodes in the future.

CHANGING THE PATTERNS
OF FAMILY COMMUNICATION

Conjoint family therapy was a treatment method that developed serendipitously from research studies of communication behavior in the nuclear family group. In order to study the family communication patterns in a relatively simple environment, researchers met with each family as a group in the clinic and passively attempted to observe open-ended family discussions. Jackson and Weakland (1961) noted that it was not uncommon for the families to report substantial benefit from the opportunity to engage in this procedure, and that improvement in the schizophrenic illness of the index patient was often evident. Furthermore, the researchers found themselves making more active interventions to facilitate these family discussions. At the same time that these experiments were being conducted in Palo Alto by the anthropologically oriented group under Gregory Bateson, Lidz and his researchers at Yale and Bowen's group at NIMH were conducting very similar studies, and were observing similar beneficial effects from their family discussions. The researchers' interest centered primarily on aberrant communication patterns in the families, so that the patient's illness *per se* was a confounding variable that was given minimal attention and considered somewhat irrelevant.

This research basis offered an important perspective for some of the theories and practice of family therapy for schizophrenia. The systems theory formulation and treatment model was the most influential of these. This approach conceptualized the family as an interactive system in which each component individual functioned within certain prescribed limits and contributed to the combined productivity of the family group. In the case of families in which one member had schizophrenia, the illness was considered to be the direct product of ineffective family interaction. The family was considered the unit of pathology—a *"schizophrenic family"*—with the index patient merely the "carrier" of the disorder, the unfortunate "scapegoat" for the family "madness." It was further hypothesized (1) that in order to understand the index patient's schizophrenia, the communication patterns of the whole family must be clearly understood (Ackerman, 1966; Bell, 1963; Bowen, 1961; Haley, 1959; Laing & Esterson, 1964); and (2) that homeostatic mechanisms exist within the dynamic transactions of family members that serve to preserve the status quo and to resist major changes. Change of one family member was always balanced by changes in one or more of the other family members that effectively canceled out the net effect of the change on the family unit. Thus, improvement of the symptoms of schizophrenia of the index patient may be accompanied by increased psychopathology in other family members. Similarly, stress on one family member may result in changes in members other than the recipient of the stress (Jackson, 1959).

This model of family psychopathology clearly implicated the family in the etiology of schizophrenia, but apart from pointing to family management as the preferred mode of therapeutic intervention, it offered few specific strategies to foster lasting change. The frustrations experienced by the early family therapists in producing sustained changes in the patterns of family transactions appeared to have been captured in the theory of homeostasis and the associated notion that the family is a closed system that effectively isolates itself from the other systems of work, education, and social contacts, and from the potential benefits offered through social network inputs, including family therapy. Some validation for the social isolation of families with schizophrenic members has been presented in Chapter 1. However, there is little research validation for this conceptual model (Leff, 1979).

Several family therapy approaches have been derived from the belief that schizophrenia is essentially a disorder of family communication, and that its cure lies in unraveling the observed distorted communication patterns and facilitating increased clarity of verbal and nonverbal communication among all members of the family. Probably because few of the pioneers of this approach, with the notable exceptions of Don Jackson, Carl Whitaker, and the Philadelphia group of Friedman, Boszormenyi-Nagy, Rubenstein, Sonne, Speck, and Haley, were interested primarily in developing clinical methods, they emphasized the *process* of the family interaction they observed in family therapy sessions rather than the *outcome* of the treatment. Clarifying communication processes was considered of prime importance, and attention to the index patient's schizophrenia and associated handicaps was thought to be counterproductive.

The specific interventions employed in these communication-based approaches are not clearly defined in the literature. In most, but not all, cases the family meets together as a group with one or more therapists to discuss problem issues in their mutual relationships. Discussion about schizophrenia and its management is eschewed. The therapist facilitates an open discussion of the feelings, attitudes, and behavior toward one another, with specific feedback aimed at fostering clarity in the communication of information and emotions. Family rules, the boundaries of parent–child roles, and mutual expectations of all family members are elucidated. The emphasis is on here-and-now interaction, with less concern about the intrapsychic developmental issues addressed in traditional psychoanalytic therapy. However, "inheritance" of family behavioral patterns is sometimes addressed in reconstruction of the family's recollection of past generations of the family.

Individuation of the index patient and adult children from over-involved, enmeshed family ties is encouraged. As well as supporting plans for physical separation, family members are encouraged to allow other persons to think, speak, and make decisions for themselves and to avoid intrusive "mind reading" of other persons' thoughts and feelings. The statements of every family member are accorded equal status, and the less involved, noncommunicative family members are prompted to participate more overtly in the decision making and problem solving of the family.

Family members are all supported in their efforts to become more fully involved with activities and supportive relationships outside of the immediate family. A strategy known as "network therapy" involves relatives, family friends, neighbors, and other family contacts in group sessions that aim to enhance support and reduce the social isolation of the family (Speck & Attneave, 1973).

In more hostile families the therapist may function as a go-between to prevent overt conflicts exploding during sessions. This is often the role taken by the index patient in families with serious parental discord. In such cases the therapist's assumption of the mediation role reduces the patient's stress substantially.

The emotional significance or meaning of family communication is considered more relevant than the verbal information content; that is, what is said is less important than how it is expressed. Communication of emotions is highly dependent on nonverbal expression, and the emotional tensions in families are often generated by voice tone, facial expression, gesture, and other cues that are less explicit and often expressed and received at a subconscious level of awareness. The therapist seeks to observe not only the verbal content of messages, but also the nonverbal cues that determine the overall impact of communication. These nonverbal messages are made explicit through feedback from the therapist and the other family members. A simple example of this is the therapist telling a husband that, although he verbally consented to assist his wife with the household chores, he spoke in an offhand manner and looked disinterested so that the message he conveyed was that he was somewhat reluctant to follow through on this plan. The therapist asked the wife whether she had perceived his communication similarly. She said that she had and that he often responded in this way to her requests. She had formed the impression that he didn't want to support her and that this contributed to her feelings of frustration and hopelessness. In this manner the focus on the communication process leads to an increased understanding of family problems and the potential to seek more effective solutions.

There have been no adequately controlled studies to support the efficacy of the systems approach to family therapy with adult schizophrenia. Reports of series of cases treated by the pioneers of these methods have indicated that even with long-term family therapy only modest changes in the communication patterns and social functioning of family members have been achieved (Bowen, 1961; Friedman et al., 1965; Jackson & Weakland, 1961). Improvement in the index patients' schizophrenia and social status has been small. It is not clear whether these gains, small as they are, could have been achieved more efficiently by other therapeutic modalities. Two uncontrolled studies that merit further discussion do point to potential advantages for the family therapy approach. The first was conducted in Philadelphia by a group of clinicians who have subsequently made influential contributions (Friedman *et al.*, 1965), and the second by a London-based group under the leadership of R. D. Laing (Cooper, Esterson, & Laing, 1965).

The Philadelphia study represented a dramatic break away of a group of psychoanalysts from their traditions, not merely because they met with the entire family as a group, but because they went to the patient's home to conduct the treatment. The original conceptualization of the home-based approach was derived from a pragmatic attempt to involve fathers in the family treatment. However, the experience of observing patients and families in their own homes resulted in many valuable clinical insights that are well documented in their book *Psychotherapy for the Whole Family*. The theoretical concepts that were readily applied to the family group in the clinic proved less fruitful in the natural family environment, and the power experienced by the therapists in the clinic gave way to more sanguine attitudes about the ability to change the family system in a profound manner.

Practical problems of living with a disturbed patient were strikingly evident. Issues such as privacy, family pets, accepting snacks, dealing with a patient barricaded in the bathroom, and the physical constraints of cramped living conditions were among the problems that confronted the therapists. The discomfort of having to face the family as a visitor to their home was evident in remarks by several therapists of feeling "swallowed up" and being in "enemy territory."

It was noted that when therapists could demonstrate calm problem solving in the face of bizarre behavior and threats of violence they functioned as excellent models for family members. The more active and controlling therapists appeared less likely to have crises in their sessions, and at times would give patients and other family members firm lectures on behaving appropriately and "pulling themselves together" (p. 179). This no-nonsense approach to setting limits assisted parents in adopting similar firmness in controlling behavioral disturbance in the families. The intensity of feelings generated in the home environment was considerable, and an approach somewhat removed from that adopted under psychoanalytic models of transference was required.

About 100 families were treated in this study and data were gathered on most of them, including psychological tests, interviews, and therapist observations. Unfortunately these data have not been fully presented. Four detailed case studies are described in their book along with snippets of other data. Only two of the first 25 patients were admitted to hospital during the 1–2 years they were treated in the study. This suggests that substantial improvements in the families may have occurred, at least in their management of schizophrenia. The advantages of the home-based family approach were clear and appeared to outweigh the disadvantages. However, the reasons why this apparently successful approach was not developed further are somewhat mysterious. One might speculate that therapists' trepidation to venture into the home environment played no small part in its demise.

A second study of 42 inpatients treated by an existential family therapy approach suggested that hospital admission could be substantially lowered by family therapy accompanied by continued family crisis intervention, including home visits, over a 1-year follow-up period (Cooper et al., 1965). This treatment approach involved clarification and unraveling of distorted communication models in the family. Similar clear communication models were encouraged between staff and patients in the ward environment. Small doses of neuroleptic medication were employed for most patients during the hospital phase, which lasted several months. During follow-up, fewer than half the women and one-sixth of the men continued to take medication. A large percentage of the patients (approximately 80%) returned to productive jobs after discharge, with 70% earning their living. Only 17% were readmitted in a subsequent year of follow-up, and they tended to remain in the hospital for briefer periods.

The researchers went to pains to clarify that the diagnosis of the patients was unequivocally schizophrenia, and compared the outcome of their cohort with other surveys of community tenure and social functioning in British populations. However, in both these studies it is not clear whether it was the family therapy itself, the crisis management provided, or the judicious use of neuroleptic drugs that may have contributed to the good outcome. Gould and Glick (1977) suggest that patients who maintain contact with their families during and after hospital treatment for schizophrenia show a better clinical outcome than those without any family involvement. In their uncontrolled study of brief family interventions, casework contact with the patient's family members on an inpatient unit was as effective as conjoint family therapy, with or without multifamily group sessions. Involving the family unit in the treatment of schizophrenia appears to be the important ingredient.

Thus, as Mosher (1976) has concluded, the communication systems approach to family therapy has "not been demonstrated definitely effective in schizophrenic patients, neither has its use been *discredited*. . . . the problem is not that systematic, controlled research has failed to yield positive results, but that systematic, controlled research has yet to be undertaken in this area" (p. 162). The promise of cure has faded somewhat, but there are definite indications that the course of the illness may be modified by family treatment approaches that attempt to enhance family communication skills. The early enthusiasm for these family systems interventions has diminished and the techniques have found a more receptive population in child psychology and psychiatry, where controlled studies have supported their efficacy (Ro-Trock, Wellisch, & Schoolar, 1977).

The preeminence assumed by drug therapies, and their relatively low risk–benefit when administered by skilled clinicians, mediated against the widespread use of family treatments that were postulated as humanistic alternatives of similar efficacy. The acceptance of schizophrenia as a biological disorder—at least in part—and the labeling of the index patient as having an illness treatable by physical means were an anathema to the pioneers of family therapy. Failure to acknowledge the growing body of scientific and clinical support for the substantial yet incomplete benefits of drug therapies contributed to the premature demise of an exciting new development.

However, a new generation of clinicians raised in an era in which drug treatment is an accepted and crucial component in the community management of schizophrenia may be willing to reestablish family systems therapy as an important intervention in a comprehensive treatment program. In particular, the Milan group led by Mara Selvini-Palazzoli has been responsible for rekindling interest in the systemic family therapy of schizophrenia (Selvini-Palazzoli, Cecchin, Prata, & Boscolo, 1978). Although few of the cases described by this group would meet stringent DSM-III criteria for schizophrenia, the family management problems appear similar. A feature of this approach is the specific use of intervention strategies that take the family focus away from changing the symptoms of the index patient, and on to the stress experienced by other family members that may be preventing symptom resolution. A series of ingenious prescriptions, often involving paradoxical intention, are provided at the end of family sessions. Prescribing "no change" in the symptom behavior of the index patient or the symptom-contingent behavior of other family members at that time appears to facilitate the ability of the family to seek new alternatives to their problem-solving efforts. Unfortunately, as is the case with so many exciting clinical methods, its proponents have not yet sought to validate the utility of their model in controlled outcome studies.

FAMILY TREATMENT BASED ON THE STRESS–DIATHESIS MODEL

A resurgence of interest in family treatment modalities has occurred in recent years. The reasons for this renewed enthusiasm are far from clear. Speculation ranges from the acknowledgment of the oppression of women care givers in the home to a greater understanding of the family factors implicated in relapses of schizophrenia. Although comforting to social-science researchers, who so infrequently witness the results of their studies translated into meaningful clinical advances, it is doubtful that the family stress work of George Brown and his colleagues was the major perpetrator of these changes. Indeed, this initial work on family stress led clinicians to advocate widespread separation of patients from thier families. Perhaps the gradual acceptance of family therapy approaches into the mainstream of psychiatry, which coincided with the finding of deleterious features of some family environments, contributed to a reexamination of family treatment methods in schizophrenia. The rapid benefits of neuroleptic medication and a supportive hospital milieu in the treatment of acute episodes have led to an increased focus on sustaining improvement after the patient returns to his or her home in the community. Prevention of relapse and readmission to hospital became the focus of these newer approaches, with decreased concern devoted to the social functioning of the index patient and his or her family members. The replicated finding that high levels of family stress directed toward the index patient may have contributed to relapse and rehospitalization induced clinicians to adapt family therapy methods that seek to minimize the expression of negative attitudes and feelings toward that one person.

Three different versions of family therapy that focus extensively on reducing stress on the index patient have been developed systematically. These methods have been reviewed in a volume edited by Michael Goldstein (1981). They include Goldstein's brief aftercare approach (Goldstein, Rodnick, Evans, May, & Steinberg, 1978), Anderson and Hogarty's psychoeducational method (Anderson, Hogarty, & Reiss, 1980), and the family members' support group developed by Julian Leff and his team (Berkowitz, Kuipers, Eberlein-Vries, & Leff, 1981). A fourth variant that employs a more family-oriented approach based on the stress–diathesis hypothesis was developed over several years by Falloon, Liberman, and Lillie (Falloon, Liberman, Lillie, & Vaughn, 1981; Falloon & Liberman, 1983b). This last approach employs behavioral psychotherapy methods to reduce family stress as well as to enhance family rehabilitation. Its development is described in the next chapter. In striking contrast to many of the previous innovations in this field, all of these methods have been (or are in the process of being) evaluated in controlled outcome studies.

THE BRIEF FOCAL FAMILY APPROACH

Goldstein and his colleagues (1978) devised a six-session family treatment model for patients who had been discharged home to their families after brief inpatient treatment of acute episodes of schizophrenia. Patients were often discharged after only the most disturbing symptoms had remitted, and were often still in the restitution phase. It was clear that such patients were at high risk for subsequent relapse. For this reason an intervention that assisted the family in understanding the nature of the patient's illness and the need for stress reduction in the period immediately after discharge appeared indicated.

The crisis-oriented method involved six weekly (1-hour) sessions during which a psychologist met with the patient and family members in a problem-focused group. The major issues of these sessions were current, and anticipated future stress. The families discussed ways to reduce their current difficulties and possibly prevent past difficulties from recurring. Patients and families were encouraged to adopt realistic expectations for their full recovery from the illness and to reduce the pressure on the patient to return rapidly to his or her premorbid social status. A gradual return to social functioning was advocated. Although sessions were relatively unstructured, the therapists were provided with four target objectives to achieve in the six sessions: (1) The patient and his or her family were able to accept the fact that he or she had suffered a psychotic illness. (2) They were willing to identify some of the probable precipitating stressors in the patient's life at the time the illness occurred. (3) They attempted to generalize from that to identification of future stressors to which the patient and his or her family were likely to be vulnerable. (4) They attempted to do some planning on how to minimize or avoid these future stresses.

The first of these aims involved discussion about the nature of schizophrenia, with the therapist educating the patient and family about the association between stressful events and precipitation of the illness, as well as the serious nature of schizophrenia, its prognosis, and the need for drug treatment and stress management to prevent further episodes. This educational component was not standardized.

Once the family had a clear grasp of the stress–diathesis principles, a problem-solving format was employed to identify stressors, to explore strategies for avoiding or coping with stressful situations, and to plan and evaluate attempts to use stress-management strategies. Coping with current symptoms of schizophrenia and practical problems of living were commonly identified stressors. Some intrafamilial stresses were dealt with, but attempts to restructure family communication patterns were generally avoided.

A controlled study of the effectiveness of this approach compared the family therapy approach with standard aftercare procedures in a population of predominantly first admission patients who were diagnosed on broad-based criteria for schizophrenia. Patients were all maintained on injections of fluphenazine, either 25 or 6.25 mg every 2 weeks. Measures of psychopathology and community tenure were collected before treatment, after 6 weeks, and after 6 months.

After the 6-week treatment period only two of 46 (4%) patients who received family treatment were readmitted to the hospital, compared to eight of 50 (16%) patients who had standard aftercare. The differences between the high and low dosages of drugs were not striking, although only one readmission occurred among the cases who received both family therapy and high-dose neuroleptics, whereas 24% of those in the low-dose neuroleptic and standard aftercare were readmitted. Patients treated with family therapy had significantly lower ratings of psychopathology on withdrawal, affective disturbance, and thought disorder factors of the Brief Psychiatric Rating Scale (BPRS). These advantages for family therapy were less pronounced 6 months after discharge, although there were still no admissions in the high-dosage plus family therapy condition. Almost half the low-dosage plus standard aftercare patients had reentered the hospital.

The authors equated relapse of schizophrenia with hospital admission, not with exacerbations of florid symptoms of schizophrenia. Clearly, hospital admission is often preceded by an exacerbation of symptoms, but not infrequently it results from social crises, and at other times by affective disturbance and suicidal threats. Thus, while it is evident that this family intervention was effective in preventing rehospitalization in the short term, it is less clear whether this was associated with sustained improvements of the illness or by a greater willingness of families to tolerate the patient's persistent abnormalities. Unfortunately, the data did not include any measures of social functioning. The reduction in social withdrawal attributed to family treatment may suggest that reduction of stress was not achieved at the expense of diminished participation in social activity. The importance of optimal neuroleptic treatment in achieving and sustaining the benefits of psychosocial treatments is underscored by this study, at least in the first few months after an acute episode of schizophrenia.

THE PSYCHOEDUCATIONAL APPROACH

Hogarty and Anderson at the University of Pittsburgh have developed a family therapy model that addresses the stress–diathesis hypothesis directly (Anderson et al., 1980). They contend that persons with schizophrenia suffer from a "core psychological defect" that interferes with the cognitive processes essential to problem solving and is manifest in excessive physiological arousal under conditions of everyday stress. Additional stress readily overloads the cognitive processing capacity of the individual and precipitates episodes of schizophrenia. Thus, the goals of their approach are to diminish environmental stimulation while reducing psychophysiological vulnerability through neuroleptic drug therapy. The focus is clearly on reducing florid symptom exacerbations while gently prompting social rehabilitation. The family therapy intervention aims to increase the stability of the home environment by reducing the apprehension of family members about schizophrenia and promoting effective stress management. Attention is given to four main areas: (1) increasing family understanding of schizophrenia and strategies for managing symptomatology; (2) reduction of family stress through promoting more effective coping behavior to deal with crises; (3) promotion of extrafamilial social relationships for all family members; and (4), in some cases, resolving longstanding family conflicts.

The family intervention is divided into four temporal phases stretching over a period of 1–2 years (see Table 5-1). The first phase involves

TABLE 5-1. *The Pittsburgh Psychoeducational Program*

Phase 1: Connecting
  a. the family's experience of schizophrenia
  b. establishing the clinician as family ombudsman
  c. mobilizing family concern
  d. establishing a treatment contract
Sessions begun at admission of index patient to hospital with other family members only.

Phase 2: Survival-skills workshop
  a. information about schizophrenia
  b. information about medication
  c. information about management
  d. meeting needs of all family members
A daylong meeting of several families, excluding index patients. A didactic teaching format employed.

Phase 3: Reentry and application of survival skills themes to individual families
  a. family boundaries and restructuring of family coping behavior
  b. patient responsibility and rehabilitation
Individual family sessions with patient that attempt to apply survival skills to family. Lasts about 6 months.

Phase 4: Continued treatment or disengagement
  a. traditional family therapy, or
  b. maintenance sessions, or
  c. termination
Sessions may continue indefinitely.

Note. Based upon Anderson, Hogarty, and Reiss (1980).

connection with the family in twice-weekly meetings while the patient is hospitalized. The patient does not attend these sessions that aim (1) to develop a therapeutic alliance with the family; (2) to establish the clinician as the family ombudsman; (3) to elicit reactions to the illness; or (4) to mobilize family concern and support. This phase is supportive and empathic, with limited discussion about practical coping issues relating to the hospital management and discharge plans. Formulation of short-term and long-term goals of therapy is carried out mutually between family and therapist. The patient receives parallel relationship-building sessions from a project nurse–therapist on the ward.

Phase 2 consists of a daylong survival-skills workshop that combines four or five families new to the program. Parents, spouses, and siblings are encouraged to attend, but the index patient is *excluded*. Goals include providing detailed information on the illness and its management as well as assisting families in forming a mutually supportive network. Comprehensive discussion of the nature of schizophrenia, theories of etiology, and drug and psychosocial interventions is conducted. Specific family management strategies for stress reduction and coping with the illness in the family are outlined. Families are encouraged to attenuate their expectations for full recovery for many months after all the florid symptoms have remitted. The guilt that families may harbor concerning their role in causing schizophrenia or over what they should have done to prevent the illness is discussed openly and realistically. The importance of clear family communication is stressed. At the conclusion of the workshop, families are reported as feeling substantially less isolated and usually opting to participate in a monthly multiple-family group to continue sharing their burdens and to offer support to each other.

Phase 3 consists of weekly family sessions that are reduced in frequency to biweekly during the first 6 months after the patient returns home. The family stress-management strategies outlined in the survival-skills workshop are individualized and applied to the specific concerns and problems of each family. The patient now becomes an active participant in the family sessions, and his or her gradual resumption of role functioning is a major theme of the sessions. The second major issue dealt with in this phase is the reinforcement of structure within the family to allow increased "psychological space" for the patient and other family members. Concrete methods to deintensify face-to-face contact between the patient and family members are advocated. These include allowing family members to speak for themselves, to do things separately, to recognize each person's limitations, and to encourage "time outs" whereby the patient may retreat to his or her room or take a walk when feeling agitated or overstimulated. The importance of a strong alliance between the parents is supported. Parents are encouraged to engage in social activities as a couple and to expand their social networks.

A low-key focus on the patient's resumption of activities is maintained. Simple structured tasks are set to encourage a gradual return to the requirements of everyday living. Reinforcement is provided for small successes. The need for exceptional patience is stressed, and attempts to push the anergic patient are discouraged. As the patient becomes less withdrawn, more ambitious tasks are assigned relating to return to appropriate work and social functioning. Families are educated in the appropriate use of therapeutic resources such as when and how to seek professional help. Expectations for substantial changes in the patient's social status are kept low, and families are supported for their persistent efforts. Neuroleptic drug therapy with intramuscular fluphenazine is continued at the optimal doses throughout this phase of management.

The final phase (4) of the family intervention is attained when the index patient is able to perform expected roles in the community through work or school and when the family is coping effectively with this increased autonomy and role functioning. At this time the family can opt for one or two alternative treatments: (1) maintenance family therapy with contact decreased to monthly or less; or (2) more intensive family therapy with confrontation of long-standing family conflicts and interpersonal communication deficits. The maintenance therapy seeks to consolidate early gains and to reinforce continued stress-management efforts. This phase usually begins a year after discharge and continues for two years. In practice most families continue in Phase 3 during the second year of the program, during which time they gradually increase their community functioning.

The strength of this intervention appears to lie in its clear conceptualization, concrete objectives, and long-term commitment. The focus is clearly on the rehabilitation of the index patient and minimizing family stress associated with management of a handicapped family member. Although goal setting and homework tasks are employed, the teaching of some rather complex behavioral strategies—for example, time out—is accomplished through family discussions. Little attention is paid to the process of communication or problem solving; instead, the therapist outlines basic principles for the family to follow. It is not clear how compliant family members are in adhering to such rules in dealing with stressors at home.

A major criticism of the method is the exclusion of the index patient from the initial phases of treatment. Not to involve the patient in education about his or her illness and its management as well as in defining the treatment objectives, of which he or she is clearly a central figure, seems likely to engender some negative attitudes toward the therapeutic process and to foster passivity. It also denies the potential of the patient to take responsibility for his or her own recovery and control of stress. In this respect this method differs substantially from the systems-oriented methods in which the patient is always considered an equally effective member of the family, and the illness is considered not merely a family responsibility but a core part of the pattern of family life, requiring changes in the structure of transactions between *all* family members to achieve lasting improvement.

A controlled outcome study of the psychoeducational approach is in progress at the University of Pittsburgh. The family approach is being compared with an equally intensive patient-oriented, social-skills training program and a program that combines the family and social-skills approaches. All patients receive intramuscular neuroleptic drug maintenance, and a control group receiving drug therapy only is employed. Four randomly assigned groups of 20 patients each are being evaluated on a battery of clinical and social-outcome measures. Patients are diagnosed schizophrenic on the RDC and all come from families rated as having high "expressed emotion," but including spousal, child, and sibling as well as parental family units.

Although definitive data are awaited, preliminary reports favor the psychosocial interventions (Anderson, Hogarty, & Reiss, 1981). Of 28 patients assigned to the two family treatment conditions, only two had relapsed after an average of a year in the program. Problems of social functioning have been prominent in many patients. A relapse rate of one-third has been noted in the medication-only group, suggesting that the family intervention may be reducing the risk of relapse of schizophrenia. One of the relapsed patients who began the family therapy program was a 52-year-old single parent who was living with her children and had a 22-year history of schizophrenia. Her attendance at family sessions was poor, and the investigators suggested that the model may not be appropriate for such individuals who lack an adequate family support system (Anderson et al., 1980). However, most other families appear to find this model of family support satisfactory, and early data suggest that the outcome is very worthwhile.

THE FAMILY MEMBERS' GROUP

A variant of the stress-reduction models of family treatment has been developed by the London-based group of Berkowitz, Kuipers, and Leff (Berkowitz et al., 1981). This is most notably an extension of the work on "expressed emotion" in families conducted earlier at the same department (see Chapter 2). A high level of criticism and/or overinvolvement expressed by one or more household members was predictive of a high rate of relapse of schizophrenia. This effect was found to be less prominent where maintenance drug therapy was sustained and where the index patient and the high-EE relatives were physically separated for much of the time. A highly pragmatic approach based on these studies was to provide maintenance drug therapy through intramuscular administration, and to maximize interpersonal separation. Furthermore, an analysis of the content of most criticisms made of the patients revealed a considerable confusion about the nature of the illness. This suggested that a further intervention might involve educating the family members about schizophrenia. The need for flexibility in meeting the heterogeneous needs of patients with schizophrenia and their relatives led to the development of several therapeutic modalities to supplement drug therapy: (1) joint family interviews; (2) mental health education; (3) a relatives' group; and (4) occasional home visits to counsel relatives.

Patients were chosen for the program on the basis of a Present State Examination (PSE) diagnosis of schizophrenia, and a Camberwell Family Interview (CFI) with each household member. Patients who lived in close contact with one or more relatives were included in the program. The initial session took place soon after the patient was discharged from the hospital. Explicit instructions were given to the patient and his or her relatives that "it is better that the relative(s) and the patient spend less time together because it is better for the patient" (Berkowitz et al., 1981, p. 35). This statement was followed by a problem-solving discussion about ways in which such physical separation could be achieved through constructive activities, such as the relative getting a job or the patient attending a day center.

The mental health education modality consisted of four short talks about schizophrenia delivered in two sessions. These prepared talks were delivered in a lecture format followed by a question-and-answer period and written materials to take home. They dealt with the nature of schizophrenia, but, unlike the education provided in the Goldstein and Pittsburgh programs, excluded information about management of the illness. The index patient was excluded from these sessions.

The relatives' group consisted of an open-ended meeting held biweekly to provide support, catharsis, further educational material, and enhancement of personal coping and management strategies for dealing with the patient's symptoms. Relatives who were rated low on the expressed-emotion (EE) index of the CFI were invited to participate, as well as those who were rated high-EE. The notion was that the low-EE relatives who tended to be more effective at coping with the index patient might participate as models for the less competent and more highly emotional high-EE relatives. Of course, reverse modeling might equally well have occurred unless the group had been specifically structured to avoid that possibility. A semistructured, problem-solving discussion format about specific difficulties in the management of the index patient was employed. Relatives were invited to share their experiences of coping with patients' deviant behavior. High-EE relatives were encouraged to become more empathic listeners and to focus their attention less on their own emotional needs and more on the concerns of others, both in the group and at home. Efforts to have the group members form a supportive social network outside of the sessions were promoted.

Home visits were not a consistent part of the program, but were provided on an *ad hoc* basis for relatives who were unable or who refused to attend the group. Similar supportive problem solving about ways to cope with the index patient were conducted, but in this instance the patient was permitted to attend the sessions.

While the relatives' group resembled the multiple family group therapy of Laqueur and others (see pp. 94–96), the absence of the index patient in sessions that focus almost exclusively on his or her illness and behavioral deficits distinguished this approach from earlier attempts at family group support. The method implies that unilateral change of transactional behavior is the most efficient way to change emotionally charged relationships, and that the association between expressed emotion and relapse is one of cause and effect. The association found in the earlier studies between the patient's behavioral disturbance and relatives' expressed emotion suggests that mutual changes might provide even greater and more lasting benefits. In a similar vein, the association between separation of the patient and relatives and a reduced risk of relapse could equally well be postulated as predictive of a good prognosis on the basis of patients who are less symptomatic and less disturbed, have better premorbid skills, are better able to work or leave the house, and consequently have relatives who are less concerned about leaving them to function independently. Thus, working together with the whole family unit might enable separation to occur as a result of mutual improvement.

Despite these criticims of the model, the results of a study that compared supportive family therapy with standard aftercare suggested that such family treatment may indeed reduce the rate of relapse of schizophrenia in the index patients (Leff *et al.*, 1982). This was considered to have accrued through lowering the household tension and increasing the tolerance of relatives for the patient's disturbance (i.e., lowering EE), as well as through reducing high levels of interpersonal contact between the patient and stressful family environments.

CONCLUSIONS

Over the past 30 years several family interventions have been employed in the management of schizophrenia. Initial approaches focused on attempts to unravel the distorted patterns of communication that were noted in family discussions with the index patient. Recent trends in family treatment have attempted to reduce everyday stress levels through education about schizophrenia and teaching the family members more effective methods of coping with the patient and his or her illness. The stress-reduction approaches have been employed in combination with continued neuroleptic medication. Although more circumscribed in their goals, these approaches show very promising results. Preliminary data from controlled outcome studies suggest that the frequency of florid relapse of schizophrenia can be substantially reduced. After many years of neglect it is now becoming apparent that the family support system has a vital role in the community treatment of mental illness.

BEHAVIORAL FAMILY THERAPY: THE METHOD

CHAPTER 6

BEHAVIORAL FAMILY THERAPY
FOR MAJOR MENTAL ILLNESS:
DEVELOPMENT OF THE MODEL

The behavior therapy approach to the family is little more than a decade old. However, in that time these methods have burgeoned into a major field of psychotherapy. Behavioral marital therapy and parent-training methods are now among the interventions most frequently applied for marital discord and child-rearing problems, respectively (Jacobson & Margolin, 1979; Patterson, McNeal, Hawkins, & Phelps, 1967). Most of these methods have been employed to deal with marital and parental distress unassociated with major psychopathology. Applications in the treatment of schizophrenia have been more recent. This chapter will trace the development of a behavioral family therapy approach from the early basic efforts to the more sophisticated approaches currently employed.

The behavioral approach to family therapy is often equated with specific techniques, such as the behavior-exchange methods of contingency contracting or operant reinforcement strategies. Behavior therapy, although principally based on social learning theory paradigms, is unique in its essentially empirical and relatively atheoretical framework. Exponents of the behavioral approach experiment with a broad array of intervention methods unrestricted in any way, provided the strategies can be empirically validated for effectiveness in achieving the goals targeted for a particular patient. The measurement of effectiveness of a clearly operationalized treatment modality upon a person, group, or family is more basic to the approach than a rigid adherence to learning theory, a specific intervention, or a package of interventions. In this manner the unique potential of every individual and his or her interpersonal environment is stressed. For this reason, an exposition of the methods employed by a behavioral family therapist may lack the satisfying completeness and cohesion of a method derived from a more rigid theoretical framework. The behavioral approach does not demand that the pieces all fit together smoothly, since they may be employed in many different ways with each family that enters treatment.

The clear emphasis on empirical evaluation of the effectiveness of treatment of each family is an essential feature of the behavior therapy approach. The early single-case studies of approaches derived from operant conditioning methods demonstrated the specificity of change associated with the careful application of these techniques with problems of marital discord (Stuart, 1969) and childhood behavioral disturbance (Patterson, 1974). These methods involved a systematic restructuring of the rewards and punishments meted out within the family relationships so that desired behavior was increased as undesired behavior was reduced. Such methods were effective at changing the specific target behavior of family members in the specific manner determined before therapy onset. Subsequent control-group studies have confirmed the early promise shown by the case studies of marital therapy (Crowe, 1978; Jacobson, 1978; Liberman, Levine, Wheeler, Sanders, & Wallace, 1976; O'Leary & Turkewitz, 1978) and the treatment of the families of disturbed children (Alexander & Parsons, 1973). Moreover, the feedback obtained from these empirical studies has enabled improvements in the treatment procedures. Problem-solving and communication training methods have become increasingly prominent (Robin, Kent, O'Leary, Foster, & Prinz, 1977), with contingency contracting and other behavior-exchange strategies serving as potential solutions to specific problem issues.

Enhancement of parenting skills through communication and problem-solving training has been employed in the prevention of childhood behavioral disturbances. Such "parent effectiveness training" has not been empirically evaluated, so it is unclear whether such "training before trouble" does indeed reduce the potential for behavioral disorders in children (Gordon, 1977). In the same vein, marital enrichment programs with nondistressed couples have not yet demonstrated any clearly defined preventive functions (L'Abate, 1977). Such preventive methods are probably applied most effectively when persons are at high risk of illness or when functional disturbance (e.g., delinquency, divorce) can be identified. Although these enrichment programs employ behavioral techniques, they tend to be delivered as packaged courses that are not accompanied by the crucial ingredients of comprehensive behavioral analysis and follow-up assessments.

The cornerstone of behavioral family therapy is the behavioral analysis of the family unit (Kanfer & Saslow, 1965; Liberman, 1972; Wolpe, 1969). It is the information provided by the careful analysis of the behavior of each individual family member and his or her interactions with every other member that provides the basis upon which the family therapy interventions are planned. This assessment assumes that at any given time, each member of the family unit is performing at his or her best possible level of function, given the unique set of contingencies that he or she is experiencing. At times, coping behavior that may appear undesirable to an observer (e.g., social withdrawal, aggression, intrusiveness, or criticism) represents each person's *best effort* to respond in that environment at that particular time. The behavioral family therapist notes these deficits as areas where more effective coping behavior might be sought, but first validates the individual's current coping efforts.

Any attempt to modify family interaction is considered carefully for the consequences (both positive and negative) of that change on the functioning of all family members. The therapist aims to pinpoint where intervention may result in maximal improvements of the social functioning of *all* members of the family. To accomplish this, a detailed systematic analysis of family behavior is conducted before therapy. This behavioral analysis is not conducted only at the pretreatment assessment but continues throughout the entire treatment phase. It involves three levels of assessment: (1) identifying the specific assets and deficits of individual family members; (2) identifying the assets and deficits of the family group as a whole; and (3) identifying the role that specified "problem" behaviors play in the overall functioning of the family unit. This information is gleaned from semistructured interviews with individual family members; observation of family transactions in a variety of settings, including the home, clinic, participating in laboratory tasks, as well as observation of one another by the family members themselves; and the observations made by therapists during conjoint family sessions.

The behavioral assessment of family behavior can be a lengthy process—in some cases longer than the treatment phase. The therapist plays the part of a skilled detective, sifting through a variety of clues with the aim of fitting the pieces of the puzzle together so that he or she can develop a comprehensive understanding of the family—their unique assets and deficits that may contribute to their potential in coping with each specific problem they may encounter. The therapist seeks to pinpoint a few critical deficits of the family members' communication and problem-solving behaviors that, if improved, would be expected to facilitate positive changes in family functioning. Once each critical deficit has been operationalized, a clearly specified intervention procedure is systematically applied for a prearranged period of time, after which changes contingent upon the intervention are carefully evaluated and the next step in the process is determined. Changes (both positive and negative) are continuously evaluated and further interventions planned that are based upon the status of the problem—improved, partially improved, minimally changed, or worse. Each family represents a new experiment calling for a combination of treatment modalities different from that of the preceding family. This behavioral analysis and therapy framework is described in greater detail in Chapter 7.

Within this framework of sequential assessment, intervention, and review, the present authors and others have developed several therapeutic modalities that address the varied needs of members suffering from schizophrenia in its various forms. The first description of behavioral family therapy with schizophrenia was published in 1970 (Liberman, 1970). This paper described the use of operant conditioning methods after careful behavioral analysis with adult cases of schizophrenia living with spouses or parents. Many of the methods described involved a more mutual sharing of emotional resources by family members through behavior-exchange techniques similar to the marital contingency contracts developed by Richard Stuart (Stuart, 1969). Liberman explained that the behavioral approach did not attempt to reduce all family interaction to simple behavior exchanges, but merely attempted to devise highly specific methods to effect change in the complex family system. He noted that the behavioral contingencies within family systems are complex and variable, and gave clear examples of instances in which thorough behavioral analysis assisted in pinpointing areas where specific interventions appeared to induce significant and lasting changes in the functioning of the family system. The precise features of behavioral interventions chosen are determined primarily by the findings of the behavioral analysis, and although strategies derived from the empirical social learning theories are commonly employed, behavioral family therapists are unrestricted in their selection of therapeutic modalities and format, provided they adhere to the specificity dictum—*specific assessment, specific intervention*, and *specific review* of results.

FAMILY PROBLEMS SPECIFIC TO SCHIZOPHRENIA

The view espoused by some family therapists that schizophrenia is a disease of the family unit, and that family members demonstrate idiosyncratic communication patterns, has not been supported by adequately controlled research studies. Most families appear to respond in a readily understandable, "normal" way to the often extraordinary stresses associated with the long-term care of a disturbed individual. Many of their problems and conflicts are qualitatively similar to those experienced by families with a member suffering chronic physical illness. Clearly, a large proportion of families are unable to cope adequately with the added stress associated with living with a functionally impaired individual. Somewhat surprisingly, at least half the relatives of schizophrenic patients appear to cope exceptionally well. The need for basic social supports for family members who are caring for any person with a handicapping disorder is self-evident. In addition, the effects of stress are likely to heighten pre-existing family problems such as marital discord, sibling rivalry, or social isolation. However, a careful review of the literature suggests that certain family problems may be more common in the families with members who suffer from schizophrenia. These include (1) a lack of understanding of the complex nature of schizophrenia and its social impairments; (2) a lack of skills to cope effectively with acute and chronic symptoms of schizophrenia; (3) difficulties in expressing feelings, both negative and positive, especially toward the index patient (this may result in hostile criticism or overconcerned behavior); (4) difficulties in reducing tension in the family through effective problem solving; and/or (5) a tendency to feel stigmatized and to limit social contact outside the family circle.

Apart from the first two, these problems are essentially nonspecific to schizophrenia. However, the vulnerability to relapses of schizophrenia is great under conditions of high environmental tension, and the reduction of all sources of family stress may have a profound effect on the course of the illness. Persistent family tension not only affects the patient but may lead to stress-related physical and mental disorders in other family members.

From the point of view of relatives, schizophrenic family members living at home display two types of behavior that are distressing and difficult to cope with: Aggressive, bizarre, and disruptive behavior on the one hand, and social withdrawal and apathy on the other, are found in varying degrees at different points in time during the course of the illness. Social withdrawal, which may be profound to the point of rarely engaging in everyday conversation, is the more common pattern, and it generates helpless frustration in relatives whose sustained social support for the patient requires a modicum of appreciation. Another facet of behavior for which few relatives have adequate means of coping is the apathy and indolence of the more disabled patient; they tend to view the patient as physically able to function, and cannot comprehend the almost complete absence of productive activity.

Family members who have experienced several relapses of the patient's schizophrenia speak of being "constantly on a knife edge," "living on your nerves," or "feeling a constant dread of flare-ups of symptoms." Their inability to cope may lead to guilt, exhaustion, anxiety, anger, and depression. The buildup of such strong emotions is undoubtedly a factor in the high "expressed emotion" responses of families. The criticism, hostility, and emotional overinvolvement are an understandable reaction of concerned family members, who are at a loss to know how to assist their disabled relative. Overinvolvement can lead to the family's devoting excessive amounts of time and energy to the care of their relative, and to their sacrificing their own leisure pursuits and friendships, particularly if they are led to believe that they themselves may have contributed to the development of the schizophrenic illness. Criticism and hostility can lead to rejection of the patient and, ultimately, to a breach of the relationship.

Thus, within the framework of a behavioral analysis that recognizes the unique potentials and deficits of each family system, several programs that deal with these common issues have evolved. Collaboration with Robert Liberman at UCLA has been a crucial impetus to the development of these methods.

EDUCATIONAL WORKSHOPS FOR PATIENTS AND RELATIVES

In 1971, as a response to the needs of families who were living with chronic mental patients currently attending a day hospital, Liberman convened weekly evening meetings for patients and their relatives. The sessions reviewed the nature and management of the major mental illnesses, including schizophrenia. These seminars extended over several weeks and usually involved individual counseling with families concerning their specific problems.

Leaders were provided with curricula (see Table 6-1) and guides, exercises were employed to promote family interaction and to illustrate specific points, and the families were given handouts. Assessment before and after the series of meetings indicated that patients and their relatives had increased their knowledge about mental illness and its management, and had experienced the courses as assisting them in their coping efforts. The main presentation of didactic material was conducted by a psychiatrist who was assisted by other mental health professionals. The information and coping methods were conveyed through lecture–discussion, films, case studies, and role rehearsal.

The 4-month sequence of continuing educational sessions included topics about the different types of mental illnesses and their biosocial determinants; operant conditioning principles, reinforcement, shaping, family contracting exercises, drug therapies and coping with side effects, and recognizing the early warning signals of an impending relapse. These educational workshops provided considerable information of general interest to the families but were not specifically directed toward any

TABLE 6-1. *Topics Covered in Family Education Workshop*

1. Translation of mental illnesses as "problems in living."
2. Determinants of illness behaviors, symptoms, and impairments: the central nervous system ("the world inside") and the environment ("the world outside").
3. Social learning principles: the ABCs of behavior modification (learning through imitation and reinforcement).
4. Reinforcing small steps in the desired direction (shaping).
5. The power of social reinforcement: shaping behavior, especially the amount and content of conversation.
6. Family contracting: giving and getting needs and rewards through negotiated exchanges.
7. Description of social psychiatric programs at the day hospital: educational workshops, personal effectiveness training.
8. Psychoactive drugs: effects, side effects, and indications.
9. Recognizing the early warning signals of relapse.

diagnostic group. Although efforts were made to individualize the content, only limited family treatment was provided. Unlike the psychoeducational methods of Leff, Anderson, and others (see Chapter 5), patients were encouraged to attend with their relatives and to participate fully in the discussion about their illness and its management. The behavioral training of families were limited to an orientation to these methods.

BEHAVIORAL COMMUNICATION TRAINING WITH FAMILIES

In 1975 Liberman and Falloon teamed up at the Institute of Psychiatry in London when the former was on an NIH Fogarty International Fellowship. Falloon had been developing behavioral family therapy for severe depression and anxiety disorders. The educational workshop approach was extended. A pilot study was undertaken to explore the efficacy of a comprehensive behavioral approach to the rehabilitation of chronic schizophrenics. In addition to extensive social-skills training of the patients, a family intervention that employed similar skills training procedures was developed. The focus of this intervention was enhancement of the communication of feelings (Falloon, Liberman, Lillie, & Vaughn, 1981). A somewhat similar approach had proved effective in marital therapy (Liberman *et al.*, 1976).

The emphasis on the appropriate expression of feelings was derived directly from the results of a further replication of the "expressed emotion" research of George Brown by Christine Vaughn and Julian Leff (1976). They had found a strikingly similar association between highly critical and overinvolved expression toward the schizophrenic family member at the time of hospitalization and the risk of further relapses after returning to live with the family upon discharge. These data could be interpreted several ways (see p. 51), but the implication that family attitudes expressed in a negative or intrusive manner were in some way contributory to the prognosis of the illness presented a clear rationale for restructuring family communication patterns. At the same time the source of most criticism and the apparent stimulus to overinvolvement appeared to be the patient's deficiencies in social competence. Thus, an extensive individualized behavioral rehabilitation program based on social-skills training, but employing a broad range of strategies, was devised for each patient. It was contended that the most effective intervention might involve intensive psychosocial rehabilitation of the patient to enhance his or her own interpersonal effectiveness combined with a family intervention to foster more appropriate communication of emotions between family members and to lower tensions in the family milieu. In keeping with the concept of detrimental impact of the family a further thrust of this approach was to effectively separate the patient from the family household, while maintaining supportive contact with the family. It was recognized that this separation was predominantly one of breaking emotional bonds, and success depended more on the establishment of mutually satisfying independence than on merely physical separation. The old adage "distance maketh the heart grow fonder" applies readily to the mutual dependence of overinvolved parents and their disabled offspring. It is important to note that despite the extensive focus on behavioral treatment of the index patient, the behavioral analysis involved the entire family unit, and planning and implementation of all therapeutic interventions took into consideration the potential impact it might have on the family system.

Three single male patients who had clear diagnoses of schizophrenia were chosen for this pilot study (Falloon et al., 1981). All three had multiple episodes of schizophrenia with lengthy hospital stays, and all had been living with one parent who had previously exhibited high expressed emotion on the Camberwell Family Interview (CFI). The patients had been participants in Vaughn's recently completed study of expressed emotion (EE). The patients were transferred to the Behavior Therapy Unit at the Bethlem Royal Hospital where they were treated as a small group.

All the parents were currently single, although one mother had been living with a man friend for several months. Two of the parents were overinvolved and moderately critical, and the third had been highly critical without overinvolvement. Throughout a 15-week period the parents and their sons met together for 2-hour sessions in a multifamily group. During the first 10 weeks, while the patients were in the hospital, twice-weekly family sessions were conducted. After discharge, weekly sessions were held for a further 5 weeks.

The family intervention formed a major component of a multiple-baseline design that included 3 hours per day of social-skills training for the patients. After 5 weeks' focus on skills relevant to independent community living, the social-skills training program's focus switched to communication and problem solving within the family. In an effort to avoid an extensive family intervention prior to that point, so that the impact of the social-skills training could be discretely and sequentially analyzed, no specific family therapy was conducted during the first 5 weeks of family sessions. Instead, a series of educational seminars closely based upon the Educational Workshop program were employed. The major difference was a greater focus on specific education about schizophrenia and its management. This included discussion about topics such as the characteristic symptoms; the associated impairment and disability; theories of etiology, including biochemical, genetic, environmental stress, and family factors; and the role of pharmacotherapy and psychosocial interventions.

All family members, including the patient, were encouraged to share their experiences with schizophrenia and their fears and difficulties in understanding and coping with the illness. Parents were explicitly told that it was highly unlikely that they had caused the illness, although it is possible that any environmental stress, including family tension, may serve to trigger off an episode of schizophrenia in a person predisposed to the condition. During the last 2 weeks of the "baseline" period, behavioral principles were discussed that focused upon operant reinforcement strategies for developing a supportive family milieu. However, no specific attempts were made to alter family interaction and communication patterns during this baseline phase of family involvement.

Communication Skills Training

At the end of the 5-week baseline period the targets of the social-skills training and the family sessions were shifted to specific family communication deficits. The specific areas that were targeted for intervention in each family had been identified from the pretreatment CFIs as well as direct observations of family communication and problem-solving behavior during the baseline family sessions. Problems that appeared to contribute to the high criticism and overinvolvement components of the EE index were given high priority. These included unrealistic goals and expectations; nonspecific critical remarks; intrusive behavior of parents, such as speaking for the patient; a lack of reinforcement of desired behavior; an inability to ask for behavior change in a constructive manner; a lack of ability to promote independent behavior.

Each 2-hour session was structured to allow a multifamily group format for the first hour followed by an hour of individual family therapy. During the first hour progress in the families was reviewed, including the specific homework tasks assigned at the previous session. This was followed by presentation of the main training theme for the session. Therapists met together before the group and set an agenda for each session; this was based on ongoing behavioral analysis of each family system. Issues were chosen that were shared by the group of three families, as well as specific topics for each family separately. While some structure was imposed by the agenda, considerable flexibility existed to follow themes that developed during the sessions.

All families were trained in effective interpersonal communication, such as identifying and giving praise, compliments, criticism, and requests for behavior change. Expression of feelings in a generalized manner was eschewed in favor of emotional expression that specified the behavior that was being praised, criticized, or prompted. Training in empathic listening behavior was provided for the families that showed clear deficits in this skill. Family members were encouraged to set specific, realistic goals for themselves, and to make independent decisions about their own future life plans.

The personal effectiveness format was used throughout these sessions (Liberman et al., 1975). This consists of repeated role rehearsal of typical family interaction in which family members were provided constructive feedback and coached with instructions, modeling, and positive reinforcement to improve their performance. The therapists encouraged other family group members to provide feedback, to suggest and demonstrate alternative modes of expression, and to praise small steps toward increased effectiveness. The same approach was employed in the family subgroupings.

While the early family therapy sessions tended to deal with the more general issues of effective communication of positive and negative emotions, the later sessions dealt with specific problem behavior that had been pinpointed as triggering family disputes or tension. The repeated role rehearsal of alternative strategies of coping with those problems was used to develop more effective coping behavior. The focus of these interventions was the patient, and usually concerned training the parents in the management of a chronically handicapped young adult, such as a father getting his son out of bed in time to attend a day treatment program.

Homework

To expedite transfer of skills learned in the family sessions to the home environment, specific homework tasks were assigned at the end of each session. These tasks had been researched during the session and were crucial areas of conflict for that family. Homework assignments were recorded in pocket books carried by all participants, who were instructed to note the completion of the tasks and the level of competence attained during performance. In addition to these tasks, which were tailored to each family, a standardized list of 15 common family interactions, such as praising or complimenting another family member, or requesting a change in an undesirable family routine, was given to each family member with instructions to carry out as many of these interactions as possible during the week. While the patients were in the hospital family contact was limited to weekend visits home, telephone conversations, and time before and after family sessions. At the beginning of each session progress with homework assignments was reviewed. Family members were praised for *all attempts* to carry out interactive tasks. Both success and failure were closely examined to determine the essential components contributing to the outcome. Where further problems were pinpointed work continued during the session until a more effective strategy could be found.

Evaluation of Outcome

The most important question we hoped to answer in this pilot study of behavioral family therapy in schizophrenia was whether the families were able to learn more effective communication skills that could in turn reduce the levels of criticism and overinvolvement in family interactions. A simple measure of the frequency of completed family interactions that were assigned weekly indicated that at least on these specific areas change had occurred (see Figure 6-1). Constructive family communication occurred with greater frequency during the 5 weeks of active communication training than in the preceding 5 weeks when family sessions employed an educational format. Further confirmation was provided by CFIs conducted at the end of the treatment period. All three parents showed evidence of reductions in the EE index. One mother was much less overinvolved, and another was less critical. The third parent, an overinvolved and critical father, made fewer criticisms and was more

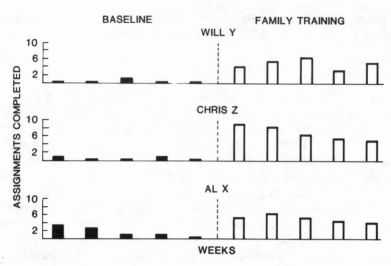

FIGURE 6-1. *Family communication assignments completed after family training.*

positive toward his son, but was still high on the overinvolvement scale. The patients and families were very enthusiastic about the family therapy, and expressed their regret that the program could not continue for a longer period.

It was concluded that the family intervention probably led to changes in both the quantity and quality of family communication, and to some changes in the behavior and attitudes of parents and their sons toward each other. These changes seemed difficult to sustain, and once the intensive program was completed families reverted to their former patterns of interaction. One father articulated this problem when he said, "You can't change a lifetime of doing things this way in a couple of months." Further indication of the difficulties of changing these families in a lasting fashion was the fact that despite the hundreds of hours of social-skills training, not one of the three patients succeeded in living away from the family for more than a month. The impact of the education about schizophrenia was similarly time-limited. One mother supported her son's efforts to discontinue his medication and to take a proprietary tonic in its place. Several months later, after he had dropped out of his aftercare program, he committed suicide. Although the two remaining patients were followed up for 1 and 3 years respectively, neither was readmitted to the hospital or suffered major exacerbations of their schizophrenia but their social functioning remained only marginally improved.

DEVELOPMENT OF A PROBLEM-SOLVING APPROACH

Behavioral family therapy in a group setting appeared feasible with severely impaired patients, and at least temporary changes in family communication may have accrued. However, it was apparent that clear communication of feelings was only one part of the problem-solving process that contributed to reduced family tension. Attention to small increments of desirable behavior and the communication of positive feelings helped create a supportive milieu in which effective problem solving could be conducted. However, when difficulty arose that called for expression of negative feelings, it seemed crucial that the family members be able to find a satisfactory resolution to the problem. Identification of problems in a clear, appropriate manner is a vital step in conflict resolution, but it is the *first* step, and it cannot be assumed that the family unit will readily find and implement a satisfactory solution. Thus, formulation of family difficulties based solely on communication deficiencies appears limited.

On the basis of the London pilot study funds were secured from the National Institute of Mental Health to conduct a controlled study of the combined social-skills training/family therapy approach at the Camarillo/ UCLA Mental Health Clinical Research Center. Again the EE research formed the basis for the methods employed. Single males living with high-EE parents were most vulnerable to relapse in these studies and were thus selected for this study. The goals of separating patients from their families and of ensuring long-term neuroleptic medication were considered important in reducing the risk of relapse. The limitations of these clinical approaches led to a more searching exploration of the process by which high expressed emotion operates on a vulnerable person to produce breakdowns of interpersonal functioning and symptom exacerbation (see Figure 6-2).

While it is probable that neuroleptic medication, even in low doses, reduces the impact of environmental stressors upon a vulnerable individual, it is not clear why many persons suffer exacerbations of schizophrenia that appear to be triggered by relatively mild stress. One possible explanation is that acute symptoms of schizophrenia become manifest at any time a person is overwhelmed by situational challenges that he or she lacks the interpersonal coping skills to handle. In other words, relapse of schizophrenia may be determined by the balance between life stress and problem-solving potential. Excessive environmental stress, such as persistent, high family tension, or a major extrafamilial life event, associated with ineffective problem-solving behavior to cope with these stresses, results in an increased risk for recrudescence of symptoms.

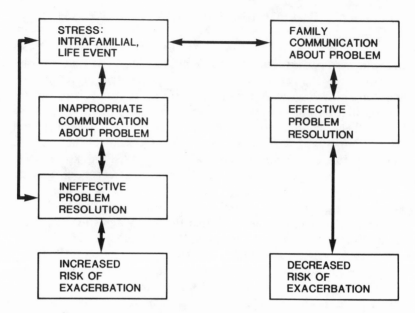

FIGURE 6-2. *The roles of family communication and problem resolution in exacerbation of schizophrenia.*

It was assumed that through enhancing the problem-solving capacity of the vulnerable family member, as well as that of the family support network, the prognosis of schizophrenia could be improved. Thus, a comprehensive problem-solving therapy model superseded the earlier communication training approach. The approach differed from the earlier model in that structured problem solving was emphasized to a greater extent. Communication skills training was closely integrated into the process of problem solving. The concomitant social-skills training for the patients employed a similar problem-solving model and was conducted over a 9-week period when the patients were admitted to a behavior therapy unit in a similar fashion to the London study (Snyder & Liberman, 1981).

The multiple family group of three to four families was again employed over a 9-week period. The groups were conducted in an office above a shopping center midway between Los Angeles and Camarillo (where the hospital was located). During the first hour the therapist employed an educational workshop structure with lecture–discussions, demonstrations, and instructional worksheets. After a brief coffee break a second hour was spent working separately with the specific problems of each family, before reconvening the family group to assign homework tasks.

The first two sessions were used to educate the patients and families about schizophrenia. Detailed information was presented about the causes, management, and course of schizophrenia, and index patients and family members were encouraged to discuss their own experiences of the illness, their fears and concerns, and the difficulties they had encountered in coping with the symptoms, including the side effects of medication. Clear answers to all questions were provided wherever possible, and the limitations of current knowledge were explained. The guilt, helplessness, and confusion of family members were shared by most of the families. The importance of resolving problems with medication was discussed in light of its importance in preventing relapse. Patients and families were encouraged to assess their problems of living with substantial handicaps that can be overcome with time. Unrealistic views of rapid return to premorbid functioning levels were addressed. The final session was devoted to the effective use of community resources after discharge. Although the contents of these sessions were similar, the presentations were more structured than the ten sessions provided in the baseline period of the London study.

A more structured workshop approach was also employed in training communication and problem-solving skills. The six sessions were each devoted to one component of problem solving with training in the relevant communication skills. Three leaders attended each group and were each allocated one family. In the first hour a workshop format was used to outline and demonstrate the skills that were being trained. Families practiced these skills in the group with guidance from the therapists. In the second part of the session the families employed these skills in their attempts at solving current and anticipated problem issues. Once again the lack of family contact while the patient was in the hospital limited homework practice of these skills in the home environment. Initially the therapist took an active role in the family problem solving, but as the family acquired greater problem-solving skills the therapist became a less active participant and merely coached the family in their efforts.

The brevity of this intervention, combined with the more complex problem-solving method, necessitated a more structured workshop approach with less focus on the comprehensive behavioral analysis of each family system. However, therapist observations during sessions indicated that most families spontaneously employed the communication and problem-solving skills they had been taught. The Schizophrenia Knowledge questionnaire showed that relatives and patients answered 80% of the questions correctly after the family education sessions, compared with 40% before the sessions (Liberman, Falloon, & Aitchison, 1978).

The assessment of the effectiveness of the family intervention was hampered by its combination with individual social-skills training for the patients. Any benefit could be attributed equally well to changes in the patient's social competence. Nevertheless, all family members of the 14 single males assigned to the social-skills training/family therapy condition were interviewed on the CFI before and after the multifamily group. The number of critical comments made about the patient was reduced 60% after treatment. Family members in a standard therapy control group showed a 16% reduction in criticism. One father, who refused to attend the family therapy, showed increased criticism on the posttreatment interview, whereas his wife showed substantial improvement in both the criticism and overinvolvement components of the EE index. This supported the tentative conclusion that the family therapy was a specific factor in reducing the "expressed emotion" of the family members who participated in the sessions. Two-thirds of the families were rated low on the EE index after treatment. The frequency of occurrence of 49 common situations that result in conflict in families with a schizophrenic member decreased substantially after the family intervention.

After 9 months of community follow-up, three of the 14 patients had relapsed. This 21% relapse rate compared with a relapse rate of 56% among the matched control group. Aftercare treatment was again provided by standard community services. With such limited control over the quality of aftercare treatment, the apparent reduction in relapse rate may well have been attributable to the reduction in family criticism and overinvolvement. But advocates of the social-skills training approach would argue that it was the strengthening of the individual patient's coping repertoire that made the difference. Thus, the efficacy of a combined treatment package consisting of extensive individual behavior therapy and behavioral family treatment in producing changes in the family had been tentatively established. However, the relative contribution of the family intervention component remained unanswered.

The multifamily group seemed well suited to the educational approach. Families reported considerable support from their sharing of common experiences, giving advice, encouragement, and praise to one another, and suggesting possible solutions to common problems. Attendance was good for the six groups conducted in these programs, with only one family dropping out after the index patient left the social-skills training program. Family members, as well as index patients, appeared enthusiastic participants. The more severely impaired patients had some difficulty processing information in the groups but did not appear to suffer any adverse effects. The one clear contraindication for family therapy in the group setting is the floridly thought-disordered patient who is unable to process information and becomes overstimulated by the family group, which inevitably focuses on his or her impairment (Guttman, 1973).

The attempt to integrate communication skills with problem solving was somewhat cumbersome, and more intensive work with individual families appeared necessary for families to achieve mastery of these complex skills. A more extensive behavioral analysis of family communication would have provided a clearer picture of the assets and deficits of each family and enabled the therapist to concentrate on each family's unique deficits in the problem-solving process. Group approaches are most efficient when specific deficits are common to all participants. Although all families shared a member with schizophrenia and all were rated high on the EE index, the precise behavioral problems varied considerably. The provision of individual family sessions in the second part of the group proved a partial answer to this problem.

BEHAVIORAL FAMILY THERAPY: A COMPREHENSIVE, LONG-TERM, HOME-BASED APPROACH

The educational approaches described to this point all employed multifamily groups as supplements to the individual behavioral treatment of the index patient. They were conducted when the patient was in the hospital in limited contact with the family. One major limitation of this family approach is the difficulty ensuring transfer of performance of behavioral skills acquired in the treatment sessions to the actual home environment. Interpersonal transactions that may be performed with ease in the hospital or in multifamily groups may be less readily replicated under the differing contingencies of everyday family life. Although homework tasks were assigned to foster this generalization, the restricted opportunities available for practice of these skills by patients and their relatives may have contributed to the lack of effective generalization noted in several families. Upon return home many patients readily settled back into their former roles, and their family members responded in a manner similar to before treatment. The need for more effective methods of ensuring transfer of communication and problem-solving skills to the naturalistic situation was identified.

The social-skills training of the index patients placed considerable emphasis on living independent of the parental home. Indeed, several patients in the Camarillo/UCLA project did leave home, but this usually involved moving to a board-and-care home—an often substandard residential facility. These environments have few qualities to recommend them and offer very limited support for community rehabilitation (Lamb, 1979). Recent evidence supports the contention that residential care holds no advantage over family care, save perhaps that it relieves the burden of primary care from the relatives (Blumenthal, Kreisman, & O'Connor, 1982). Moreover, social-skills training, of the intensity provided, is a costly rehabilitation procedure, the benefits of which have not been assessed independent of family therapy. It is conceivable that the gains, in terms of improved prognosis, were achieved largely through the relatively low-cost family intervention.

The earlier notion that reduced contact between the index patient and his or her high-EE relative(s) would "protect" him or her from the negative impact of the relative has not been replicated in the recent UCLA/Camarillo study of expressed emotion (Vaughn et al., 1984). A stressful relationship does not cease to be stressful merely because of temporary physical separation. Thus, the rationale for increased social distance between the patient and his or her family may be less clear than in earlier formulations. In an environment rich with rehabilitation resources the index patient may find considerable support for his or her efforts to return to effective community functioning. However, the supportive involvement of the family in the rehabilitation process may be vital. Practical considerations requiring family support may include ensuring that the patient arrives at programs on time, that his or her participation is sustained when difficulties arise, and that changes in his or her personal and social behavior are positively reinforced by family members. Where rehabilitation resources are scarce the family may represent the best available resource for the psychosocial rehabilitation of the patient—after all, the family provides a major source of training in interpersonal functioning in the normal development of the individual.

A further critique of the previous approaches based on the expressed-emotion paradigm involves questioning the benefits of a low-EE family milieu. While short-term reductions in the relapse rate have been reported, longer follow-ups have revealed that a substantial number of patients do relapse in the second year of follow-up (Leff & Vaughn, 1981). The benefits in terms of relapse appear short-lived. Secondly, although a reduction in the number of major exacerbations of schizophrenia is undoubtedly worthwhile, there is no evidence to suggest that low-EE families promote better social functioning in the index patient.

Some reports hint at a greater degree of social withdrawal in low-EE households. It is possible that the more demanding, concerned, high-EE families more effectively support the patient's rehabilitation efforts. Finally, patients living in low-EE families continue to relapse when confronted with extrafamilial stressful life events (Leff & Vaughn, 1980). The family is not able to effectively buffer the vulnerable patient from this stress. It may be concluded that an effective family system not only reduces the risk of major symptomatic exacerbations of schizophrenia, but also maximizes the potential of the index patient, as well as the potential of every other family member. This optimal family milieu is characterized not merely by low expressed emotion, but by effective communication of positive and negative feelings, and effective problem-solving and coping skills. The potential of the family as a resource, not merely to protect the patient from life stressors, but also as a framework for effective psychosocial habilitation of its members, may obviate the need for extensive and costly rehabilitation procedures such as social-skills training and day treatment. This ambitious role for the family clearly demands a longer-term family intervention and must be evaluated in terms of the costs (emotional and financial) and benefits to *every* family member.

The development of a comprehensive home-based family management program for schizophrenia was achieved by the three authors with the support of an NIMH research grant to evaluate its effectiveness. The remainder of this book will be devoted to a detailed presentation of this family therapy model and a discussion of its efficacy.

This method was an extension of the multifamily problem-solving approach with some major differences. Whereas the previous methods were almost exclusively based on the stress-reduction concepts derived from the studies of expressed emotion, this model encompassed a broader theoretical base. Relapse of schizophrenia was considered the multidetermined end point of a failure to cope effectively with stress originating from extrafamilial life events and ongoing social difficulties; intrafamilial stressors such as negative attitudes, intrusive overinvolvement, and confusing communication patterns; and intrapersonal stressors such as low self-esteem, poor judgment, anxiety, and limited interpersonal skills. In designing a family intervention that aims to minimize florid episodes of schizophrenia, a vital component would be methods that enhance the problem-solving capacity of both the patient and his or her family members to cope with this wide variety of potential stressors. But mere prevention of relapse is not a sufficient goal for community management. Restoration of the patient to a level of effective psychosocial functioning is an even more important goal. Although the extensive social-skills training intervention could not be readily adapted for family application, a somewhat similar approach may be employed to enhance the interpersonal skills of all members of the family. The aim is not merely to provide rehabilitation for the patient, but to improve the social functioning of *every* family participant. Each member of the family was considered a potential beneficiary of the treatment through enhanced communication and problem-solving skills and through a reduction in tension in the family as a whole. The components of the therapy included (1) behavioral analysis of the assets and deficits of each family member and the family as a unit; (2) treatment sessions conducted in the family home; (3) education about schizophrenia and its management; (4) training effective nonverbal and verbal communication for all family members with functional deficits (the appropriate communication of positive and negative emotions are included, so the detrimental consequences associated with high expressed emotion might be minimized); (5) training more effective problem-solving behavior to assist family members in efficient resolution of a wide range of intra- and extrafamilial stressors; and (6) specific behavior therapy strategies to assist with specific problems in the psychosocial rehabilitation of patients and family members (e.g., marital discord, medication compliance, anxiety management).

The emphasis of this approach is more strongly that of family-centered problem solving than the previous methods described in this chapter. There is no attempt to reformulate the patient's illness in terms of a familial disorder, but the capacity of the entire family to cope effectively with their mutual problems is considered to be of major importance. In the early stages of therapy, when the patient is still recuperating from a recent exacerbation of schizophrenia, or in cases where disturbing symptoms persist, the patient's illness is usually the gravest problem confronting the family. For this reason the program inevitably begins with the educational seminars. These serve as an entry to the family and provide a crucial framework to patient and family attempts to cope with illness problems when they arise. The communication training similarly serves to create a problem-solving milieu for the family.

The methods are designed so that they can be readily employed by family members in their everyday lives, and that eventually the therapist can withdraw from the family, once they have effectively become their own therapists. To this end, guide sheets and workbooks are provided and therapy occurs in the family home. The therapy attempts to build on the problem-solving skills already present in the family and to facilitate development of more effective behavior. Problems and goals are selected by the family members, and the therapist seeks to teach the process of problem solving rather than become immersed in the content of the problems. The treatment sessions are considered training exercises with the "real" work occurring when the family copes with problems outside the sessions. On occasion the therapist may assist in finding solutions to important problems, but wherever possible, the therapist encourages the family to make their own decisions.

A final major difference in this home-based problem-solving approach is its duration. The family treatment is employed over an indefinite time period, according to the needs of the family. The aim is to reduce therapist time to a minimum as soon as feasible, but to continue to provide support and consultation for family problem-solving efforts as necessary. Families have been treated for over 5 years in some instances. In most families treatment after 1 year is supportive and consists of reviewing family problem-solving efforts and progress toward long-term rehabilitation goals.

While there have been some structural differences in this long-term approach, the major behavioral interventions remain similar to those employed earlier. An overview of the major components will be provided in this chapter with detailed descriptions of the methods and their application with families provided in subsequent chapters.

Behavioral Family Therapy in the Home

The main rationale for conducting the family intervention in the home concerned the issue of generalization. Skills learned in a clinic setting are not automatically transferred to the home environment. This has been found particularly true for patients with schizophrenia. Patients and families are more relaxed in their own homes and are more willing to assimilate new patterns of behavior that, once established in the home setting, tend to be retained. Thus, problem-solving methods rehearsed in the family are perceived as "real" family interaction. Feelings communicated by family members during discussions at home, even when members are participating in behavior rehearsals, are similarly part of real family interaction. This integration of therapeutic interventions into the family system is crucial to effective and lasting change, and appears to be facilitated by conducting treatment at home. A further benefit is the increased participation of household members who might resist attendance at a clinic.

Family Education

Two sessions of family education are employed with content similar to that described earlier. The individual family group allows greater scope for family discussion about the specific features of schizophrenia, its impact on each family member, and problems of management. The patient is encouraged to take the role of the "expert" and to describe his or her experiences to the family. Throughout the course of treatment the therapist may refer back to these seminars. All family members are provided with detailed pamphlets that have been specially prepared for these sessions.

Communication Training

The two educational seminars are conducted in a semididactic style with visual aids and written materials. The subsequent family sessions are conducted in the more traditional, conjoint family therapy format, although therapists may give specific instructions and use written materials and chalkboards to prompt family participants during sessions. The agenda for the sessions is based on the behavioral analysis conducted prior to starting family therapy as well as a here-and-now analysis of behavioral deficits. Although a "core curriculum" of communication and problem-solving behaviors that are considered the minimal sufficient repertoire provides the therapist a general framework in the initial months of treatment, the issues that form the basis for enhancing these skills are the areas identified as problems by the family. Top priority is given any crises or impending crises. These are worked on during the sessions. In the absence of crises, the initial phase of therapy is used to enhance the communication skills of family members—in particular, the expression of positive feelings, prompting and reinforcing mutually rewarding behavior, and attentive listening skills. The aim of the early stage of family therapy is to maximize mutual family support and group cohesion. Family members are encouraged to look at the positive qualities of their transactions and to recognize the good points of one another. Once the family appears to be operating as a cohesive, supportive group in which solving of intrafamilial tensions is feasible, they are encouraged to identify specific behaviors they would like others to attempt to change and to make appropriate requests and suggestions for that change. Finally, they are prompted to express negative feelings about issues of major conflict and long-standing problems within the cohesive, problem-solving milieu of the family sessions. Family members are encouraged to express specific negative feelings to one another about their specific irksome *behaviors* rather than making generalized *ad hominem* attacks which are more likely to generate hostility and resentment in the recipient and seldom contribute to effective problem resolution. Similar family discussions about both good and bad issues are promoted outside the treatment sessions.

Problem-Solving Training

Adequate communication skills are a prerequisite for effective problem solving. The ability to specify a problem within the family group and to discuss it clearly and empathically can only be carried out by families that have competent communication behaviors. Specifying a problem is the vital first step in a six-step problem-solving approach that is taught the family. The further steps of problem solving involve the time-honored "brainstorming" method, and are relatively straightforward once the problem is behaviorally defined. Particular importance is attached to the detailed planning and implementation of the problem solution. Many families are able to agree on the "best" solutions to their problems, but lack the organization and resources to implement those desired solutions fully.

To foster participation, family members are invited to take turns at chairing family problem-solving discussions and recording the problem-solving process, including the detailed plans. A folder is kept by each family in which they keep an ongoing record of all problem-solving attempts. A sheet outlining the six steps, with space for note taking, is employed on each occasion the family convenes a problem-solving discussion. The folder is kept in an accessible spot in the home so that any family member may refer to it at any time.

Specific Problem-Solving Strategies

In addition to the communication and problem-solving skills, families may be trained in the use of a range of behavioral strategies for dealing with specific problems that arise and are not readily solved by the creative family problem-solving approach. These may include contingency contracting for parental discord, token reinforcement programs for enhancing constructive daily activities, social-skills training for interpersonal inadequacy, and/or behavioral management strategies for weight reduction, sleep disturbance, anxiety, or depression. In these instances, any family members may be the target persons for these interventions, which usually involve all family members in their effective execution. Some specific interventions directed toward the symptoms of schizophrenia and its treatment may involve the index patient as the target person, but, aside from methods of ensuring medication compliance, these problems are not common. Even in these cases the context of the problem solving is always related to the family system, and the question is asked, "What can we as a family do to overcome this family problem?" However, while the approach is clearly family-centered, it should not be concluded that schizophrenia is construed as a disturbance of family functioning. Throughout, schizophrenia is defined as a biologically mediated, stress-related disorder of unknown cause that is most effectively treated by low doses of neuroleptic drugs combined with psychosocial interventions that reduce stress from all sources. Active vocational and social rehabilitation is considered an important component of long-term stress reduction and the reduction of morbidity for the patient and family members. While intensive rehabilitation, including family therapy, may itself be a source of stress, these efforts to promote changes in the quality of life of each family member are not compromised, in order to minimize the short-term risks of relapse.

Assessment of Progress

Behavioral assessment involves a constant reappraisal of treatment goals and strategies based on empirical evidence of change. This is a basic concept in behavior therapy. The specific behavioral deficits targeted throughout therapy are resolved before moving to the next step. This model is identical to the problem-solving model presented to the families, and integrates therapy and assessment in a highly constructive manner. Both the family and the therapist are observing the same targeted behaviors and draw the same inferences from their observations. Crises may appear to interrupt the therapy process, but, wherever possible, they are used to observe the overall problem-solving capacity of the family system as they gradually acquire a more effective repertoire of coping skills. At times of crisis, competent problem-solving skills are essential to develop and implement effective strategies to reduce short-term and long-term stress. Where deficits are observed, the therapists may target interventions. The effectiveness of this home-based program has been assessed in a controlled outcome study with support from the National Institute of Mental Health. This study and its results is described in Chapters 13 to 15.

CONCLUSIONS

Behavioral family therapy has been employed in the community treatment of schizophrenia in a variety of approaches. These have included (1) educational workshops; (2) communication training in a multifamily group; (3) combined communication and problem-solving training in a multifamily group; and (4) a comprehensive, home-based, problem-solving method. Each of these approaches has been based on the behavior therapy principles of specificity of goals, methods, and assessment, to meet the varied needs of families. Although stress reduction and expressed-emotion research has strongly influenced the development of these approaches, the limitations of these concepts have become apparent as increasingly sophisticated family therapy methods have been devised. A high proportion of families have expressed satisfaction with their therapy, and objective assessments of change have indicated a favorable clinical response.

The comprehensive approach incorporates many features of the earlier methods, but aims to employ the family as the basic resource for the overall community rehabilitation of the individual who has suffered schizophrenic illness. This includes not merely the prevention of future attacks of schizophrenia, but the prevention of morbidity and the promotion of effective social functioning. The major components of the approach conducted in the family home include behavioral analysis, family education, communication training, problem-solving training, specific behavioral strategies, and evaluation of effectiveness. The remainder of this volume will provide a detailed description of the implementation of this approach.

CHAPTER 7

BEHAVIORAL ANALYSIS AND THERAPY:
A FRAMEWORK FOR SOLVING PROBLEMS

INTRODUCTION

The sources of family stress and the collective aspirations of family members are protean. Despite attempts to isolate pathogenic aspects of family interaction, it is evident that families with a member who develops schizophrenia have the same range of stressors as any families that seek assistance from the mental health professionals. In addition, the family may suffer some stress and limitations associated more specifically with the deficits of the condition. The latter, especially when the index patient is in a state of florid exacerbation, may be identified as the major source of family stress. However, with the advent of effective medical treatment of the acute episodes of mental illness, the focus of intervention is on the reduction of the stresses that appear to trigger subsequent episodes, and on maximizing the interpersonal functioning of *every* family member. This combination of minimizing stress and maximizing social adjustment is the goal of all families, regardless of their presenting problems. Thus, the approach outlined in this volume has been applied to a wide range of presenting problems, from depression, schizophrenia, and anxiety disorders to marital discord and children's behavioral disorders. All these problems and a host of others are often presented in the long-term management of schizophrenia. Indeed, in a recent survey, episodes of depression and anxiety occurred almost as frequently as episodes of schizophrenia in patients followed for 2 years after a definite schizophrenic illness (Falloon, 1982). Although the focus of this volume is the application of behavioral family therapy with families in which one member has been diagnosed as having DSM-III schizophrenia, the problems illustrated will undoubtedly cover issues common to almost all families.

The behavioral family therapy approach is less concerned with the content of problem issues or the goals of family members than with enhancing the problem-resolution capacity of the family unit. Early attempts involved training family members in the application of operant reinforcement strategies such as parents' use of positive reinforcement and punishment in the modification of the behavior of their children, or the exchange of mutual rewards by distressed couples. These problem-resolution strategies are useful, but are limited to specific family problems. The current behavioral family approach has considerably broadened the scope of this method through providing a problem-solving framework that facilitates the family's potential to derive and plan their own unique solutions to their own perceived problems. It is assumed that there are no right or wrong ways to deal with problems or to achieve life goals, but merely a wide variety of solutions from which the family group may choose the one they feel most comfortable and competent in applying.

The framework within which a problem is identified, and a solution implemented, differs from family to family. In some, a vertical decision-making structure is observed, where one dominant family member imposes his or her solutions upon the remainder. This may prove highly effective in families that accept this pattern of problem solving, whereas others may greatly resent this often dictatorial domination and prefer more democratic problem resolution. The behaviorist is not bound to theoretical assumptions that any one method is any better than any other. However, faced with a specific family unit that is having trouble with problem solving, the therapist provides a stimulus to try alternative methods until they devise a more effective plan of action.

Crucial to effective family problem solving is a minimal repertoire of interpersonal communication skills so that all family members can sit down and discuss their problems and goals in an open, empathic, and supportive framework. Major deficits in this area may necessitate considerable therapeutic guidance before the family can be expected to flourish as an independent problem-solving unit. However, it is important to note that training in communication skills is not an end in itself, merely a crucial step toward enhancing problem-solving effectiveness. Obvious communication deficits that do not appear to interfere with the problem-solving process may receive only limited attention, whereas those deficiencies that reduce the family problem-solving capacity become the focus of therapy. This functional analysis of deficits is a major feature of the behavioral family therapy method.

BEHAVIORAL ANALYSIS OF THE FAMILY

The behavioral analysis of family interaction involves a multifaceted assessment process that attempts to define operationally one or more deficits of family problem-solving behavior. The family may be interviewed conjointly or seen in a series of individual interviews or in various combinations. The initial interviews serve to accomplish several goals:

1. To gather detailed information about each family member's observations, thoughts, and feelings about family attempts to resolve everyday problem issues.
2. To gather information about each family member's interaction within the family system; his or her attitudes, feelings, and behavior toward other members; motivation to change presenting problems; and his or her potential as a mediator of change within the family system.
3. To gather information about each family member's function outside the family unit; his or her personal assets and deficits.
4. To build rapport with all family members.

The focus is problem-oriented with problem issues presented by the family being used as stimulus material for a fine-grained analysis of the family system. Each component of the system is examined extensively with an eye to pinpointing the dysfunctional problem solving that underlies the current problem issues. Once each household member and any other involved person has been interviewed, the picture of the problem behavior becomes more sharply focused and a more precise definition of deficits can be made in readily observable everyday terms. In addition, a number of testable hypotheses may be made concerning the meaning or function of problem situations within the family system. It is assumed that the unresolved problems are the result of the family's best efforts at coping with their current life situation. The family presents for therapy because they are unable to sustain their coping efforts, are suffering from the wear and tear of their coping efforts, or anticipate a breakdown in their coping performance. This is not to say that presenting problems are *caused* by deficits of problem solving, but that with more effective problem resolution, the distress associated with the problem issues may have been contained within the family unit and may not have led to professional consultation.

In addition to the exhaustive behavioral analysis of individual family members, the behavioral therapist seeks to examine the interaction between family members. While traditional family therapists examine the interaction of family members in a group-therapy setting, a behavior therapist will attempt naturalistic observations. This approach was pioneered by Gerald Patterson in Eugene, Oregon, where he coded in detail the behavior of families at home (Patterson et al., 1967). Although a tremendous amount of additional information may be acquired from a single home visit, alternative methods of obtaining behavioral observations of the family pattern of interaction have been developed. Perhaps the most widely used method is to observe the family attempting to solve a family problem in the clinic. This method has been used to assess problem-solving deficits in marital (Weiss, Hops, & Patterson, 1973; Liberman et al., 1976) and family therapy (Falloon et al., 1982). Some communication deficits that may mediate against effective problem solving include poor eye contact, interruptions, speaking for the other person, talking off the subject, and inappropriate nonverbal expression. Problem-solving defects may include lack of problem definition, lack of discussion of potential solutions, lack of acknowledgment of alternative suggestions, lack of evaluation of the consequences of a proposed solution, and lack of realistic planning for implementation of the proposed problem solution.

Assessments of family problem solving may be recorded for detailed analysis later and may be repeated at intervals during and after treatment to provide an assessment of progress. In addition to examining the general components of problem solving, specific behavior sequences may be closely examined. Patterns of interaction, excessive use of criticism or coercion, sequences leading to aggressive behavior, or intrusive comments may be assessed when a particular hypothesis is being considered. For example, a man and his obsessive–compulsive wife were observed attempting to solve an everyday problem. Each time the wife attempted to state her point of view, her husband interrupted her and attempted to contradict her. She raised her voice a little and repeated her statement, and her husband again interrupted with a contradiction. She raised her voice a little more and repeated her statement and was interrupted yet again. This sequence continued for a few minutes in slowly escalating fashion until the exasperated wife shouted "Stop" and insisted that her husband perform a series of rituals to her satisfaction. After a brief interval, the sequence of interrupted statements and rituals was repeated. It was noted that each partner refused to acknowledge the other's statements. This deficit was pointed out, and a program aimed at improving their empathic listening skills was instituted. Within a matter of weeks a substantial improvement in the obsessive–compulsive features was noted, and for the first time in many years the couple were able to communicate their feelings to one another without bitter arguments or obsessional rituals.

These changes were recorded on a graph and shown to the couple (see Figure 7-1). This feedback provided an understanding of a problem that had previously mystified them—and a long series of frustrated therapists!

Not all family problems are so readily pinpointed and responsive to straightforward solutions. However, a behavioral analysis is a dynamic process (Table 7-1). Each specific problem is highlighted in turn, and the hypothesis that its correction will lead to positive change is proved or disproved, and forms the basis for further observation and for generation of further hypotheses. The *specific focus* almost always leads to clarification even when it does not result in totally effective treatment. For example, it was hypothesized that the parents of Liza, a 20-year-old girl, who scapegoated her with incessant criticism and gave her minimal encouragement to develop independence, contributed to her feelings of insecurity and incapacitating fears of sharp objects. While attempting to have her parents identify and express positive feelings toward Liza, it became clear to the family therapist that the major family problem was not *her* fears but her *father's* lack of confidence. This was manifest in a serious drinking problem. Liza's anxiety appeared linked to her father's alcoholic binges and consequent unpredictable behavior toward both her and her mother at those times. Liza feared leaving her mother alone with her father lest he seriously harm her. She had noted that her fears were related to gestures her father made which appeared threatening and to sharp objects, particularly when her father held them. She feared the sharp objects might fly out of control and damage her eyes or genitals.

The initial therapeutic emphasis on communication of positive feelings proved surprisingly difficult for the family in the knowledge that a more serious problem existed. After three sessions, the family secret was revealed and a new hypothesis was generated, necessitating further behavioral analysis of the functional impact of her father's drinking behavior on the family system. It was ascertained that her father began drinking after her mother nagged him about his lack of career success.

The problem-solving deficits pinpointed in this family included (1) an inability of the family to sit down and openly discuss serious manifest problems; (2) excessive nonconstructive criticism of Liza by her parents; (3) minimal parental support for Liza's attempts at individualism (e.g., dating, moving out of the home); (4) father's ineffective solutions to his lack of confidence (e.g., excessive alcohol intake); and (5) mother's nonconstructive criticism of father's lack of success.

This more detailed list of issues prevalent in the family clearly mediated against effective treatment of an irrational fear response by straightforward desensitization procedures in the absence of enhanced family problem solving. However, merely listing the observed deficits and correction of each in turn is unlikely to be the most efficient intervention

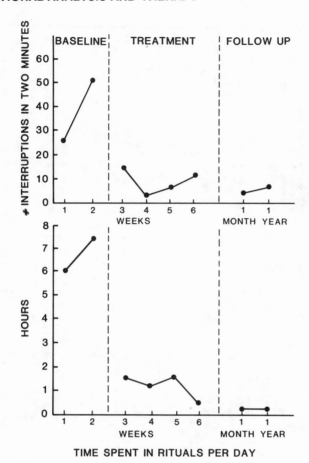

FIGURE 7-1. *Frequency of interruptions by spouse.*

in a family system, where such problems are often interwoven in the family transactions. Further assessment is necessary to clarify these inter-relationships and the functional links between them. This is known as *functional analysis*.

FUNCTIONAL ANALYSIS: A BEHAVIORAL SYSTEM

The behavioral approach postulates that patterns of family interaction are learned over repeated episodes and many trial-and-error experiences. With time, the behavior that is most frequent is that which proves the

TABLE 7-1. *Behavioral Analysis of a Family System*

Targets	Methods	Primary goals	Secondary goals
Individual family members	Interviews Questionnaires Self-observation Therapist observation	Identify assets Identify deficits Define problem behaviors Determine reinforcement patterns Determine motivation to change	Develop therapeutic alliance Identify responses of other members to index patient's problem behaviors Identify responses to problem behaviors of other members Determine motivation to change index patient's responses to problem behaviors of others
Family group	Family interview Questionnaires Self-observation Structured family interaction tasks Role playing Naturalistic observation (e.g., at home)	Identify group assets Identify group deficits Define individual roles in group Define communication and problem-solving patterns	Develop cohesive problem-solving milieu Determine mutual reinforcement patterns
Specific problem behaviors	All of above	Pinpoint discrete problem behaviors that induce a negative effect on the family as a whole, and/or on individual family members	Determine whether family therapy or individual therapy or both are indicated
Functional analysis of specific problem behaviors	All of above	Identify all contingencies surrounding each specific problem: • antecedents • consequences } short and long term • modifying factors	What triggers problem behaviors: what maintains them; how people cope with them Determine problems most readily modified Determine probability of obtaining maximum benefit from potential interventions on family system
Treatment goals	Family interviews	Choose one or more problem behaviors likely to produce maximum benefits for family system if effectively resolved Define a treatment plan that details specific goals, specific interventions, specific duration of interventions, specific assessment procedures	Define subgoals and substeps Define therapist assets and deficits in conducting desired intervention procedures
Review	Therapy observations Family members' reports Structured assessments	Define progress toward specific goals Identify further problem behaviors Continue functional analysis Prepare future specific goals and intervention	Provide feedback to family and therapist

most rewarding for each member of that family system, given the constraints placed upon him or her within the system. In an optimal family setting, the individual potential of each member is enhanced by the reciprocal exchange of reinforcement from other members. In a dysfunctional system, the converse applies: Each person's potential is thwarted, and only his or her weaknesses are reinforced. The individual's "pleasing behavior" is ignored or taken for granted, while unpleasant behavior is accorded considerable attention. However, even deficits and negative interaction patterns may be considered to be coping mechanisms, and may represent the best efforts of the family to deal with their mutual problems. This mutual-reinforcement paradigm has much in common with the systems theory concepts employed in other models of family therapy.

When one member of a family develops symptoms of a mental (or physical) illness, the behavior therapist does not consider those symptoms direct manifestations of family dysfunction. However, it might be postulated that excessive family stress or ineffective support may contribute to the pathogenesis of the illness. Moreover, patterns of support provided by the family may play a major part in the *recovery* from illness. Where recovery is incomplete and symptoms persist despite adequate therapeutic interventions, the pattern of reinforcement within the family system may play a significant role in *maintaining* the symptom behavior. An example of this was an attractive young woman who had suffered from agoraphobia for 5 years. Three years ago, she married an older man who cared for her devotedly. She sought help for her agoraphobia contrary to his expressed wishes. She made excellent progress with individual behavior therapy and began to leave the house on her own and to attend college. At first, her husband appeared pleased and supported her efforts, but quite soon he became depressed and jealous of her independent behavior. All efforts to engage the couple in marital therapy failed, and the marriage ended in divorce.

It had been noted in the initial assessment that the housebound behavior of the wife was reinforced by the husband. But he refused to participate in the assessment and treatment process, despite persistent efforts to gain his cooperation. He seemed at a loss to cope with an independent wife who previously, while symptomatic, had met his needs admirably.

In this example, an incomplete functional analysis of the significant role the wife's behavior played in this marriage may have led to the marital crisis. However, it was clear that the wife was aware that one probable consequence of giving up her housebound behavior was dissolution of her marriage. Had she feared this consequence, she might have either persuaded her husband to become involved or given up the treatment; or, possibly unwittingly, not improved with the therapy.

Thus, a functional analysis defines the manner in which an individual, his or her family members, and social network resolve specific problem behavior, either to reduce its threat or to incorporate it into their accepted pattern of interaction (i.e., to cope with it). Coping solutions may range from passive acceptance of the problem to active attempts to eliminate the problem to active support of the problem. It is important to determine how this problem solving occurred—whether through problem-solving discourse and planning or through less specific means. It is assumed that the problem behavior provides positive as well as negative functions within the family system. The housebound behavior of the wife above pleased the insecure husband but became intolerable for the wife, who expected to function with greater independence.

In a functional analysis, the family therapist seeks answers to the following questions:

1. How does *this specific problem* handicap *this person* (and his or her family) in everyday life?
2. What would happen if this specific problem was *ignored*?
3. What would happen if this specific problem was *reduced in frequency*?
4. What would this person (and his or her family) *gain* if the specific problem was *removed*?
5. Who *reinforces the problem* with attention, sympathy, or support?
6. Under *what circumstances* is the specific problem *reduced in intensity*? Where? When? With whom?
7. Under *what circumstances* is the specific problem *increased in intensity*?

An example of the functional analysis process was provided by the further assessment of Liza, the case described above of a 20-year-old girl who was living with her mother and alcoholic father. Her major complaint was a fear of sharp objects, especially those associated with her father. This problem handicapped her in her family life, so that she became filled with dread when she was at home with her father. However, when she visited women friends, she was much less fearful. Men friends who appeared attracted to her increased her phobic anxiety. So she avoided anything more than superficial contacts with men. She had obtained several clerical jobs but all had been short-lived. Invariably, casual contact with a man in the work situation had upset her and led to her leaving the job. Her fear of sharp objects was maximal in the presence of her father, particularly if he had been drinking. It was minimal when she attended a women's exercise group at a community college. The neuroleptic medication that several psychiatrists had prescribed, on the basis of a tentative diagnosis of schizophrenia, did not reduce her fears, but slowed her thinking and made her feel tense inside, and to pace excessively.

Had the problem been reduced in intensity, she believed she would lead a near-normal life. She would want to leave home and share an apartment with a friend, get a job, and begin dating men. She thought the stress this problem caused at home would be relieved, her mother would be happy again, and her father would stop drinking. Her mother agreed that there would probably be less tension in the household, but did not believe this would change the father's drinking habits. Her mother said she would miss Liza's company and "wouldn't know what to do with her time." The father wholeheartedly blamed Liza and insisted that his drinking would be controlled if his daughter were "cured."

Liza and her parents claimed that on occasions they had all ignored the problem. This had resulted in brief improvement, after which her fears became worse. The mother and father focused a substantial portion of their shared time discussing Liza. Their conversations with Liza centered around "how her fears were"; "Did she feel well enough to do [such and such]?" Her mother accompanied Liza almost everywhere, never went to bed before her, and carefully planned family interaction to minimize her fears—for example, Liza was prepared special meals which she ate alone in her room, so that she would not have to interact with her father while he was eating with a knife and fork.

It can be seen that the problem of fearing sharp objects was accorded special status in this family. It not only kept the mother and father from discussing their own problems, but was also considered, rightly or wrongly, to be the major contributing factor to the problems of other family members. Avoidance of her father and leaving the house were two coping methods described. However, as described earlier, Liza feared the consequences of leaving her mother alone with her alcoholic father. Her commitment to her mother was strong; and although she appeared to gain much from leaving home, she was unwilling to move out until her father had conquered his alcohol dependence. She daydreamed of a wonderful man rescuing her, but believed she could not leave home without help from a person her mother would listen to, probably a doctor. She would not consider making any decision her mother would not fully endorse.

As a result of this functional analysis, the following treatment plan was devised:

Goal: To enable Liza to live an unrestricted life, regardless of her fears.

Steps:

1. Father to attend alcohol rehabilitation program regularly.
2. Mother to praise father for his self-improvement efforts.
3. Mother and father to discuss their personal difficulties twice a week for 20 minutes without mentioning Liza's problem.
4. Family eating evening meal together three nights a week with conversation about everyday events—avoiding any mention of Liza's fears.
5. Liza to spend 1 hour 4 days a week visiting friends on her own, without consulting her mother for approval.
6. Family therapy sessions to be held weekly to assist in the implementation and monitoring of progress of the plans.

PATTERNS OF FAMILY REINFORCEMENT

Patterns of human behavior are seldom random, although at times they may appear confused and disorganized. If we take the time to observe a family in their everyday lives, we will tend to see sequences of behavior being repeated. Such patterns that emerge have been learned by the family members to have the most reinforcing consequences for the family system. In other words, families do the things that bring them the greatest rewards, and do not do the things that result in few rewards. Although the sum of the rewards is usually positive, this is not always the case. At times, finding the least undesirable solution may be the best possibility. Not every family member may find the solution selected by the family rewarding for himself or herself. He or she may be the scapegoat from time to time. Nevertheless, no matter how unpleasant or destructive the pattern of behavior may appear to the extrafamilial observer, if it is the most frequent response to a specific situation then it is probably the best alternative the family has in its current repertoire. That does not imply it is the *only* alternative the family employs, or that the family cannot be taught to adopt more effective and more rewarding solutions to the problem.

How can we assess which problem-solving strategies are most frequently employed by our families? There are several methods. The first would be the age-old standby, the clinical interview. We can simply ask each family member what happens in response to any specific problem situation. This method is straightforward but has the major failing of being subject to the perceptual distortions of the reporter. Each may observe different aspects of the response or remember only those sequences that involve him or her most dramatically. Few families report consistent agreement on these behavioral patterns when more than one member is interviewed. Therapist observation of spontaneous interaction between family members is less practical in clinical settings but provides more objective data. A compromise involves getting the family to observe their own responses to a specific situation and to complete a diary or chart themselves. This record may reveal patterns of which the family members themselves are quite oblivious and itself prove an effective therapeutic intervention.

An example of the use of such charting of interaction is the case of a couple who complained that they seldom went out together. Jean, the wife, complained that George "always said he was too tired to do anything after work." George related that he "would *always* do it if it was something she really wanted to do." The therapist did not attempt to resolve this clear difference of opinions. Instead, he gave each spouse a chart on which to record the times Jean initiated a request that they do something in the evening and the response that followed. Over a 4-week period, the following responses were noted:

George's responses to Jean's request	Jean's chart	George's chart
"I'm feeling rather tired now, darling"	5 (42%)	4 (36%)
"After I've put my feet up for half an hour"	2 (17%)	3 (27%)
"That's a good idea!"	2 (17%)	3 (27%)
"I've got a busy day tomorrow"	1 (8%)	0 (0%)
"Could we do that at the weekend?"	1 (8%)	1 (9%)
"You know I don't like that"	1 (8%)	0 (0%)

It can be seen from this recording that a consensus was reached on the responses that George provided to Jean's requests. Indeed, Jean was partially correct in her observation that George said he was tired, but he made this response on fewer than half the occasions—not "*always*," as she had previously asserted. At times, he even made the response she desired: "That's a good idea!" This was invariably followed by their engaging in a mutual activity of her choice.

It can be seen that the behavioral method does not accept potentially biased, indirect reports of family interaction, but seeks to validate these reports through observation. The examination of subjects' responses frequently reveals a considerable adaptive repertoire of problem-solving strategies *including desirable alternatives*. The therapeutic problem then resolves itself into an examination of the contingencies surrounding performance of the desired alternative so that it occurs more frequently than the less effective responses. This is a much easier task than having to train an entirely new response not currently evident in the family's repertoire. In the case cited above, further questioning revealed that the wife usually asked her husband to do something just as he had sat down after coming home from work, after a 1-hour commute through heavy traffic. When the couple acted out her request, it became clear that she spoke in a rather demanding, hostile tone of voice. After a brief session of negotiation, the couple agreed that she would allow him half an hour to unwind before making any requests, and that when she approached him she would sit down next to him and ask him in a friendly tone, giving at least two suggestions of possible activities. When this was accomplished, the husband's compliance with the requests increased considerably.

THE REINFORCEMENT SURVEY

A helpful strategy in the behavioral analysis of family interaction is a reinforcement survey (Table 7-2). Family members are invited to describe their most frequent activities and the people, places, and objects they spend most of their times with. It is assumed that these represent their most reinforcing situations. They are then asked which activities, people, places, and things they would like to spend more time with in the ideal situation, where current problems were disregarded. Discrepancies between *present* interaction and *desired* interaction are noted and may help to shed light on the individual's daily goals and motivations. A comparison between family members may reveal current or potential sources of conflict that may need to be considered in the treatment plan. A mother wanted her son to spend more time with her pursuing church activities, but the son wanted to substitute his mother's company with that of a girlfriend, and church activities for a sport or social club. Such a conflict of short-term goals did not appear to lend itself to an easy compromise, and restructuring the mother's expectations of her son was an essential component of problem resolution.

As well as an examination of current and desired positive reinforcers, situations that are avoided or escaped from are noted. These aversive stimuli may vary widely and, in addition to common phobias, may include a variety of family situations, such as arguments, sex, discussions about finances, family meals, or family outings.

The reinforcement survey provides a fascinating picture of the everyday activities of the family members and their intertwining sources of mutual reinforcement. In some families, a clear pattern of avoidance of

TABLE 7-2. *Reinforcement Survey*

Positive reinforcers

People
Current behavior: With whom does the subject spend most time (e.g., family members, friends, co-workers, etc.)?
Desired behavior: With whom would the subject like to spend *more* time?

Places
Current behavior: Where does the subject spend most time (e.g., work, bedroom, kitchen, living room, yard, car, stores, church, etc.)?
Desired behavior: Where would the subject like to spend *more* time?

Activities
Current behavior: What activities does the subject spend most time doing (e.g., work, social pursuits, hobbies, doing nothing)?
Desired behavior: What activities would the subject like to spend *more* time doing?

Objects
Current behavior: What things does the subject spend most time (e.g., books, hobbies, foods, drink, clothes, TV, stereo, etc.)?
Desired behavior: What things would the subject like to spend *more* time with (buy, possess, etc.)?

Negative reinforcers

What situations are aversive stimuli for subject? What situations are *escaped from* or *avoided* (e.g., people, activities, fears, social isolation, etc.)?

intimacy may be noted; in others an overinvolved, interdependent pattern may be inferred. Such reported behavior is used merely as a guideline to suggest avenues to explore at greater depth, and is not in itself a valid representation of actual interactions. As we have already seen, reports of interaction behavior are subject to considerable distortion. In addition to the reinforcement survey, we frequently ask family members to keep diaries of their daily activities. The diary provides an ongoing assessment of everyday behavior and is an extremely useful clinical tool.

The reinforcement survey may reveal current or potential sources of reinforcement that could be valuable resources in the treatment program. These people, activities, or objects that are current reinforcers provide a positive basis upon which to mediate change. For example, a meal that an adolescent son finds very enjoyable may be used to reward him for assistance with the household chores, or an activity he would like to increase, such as playing baseball with his father, might serve as the basis for increased positive interaction between them. A knowledge of such reinforcers greatly enhances the power of the therapist to facilitate positive changes within the family system.

OTHER BEHAVIORAL ASSESSMENT PROCEDURES

Behavioral assessment of families goes beyond the clinical interview. A number of other procedures, including standardized rating scales, are employed in order to obtain further reliable and valid information about family behavior. It is important to realize that standardized procedures are always regarded as adjuncts to naturalistic clinical observations of the family that continue throughout therapy.

Journal Recording

A simple, yet effective means of recording family behavior is the diary or journal. Although somewhat out of fashion in the hustle and bustle of modern living, the diary offers a ready source of information. We have encouraged family members to keep daily records of their activities. When specific topics are dealt with in the ongoing family therapy, evidence of generalized behavior change can often be monitored through the daily records. At times, family members may be instructed to record *specific* events on a daily basis. As well as providing an information source, the diary provides its author with an opportunity to sit down and reflect on his or her family interaction on a regular basis. This self-monitoring procedure is in itself a potentially powerful therapeutic intervention.

Family Self-Observation

A specific variant of the daily journal is a checklist or chart to be completed by family members to record the frequency and responses associated with specified events: arguments, bedwetting, pleasant events, and so on. A version of this approach is the Spouse Observation Checklist (SOC). This was developed by Robert Weiss and his colleagues at Oregon (Weiss *et al.*, 1973) to measure the frequency of pleasing and unpleasant behavior in couples. It is important to obtain information on rewarding exchanges as well as negative interaction in the behavioral analysis of families.

The SOC consists of a checklist of more than 400 items which have been classified as pleasing and displeasing events—for example, "*spouse initiated sexual advances*," and "*spouse was tolerant when I made a mistake.*" Couples are invited to complete the entire SOC inventory each evening, checking those items that have occurred during the previous 24-hour period. Typically, the couple are invited to record their observations of interaction with their spouse for a 1-week period. The SOC items have been further classified into 12 content areas of interaction: affection, sex, companionship, communication, coupling activities, financial decisions, child care, consideration, household management, personal habits, independence, and employment.

This instrument suffers from its length. An abbreviated version is known as the Marital Activities Inventory, and with 85 items it can be applied more readily in clinical practice. Further criticism by Gurman (1978) concerns the basic assumption that activities can be neatly divided into "pleases" and "displeases." This has led us to ask family members to record their own examples of pleasant and unpleasant events and their responses to them.

Direct Observation Procedures

We have already discussed the observation of family interaction in the home setting. This entails an assistant visiting the family on several occasions, usually around the dinner hour, and recording the family interaction with the aid of a reliable coding system. Another version of this approach involves having the family switch on a tape recorder at a specified time to record interaction that is subsequently coded. Sophisticated technology now enables recorders to be activated at random intervals from the clinic, providing even less potential for the family interaction to be affected by their knowledge that the recorder is on (Christensen, 1979).

A somewhat less expensive procedure is to attempt to generate naturalistic family interaction in the clinic setting. A wide variety of interaction test situations have been developed in family research programs. All have the common aim to provide the family with a specific task to focus their interaction over a 5- to 10-minute period. Most of these tasks have involved some form of problem solving, but have ranged from solving a puzzle (Reiss, 1967, 1968, 1969), to planning a vacation (Riskin & Faunce, 1970), to completing a Rorschach together (Wynne, 1968), to resolving a "hot issue" in the family (Goldstein, Judd, Rodnick, Alkire, & Gould, 1968). The resulting discussions may then be coded according to the interaction parameter considered most relevant. The Oregon group employs the Marital Interaction Coding System (MICS), which codes verbal and nonverbal behaviors that occur as couples attempt to resolve a specific problem in a discussion format (Weiss, Hops, & Patterson, 1973). Examples of the 28 behaviors coded are approval, disagree, agreement, criticism, compromise, acceptance of responsibility, and humor. Robin *et al.* (1977) have developed a similar coding system for recording problem-solving behavior in family groups that includes items such as problem specification, suggested problem solution, and approval.

Doane (1978) has coded statements reflecting positive and negative affect while a family resolves a problem situation. Criticism, supportive statements, guilt induction, and intrusiveness are included in the "affective style" ratings. Wynne and Singer (1965) and Al-Khayyal (1980) have coded the verbal communication behavior of family members while they identify patterns on Rorschach cards. While all these methods have been used in family interaction research, we have adapted several of these methods to measure changes in family problem solving that result from family therapy interventions (Liberman *et al.*, 1976; Falloon *et al.*, 1980). Many of these structured tests are relatively straightforward and can be administered in 10–20 minutes, although precise coding may take longer. The additional information provided usually justifies the effort.

Camberwell Family Interview

This interview assessment has gained considerable interest since the publication of a series of replicated studies that have shown that an index of "expressed emotion" can be a highly effective predictor of the outcome of persons suffering a depressive or schizophrenic illness (Brown, *et al.*, 1972; Vaughn & Leff, 1976). This semistructured interview is conducted with each family member individually. The family member's relationships with other persons in the household are explored, particularly the informant's emotional responses to each person. The interview is recorded for subsequent analysis of critical remarks, hostile comments, positive comments, and intrusive and overinvolved expression directed toward the index patient. On the basis of these ratings, an overall index of expressed emotion (EE) is made. High EE toward a hospitalized family member appears to increase his or her vulnerability to further episodes of mental illness. It is not clear whether the same high-EE response is predictive of behavioral disturbance in the absence of prior major psychopathology. The advent of this standardized instrument has provided considerable renewed impetus to family therapy approaches in the rehabilitation of schizophrenia. Although the assumption that the reported interaction patterns do indeed occur in spontaneous family interaction has not been validated, some preliminary data suggest that the reported behavior is similar to that directly observed in family problem-solving discussions.

INTEGRATING THE FAMILY SYSTEM: PROVISIONAL TREATMENT PLANS

The focus to this point has been on several assessment procedures employed in the behavioral approach to family problems. It may be noted that a considerable amount of time is required for a comprehensive behavioral assessment. The interviewer, like a skillful detective, aims to build up the pieces of reliable evidence until he or she can provide an unimpeachable case for the relevant function of the unwanted behavior within the entire family system. Like a detective, the approach must be flexible, include interviews as well as on-site inspection, and observation of interaction. Inference is minimized. Wherever possible, observable data support the therapist's hunches. Until the therapist is clear in his or her mind what part the dysfunctional behavior plays in the family, he or she refrains from making a definitive intervention. Moreover, after a treatment strategy has been defined, the therapist consistently monitors the changes so that the plan can be further modified to provide more efficient progress toward the specific goals. Sessions with family members may employ various combinations of therapeutic interventions, with various formats. No one format is considered useful for every case. The success of the approach depends more on the adequacy of the assessment phase than on the treatment techniques employed subsequently. An incomplete assessment results in a situation akin to driving in a foreign city with an incomplete street map—a considerable amount of time may be spent trying to reach an unseen goal. The few extra hours spent to obtain a complete understanding of the "map" may uncover remarkably few steps to the destination.

The behavioral analysis of the family system attempts to gain an integrated picture of the function of the family. This picture is in two parts: (1) the strengths and assets of the family, and (2) the current problems and weaknesses. In a dysfunctional family, it is assumed that the assets of individual family members are not being effectively utilized to solve the problems of the family system. Reinforcement for maladaptive behavior or coercive sequences which lead to escape, withdrawal, or retaliation can maintain family dysfunction and symptoms. One common cause of this inefficient use of resources is a breakdown in the communication process. This leads to a lack of effective problem-solving behavior in the noncohesive family group. The therapist attempts to elucidate the critical areas of breakdown and to negotiate short- and long-term treatment goals that will provide more effective coping with problems.

The behavioral assessment is directed toward a clear definition of problem areas, to determine the strengths and weaknesses of each individual and the group as a whole. Standardized assessment measures such as structured interviews, rating scales, questionnaires, and real-life observations are used to supplement the therapist's interviews with individual family members and the family group.

The functional analysis attempts to evaluate the way in which specified problem issues and goals fit into the family system. This involves an interactive assessment of the potential positive and negative consequences of change that will result from successful resolution of the problem behavior. The initial functional analysis sets up hypotheses that are tested only when an intervention program begins.

Feedback obtained after the treatment has been applied provides continuously monitored evidence of the complex interrelationships between family members. Adjustment in the intervention procedures is essential to their short- and long-term success. Lasting changes will occur only when all family members find that their new behavioral patterns are more rewarding than their former interactions. Resistance to change occurs when the cost to the individual exceeds the benefits experienced (or perceived) as a consequence of the change. Pretreatment functional analysis provides an assessment of the perceived cost–benefit equation.

This assessment may be relatively straightforward, but at times it is a complex and lengthy procedure requiring many hours to complete. However, a comprehensive assessment will substantially reduce the complexity and duration of subsequent successful interventions. The therapist will be assured that he or she has pinpointed key areas of dysfunction in the family system and has at least a rudimentary grasp of the probable consequences of his chosen treatment procedures.

It should be repeated that the behavioral assessment process is never completed, and that the behavioral analysis is constantly modified by the information gathered during therapy. This dynamic aspect of the behavioral approach retains a structured framework in which specific behavior is pinpointed, its function with the family system clarified, strategies to resolve the problem are developed, and mutual reinforcement for the changes in behavior patterns is predicted. Life change is somewhat less predictable in the home environment, where the family system is affected by stressors from the wider social and cultural systems in which they live. Thus, family problem solving must address issues of coping with extrafamilial as well as intrafamilial stressors. The behavioral approach retains a flexibility to consider these broader systems as well as intrapersonal systems, including the cognitions of individual family members and their biological systems. Thus, problem issues may range from housing and finances to paranoid beliefs, or from hallucinations to the taking of street drugs or plasma levels of prescribed drugs. However, each problem is assessed with the same specific functional approach. For example, a young girl who took her prescribed medication irregularly was found to have a mother who believed that *any* "mind-altering" drugs were harmful. Although the mother trusted the doctor who prescribed the drug, and generally supported his suggestion that the drug be taken every day, she readily took her daughter's side whenever the latter attributed the slightest discomfort to the medication, and advised her to skip her dose. The intervention to solve this problem involved primarily changing the cognitions of the mother through education about the beneficial and unwanted effects of the prescribed medication, including information that the side effects were maximized by her irregular ingestion. This relatively simple procedure quickly solved a problem that had been a source of family tension for several years, and resulted in substantial benefits for all family members.

ESTABLISHING A PROBLEM-SOLVING FRAMEWORK

Behavioral psychotherapy is an approach to solving problems that has been applied to a wide range of disorders. The essence of the method is the specificity of problem solving employed. Each problem is defined after a detailed behavioral analysis. This is followed by careful selection of a specific treatment approach that has usually been validated experimentally as effective in resolving the specific problem. The approach is applied within a clear intervention plan to enhance the efficiency of the treatment. Finally, the effectiveness of the intervention is assessed and further treatment plans are developed as necessary. We have described the first step in this approach: problem definition through behavioral analysis. The second step involves choosing an appropriate intervention, and will be dealt with in later chapters of the book. The remainder of this chapter will describe the planning and structural framework in which the myriad of specific interventions are posited. These include setting goals, assessing progress, and developing a therapeutic alliance, as well as the basic therapeutic techniques employed in the behavioral family therapy group setting.

Setting Goals

Once the initial behavioral analysis has been completed, the therapist reviews his or her findings with the family and together they seek to define one or more specific goals for their therapy. Such goals must be clearly defined prior to the start of any specific intervention, and are structured so they can be readily achieved within an agreed-upon duration of therapy.

Example: Daniel, a 31-year-old single man, lived with his widowed mother. He complained bitterly of her "overmothering." This involved her constantly checking up on him when he went out in the evening, and expressing her concern for all the difficulties he might encounter when out of her sight. She reported that she was afraid he might attempt suicide again as he had a year ago, quite unexpectedly when he gave no indication of unhappiness or other warning signals. After detailed assessment and some negotiation, a goal was set that "Daniel would move into his own apartment in 2 months' time."

Although this goal appears straightforward, the steps toward this desired outcome may involve substantial changes in the mother–son relationship. A goal such as "reduce mother's overconcern" is clearly a major therapeutic issue, but in itself does not relate to specific change. Such goals are avoided unless the precise changes in the protagonist's behavior or attitudes can be described with sufficient clarity that therapist and the family are able to readily assess progress toward the goal and can set themselves a clear course to aim for. Shared feedback of progress is an important therapeutic factor that provides motivation and direction for the therapist and the family.

The goals of the behavioral treatment are agreed on before therapeutic interventions are applied. Whenever possible, the goals are chosen by the family, not imposed by the therapist. Throughout the therapy process, the therapist seeks to maintain a role as a teacher and facilitator of learning and change. There are occasions when he or she may need to take greater control over the family situation. In such situations, usually a major crisis, the therapist may take major responsibility for leading the problem-solving effort; at other times, he or she may encourage the family to attempt their own problem solving of less critical issues while he or she coaches them from the sidelines.

The choice of therapeutic strategy and the method by which it will be applied are determined by the behavioral goal to be achieved and the unique contingencies that have been elucidated in each family through the behavioral analysis. In the case above of the overinvolved mother, an agreement by the patient that in the future he would talk to her before attempting suicide provided she not call the police went a considerable way to alleviating her overconcern. It may be helpful to consider each family intervention as a separate experiment in behavior change. The therapist and the family collaborate closely to develop novel solutions to their unique problems through the use of their specific assets. Small, well-defined goals are chosen initially so that a successful collaboration can be developed. This leads to increased confidence in the family's ability to change successfully; to an increased willingness to take responsibility for change; and to the generation of further data that can be utilized in defining subsequent interventions.

Example: Joe had never been able to get his 30-year-old son, Walter, out of bed in the morning. He had tried everything, but Walter refused to move. Walter had indicated that he viewed this as a sort of game he could always win with his father and did not want to give it up. However, he was frequently late for work and this caused him some problems. The therapist suggested that Joe might stop trying to wake his stubborn son and hand over that responsibility to his son. Walter considered a variety of possible solutions to his problem of getting up and decided to wake up at the time *he* desired. This plan was carried out and led to Walter's getting to work on time four of the six workdays the following week. Father and son were very impressed with their success and subsequently were eager to tackle some more complex issues in their relationship.

Assessing Progress toward Goals

The techniques employed in behavioral family therapy are not rigidly ordained. Any problem-solving strategy that makes common sense to the family as well as the therapist may be prescribed for a highly specific problem. The effectiveness of the intervention is assessed, on a session-by-session basis, by the most reliable and efficient means—often a count of the frequency of a behavioral sequence before and after the intervention, but at other times an assessment of mood or cognitive changes. While behavioral assessment is often extremely direct, simplistic, and a grossly inadequate measure of the complexity of human interpersonal relationships, it does offer a readily available source of feedback to the patient and the therapist to monitor the progress toward the specific treatment goals.

Example: Sarah counted the number of times her mother interrupted conversations with her friends before and after a plan was instituted that involved this issue. Sarah's rough figures suggested that her mother had reduced this major source of irritation by 75% over a 2-week period. Sarah was pleased but her mother was disappointed because she did not remember *any* time that she had interrupted. Sarah recounted those few occasions and her mother was subsequently able to cue herself to eliminate this behavior almost entirely. She realized that she had been treating Sarah like a small child, and began to respect her as an adult who could fend for herself more than adequately.

Thus, the tendency to be highly specific often involves simplification of measurement. However, the behavioral family therapist aims to provide a framework for problem solving that the family can continue to use *without the therapist's presence*. The emphasis on direct communication, clearly operationalized goals, and ongoing assessment to monitor observable changes and provide objective feedback to patient and therapist are the most critical elements of the behavioral approach. Comprehensive assessment of the outcome of a treatment program is employed at less frequent intervals, but is not a substitute for assessing day-by-day progress.

COMPONENTS OF BEHAVIORAL
INTERVENTION STRATEGIES

It has often been noted that behavioral psychotherapy interventions are derived almost exclusively from learning theory. While the early work of behavior therapists was derived from the classic laboratory experiments on animal learning of Pavlov and B. F. Skinner, and the human experiments of Watson and Mary Cover-Jones, recent advances have included an extraordinary array of strategies derived from a much broader perspective. This has included the use of role playing from the psychodrama methods of Moreno, imitative learning of Bandura, reciprocity of marital exchanges from Stuart, and cognitive responses of Ellis, Beck, and Meichenbaum. Other strategies have been derived from the common stock of social knowledge (common sense), such as the graduated exposure to fear of Marks, the social skills of Argyle, and the problem-solving methods of Spivack. Thus, in clinical practice the behavioral psychotherapist employs a potpourri of ingredients that are blended together in a varied manner to fit the individually specified goals of each patient or family. While reports of behavioral methods emphasize the specific therapeutic ingredients, less space is devoted to discussion of the supportive framework on which the specific interventions are built. This framework will be discussed, as well as several of the more commonly utilized intervention strategies that form the basic components of many behavioral programs.

Therapeutic Alliance

The establishment of a strong therapeutic alliance is as vital to behavior therapy as it is to other forms of psychotherapy, and possibly more so. The behavior therapist tends to place the patient in a situation where high demands for changing often long-standing behaviors and attitudes are made. This necessitates a strong degree of trust and confidence in the therapist's ability to guide and support. This is seen most clearly in patients with phobias who undertake to expose themselves to objects that have formerly induced terror. To a lesser degree, family members who are attempting to change their methods of communicating angry feelings may feel the need for a guiding hand they can use to support their initial tentative attempts.

The Temple University study indicated that expert behavior therapists showed a high level of warmth and concern for their patients (Sloane, Staples, Cristol, Yorkston, & Whipple, 1975), while Crowe (1978) found that the majority of therapist statements in behavioral marital therapy could be classified as "supportive." Thus, the collaborative set is clearly valued by behavior therapists and undoubtedly contributes substantially to the effectiveness of this method.

In addition to the supportive concern shown toward family members, some specific components are employed to aid the development of a therapeutic alliance:

1. Focus on the present strengths of the family unit. The therapist acknowledges that each family group has considerable assets and that at all times their behavioral responses represent their best possible effort for coping with the specific situation given the constraints they find imposed on them at any particular moment. Rather than confront incompetent or inappropriate responses, the therapist views them as partially effective coping efforts to be fashioned into more successful responses.

2. Collaboration in developing specific goals. The therapist avoids imposing his or her own goals and values on the family. Instead, goals are developed in close collaboration with the family and are clearly related to each family member's functional life situation. The level of participation in this goal-setting process has been shown to affect the ultimate achievement of the goals during therapy (Falloon & Talbot, 1982).

3. Specific therapeutic contract. In addition to mutual agreement on the outcome goals, the therapist and family agree upon the strategies to be employed in the therapy. A clear rationale for the use of all interventions is provided to the patient and his or her family prior to the start of treatment; in addition a time frame is clearly contracted (five sessions, 6 months' treatment, etc.). At times, therapists may employ simple written contracts that outline the mutual patient–therapist responsibilities; however, a clearly understood verbal contract is more common. Informed consent is considered important to building a strong therapeutic alliance, particularly when family members are reluctant to be labeled "patients" or fear they will be "analyzed" if they participate in family therapy.

4. Therapist modeling of appropriate behavior. The therapist presents a successful model of the appropriate responses he or she seeks to achieve with the therapy. Thus, the therapist demonstrates effective communication and problem-solving skills and demonstrates skills for coping with the contingencies of therapy. He or she assiduously avoids negative modeling—losing temper, forgetting appointments, making ambiguous or sarcastic comments, and so on. The behavioral therapist conforms with the "good parent" model who is firm, supportive, directive when necessary, but attempts to elicit the appropriate responses from the family members before proposing his or her own suggestions.

Operant Reinforcement Strategies

The paradigms of operant conditioning occupy a central position in all behavior therapy interventions. Family interventions prove successful when the therapist is able to guide the family members into changing their modes of dealing with each other. In behavioral terms, we can translate "ways of dealing with each other" into consequences of behavior or *contingencies of reinforcement*. Instead of rewarding maladaptive behavior with attention and concern, the family members learn to give each other acknowledgment and approval for desired behavior. It is clear that in the course of daily interaction, relatively few of the actions performed in the family system engender either a positive or negative reaction. Most of our responses pass without comment. Observations of distressed families reveal a higher rate of attention for displeasing behaviors in an angry manner that precludes effective problem solving. This anger may be focused on one member, the scapegoat, or be shared among a number of family members. Such punishment, which is apparently aimed at suppressing undesired behavior, often has the paradoxical effect of perpetuating the deviant behavior as a result of the attention and recognition it receives. This is particularly the case when attention for pleasing behavior is simultaneously reduced. The mother who says, "Why should I praise Jimmy for all the good things he does when he wets the bed every night?" illustrates this dilemma.

Anything that tends to increase the future occurrence of the behavior that immediately preceded it is termed a *positive reinforcer*. In everyday terms, people do the things that produce the rewards they want. Verbal and nonverbal means of giving attention and recognition (praise, pats on the back, smiles) are termed *social reinforcers*, in contrast to food or sex, which are termed *primary reinforcers*. Primary reinforcers are considered *innate drives*, whereas social reinforcers gain their rewarding qualities through *learned associations*. Social reinforcers and specific objects that also acquire reinforcing properties as a result of cognitive mediation (e.g., money, privileges, possessions) are termed *secondary reinforcers*. However, much of this theoretical work has been conducted with animals, and in the higher-order human species, reinforcers are highly individualized and of variable potency in different settings and contingencies even within the same individual. Drug addicts report considerable variation in their experiences when identical drugs are taken under different contingencies—the setting, company, or time since the last fix. Food eaten in a pleasant restaurant with felicitous company is experienced as more enjoyable than that served in a dank, dingy prison cell. The fickleness of the sophisticated adult human mediates against simple reinforcement paradigms.

A further level of complexity is added by the important element of timing and scheduling of reinforcement: "Darling, you are so boring—the same old routine every time. I want excitement, a bit of surprise, something new!"

The oft-heard pleas for changes in the reinforcement pattern in order to preserve the potency of the response are somewhat more complicated than merely changing from a one-to-one stimulus → response ratio (go to bed → have sex) to a one-in-two-to-three ratio (go to bed → have sex on Monday, Wednesday, and Saturday)! However, to *maintain* a behavioral sequence, *intermittent reinforcement* is more efficient than *continuous reinforcement*, while the latter is more effective in enhancing the *acquisition* of new behaviors. Thus, it is important for the therapist to reinforce every attempt to change a specific behavior, and then, once the behavior has been effectively established, to periodically reinforce its performance. Eysenck (1965) has shown that conditioned learning also varies with personality variables. Without a detailed exposition of reinforcement theory, it seems clear that this potentially powerful tool requires an adequate training in its application before it can be fully exploited by the family therapist. However, this investment is probably worth the effort in view of the wide applicability of this paradigm. All therapists employ reinforcement strategies in their therapies, but the skilled behavioral psychotherapist employs them more specifically and consistently.

Positive reinforcement, usually praise and attention, is used during the sessions with the family group to increase the frequency of the following:

- Specific positive remarks
- Specific requests
- Problem-solving statements
- Coping attempts
- Homework attempts

Families often communicate their mutual reinforcement in well-disguised fashion, with subtle, nonverbal cues having acquired special meaning after many years. Thus a frown, wink, smile, tone of voice, or specific word may have considerably more impact on the behavioral responses of family members than the more overt methods employed by the therapist. Very often, however, these reinforcers may become habitual and function at a covert level to control family behavior. Retraining the family in more overt reinforcement methods may serve to clarify these subtle yet powerful reinforcement patterns.

Punishment is considered to have occurred when an event tends to reduce the likelihood that the behavior that immediately preceded it will recur. In other words, people tend to stop doing things that produce unpleasant results. Some forms of aversive events (e.g., electric shock, pain, vomiting) have been used therapeutically to modify behavior. Induced vomiting caused by consumption of alcohol when taking disulfiram (Antabuse) may reduce alcohol intake in an alcoholic. However, another form of "punishment" is the withdrawal of positive reinforcement. Withdrawal of recognition, attention, and support may have a powerful effect in reducing the behavior that precedes it. A parent's ignoring a child's tantrums will tend to reduce their intensity and frequency. On the other hand, the lack of adequate attention, interest, and encouragement for desired behavior (e.g., cooking, cleaning, working efficiently, appropriate social behavior) may have a profound effect on family relationships, where desirable behavior is taken for granted so that attention is focused exclusively on deficient behavior. Recognition is provided for family members only when they perform inadequately or behave in a disturbing fashion. To maximize positive reinforcement (e.g., attention) in such a family system, the family member must act in a disturbed manner. This distortion of reinforcement patterns is frequently seen in families overburdened and demoralized by persistent life stress. The reinstitution of more effective reinforcement patterns may be an important element in restoring the mutually supportive potential of such families.

Within family therapy sessions, in addition to positively reinforcing effective communication and problem-solving behaviors, the therapist specifically ignores various unwanted responses, such as (1) hostile remarks, (2) nonspecific criticism, (3) interruption of the other person's speech, (4) symptom behavior, and (5) intrusive statements (e.g., speaking for others; "should," "must," "ought to" comments).

On such occasions, the family member may be invited to rephrase his or her remark in a more appropriate manner that may facilitate the problem-solving potential of the group. In this manner, attention is provided for effective communication behavior, not for the undesirable responses. Negative emotional responses are not suppressed; their effective communication is strongly reinforced. When a family member persists with hostile comments, the therapist may need to shout "Stop" (i.e., an aversive, punishing stimulus) to terminate the flow of acrimony before attempting to restructure the communication into constructive criticism and effective problem solving.

Shaping

The process of encouraging a person to approximate his or her behavior closer and closer to a clearly defined goal is known as *shaping*. A parent encouraging a baby to walk demonstrates this skill. With each attempted step, the parent praises the child's efforts as he or she shows slowly increasing competence. Negative features are ignored. Successive approximation through small steps is an extremely useful strategy in rehabilitation of the mentally as well as the physically ill.

Example: Mrs. P was a 72-year-old woman living with a 43-year-old disabled son. She had been depressed since her husband's death 6 months earlier. Although an excellent cook who enjoyed preparing meals for her son and herself, she had not cooked for several weeks and had depended on her two married daughters to visit at least twice a day to prepare food. One goal of therapy was for her to cook lunch every day. A shaping paradigm was used to achieve this. Her son and daughters were instructed to praise her for initially putting the kettle on, later to make a pot of tea, then to make toast, then to prepare eggs, and so on, until she was again creating exotic dishes. In a stepwise fashion, the goal was achieved over a 4-week period, after which one of her daughters visited twice a week to continue intermittent reinforcement of the lunch preparation behavior.

Extinction

As we have noted, the absence of any reinforcement for a specific behavior leads to a reduction in its performance. This rationale forms the basis of a strategy known as "extinction." Simply stated, family members are instructed to selectively ignore any undesirable behavior they wish to "extinguish" in other family members. This strategy has several pitfalls that limit its applicability, the most obvious detractor being that the behavior to be extinguished must be ignored by *all* members in the target person's environment. This may extend beyond the immediate household to any persons who may acknowledge, attend to, or sympathize with the selected behavior. Furthermore, the attention-seeking person may escalate the undesirable behavior in an attempt to provoke greater reinforcement. Family members need to be warned that a temporary worsening of the behavior may precede improvement; otherwise they will conclude understandably that the extinction strategy is not working. However, when used in combination with selective reinforcement of desired behaviors, extinction may make a useful contribution to the therapeutic endeavor.

Here is an example of the use of the extinction paradigm in a multiple family group:

One young man became anxious in group settings. He frequently interrupted the group discussion with irrelevant questions or comments, or by abruptly getting up and leaving the room and then returning. After several unsuccessful requests by the group leaders that he attend to the group discussion, the leaders agreed to ignore the disruptive behavior and instructed the group to do likewise. At the same time, all relevant comments were clearly acknowledged and praised, as were periods when he sat quietly in the group for 5 minutes. Subsequently, a decrement in this disruptive behavior was noted and problem-solving discussion proved feasible.

Time Out

This involves a more structured form of negative reinforcement than the previous example, and is usually employed in circumstances where the social reinforcement of undesirable behavior is almost unavoidable. The family member exhibiting the unpleasant behavior is removed from contact with others for a brief period of time. This strategy has proved useful in the modification of severe behavioral disturbances such as temper tantrums or violent behavior by sending the offender to a nonrewarding room for several minutes (duration clearly specified) with minimal fuss. The goal is to change the environment from one that is highly reinforcing of the problem behavior to one where there is minimal reinforcement for that behavior.

Example: Janet, age 8, often behaved aggressively (slapping, kicking, and pulling hair) toward her 12-year-old brother. Her parents were instructed to send Janet to the utility room immediately following such behavior. If she did not go when requested, they were told to walk her to the room with minimal attention. She was told to stay in the room for 2 minutes, after which her parents would call her. The reason for the "time out" was explained and she was requested not to repeat the specific aggressive act in the future. After institution of the time-out procedure, a substantial reduction in this undesired behavior was noted.

Application of time-out procedures to adolescent and adult family members is somewhat more difficult but has been successfully employed with them as a means of reducing excessive family tension. Persons with schizophrenia and other family members have been trained to monitor their own tension levels and to excuse themselves from stressful discussions and take a walk or relax in their rooms. Family members have been similarly taught to cut short a discussion that appears to be getting out of hand and leading to ineffective, potentially destructive problem solving.

Rules and Setting Limits

A specific definition of the rules for family behavior is an important therapeutic intervention. Where family members clearly infringe upon the rights and expectations of the family as a whole, setting specific limits may help define the structure of family interaction. Covert rules exist in most families. The process of making such rules explicit and clearly specified may in itself serve as a control over inappropriate behavior. In other cases, limit setting may facilitate a consistent approach to modifying behavior considered undesirable by the family group.

Example: A 23-year-old man was living with his mother, brother, and sister. Although he earned over $1000 a month, he spent large amounts on drugs and was frequently unable to pay his share of the rent. As a result, his mother was forced to work at two jobs to make ends meet. The therapist helped the family to establish the rule that everybody has to pay an equal share of the rent on the first day of each month, that no excuses could be considered, and that defaulters would have to move out immediately. It was also agreed unanimously that mother would work at one job and would not be solely responsible for the rent bill. Problems with payment of rent were greatly reduced once these limits had been explicitly laid down.

Behavior Rehearsal (Guided Practice)

This modality has been employed extensively in behavior therapy. It involves having a subject perform a behavioral sequence in the therapy session in a manner that approximates real-life performance. This may involve the use of role-playing methods derived from psychodrama. The subject imagines that he or she is in a particular setting interacting with a specific person—parent, boss, date. The therapist utilizes his or her skills as a director to enhance the realism of the rehearsal. When the role playing cannot readily approximate the real-life setting (e.g., taking off in an airplane, driving a car for a license test), it may be more effective to employ *covert* rehearsal. The patient closes his or her eyes and imagines performing the behavior in step-by-step detail. At other times, it may be advantageous to rehearse behavior in the real-life setting. This often necessitates having the behavior therapist leave the clinic with the patient and venture into the real world. Persons with agoraphobia and social phobias have been successfully treated in this manner (Hafner & Marks, 1976; Falloon, Lloyd, & Harpin, 1981). When patients are confronting feared situations in real life, this variant of behavior rehearsal has been termed "exposure *in vivo*" (Marks, 1976).

In addition to providing exposure to feared situations, behavior rehearsal is used as a component of behavior therapy in several different ways:

- practice in a nonthreatening environment;
- performance of interpersonal behavior that may be positively reinforced by observers;
- performance that can be reinforced by the subject himself or herself;
- performance that can be analyzed with constructive feedback from self and others;
- repeated practice employing alternative methods;
- as an assessment procedure (behavioral test);
- as a means of increasing attention and contact between members of a group or family;
- as a means of testing coping strategies.

Once again, this technique requires skillful application to maximize its utility. In a warm, supportive, therapeutic milieu most family members will engage in behavior rehearsal without substantial discomfort. However, if persons perceive that their best efforts will be laughed at or scorned, resistance to this technique may arise.

Modeling (Demonstration)

"Modeling" is the term used to describe demonstrations given by the therapist or other members of a group or family. A highly specific aspect of behavior is demonstrated so that the participants can focus with minimal distraction on the skill that is modeled. Modeling would appear to be most effective when a complex behavioral sequence is demonstrated to people who lack these skills in their repertory, and/or who lack the verbal skills to follow adequately the sequence of steps. Such modeling has been used extensively in training social behavior in mentally retarded and autistic children (Rosenthal & Kellogg, 1973; Lovaas, 1967); it has been less effective with assertiveness training of college students (McFall & Twentyman, 1973).

The most effective model is a person who is perceived as being on a similar performance level to the subject's expected performance, shows signs of discomfort, but appears to be in control of the situation throughout (Meichenbaum, Gilmore, & Fedoravicius, 1971). For these reasons, another family member is often the most effective model in behavioral family therapy.

This formal modeling procedure enables the subject to focus clearly on a specific element of the model's behavior. At the same time in family therapy, or other groups, members may informally imitate features of other people in the group.

Feedback

Feedback is a crucial element of all biological and social systems. It may be defined as the information that is processed during a response or sequence of responses, that may serve to modify the future performance of the response. In a family, this may operate at several levels at the same time—behavioral, interpersonal, affective, cognitive, and physiological. We have already considered the behavioral–interpersonal component of feedback in the discussion of reinforcement strategies and behavior rehearsal. But aside from the feedback obtained by interpersonal responses to specific behavior performance, feedback concerning other parameters may be important in facilitating behavior change.

To obtain comprehensive feedback on the performance of a particular interpersonal transaction, the following questions may need to be answered:

- *Behavioral:* "What did you do?"
- *Interpersonal:* "How did other(s) respond to your behavior?"
- *Affective:* "What were your feelings?"
- *Cognitive:* "What were you thinking, imagining?"
- *Physiological:* "How did you feel?"—bodily changes: sweating, blushing, tensed up, and so on.

In describing different psychotherapeutic strategies, greater or lesser attention is given to each of these feedback levels. Psychodynamic approaches stress affective and cognitive feedback; operant approaches stress behavioral and interpersonal; biofeedback and medical approaches focus on physiological features. While it is cumbersome to obtain feedback on all levels at all times, the family therapist may enhance his or her effectiveness by skillful choice of the focus of feedback when examining any interaction. It is postulated that a comprehensive integration of all these feedback sources facilitates change more efficiently than narrow attention to one or two areas.

Homework

Behavioral family therapy sessions may be conceptualized as training workshops in which family members can try out different response patterns to overcome problems they consider important. It is emphasized that performance between sessions in the everyday home setting is absolutely essential for ensuring durable and generalizable improvement. To aid this process, specific homework assignments are prescribed at the end of each session to enhance the transfer of skills acquired during the sessions into the family's repertoire. These homework tasks usually involve carrying out the skills rehearsed in the sessions, or following problem-solving plans. The success of the therapy is measured in terms of *changes in the real-life environment*, and considerable effort is expended in therapy to ensure that these changes occur and are sustained.

SUMMARY

The behavioral family therapy approach tends to follow a commonsense problem-solving structure. Five components are integral to this method:

1. Specific assessment of deficits before, during, and after intervention in order to provide feedback for the family and therapist. This knowledge of results enables the therapy to be directed efficiently and effectively to maximize progress toward functional goals that have been selected primarily by the family.

2. Development of a problem-solving milieu in the family. Emphasis on strengths, strong therapeutic alliance, functional goals.

3. Enhancement of interpersonal communication effectiveness so that stressful problems can be discussed openly without excessive tension and discomfort.

4. Enhancement of problem-solving skills to effect creative yet realistic strategies to overcome problems.

5. Intervention techniques are derived as the best solutions to the individualized goals of each family. Although social learning theory paradigms are almost always employed in some fashion, they are frequently not the primary intervention procedures. Strategies are derived from the active body of psychotherapeutic endeavor as well as from the social stock of commonsense knowledge. Each strategy is rigorously tested for efficacy in facilitating progress toward the specific goal of a specific family.

This approach has been widely utilized in the treatment of dysfunctional families with varied presenting features. The other chapters in this section will focus on the adaptation of this model to dysfunctional families in which one member has suffered an episode of schizophrenia and is living at home with his or her parents. Apart from the next chapter, which deals with family education about schizophrenia, the remaining discussions of the behavioral family therapy communication and problem-solving interventions have applicability across the spectrum of psychiatric problems and have been applied in a similar fashion with family members who have suffered depressive disorders, anxiety disorders (generalized anxiety, agoraphobia, social phobia), obsessive-compulsive disorders, alcoholism and drug dependence, marital distress, adolescent behavior disturbance, school phobia, and child abuse. Where assessment is based on a comprehensive behavioral analysis of functional problems, no contraindications for this approach have yet been reported. However, realistic limitations regarding behavioral family therapy as the primary treatment intervention are clear in the major mental disorders, and care should be taken to ensure that the family interventions clearly support associated medical, psychological, and social interventions when these are indicated.

CHAPTER 8

EDUCATING PATIENTS
AND THEIR FAMILIES
ABOUT SCHIZOPHRENIA

INTRODUCTION

Mental health professionals have often avoided detailed discussion of diagnosis, symptoms, and prognosis of schizophrenia and other psychiatric illnesses. Commonly cited reasons for doing so include lack of diagnostic clarity, the ill effects of stigmatization, discomfort with imparting such information, or the potentially harmful effects of a distressed reaction on the part of the individual with the illness.

When a patient is admitted to the hospital with an episode of schizophrenia, it is quite likely that neither the patient nor his or her family will be told much, if anything, about the illness. Factors mediating against this include notions implicating families in the cause of schizophrenia, issues of patient confidentiality, and the patient's disorganized mental status.

Usually an individual is discharged to the community after a brief period of hospitalization on a high dosage of neuroleptic medication with a referral to an outpatient facility. However, numerous studies have documented the low rate of patient follow-through on referrals, and others have described the period immediately following discharge from the hospital as a particularly vulnerable one for relapse. The family has been identified as an important system of primary care, and yet few interventions acknowledge the crucial role that the family may play in the patient's recovery. Several surveys have documented the lack of attention paid to family members and their need for support, information, and resources (Chapter 2, pp. 31–36).

A basic assumption underlying family management training is the necessity of providing a cognitive framework by which the family and patient can understand the illness and rationale for treatment. Our educational hypothesis is that provision of educational material may contribute to changes in attitudes and coping mechanisms within the family which may in turn lower family tension and the stress associated with dealing with chronic illness.

Several methods of providing education about mental illness have been tested by our group and others for use in different settings. Evaluation of group and individual family approaches, with or without the index patient present, day-long workshops, or weekly sessions have not established any clear consensus as to the best way to disseminate information and to facilitate family understanding about schizophrenia (Goldstein, 1982). In the absence of any comparative outcome studies, we chose to work with individual families, to include the index patient, and to conduct the sessions in the family home. We made these choices because we believed that the families would be more relaxed in their own homes, that disclosure about symptoms experienced by the index patient and other family members would be facilitated, that the patient would be an important source of information about schizophrenia, and that a wider network of family members would attend home-based sessions.

The 2- or sometimes 3-hour sessions are scheduled as soon as the index patient is discharged from the hospital and has been adequately stabilized on neuroleptic medication. However, although this is usually the first visit to the family home, all members of the household have been interviewed at the clinic on at least one occasion and the initial behavioral analysis of family functioning is usually near completion. It is important to note that these sessions mark the beginning of conjoint family meetings and serve the additional purpose of providing a clear rationale for the subsequent family management of schizophrenia. Education is considered a continual process that is initiated at this point but that may be addressed at any point throughout the treatment program.

This component of the family management program is specific to families who have a member who had had a clear-cut episode of schizophrenia. Similar educational approaches have been employed by the first author in the management of depression, agoraphobia, obsessive–compulsive disorders, and anxiety states. The content of the educational material obviously differs, but the basic methods are similar.

SESSION 1: THE NATURE OF SCHIZOPHRENIA

The first family therapy session is devoted to discussing the nature, course, and treatment of schizophrenia (Table 8-1). In addition to didactic presentation of educational materials to the family, family members are encouraged to share their own thoughts and feelings, fears and hopes,

TABLE 8-1. *Education about Schizophrenia: Summary of Part 1—"What Is Schizophrenia?"*

1. Schizophrenia is a major mental illness that affects one in 100 people.
2. The symptoms include: delusions—false beliefs; hallucinations—false perceptions, usually voices; difficulties of thinking, feeling, and behavior.
3. The exact cause is not known, but appears to produce an imbalance of the brain chemistry.
4. Stress and tension make the symptoms worse and possibly trigger exacerbation of the illness.
5. People who develop schizophrenia possibly have a weakness, which may run in families, that increases their risk of getting schizophrenia.
6. Some people recover from schizophrenia completely, but most have some difficulties and may suffer relapses.
7. Although there are no complete cures available, relapses can be prevented and life difficulties overcome.
8. Family members and friends can be most helpful by encouraging the person suffering from this illness to gradually regain former skills and to cope with stress more effectively.

about the illness. The specific objectives of this first session are (1) to encourage the patient to describe his or her experience with schizophrenia to the rest of the family; (2) to discover and correct misconceptions family members might have about schizophrenia; (3) to impart knowledge to the family regarding what is currently known about the causes, course, and treatment of schizophrenia; (4) to lower, where they might exist, unrealistic family expectations of complete recovery and rapid return to premorbid levels of functioning; and (5) to lay the foundation for subsequent family interventions by providing a conceptual framework of the factors that positively and negatively influence the course of the illness.

To facilitate learning, an eight-page handout on schizophrenia has been prepared by the authors, which is given to each family member at the beginning of the session.

The therapist then guides the family through the materials presented in the handout, providing supplementary information as required or requested by the family. Additional visual aids are provided through the use of a chalkboard or a posterboard upon which Velcro-backed summary cards are placed to highlight the main points of the discussion.

Correcting Misconceptions about Schizophrenia

It is good to start with the basics; we recommend beginning with a simple statement that the patient has been diagnosed as suffering from schizophrenia. Some families will already be aware of the diagnosis and a few will be quite sophisticated about the illness. For the families that are discovering the diagnosis for the first time, it is generally helpful to say something like this:

As you know, I have seen Bill [or whomever] on several occasions now, and have conducted a very thorough and careful evaluation. It is clear to me that the cause of Bill's recent difficulties is that he has been suffering from a mental illness called schizophrenia. Now, schizophrenia is a word that we've all heard before and I'm wondering what "schizophrenia" means to each of you.

At this point each person's notions about schizophrenia are elicited, including, of course, those of the index patient. Family members may respond that schizophrenia means "you have a split personality," or that schizophrenics are "insane," "crazy," or are "dangerous and violent." These notions are corrected. Even if none of these common misconceptions is expressed, it is still advisable to go over them. We recommend stating that:

First of all, there are several things that schizophrenia is not. It is not the same thing as "multiple personality" or "dual personality." Although many people think that schizophrenia means having more than one personality, this is actually a very rare mental illness called "dissociative neurosis" that is seen more often on television shows than it is in real life. The person with schizophrenia has only one personality, but during times when symptoms are present the person may have difficulty controlling his or her thoughts and deciding what is real and what is not real, and consequently may seem to have a change in personality. Moreover, although the actions of a person going through a schizophrenic episode may be very peculiar or strange at times, it is usually not the case that he or she is insane or crazy. Most odd behaviors or statements are logical and make sense in the context of the patient's distorted experience of reality. Thus, although many families fear that schizophrenia can cause violent or dangerous behaviors, this is generally not the case. The incidence of violent behaviors among individuals with schizophrenia is probably no higher than among persons not having schizophrenia. In fact, if anything, most people having schizophrenia tend to be more quiet, timid, and frightened, given to violence only when they are confronted. Even where this is not the case, patients who might be irrational and violent while having symptoms will return to behaving more appropriately when their symptoms improve with optimal treatment.

Some families will ask about the difference between schizophrenia and manic–depressive illness. It is not uncommon for persons with schizophrenia to have been told at one time or other that they have a manic–depressive illness. Where this is the case, the therapist should explain that manic–depressive illness is a disorder of moods characterized by severe bouts of depression and elation that often last for weeks at a time. Although persons with schizophrenia can become very depressed at times and become excited and hyperactive at other times, the two illnesses differ in the specific phenomenology presented. The therapist avoids being drawn into a debate about the index patient's diagnosis, or even the issue of whether the stabilized patient has a mental illness or not.

It is crucial that the therapist be highly confident that the diagnostic assessment is valid, that he or she has reviewed the acute symptoms of the index patient in detail, and that any doubts have been clarified with the diagnostic assessor prior to this session. Comments detracting from the credibility of the diagnostic assessment should be avoided.

What, Then, Is Schizophrenia?

After correcting any misconceptions about schizophrenia that are expressed by the family, we recommend a straightforward didactic presentation of some basic facts about the illness. This provides a background about the illness as a major medical disorder associated with substantial morbidity in many cases. It is explained that schizophrenia is a mental illness that affects approximately one of every 100 people in all countries throughout the world; that as many as 2 million people in the United States alone have suffered episodes of schizophrenia and that more hospital beds are filled by people suffering schizophrenia than any other medical illness.

The diagnosis is based on the presence of some very specific symptoms. It is considered a serious mental illness because the symptoms, when present, can have a great effect on nearly every important aspect of a person's life. Although the exact symptoms may vary somewhat from person to person, they nearly always produce a handicap in everyday functioning. The person suffering from schizophrenia may have difficulty handling problems because his or her thinking is inefficient, disorganized, or disrupted. He or she may not be able to work as well as before because of a reduced ability to concentrate and to think quickly and clearly. There may be similar difficulties in pursuing leisure activities. Interpersonal relationships are likely to be hampered by difficulties in conversation, or by a lack of normal feelings and emotional responsiveness. At times persons with schizophrenia can become so preoccupied with their thoughts and feelings that they fail to take proper care of even most basic needs for sleep, food, and shelter. Fortunately, these problems, which can be very serious during florid episodes of the illness, will generally be greatly improved when the symptoms are reduced or eliminated by effective treatment.

At this point, it is helpful to ask the patient and other family members to describe how their lives have been affected by schizophrenia. The changes in social performance that many families have attributed to laziness or stubbornness are reframed in terms of disabilities of an illness. Several families have commented that even though they had spoken to doctors for years, they had never been told that these social handicaps were a feature of the illness. Their persistent criticism of these behavioral problems had been a major source of ongoing stress in the family.

The Symptoms of Schizophrenia

In this section, the characteristic symptoms of schizophrenia are described as clearly as possible. The index patient and other family members are invited to describe in their own words those symptoms they have experienced.

The family is told that schizophrenia is diagnosed by recognizing certain characteristic symptoms involving changes in a person's thoughts, feelings, speech, and behavior. They are told that because there are no special blood tests or X-rays for schizophrenia, therapists depend on the individual's description of his or her experiences, so it is important to tell the therapist exactly what appears to have been happening. The therapist describes the characteristic symptoms of schizophrenia and invites the patient to discuss his or her own experiences of similar phenomena.

Thought Interference

There are several kinds of disturbances of thinking that persons with schizophrenia sometimes experience. These disturbances of thinking all involve ways in which one's thoughts are disrupted or interfered with, no matter how hard one fights against it. One example is experiencing thoughts being put into your head that are *not* your own thoughts. It might even seem like these alien thoughts are being put into your head by some kind of telepathy or radio waves. You might also have the experience of having your thoughts suddenly disappear, almost as though they were being withdrawn from your head. Your mind goes blank, and you are completely unable to think about anything. Another experience you might have is hearing your thoughts out loud, as if someone standing nearby would be able to hear them. It might even seem as if your private thoughts were somehow being transmitted or broadcast, so that everybody knew what you were thinking and none of your thoughts were private.

Following this, family members are asked if they have experienced any of these forms of thought interference.

Example:

THERAPIST: (*after describing the various kinds of thought disorder*) Bill, have you experienced any of the things I just described?

BILL: Yeah. I hear my thoughts real loud lots of times.

THERAPIST: What is that like for you?

BILL: It's embarrassing when other people can hear my thoughts. If it's happening I usually just stay in my room.

THERAPIST: (*to parents*) Were you two aware that this happens to Bill?

MOTHER: No, he never told us that.

FATHER: I thought he stayed in his room because he wasn't interested in anything but his music.

THERAPIST: This kind of symptom can be very difficult to cope with because it seems perfectly real when it is happening. Although other people really can't hear Bill's thoughts, it seems quite certain to him that they can when this symptom is occurring.

Delusions: False Beliefs

After a discussion of the different types of thought interference, we go on to discuss the nature of delusions:

Another disturbance of thinking is called a "delusion." This is a clearly false belief that seems quite real to the person with schizophrenia, whereas other people do not share this belief or idea. Some examples of delusions that commonly occur in schizophrenia are:

• A belief that something or someone is controlling your thoughts or actions, and that you are powerless to resist. It is as though some outside power takes over your will and makes you do things.

• A belief that somebody is trying to harm you, make your life miserable, or even kill you. Even though you feel you don't deserve to be treated like that, it seems to be happening nevertheless.

• The experience of seeing special messages or meanings in trivial everyday events that seem to be meant especially for you. It may seem, while watching TV, that somehow they knew you'd be watching, and so the show was done in a special way to communicate a message to you. Or it may seem that ordinary things take on special meaning; for example, one man had the delusion that every time a car horn was honked, it meant that people were accusing him of being a homosexual.

• A belief that you are a very special person with unique powers or abilities. It might seem that you are a famous person, or that you can cause earthquakes, floods, or other natural disasters.

In short, a delusion is simply a false belief that other people not only do not share but in fact recognize to be quite impossible. For the person having delusional thoughts, however, it is usually perfectly realistic. Often, after the person has recovered, he or she may also realize that it had all been a delusion. It can be a little like waking up from a dream. It all seemed quite real in the dream, but when you wake up you realize it was not really true.

Example:

THERAPIST: (*after describing delusions*) Bill, have you had any experiences like this?

BILL: Yeah. Last week I was watching TV with Mom and something made me get up and walk over to the park.

THERAPIST: Could you have stayed at home if you had wanted to?

BILL: I did want to stay at home. But it just kind of took me over and I had to go to the park.

THERAPIST: (*to the mother*) Were you aware of all this at the time, Mrs. Candy?

MRS. CANDY: No. In fact I was mad at Bill for leaving like that, just when we were about to go out for dinner.

The above example illustrates how family members may often mistakenly believe that the patient is choosing to behave in a manner that may aggravate them. In this case, the patient was experiencing a delusion of external control that he felt powerless to resist. This is not to say that persons with schizophrenia do not volitionally do things that other people dislike; however, it is important during the educational sessions, as well as in subsequent sessions, to help family members to clarify which inappropriate behaviors may be illness-related and which are not.

Hallucinations: False Perceptions

The most characteristic symptom of schizophrenia is auditory hallucinations, though surprisingly some patients manage to keep their families (and even therapists, at times) quite in the dark about them. We have found that even guarded patients, who have repeatedly denied hearing voices during interviews at the clinic, will frequently acknowledge for the first time that they have heard voices, when the topic is discussed in the family education session. This is especially true when the session is conducted in the home. We generally proceed as follows:

Another common set of symptoms of schizophrenia is hallucinations. An hallucination is a false perception; in other words, if someone hears, sees, smells, or feels things that other people don't, then that is termed a hallucination. Sometimes people will think they hear their name being called, often when they are half asleep, or see things under the influence of drugs or alcohol, or even hear what seems to be the voice of a dead relative with whom they were particularly close. These hallucinations can occur with schizophrenia but are not the characteristic ones we are referring to here. The type of hallucination that occurs in schizophrenia happens when a person is quite wide awake and completely sober. The most common hallucination is hearing voices talking when there is nobody around. These voices will seem quite real and most often seem to be coming out of the air above one's head, or maybe in the next room or outside. Sometimes they sound like they are coming from inside the person's head or other parts of the body such as the stomach or throat. Often there are several voices talking among themselves and referring to the person as "him" or "her." They might say sometimes like, "There she goes again, walking up the street. Walk, walk, walk always walking."

Have you had any experiences like this? What did the voices say? What was it like for you? Were you able to make the voices go away?

Example:

THERAPIST: Sally, have you ever heard voices like I was just describing?

SALLY: Yeah. I guess so.

THERAPIST: Could you describe to us what it is like?

SALLY: Well, I hear the voice of God, especially when I'm driving.

THERAPIST: What does the voice say?

SALLY: It tells me what to do, like "Turn left here" or "Keep going straight."

THERAPIST: Does it seem that you have to do whatever the voice says?

SALLY: Sometimes it tells me to turn left when I should really keep going straight to get to where I'm driving. But I'm afraid to disobey Jesus. Sometimes I go ahead anyway.

THERAPIST: What happens when you don't do what the voice says?

SALLY: I feel really scared, Doctor. I don't know what's going to happen. Sometimes I get so scared I have to pull over.

MOTHER: Is that what happened last Sunday when you turned pale and got all wild-eyed and nervous?

SALLY: Yeah. I was disobeying the voice of God and I was afraid.

The above example illustrates not only what the experience of an auditory hallucination can be like, but also shows how this kind of open discussion can be quite enlightening for family members who are usually only dimly aware of what the patient's inner experience is really like. It is common during discussions such as this to see family attitudes change quite dramatically from criticism and hostility to greater understanding, emotional support, and appreciation of the difficulties with which the family member with schizophrenia is trying to cope.

Unusual Behavior

Although thought disorders, delusions, and hallucinations are identified as the most typical symptoms of schizophrenia, and are used in establishing the diagnosis, we go on to describe additional symptoms which frequently occur:

Another common symptom, particularly during a worsening of the illness, is speech that is very peculiar and difficult to follow. Occasionally people will make up new words or use unusual expressions. At other times their thoughts will be so jumbled or disconnected that it is difficult to make any sense out of what they are saying. Sometimes the person might stop talking altogether and be unresponsive for hours.

There are some peculiar behaviors that are considered symptoms of schizophrenia. A person may adopt unusual postures, or repeatedly go through a series of motions that don't seem to make any sense.

Although these abnormal behaviors do not occur for many people suffering from schizophrenia, most people do report changes in their feelings. For most this takes the form of having their feelings and emotions disappear or become less intense. This holds true for both happy and sad feelings. Others may experience a loss of control over their feelings, so that they find themselves laughing at times for no particular reason or crying when not even feeling sad. Most people suffering an episode of schizophrenia experience a period, which can be relatively short or last for months, during which they have a hard time becoming interested in things or deriving pleasure from activities they formerly enjoyed. People often mistake this for laziness or unwillingness to help oneself, but frequently this loss of pleasure and loss of interest can be quite profound and one of the most difficult symptoms to cope with.

The therapist concludes this section by inviting the index patient and the family members to recount their experiences of these symptoms. It is difficult to convey the unusual quality of the abnormalities associated with schizophrenia, and there is the danger that family members may consider all inappropriate behavior to be "symptoms." One father considered the "irrational" temper tantrums of his 25-year-old son a symptom of schizophrenia and was unwilling to adopt a firm, no-nonsense approach to dealing with this inappropriate behavior. Remember that the index patient is the "expert" on the experiences of schizophrenia in the family. But he or she may not be the only such expert in the family! During the course of the discussion, the therapist addresses his or her remarks about schizophrenia not only to the index patient, but also to the family members. This gives them permission to disclose symptoms they may have experienced. Not infrequently, other family members will report symptoms of schizophrenia that they have experienced. One sister described an episode of delusions and auditory hallucinations that she had recovered from spontaneously. She had never before discussed this with anyone. Her younger sister, the index patient, felt greatly relieved to hear her sister's story and to compare notes on the experiences.

Course of the Illness

Many patients and relatives fear that schizophrenia is an illness that gradually worsens as the patient gets older. Some even worry that it leads to early death. It was not long ago that it was thought that schizophrenia followed a gradual, yet inexorable downward course. Fortunately, the gradual deterioration noted in long-term patients in mental institutions turned out to result mainly from the long-term hospitalization *per se* rather than from schizophrenia. In the past two decades, the trend toward community management of schizophrenia, with brief hospitalizations in acute-care facilities when necessary, has revealed that although schizophrenia is an episodic illness characterized by exacerbations and partial or complete remissions, it is not generally a progressive illness. It is important to convey this information to the family. The following is offered as one way this might be accomplished:

Schizophrenia is typically an illness that begins in late adolescence or early adult life. It can occur at any age, although it is unusual to see a first episode of typical schizophrenia in a person older than 45. It is generally a favorable sign if the symptoms come on suddenly rather than gradually over a period of many months or even years, and it is also a good sign if the first episode occurs after the age of 35. One-third of people with schizophrenia suffer only one episode of the illness and never have a further attack. Another third have symptoms that continue without a stable remission, and a further third have a course of exacerbations of symptoms interspersed by periods without any symptoms. In any event, schizophrenia is not generally a progressive illness—it does not get worse with age. In fact, there is a tendency for schizophrenia to lessen gradually over the years, and it does not have any adverse effects on physical health. Although it does tend to improve gradually over the years, schizophrenia is, nevertheless, frequently a lifelong concern.

Schizophrenia affects many young people in the prime of their lives. It represents a significant setback in their plans and hopes for the future and, consequently, it is not uncommon for a person to become depressed and feel considerable despair. Such depression can resemble that of other psychiatric disorders and may confuse the therapist who has not seen the person when he or she was experiencing characteristic symptoms of schizophrenia.

Recovery from a major episode of schizophrenia usually takes a number of months and sometimes even longer. It is different for each individual. Occasionally, symptoms such as hallucinations and delusions persist for a long time following a relapse, though to a milder, less bothersome degree. For many individuals these symptoms gradually fade away over a few weeks or months. For other, more fortunate individuals the hallucinations and delusions go away completely in a relatively short time. During this recovery phase families often mistakenly believe that the person is just being "lazy" or is "unwilling to help" himself or herself. This is almost always *not* the case. Lack of energy, apathy, withdrawal, loss of interest, sleeping a lot, and uncommunicativeness are all very real symptoms that occur with varying severity in most people recovering from a major episode of schizophrenia. Although it is good to encourage such a person to get out periodically, join the family activities, and so forth, it should be kept in mind that these problems are usually part of the illness, that they eventually improve, and that it is important for everybody to try to be patient and allow ample time for the recovery process to take place.

The exact content of the preceding section can be modified somewhat to fit the symptom picture and progress toward a recovery of each individual case. Some families are very understanding of what the patient is going through, but others are highly critical and unsupportive, assuming that the patient has fully recovered from the illness and is now choosing to be lazy and unproductive.

Causes of Schizophrenia

Families and patients frequently ask what caused the patient to develop schizophrenia. Several misconceptions are heard repeatedly when working with this population. Many parents believe they must somehow be responsible for the mental illness of their son or daughter. In fact, just about every parent of a chronically ill schizophrenic patient can provide examples of how mental health professionals they had seen previously either implied or stated outright that they were primarily to blame for the problem of their relative. A second notion frequently encountered is that the patient has always had some kind of underlying problem or personality defect that was never properly understood and which ultimately led to their demise. People holding this belief often feel that the way to "cure" schizophrenia is to dig deep and discover the "real problem" at the core of the patient's personality and then correct it. A third commonly held belief, especially in large urban areas, is that schizophrenia is caused by using street drugs. Although it may well be that use of drugs such as phencyclidine (PCP) and amphetamines may contribute substantially to bringing on an episode of schizophrenia, it seems most probable that these individuals already had a constitutional vulnerability to develop schizophrenia and the street drugs merely accelerated the process. One also encounters individuals who believe that schizophrenia may be caused by nutritional deficiencies and that it should be treated with large dosages of various vitamins and minerals. The foundation for realistic expectations for helping the individual suffering from schizophrenia must be laid by addressing the issues surrounding its causes. We generally proceed as follows:

Biological Components

Although the exact causes of schizophrenia are not well understood at present, it does seem clear that it has biological as well as environmental aspects. For example, we know that although the incidence of schizophrenia in the general population is roughly one in every 100, the incidence among first-degree relatives (son, daughter, brother, sister, father, mother) of a person with schizophrenia is more on the order of one out of ten. Most experts view this as evidence that there is some kind of genetic link, at least in some cases, though most experts would say that what is inherited genetically is not the illness itself but rather a vulnerability or predisposition to develop the illness at a later time in life. The nature of this vulnerability is not precisely known, though there is growing evidence that persons with schizophrenia have abnormalities in the chemistry of their brains. All brain functions such as thinking, feeling, and body movements are the result of chemical exchanges in brain cells. When a person develops schizophrenia it is thought that a chemical called dopamine accumulates in excessive amounts and causes a chemical imbalance that produces the unusual symptoms. The medications that are used to treat schizophrenia seem to reduce this excess of dopamine, though the exact way they do this is not well understood. Thus, the symptoms of schizophrenia seem to be caused by a chemical imbalance, which is partially or fully corrected by the medication. We say "partially" because in some cases the medication will not eliminate all of the symptoms, though most people do report at least some improvement.

Psychosocial Components

This brings us to the psychological or environmental aspects of schizophrenia. What have you read or heard or thought about what might cause a person to develop schizophrenia?

At this point it is helpful to give family members a chance to express their own views on what caused the index patient to develop schizophrenia. Some family members will feel guilty and worry that they are somehow responsible for it. Many families have made considerable adjustments to cope with the person with schizophrenia. They often believe that if they had coped better early on maybe the illness would not have developed, or it may have been less severe. Other families will tend to blame the patient for developing the illness. They may staunchly believe that it was all the result of smoking marijuana or taking stronger street drugs. Some families believe the patients led to their own downfall by being lazy or inactive, rather than doing something constructive. One man believed that his son's illness was caused by the son's unwillingness to figure out what he wanted to do with his life after he graduated from high school: "If Jerry could just make up his mind about what career to pursue, I'm sure these problems would end."

Families frequently mistake prodromal phases of schizophrenia for a personality flaw or weakness (i.e., apathy and withdrawal might be considered evidence of being unwilling or too lazy to get out and straighten out one's life), which they then believe to have caused the later development of florid symptoms. In any event, it is advisable to cover some of this ground even with relatives who do not express these ideas spontaneously.

Some families worry that they might be to blame for schizophrenia in one of the members. We often hear the notion that schizophrenia is caused by an unhappy childhood. A lot of publicity has been given to various theories that families that raised their children in certain ways could cause them to develop schizophrenia later. However, there is no conclusive scientific evidence that families in any way cause schizophrenia. But there is abundant evidence that families may be able to help improve the outcome of the illness.

The evidence suggests that some individuals are born with a constitutional predisposition to develop schizophrenia later in life, just as some individuals are born with a predisposition to develop diabetes or high blood pressure.

The influence that a family might have on schizophrenia takes a somewhat different form. We view schizophrenia as a stress-related biological disorder. Although it appears to have a basis in the brain chemistry, a vulnerable person is most likely to have an episode of the illness during a period when he or she is under a great amount of stress. This probably explains why the first episode of schizophrenia most often occurs in early adulthood, a period of high stress for men and women.

It is a time when individuals are trying to establish close friendships, find a marital partner, have children, complete their education, make career decisions, and establish their independence from their families. Studies have also shown that major stressful events, such as a death in the family, loss of a job, or breakup of an important relationship tend to make schizophrenia worse. Another important aspect of any person's environment is the home environment. High levels of family tension will add to the stress that everyone is under and can cause schizophrenic symptoms to worsen. On the other hand, families that are helpful in coping with life events and solving the day-to-day problems of living together help reduce the amount of stress affecting each member and improve the course of the illness. For this reason we will be teaching you ways of coping more effectively so that everyone will be under less stress.

By the same token, families sometimes do too much for persons with schizophrenia, allowing them to lie around all day doing nothing. This lack of stimulation can also be harmful. The key is to find a middle ground where families are supportive, and offer encouragement to the person without being excessively critical or nagging a lot. Families that provide consistent support and can cope effectively with adverse life stress have a very positive impact on the course of the illness.

Summary

The above material can be discussed in a little under 1 hour. At the end the family are to be invited to make comments or ask questions. Following this the main points are summarized:

To summarize, then, schizophrenia is a mental illness that is quite common, affecting about 2 million people in the United States. Although it can be very disruptive during times when the symptoms return or get worse, there are very effective treatments available which can permit most people to resume their normal lives gradually. The characteristic symptoms are hallucinations—particularly experiences of hearing voices—delusions, and disordered thoughts, feelings, and behaviors.

The exact cause is unknown but appears related to an imbalance of brain chemistry. Excessive stress and tension will usually make the symptoms worse, and can trigger exacerbations. Although a third recover from schizophrenia completely, almost all people will have some difficulties and may suffer exacerbations in the future. Effective treatment, however, can reduce the symptoms substantially and cause those that do occur to be briefer, milder, and less disruptive.

The most effective treatment is to take medication to offset the imbalance in brain chemistry, and learn more effective ways to cope with stress and tensions. Families can be helpful by encouraging the person to gradually resume their former activities and to cope with stress more effectively. It is important not to expect a rapid and complete recovery, but to be content with a gradual recovery process over a period of months.

Sometimes, the person with schizophrenia may have to adjust his or her life-style, learning to take things a bit easier. However, there is usually no reason why most realistic goals cannot eventually be obtained, such as working, pursuing hobbies, making friends, getting married, becoming more independent, or what-ever they might happen to be.

SESSION 2: ISSUES RELATED TO MEDICATION

The second educational session is devoted to discussing the role of neuro-leptic medications in the treatment of schizophrenia (Table 8-2). In the vast majority of cases continued ingestion of neuroleptic medications is a vital component of the management of the illness. For this reason, we find it useful to review carefully for the index patient and his or her family the rationale for taking these medications. Many patients with histories of multiple psychiatric hospitalizations also have histories of erratic com-pliance with pharmacological interventions. This is not entirely their fault. Often, the role of these medications in preventing or reducing the severity of symptomatic exacerbations has not been spelled out to the patient and family. Many patients experience unpleasant side effects such as sedation, akathisia (an extrapyramidal reaction characterized by a strong sense of inner discomfort, restlessness, pacing, and inability to sit or lie down in a comfortable position), dystonic muscular spasms, blurry vision, dulled intellect, stiffness, lack of expression, and tremors and other involuntary movements. Public acute-care psychiatric facilities are under great pressure to treat acutely ill patients in very brief hospital stays (10–21 days is typical). This encourages aggressive pharmacological strate-gies using high-dose neuroleptics. Unfortunately, the side effects can be so unpleasant that many patients stop taking their medications at the first opportunity, and have very high rates of exacerbations in the months after discharge.

TABLE 8-2. *Education about Schizophrenia: Summary of Part 2—Medication Management*

1. *Regular* tablet taking is the mainstay of the treatment of schizophrenia.
2. Major tranquilizers are very effective medicine for the treatment of schizophrenia.
3. In low doses, they also protect a person from relapse of symptoms.
4. Side effects are usually mild and can be coped with.
5. Street drugs make schizophrenia worse.

Education about the medication seeks to enhance compliance with this important part of treatment. This is accomplished by carefully explaining the rationale for taking neuroleptics, acknowledging the unpleasantness of the side effects, and advocating the use of the lowest dosages possible, to minimize these side effects. Specific behavioral strategies are discussed for improving regularity of pill taking in cases where compliance is erratic owing to forgetfulness, conceptual disorganization, or interference with pill taking related to symptoms (e.g., a voice telling the patient not to take the pills). The following sections will demonstrate how we present this material. Again, it is important to encourage the patient and other family members to discuss their experiences with psychiatric medications.

Rationale for Maintenance on Neuroleptics

We begin by asking if anyone has any questions or comments about the material covered during the previous session. In most cases questions are raised because family members will have had an opportunity to look over the handout and consider its contents. After discussing these matters and summarizing the major points of the previous session, we distribute a handout on the drug treatment of schizophrenia. The session begins with the therapist presenting a rationale for maintenance treatment with neuroleptics:

In the previous session we discussed the nature of schizophrenia, including the difficulties it can create and its probable causes. We concluded that schizophrenia is probably caused by a disturbance of brain chemistry that can be made worse by stress. Consequently, the most effective treatment would involve correcting the chemical imbalance and reducing stress. Coping with stressful events and situations can be difficult. In future sessions we will devote considerable attention to strategies for coping with personal as well as family problems. For now, however, let's see how medication can be helpful.

Effective medications for treating schizophrenia were developed over 25 years ago and are one of the most important advances in all of medicine in the past 50 years. Largely as a result of these new medications, the number of patients needing long-term hospital care has been drastically reduced and many psychiatric hospitals have been closed throughout the country. Today, these medications continue to be the mainstay of treatment for schizophrenia.

There are several different types of drugs used in the treatment of various psychiatric disorders; those used for schizophrenia are called *neuroleptics*. Neuroleptics are also referred to at times as "major tranquilizers" or "antipsychotic drugs." All share the same beneficial effects, but some have various side effects.

There are many different types of neuroleptics. Each has both a generic, or chemical, name and a brand name. Some of the commonly used neuroleptics are the following:

Chemical name	Brand name
chlorpromazine	Thorazine
fluphenazine	Prolixin
trifluoperazine	Stelazine
thioridazine	Mellaril
haloperidol	Haldol
thiothixene	Navane
perphenazine	Trilafon
loxapine	Loxitane

Most of these come in tablet form, though fluphenazine can also be taken as a long-acting injection.

The strengths of these various drugs vary considerably. For example, 100 mg of chlorpromazine might have the same beneficial effect as only 2 mg of haloperidol. Moreover, different individuals or the same individual at different times may require very different dosages of medication, depending on the body chemistry and severity of symptoms at the time.

Which of these medications have you taken? Did one seem to work better or have fewer side effects than the others?

There are two ways in which medication is used in the treatment of schizophrenia. The first is to reduce the symptoms of an acute episode of the illness. These drugs produce substantial benefits in at least 75% of people with acute episodes of schizophrenia. However, once the symptoms of delusions, hallucinations, and thinking difficulties have been relieved, the same medicine is used to help prevent relapses. This prophylactic dose is usually much less than the amount needed during an acute episode. In fact, many people can be maintained on doses low enough to produce no side effects at all.

If the current pharmacological management requires high dosages of neuroleptics and the patient is complaining of unpleasant side effects, he or she might feel greatly encouraged to know that the dosage will gradually be decreased over time and that he or she can expect to have far fewer side effects in the future. In the next section, the benefits of continued medication to prevent exacerbations of schizophrenia are outlined. The therapist must be familiar with the literature on this issue and be able to present this summary of the data in a well-informed, convincing manner (see Chapter 4, pp. 69–75). A simple graph of the relapse rates with and without maintenance medication is referred to in the handout to highlight the benefits (see Figure 8-1).

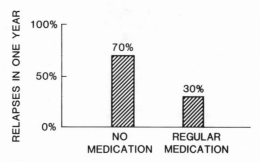

FIGURE 8-1. *Why is it important to take medicine every day?*

Continuing to take medication after the major symptoms have gone is like taking out an insurance policy against having an exacerbation in future. In the 12 months following a major episode of schizophrenia, people who do not take medication regularly will have about a 70% chance of relapse. Simply taking a low-dose neuroleptic medication on a regular daily basis will reduce the chances of relapse to around 30%. And this is only the medication effect. We have found that medication plus family therapy can lower the rate of exacerbation during the first year to around 10% or even less. Moreover, even if there is an exacerbation, it is likely to be briefer and milder for people taking medication regularly. For those not taking medications, chances are that if a further episode occurs the symptoms are likely to be more severe and more likely to interfere with everyday functioning —often resulting in hospital admission, losing a job, or major family problems. If you are taking medication and have a worsening of symptoms, most such cases can be treated effectively by temporarily increasing the dosage. Usually the symptoms will decrease within a few days and major life disruptions can be averted.

Have you had an exacerbation of your illness? Were you taking medicine at the time it occurred? How much did it disrupt your life?

One point we want to emphasize is that although medication is very important in the treatment of schizophrenia, it is not a complete treatment in itself. Medication usually helps reduce or eliminate symptoms but it cannot help a person learn new skills, get a job, make friends, or eliminate boredom. Other forms of assistance are usually necessary in combination with medication for best results. Job training, schooling, and skills training to learn to talk with people or to handle situations effectively may all be recommended as part of a comprehensive rehabilitation program following recovery from a major episode of schizophrenia.

In general, the symptoms likely to abate from taking medication are delusions, hallucinations, thinking problems, social withdrawal, agitation, confused speech, and changeable moods (laughing or crying for no apparent reason). The symptoms least likely to respond to medication, which require other forms of assistance, are boredom, lack of energy, depression, nervousness, and bodily complaints.

The therapist makes use of the posterboard to highlight features such as the symptoms that are most and least likely to improve. The perceptions patients and family members have about medication are explored in order to clear up misconceptions.

Example:

THERAPIST: Fred, in what ways, if any, have you noticed that the medication has beneficial effects for you?

FRED: It helps me sleep at night. If I don't take my pill, I can't sleep. I stay up all night. And if I don't sleep for a few nights, then the lack of sleep makes me sick again. Sometimes though, if I've drunk a lot of brewskies, then I can fall asleep without needing to take a pill, so if I've been drinking I always try to skip the pill.

THERAPIST: What do you think of that, Mrs. Samuel [Fred's mother]?

MRS. SAMUEL: Shouldn't he take his medicine rather than take beer?

THERAPIST: Yes, it is very important to take your medicine *every* day, Fred. If you are not sleeping, I'd like you to tell your psychiatrist. It may be a warning that you need a higher dose of your medicine.

Finding the Optimal Dose

Most people are not enamored with the idea of taking medication. Many patients' first experience with neuroleptic medications happens during their first hospital admission. Since inpatient treatment of an acute episode generally involves the use of comparatively high doses, many patients will associate neuroleptic medications with unpleasant side effects such as dystonic reactions, parkinsonism, and akathisia. They may not realize that the amount of medicine required in maintenance treatment is much lower, and usually need not be accompanied by the same bothersome side effects. Patients and their families are told:

It often takes some time to find the best medication and the optimal dose. Many people have received fairly high doses of medication while in the hospital and experienced such unpleasant side effects that they are reluctant to continue taking medication following discharge. Our philosophy is the use of the smallest possible dosage that still provides the protective benefits of medication. No one wants to take any more medication of whatever kind than is necessary; still, there are such enormous differences from person to person in body chemistry that it frequently takes time and experimentation to find the best medication and the best dosage. You can assist us in this part of your treatment by telling us exactly how you are feeling. Therapists rely on their patients to tell them if they are having side effects or an increase in symptoms. Thus, it is important for you to work closely with us and keep us posted about symptoms you might be having, even if they aren't bothering you particularly. Even more importantly, you can help matters by taking the medication regularly every day. This not only gives you the maximum protection, but it will also help reduce side effects. People who frequently skip days or juggle dosages on their own are likely to have more problems with side effects. Our goal is probably the same as yours: to gradually lower the dosage to the minimum amount that keeps the symptoms of schizophrenia from coming back (or getting worse).

What questions or concerns do you have about taking this kind of medication?

Some people worry that this kind of medication might be addicting or that a person can get "high" on it. There has been a lot of publicity about people abusing drugs such as Valium, Quaaludes, and various other "uppers" and "downers." In this regard, neuroleptics are among the safest drugs in medicine. They are not addicting, and you do not need an increasingly higher dose the longer you take them. If anything, the opposite is true—you may very well find that over time, you will gradually need less medicine.

Warning Signals of Relapse

A key to effective outpatient management of schizophrenia is rapid intervention during the early stages of an exacerbation. Consequently, it is helpful to teach patients and their families to recognize warning signals that may predict an impending exacerbation. If an exacerbation can be detected in the early stages, psychotherapeutic and pharmacologic interventions can usually prevent the development of a major episode of the illness. One of the major advantages to involving the entire family in the treatment is that the therapist does not have to rely solely on the patient to contact him or her at these times. Other family members, educated in the nature and course of schizophrenia, can get in touch with the therapist in those cases where the patient lacks the good judgment or social skills necessary to notify the therapist when experiencing symptoms:

Relapses of schizophrenia rarely happen suddenly. They are usually preceded by several days of tension, changes in thoughts and behaviors, or feeling "out of sorts." You can learn to recognize these warning signals and take measures that may forestall or prevent the imminent relapse. The most common warning signals are sleep difficulties, increased feeling of tension, or the return or worsening of symptoms such as hearing voices. Other warning signals include irritability, restlessness, talkativeness, increasing withdrawal, changes from usual behavior, and poor concentration. Each individual will have his or her own pattern of warning signals.

What has been your own experience? Are there certain changes that represent definite warning signals for you?

When these warning signals occur, there are several things you can do that might prove helpful. You can contact your therapist, you can take extra medication on your doctor's advice, you can discuss your difficulties with your family, and you can try to find ways to cope with stress and keep up daily activities.

Some of these warning signals may be similar to side effects of your medication. If so, do not stop or reduce your medication. Get in touch with your therapist and let him or her know how you are feeling. At other times, these tension symptoms may seem like a physical illness such as the flu. Staying in bed, however, is not usually helpful. It is better to try to keep doing your regular daily activities unless they are causing you considerable stress.

The therapist assists the index patient and his or her family to compile a list of the specific warning signals that have preceded acute episodes. This list is filed in a folder along with the educational handouts and subsequent written materials provided in the family sessions.

Side Effects

Many patients experience unpleasant side effects while taking neuroleptics, especially during treatment of an acute exacerbation of schizophrenia, when higher doses are required. Some of these side effects, such as dystonic reactions, parkinsonism, akathisia, and tardive dyskinesia, are readily recognized by knowledgeable clinicians to be secondary to the medication. Others are not so obvious and can be correctly diagnosed only by careful examination of the patient. One such symptom is akinesia, characterized by decreased movements and decreased facial expressiveness, which can easily be mistaken for depression or emotional blunting secondary to the illness. Some patients dislike certain neuroleptics but are unable to articulate the exact reasons. In such cases, there may be subtle "cognitive" side effects such as mental dulling, slowed thinking, reduced attention span, less vivid thoughts, or a foggy feeling in the head. We therefore recommend making careful and frequent inquiries regarding side effects.

Patients' complaints deserve careful consideration. In most cases, adjustments can be made that eventually will eliminate the side effects.

Therapists should acknowledge that they share with the patient the goals of eliminating bothersome side effects. In the educational session, we recommend spending a fair amount of time discussing issues related to side effects where poor compliance has been a problem:

The major tranquilizers are a remarkable group of powerful medications. Chlor-promazine (Thorazine) was one of the earliest developed and in some countries it is known by the name of Largactil, so called because it has such a *large* range of *actions*. Indeed, it affects nearly every system of the body, from the brain to the circulatory, alimentary, neuromuscular, and endocrine systems. The other major tranquilizers are similar. In the treatment of schizophrenia we are interested only in its effects on the brain chemistry, and these other actions are rather a nuisance. These unwanted side effects often include drowsiness, shakiness, restlessness, blurry vision, dryness in the mouth, muscle stiffness, occasional dizziness, and increased appetite. Most of these symptoms are mild and go away on their own after awhile. Some other side effects that are not as common include sensitivity to sunburn, muscular spasms, mouth movements, and temporary sexual difficulties.

What symptoms or side effects have you had that you thought were caused by the medication? What did you do about them?

Any of these unwanted effects are unpleasant, but because the medication is so effective in the treatment of schizophrenia and prevention of recurrence, ways of coping with these problems have been developed. These include:

1. Wait awhile. Most of the side effects are worse when you first begin to take the medicine. After a few days, or at the most a week or two, many of these effects will have worn off. There is no reduction in the beneficial effects. So the first and often best way to cope with any bothersome side effects is just to wait awhile.

2. Reduce dose on doctor's advice. It is very difficult for your doctor to calculate the exact dose for you when he or she first prescribes your medicine. Sometimes he or she will prescribe a little too much. If particularly troublesome side effects occur, contact your doctor if they do not show any signs of abating. He or she may recommend reducing the dose. The blood tests your doctor takes will be a helpful guide to the dosage he or she will recommend [when plasma levels or serum prolactin assays are being conducted].

3. Change to another neuroleptic on doctor's advice. Some people who are extra sensitive to the effects of one medicine are less troubled by another. If after waiting a week or so, and reducing your dose, troublesome side effects remain, your doctor may recommend a change to another neuroleptic that is less likely to have the specific effects that bother you. For example, chlorpromazine and thioridazine tend to cause drowsiness, whereas fluphenazine is less likely to cause this problem, but is more likely to cause shakiness.

4. *Take a medication to control the side effects.* When the above methods have proved unsuccessful at helping you to cope with the side effects, your doctor might recommend taking a medication to reduce some side effects. The medications commonly used include: trihexyphenidyl (Artane), benztropine (Cogentin), and diphenhydramine (Benadryl). These medicines are sometimes helpful in reducing the neuromuscular complaints such as shakiness, stiffness, and muscle spasms. However, they themselves have side effects such as dry mouth, blurred vision, and difficulty urinating, so are not very helpful for long-term use.

5. *Additional remedies for common side effects. a.* Drowsiness. This can be often overcome by taking your main daily dose of medicine before you go to bed. The drowsiness at that time will be helpful in getting a good night's sleep and may have worn off by morning.

b. Sensitivity of sunburn. Some neuroleptics may increase your tendency to burn in the sunshine, especially if you have fair skin. You can cope with this by avoiding exposure to the hot sun and by using a strong sunscreen cream or lotion when you are in the sun. Several excellent brands are sold in all drugstores. The best contain an ingredient known as PABA, or paraaminobenzoic acid. Ask the pharmacist which one is the best.

c. Restless legs. Two methods of coping with this bothersome side effect are physical exercise, such as walking or jogging, and muscle stretching exercises. Tense your muscles as tightly as you can, count to five, then slowly let them relax.

d. Dizziness. The dizziness occasionally produced by some medicines usually occurs when you get up suddenly, especially from a warm bed or a hot tub. This can be avoided if you rise more slowly.

e. Increased appetite. This is no problem in itself, but may lead to weight gain. Take care to eat good, healthful food and avoid a lot of fattening foods such as breads, cakes, candy, rice, and potatoes. If you gain 10 pounds or more, you may need a reducing diet.

Nearly all side effects can be eliminated or at least reduced to levels where you can cope with them with minimal discomfort. Unfortunately, on occasions people will develop side effects that persist no matter what is tried. These are more frequent when a high dose of the medicine is given over long periods. One type of side effect that may occur is that of mouth, lip, and tongue movements. There is considerable controversy over this symptom, called "tardive dyskinesia." If it does occur and becomes severe, your doctor may recommend stopping your medicines, particularly if you have been quite free of any of the characteristic symptoms of schizophrenia for some time.

Do you have any questions about side effects? Which of these coping methods have you tried. Were you able to reduce the side effects?

We have been talking a lot about side effects because we want you to know as much as possible about your treatment. However, these medications are in fact among the safest drugs used in all of medicine. For example, even commonly used drugs like aspirin might seem unsafe if you consider all the possible side effects they can have! So we don't want you to be unduly alarmed. In addition to the methods we have just discussed, you can also minimize side effects by developing a method to take your tablets every day. You may find it helpful to put your daily dose of tablets in a prominent place so that you can see clearly whether you have taken your prescribed dose. Other family members might remind you if you find that helpful. Or you might prefer to handle it yourself. In any event, excessive nagging is usually not very helpful, and may make matters worse.

A further source of increased side effects is taking more than one neuroleptic at a time. Combining medications usually does not increase the beneficial effects, but it may increase the side effects. That is why we usually try to stick to prescribing only one neuroleptic at a time.

Several other issues deserve comment. Many patients stop taking their medication even though it is clearly helping them and not causing many side effects. The reasons given for stopping medication are discussed so that the index patient and his or her family can be sensitive to these issues and hopefully cope more effectively:

In spite of the benefits of medicine in the prevention of recurrence of schizophrenia, many people do not take their medication every day. One reason for prematurely stopping medication is side effects. We have already discussed the problem effects of these medicines. Sometimes people stop taking their medication for a day or two and as a result feel better when the side effects go away. The beneficial effects of the medication may take longer to diminish so a relapse may not occur immediately. This may persuade you that the medicine was doing more harm than good; but remember, you will have a 70% chance of relapsing if you stop the medicine, but only a 30% chance if you stick with it.

A second reason is that taking medication is a reminder of the illness. Taking tablets every day serves to remind you of your illness. This may be rather unpleasant, particularly if you feel quite well and are free of any symptoms. However, taking the tablets will ensure that you *remain well* in the same way that taking vitamins in the winter may prevent colds or flu. It is like an insurance policy that is worth investing a little effort in every day. When a major stress occurs in your life, you will be much less likely to suffer an exacerbation of schizophrenia if you have been taking your medicine regularly. An exacerbation can be very costly for you in terms of the loss of progress toward your goals in life.

It is also important to remember that schizophrenia is not something you are, but is instead an illness that you *have*. A lot of people think that since its symptoms are psychological, there must be something wrong with the individual's personality. However, people with all kinds of personalities, talents, and intelligence have had problems with this illness. The key is to learn how to cope with it so that it doesn't interfere with your life too much. Just as a person with diabetes can usually control his or her illness by taking medication regularly, so can the person with schizophrenia reduce the problems caused by the illness by taking medication and learning ways to cope with stress.

A third reason some people give for stopping their medication is that they are searching for other cures. Some people continue to suffer from the symptoms of schizophrenia (hearing voices, having unusual ideas and thinking difficulties) even though they take the medicine as their doctor prescribes. The medication may be helping but some symptoms persist. This can be most frustrating and can cause a person to lose faith in treatment and to stop taking medication. If you have persistent bothersome symptoms, it is very important to take your tablets exactly as prescribed so that your doctor can measure the effect of different dosage schedules on your symptoms. Progress may seem slow at times, but stopping medication will almost inevitably lead to further episodes.

Have you stopped your medicine at any time? What were your reasons for stopping? What happened when you went off the medicine?

ALCOHOL AND DRUG ABUSE

Patients and families frequently have questions regarding the use or abuse of alcohol and various street drugs. We generally inquire about the family attitudes and rules concerning alcohol, marijuana, PCP, and other drugs. Following that discussion, we give the following information:

There is no clear evidence that any street drugs actually *cause* schizophrenia. But there is no doubt that they frequently make the illness worse, and can trigger off relapses. The worst offenders are PCP ("angel dust," "Shermans," "cools," "lovely"), amphetamines ("uppers," "speed"), and LSD ("acid"). Marijuana ("pot," "grass"), in small amounts is probably less harmful, but has triggered off relapses in many people and is not worth risking, especially as it may be mixed with PCP.

The effects of small amounts of alcohol on schizophrenia are not usually harmful. However, you may find that you will become intoxicated much quicker. As a rule of thumb, alcohol will have double its effect when you are taking neuroleptics. If you are planning to drink, limit yourself to one or two drinks only, and drink them slowly. Do not cut back on your medication!

DISCUSSION AND CONCLUSIONS

The need for ongoing educational intervention over the course of treatment is essential and should not be underestimated by the therapist. The authors have noted a tendency in some families to revert back to belief in prior notions, or to ignore the ongoing risk of schizophrenia, particularly after symptoms abate and there is a return to normal social function. For this reason, it is beneficial to review the material presented about the illness regularly.

In the area of medication compliance, family members may be highly influential in reminding the index patient to take the prescribed medication and in reinforcing his or her behavior. Thus, it is crucial that parent and family attitudes toward medicine remain positive. In several families either covert or overt messages were given that taking medication was no longer needed as the person was cured. This calls for an immediate refresher course on the risks of relapse without regular neuroleptic maintenance.

Families may demonstrate integration of the educational component in various ways. Some examples are illustrative of the range of responses. One family of limited intellectual function did not seem to grasp the biochemical hypothesis or other theoretical material about schizophrenia, although they accepted the need for medication. However, when the patient's daughter was born, the family was able to express concern about the role of genetic factors in the etiology of the illness and the implications for child rearing. Another patient was able to request a raise in her medication when she was feeling stress associated with her work. Another patient was fearful that he was suffering a relapse because he experienced transient hallucinations; he was able to discuss this openly with his parents, which allayed his apprehension and reduced tension. Many individuals with schizophrenia were able to discuss the presence or absence of symptoms on an ongoing basis with family members outside of family sessions.

A large amount of complex information is imparted to the families in a short time. A major concern has been how much is retained by the patient and the family. A multiple-choice questionnaire was devised to measure the knowledge acquired after the family education sessions, 3 and 9 months later. Substantial gains in knowledge about schizophrenia were evident in patients and family members after the sessions that were maintained at the 9-month follow-up. The levels of knowledge acquired by many patients and many family members approached those achieved by mental health professionals on the same knowledge questionnaire (McGill, Falloon, Boyd, & Wood-Siverio, 1983). It was striking that these results were often achieved in families of lower socioeconomic status where health education programs have been less effective. Some family members were unable to read the handouts, so a clear oral presentation was essential. The importance of gaining good attention throughout the didactic presentation and discussion is stressed. This was achieved through addressing issues specific to the patient's illness and family situation. Handouts and a posterboard provided additional visual prompts, and question-and-answer discussions to clarify issues kept a focus on the relevant content of the presentation.

The patient is identified as the family expert on the experiences of schizophrenia and its treatment and often derives considerable elevation in family status as a result of being able to describe the features of the illness. Initially, some patients deny that they have had schizophrenia, but as they are drawn into describing their experiences, it becomes abundantly clear that they have had the characteristic symptoms of that illness and they soon begin to accept the nature of their condition.

We have not experienced any patients or families who have been harmed by the knowledge provided. Patients have reported studying the handouts in detail and remarking how closely the descriptions match their own experiences. Their ability to function as informed consumers is often quite remarkable. Several patients described their ability to monitor their own stress levels and to suggest increases in their medication dosages to their physicians before any outward signs of an impending relapse. They were able to discuss issues regarding the medications and the side effects openly and assertively with their physicians. This appeared to result in more effective problem solving, and may have contributed to the somewhat better compliance noted (Strang, Falloon, Moss, Razani, & Boyd, 1981).

The education appeared to enlighten family members and to enhance their ability to cope with the patient and his or her illness. Their attitudes toward the patient became more empathic and supportive. In no case was increased scapegoating observed. Unfortunately, the dearth of community knowledge about schizophrenia and the media misinformation that portrays persons suffering from schizophrenia as dangerous, upredictable potential criminals, made discussions about schizophrenia difficult outside the immediate family group. However, many families were able to disseminate some information to their friends and neighbors and were delighted to find them receptive to learning more about this condition.

It is evident that this educational process is not a light undertaking. The presenter needs to be well versed in the diagnosis and community management of schizophrenia including its psychosocial and drug treatments. However, well-trained mental health professionals generally have sufficient knowledge and experience to conduct these sessions, and psychologists, social workers, and nurses have proved as effective as expert psychiatrists. We have prepared a videotape presentation entitled "What Is Schizophrenia?" with accompanying guidebooks for therapists and family members. This has proved a useful teaching aid for less experienced professionals.

This component of the family management program has been surprisingly effective. Families and patients have expressed considerable appreciation for relieving the confusion and uncertainty that have often paralyzed their efforts to cope with this often puzzling illness. Similar education for other types of mental illness have proved similarly effective. Apart from the direct benefits to the index patient and his or her family, this consumer education may eventually serve to enhance community support for the mentally ill.

CHAPTER 9

COMMUNICATION TRAINING

OVERVIEW

The manner in which family members communicate their thoughts and feelings has a major impact on the course of mental illness. At times of crisis, effective communication may reduce family tensions, facilitate coping efforts and problem solving, and as a consequence contribute to a reduction in the risk of stress-induced exacerbation of symptoms. On the other hand, ineffective patterns of communication may impede problem-solving efforts and contribute to these symptomatic exacerbations. At other times, communication skills such as expressing positive feelings for specific pleasing behavior, or clarifying a problem issue through attentive, empathic listening may provide effective strategies for solving interpersonal problems.

One of the key advantages to working with the entire family is the opportunity to intervene and alter dysfunctional patterns of communication. In behavioral family therapy, special attention is given to examining the ways families communicate. A careful behavioral analysis is performed for each family that focuses on how each family member communicates positive and negative feelings, listens to others, and makes requests for behavioral change. Intervention strategies are then tailored to each family's specific deficits in communication skills.

Several aspects of communication are addressed with nearly all families. These include the basic components of verbal and nonverbal communication when expressing feelings to others. Because much emotional expression is communicated at the nonverbal level, this aspect of family communication is considered very important. Elements of nonverbal communication that are a major focus of training include voice tone, eye contact, body posture, facial expression, and proximity of speakers. At times the nonverbal structuring of family conversations and discussions may require modification. Families may benefit from being able to meet together seated comfortably and without distraction in a circle. This structure, which is employed in family group discussion in the clinic, is seldom used in the home. Its effect on family problem solving may be profound as the communication process is enhanced.

The importance of being clear and specific about the positive and negative behavior that has engendered one's feelings is stressed, as well as the desirability of expressing positive and negative feelings directly and at the most opportune time. Intrusive speaking or thinking for others, making demands and threats, giving mixed messages, and invalidating the thoughts and feelings expressed by others are among the communication behaviors that the therapist attempts to restructure. The initial focus, however, is on maximizing the communication of positive feelings within the family to create a supportive, problem-solving milieu within which more challenging issues can be effectively addressed. Once the more straightforward positive communication skills have been mastered, the more difficult expression of unpleasant feelings is addressed. All these specific skills are trained within the context of enhancing problem-solving effectiveness. In some families, problem resolution is achieved despite the use of less optimal communication behavior. Such cases are rare, but raise the issue of whether empathic communication that is promoted in psychotherapy is always appropriate for all family problem-solving discussions, or whether with some issues a little shouting, screaming, or foot stamping may be even more effective, especially where a clear plan for solving the problem is agreed upon and implemented!

The communication training procedures used in behavioral family therapy have been derived from interpersonal skills training methods that have been employed in behavioral group therapy (Liberman, King, DeRisi, & McCann, 1975; Falloon, 1978). These methods make extensive use of repeated role playing as a basic format for training more effective skills. In a family group, the somewhat artificial quality of role play is reduced because the communication between family members that is rehearsed is indeed "real."

For the sake of clarity in the presentation of the specific components of behavioral family therapy this section of the book draws artificial distinctions between problem-solving training and specific communication issues. In reality family sessions provide a workshop for the family and therapist to try out a range of alternative strategies related to the immediate or anticipated family stresses. Considerable overlap between problem-solving, communication skills, and management strategies exists in practice. Any resemblance to a highly structured topic-by-session course is an artifact of our attempt to structure this written presentation, and should not be construed as an accurate reflection of the method.

Earlier group workshop approaches (Falloon *et al.*, 1981; Liberman, Falloon, & Aitchison, 1978) were structured as a topic-by-session course.

COMMUNICATION TRAINING METHODS

Communication training employs several behavioral procedures in sequence in order to rehearse specific expression of feelings in the family therapy group and subsequently in spontaneous everyday family discussions. The basic sequence involves rehearsal, feedback, coaching, repeated rehearsal, social reinforcement, and planning generalization. We will discuss each of these sequential modalities in detail (see Figure 9-1).

Rehearsal

The initial rehearsal (sometimes known as a "dry run") is conducted to obtain baseline data on the specific communication skill noted deficient in the behavioral analysis of family interaction. The therapist and nonparticipant family members observe the interaction sequence and attempt to pinpoint deficits that might be remedied in subsequent rehearsals. At times the initial rehearsal may occur during spontaneous family discussion when a family member expresses his or her feelings in an ineffectual manner. In this case, the therapist may decide to interrupt the discussion to focus on that specific segment of emotional expression. However, at other times, the therapist may prompt and set up the initial rehearsal. Whenever possible the skill that is chosen for rehearsal should be relevant to the flow of the family discussion, and the enhanced effectiveness derived from the training should contribute to the current issues under discussion. The session is a little like a preseason football game where the coach may stop the action frequently to try out new strategies. Although the coaching slows down the flow of the communication, it does not interfere with the overall progress of the discussion.

Each rehearsal is kept brief (usually less than 1 minute) in order to maximize attention to the specific skills under examination. Here is an example:

THERAPIST: Bob, I'd like you to show me how you told your mother you didn't like her interrupting your discussion with your friend Linda on Sunday night. You were sitting over by the piano and your mother was standing by the door. Is that right?

BOB: Yeah. I was sitting here and Mom came in the door.

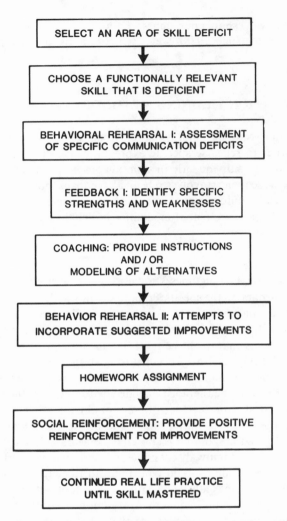

FIGURE 9-1. *Assessment and training of communication skills.*

THERAPIST: Would you come in the door like you did Sunday, Mrs. Poole, and say something similar to what you did then? (*Mrs. Poole gets up and goes to the door.*) I'll sit next to Bob and play the part of his friend. OK. Let's start.

MRS. POOLE: Bob, I was thinking you and Linda might like to go to a jazz club.

BOB: What kind of stupid idea is that? Don't interrupt us. We're trying to work out something.

MRS. POOLE: Sorry, I was only trying . . .

THERAPIST: Let's stop there. That's similar to Sunday night?

BOB: Yeah. That's just what happened. Don't you think that's unreasonable of her to come barging in . . .

THERAPIST: Well, I like the way you were direct about your annoyance with your mother, Bob. And I liked the friendly way you made the suggestion to Bob, Mrs. Poole. But it seemed that there might have been some other ways of handling that discussion. How do you think you might have replied differently to your mother's suggestion, Bob?

BOB: I could have ignored it, or I could have not got so angry.

Note the manner in which the therapist makes use of the home environment to replay a situation that occurred in the recent past. In addition, he reinforces effective aspects of the family members' communication skills while identifying elements that could be enhanced. The therapist himself models a supportive problem-solving style.

Feedback

The next step is to provide feedback on the initial rehearsal. As we have seen in the example above, this entails first providing an appraisal of specific positive features followed by an exploration of areas for potential improvement. Many of us are well practiced in the art of providing criticism, but focusing on positive features first ensures that the therapist conveys a positive constructive attitude to the coping efforts of the family. Again, specific comments are favored over generalized remarks, such as "I like the way you were direct about your annoyance"; versus merely saying "I like that."

Coaching

At this point the therapist begins to direct attention toward a specific nonverbal component that could be readily modified and lead to enhanced communication. Only one specific area is modified with each subsequent rehearsal in a stepwise fashion. Two commonly used coaching methods are the provision of verbal instruction and modeling of the communication skill.

Verbal Instruction

Straightforward instructions to change behavior are provided. Consider the following example:

THERAPIST: Bob, your brother suggests that you might try telling Mom that you are busy and would prefer not to be interrupted at the moment. I would like you to try that approach. Let's do the same situation again, and I'd like you to tell your mother that you are busy and don't want to be interrupted.

BOB: OK. She starts?

MRS. POOLE: Wouldn't you and Linda like to go to a jazz club tonight?

BOB: Mom, we're busy working on a song right now. I wish you'd let us alone.

THERAPIST: That was much better. I like the way you told your mother that you were busy songwriting and didn't want to be disturbed.

Modeling

Demonstration of communication behavior is a very effective way to coach these skills, particularly the more complex skills such as attentive listening. Research on the effectiveness of modeling suggests that where the model adopts a "coping" rather than a "mastery" style, the trainee is more likely to emulate the model's behavior (Meichenbaum et al., 1971). Here is an example:

THERAPIST: Bob, I wonder if there are any other ways you might handle your mother's interruptions in the future.

BOB: Can't think of anything right now.

JIM [Bob's brother]: You could thank her for the suggestion before you tell her to bug off.

THERAPIST: I'd like you to change places with Bob and show him how you might do that, Jim. Bob, I want you to watch and listen carefully to how your brother acknowledges your Mother's suggestion. OK, Jim?

JIM: Will Mom say something?

THERAPIST: Yes. Mrs. Poole, will you come in again and ask "Bob" if he'd like to go to a jazz club?

MRS. POOLE: Would you like to take Linda to a jazz club tonight?

JIM: (modeling for Bob) That's a good idea. Maybe I will, but I'm real busy right now. I'd rather not be interrupted while I'm writing this song.

THERAPIST: Fine. Bob, what did you notice that Jim did differently from you?

BOB: He raved on about what a great idea it was going to a club.

THERAPIST: He showed some appreciation of Mom's idea before he told her he didn't want to be interrupted.

BOB: Yeah, he did.

THERAPIST: Now I'd like you to try something similar. Remember, thank her first and then tell her how you feel about being interrupted.

BOB: (*sarcastically*) Well, Mom, I think that's a *great* suggestion, but please don't interrupt me when you can see I'm busy.

In this example the therapist changes the seating of the two brothers and takes care to frame the specific communication skill he wishes to demonstrate. This focuses the attention of observers on the specific aspects of the demonstration and reduces attention to irrelevant issues— the brother's accent, gestures, or other mannerisms. He elicits information from the person he is coaching to check whether the modeling skill had been accurately observed. An offer to repeat the demonstration may be useful where the skill is somewhat complex. The subject who is being coached is then invited to emulate the *specific* elements of the modeled performance, but to adapt other elements to his own personality style.

Repeated Rehearsal

Repeated practice of interaction sequences is the central ingredient of behavioral skills training methods. In the family group, this practice may be readily carried out between sessions so that extensive rehearsal is somewhat redundant during sessions. However, where coaching of alternative responses has been applied, repeated rehearsals serve to examine the effectiveness of suggested changes in communication skills and to provide a framework for further feedback and coaching as necessary.

During the rehearsals the therapist may actively coach through nonverbal gestures or brief prompts. "Speak up," "Look at her," "That's great," and so on. Such coaching should be unobtrusive and serve as a model for other family members to assist in the skill training after the sessions. Small increments of change are aimed for rather than major modification of communication styles.

At all times the therapist draws attention to the realism of the rehearsal and makes full use of the environmental setting to enhance the natural qualities of the role playing. Here is an example:

THERAPIST: I would like us to do that same situation again. This time I'd like you to look at your mother when you tell her that you would prefer to be left alone. Right?

BOB: Uh-huh.

MRS. POOLE: Bob, I was thinking that you might like to take Linda to a club or something tonight.

BOB: (*looking directly at his mother*) No, I'd like you to just leave us alone, Mom. We want to finish this song. But thanks for thinking about us, that's cool.

Social Reinforcement

The provision of unqualified praise for tiny increments of enhanced communication behavior is a vital step in the training procedure. As well as the reinforcement provided during prompted performances, specific praise for effective communication during spontaneous family discussion is provided. In addition to the powerful effect of this intervention on increasing the probability that the specifically acknowledged response will occur, positive reinforcement skills may be learned through observation of the therapist as he or she provides reinforcement during the sessions (informal modeling). Specific training in dispensing social reinforcement is discussed in this chapter (p. 217). Wherever possible, the therapist prompts other family members to provide reinforcement for small improvements in the performance of one another. He or she also encourages the participants in behavior rehearsals to provide themselves with objective reinforcement for their own perceived improvements (self-reinforcement). Here is an example from a therapy session:

THERAPIST: That was very good. I especially liked the way you looked right at your mother when you told her you'd rather she let you alone. What did you like about the way Bob did that, Mr. Poole?

MR. POOLE: I thought he did a good job.

Therapist: What particular things did you like about it?

MR. POOLE: Well, as you said he looked at her and he sounded as if he meant what he said.

THERAPIST: How did Bob come across to you, Mrs. Poole?

MRS. POOLE: He was polite. He didn't snap at me as he usually does. I liked that better.

THERAPIST: Bob, it seems that you got your message across very well. How did you feel?

BOB: It didn't sound like me. It was rather phoney, but if it takes that to get Mom to leave me alone and not treat me like a kid I guess I can learn to live with that.

THERAPIST: Sometimes trying a new style of saying things does feel rather strange. It's like riding a bike for the first time. But with practice, quite soon you'll find it comes more naturally. I thought you did a very good job.

Planning Generalization

Homework

The final step in the skills training sequence is perhaps the most important. This involves contracting a specific homework assignment with the family. Family members agree to practice unaided one or more of the communication skills rehearsed during the session. At the beginning of the next session, the homework is reviewed and feedback and positive reinforcement are provided. Performance of interaction sequences in the natural environment without the assistance of a therapist is the immediate goal of behavioral family therapy. The more frequent this performance, the more rapidly the behavior is assimilated into the family's repertoire. In other words, "practice makes perfect." For these reasons, considerable attention is paid to homework completion. Specific prompt sheets are employed wherever possible so that the homework task is clearly defined in writing. Family members share the responsibility for completion of homework so that blaming one or more members for noncompletion can be avoided. Families are advised to schedule regular, brief family meetings to plan and review their progress; some prefer more informal discussions. We have not made any rigid requirements as to *how* the family completes their homework, only that they do complete it to the best of their ability.

Let's look at a transcript of a therapist preparing a homework task with the family.

THERAPIST: OK. We have practiced your telling your mother you want her to leave you alone, Bob, and you seem able to do that pretty effectively. When do you expect you might need to use that skill in the next few days?

BOB: Could happen anytime. I'd say that most days I want to tell her to let me alone for some reason.

MRS. POOLE: There he goes again, always putting me down. He wants to drive me to an early grave!

BOB: Come on, Mom. That's not the point. Shut up and listen.

THERAPIST: I'd like you to rephrase that, Bob, and make a positive request.

BOB: OK. Mom, I'd be grateful if you'd stop interrupting and listen for a change.

THERAPIST: That's good. So you anticipate several times this week when you might ask your mother to do something different in a positive way?

BOB: Sure.

THERAPIST: Do you feel you would be able to make more positive requests?

BOB: Probably.

THERAPIST: I'd like you to give it a try. Would you be willing to do that?

BOB: Yeah. I'll tell her in a more polite way.

THERAPIST: That's great. Perhaps you all have some other positive requests to make of one another.

MR. POOLE: Sure we do.

THERAPIST: Here are sheets for each one of you. I would like you to record details about the requests you make. Has anyone got any questions? Bob, I'd like you to tell me what you are going to do for homework this week.

BOB: I'm going to be more polite and write it down on this bit of paper.

THERAPIST: Good. You are going to try to make positive requests and write them down on the sheet. Then at the beginning of our next meeting we will talk about how everyone got on.

The therapist carefully checks that his instructions have been understood. In our experience one of the major reasons for poor compliance with homework assignments is a lack of understanding of the exact nature of the task. It is essential that the therapist allow sufficient time at the end of the session to devote to planning the homework. Transfer of trained skills to the natural habitat is the major goal of therapy, and this step must be accorded the importance it deserves.

CORE CURRICULUM OF
COMMUNICATION OF FEELINGS

A core curriculum of communication skills has been developed that is based on the social psychology studies that have been discussed in Chapter 2. These studies suggested that deficiencies in the expression of emotional communication, in particular the expression of nonconstructive criticism and excessive concern accompanied by intrusive behavior, may have a detrimental effect on the course of schizophrenia, depression, and other major mental illness. Other studies have also implicated a lack of clarity in communication of feelings in the families of people who develop schizophrenia. In addition, the impact of life event stress on schizophrenia suggests the need for a supportive family milieu where effective crisis intervention and problem solving can occur. It is therefore important to develop a positive milieu where effective crisis intervention and problem solving can occur, where warmth, empathy, and nondemanding expectations predominate over hostility, misunderstanding, and coercion. The following communication skills are considered the minimum sufficient repertoire for such effective family problem-solving discussions: (1) communication of positive feelings for specific positive behavior—"expressing positives"; (2) communication of negative feelings for specific negative behavior—"expressing negatives"; (3) making positive requests for change of specific behaviors—"positive requests"; and (4) attentive listening behavior when discussing problems or other important family issues.

The ability of each family member to perform these skills appropriately within the family group is assessed prior to dealing with each of these areas in the sessions. Training can then be directed toward the more deficient family members, while the more proficient members assist in the training procedures. A few families show excellent skills in these four areas prior to training, but in most families there are major difficulties for one or more family members in many of these skills. The therapist adopts a matter-of-fact approach to the training and attempts to build the skills gradually into the family discussions without excessive didactic input. The family sessions are structured as living-room discussions of important family topics rather than as minilectures. A supportive workshop environment is created in which family members can help each other enhance their communication effectiveness and fully participate in the training experience. This structure is preferred because it can be more readily adopted as an ongoing feature of family life, even when the therapist is not present to act as the expert facilitator. Thus, generalization of training sessions may occur more readily and spontaneously when a naturalistic communication style is adopted by the therapist. Let us examine each of the core communication topics and describe how the training is applied.

COMMUNICATION OF POSITIVE FEELINGS

The goal of effective communication of positive feelings is for family members to be able (1) to identify a *specific positive behavior* performed by another family member; (2) to tell that person *exactly what* he or she has done that is positive; (3) to make a clear verbal statement of *how they feel* about the specific behavior that has been performed, accompanied by congruent nonverbal expression of positive feelings; and (4) to express spontaneous and frequent positive feelings for specific everyday activities.

A brief rationale for enhancing communication of positive feelings is provided by the therapist as an introduction to training in this skill. The role of positive reinforcement as a motivator for behavior change and as a morale builder is stressed. Frequent praise or acknowledgment of specific small accomplishments is defined as a major therapeutic intervention that can be used to achieve major behavioral changes in a step-by-step fashion. Rationing praise for major accomplishments or perfect performances only is eschewed.

The training proceeds through behavior rehearsal, coaching, and social reinforcement, with each family member being invited to provide examples of current or recent instances where he or she either expressed positive feelings or might wish to express positive feelings on future occasions. Competent performance of this skill or its components is positively reinforced by the therapist and other family members, who thereby demonstrate giving positives in the session. Deficient components of the skill are shaped in this and subsequent sessions. The family members are encouraged to remember the major components of expressing positive feelings and are provided with a handout sheet (Figure 9-2) to pin on a bulletin board or tape to the refrigerator door, and later to file in a family workbook. The workbook forms an ongoing record of didactic handouts, guidelines, completed homework assignments and problem-solving efforts for subsequent review and revision.

Example: Barry had been having ongoing difficulties with the nearly new car he had purchased a year earlier. His father insisted that it was as good as any other car, but Barry maintained that it was a "lemon." After his father had helped him replace a carburetor, Barry *sat on a chair near his father, made eye contact with him, and said* with a smile [appropriate nonverbal expression]: "*Dad, I was pleased* [direct statement of feelings] *you helped me fix that carburetor in my car* [specific behavior]. I was going to dump it with a dealer as a trade-in, but I guess you saved me a pile of money. I *appreciate your help* [direct statement of feelings]."

Barry was praised by his mother and the therapist for his excellent performance. The nonverbal expression and direct expression of feelings for a specified behavior were pointed out as the major components of effective expression of feelings. However, it was noted that next time Barry might improve his communication effectiveness even more if he showed his appreciation at the time his father had just finished doing something that pleased him.

Many family members demonstrate excellent communication skills during family sessions, but show little spontaneous use of these skills outside the sessions where encouragement and reinforcement of such behavior may be minimal. Thus, in addition to teaching the skills, which the majority of family members can perform adequately before the therapy, a major task is to increase the frequency of performance in everyday situations. Many family members devalue the significance of praise, encouragement, compliments, or appreciation with statements such as "She knows I appreciate her"; or "That's what parents expect their

FIGURE 9-2. *Expressing positive feelings.*

• LOOK AT PERSON

• SAY EXACTLY WHAT HE OR SHE DID THAT PLEASED YOU

• TELL THE PERSON HOW IT MADE YOU FEEL

---

kids to do, that's nothing special"; or "What about all the things he didn't do?"

While the therapist is encouraged to acknowledge that although these skills are simple and most people don't need to be taught how to perform them, they nevertheless have a significant effect on family morale and on behavior change when employed effectively. In order to demonstrate this, the therapist may solicit feedback from a recipient of praise. Here is an example of a therapist working with a couple:

BOB: Barbara, I enjoyed the lemon pie you baked for dinner yesterday. It was really excellent.

THERAPIST: What did you like about the way Bob did that, Barbara?

BARBARA: He was specific and told me his feelings. That's something he doesn't do very often, but I like it when he does.

THERAPIST: What effect does that have on your making lemon pies in the future?

BARBARA: I'll certainly make them for him in the future. Truthfully, I didn't even know he liked lemon pie until now.

THERAPIST: Bob, do you see the impact a little *specific* praise can have on Barbara?

BOB: Yeah, but don't expect me to do that to all her cooking.

THERAPIST: That's a good point you're making. It's important to choose to praise those specific things you like, not to praise everything effusively. Feelings have to be sincere. But showing your appreciation for those things people do that please you, even if it is only just a little amount of pleasure, helps communicate to people *what you like them to do*, whether it's to make lemon pies, or to help in the garden, or to clean the kitchen.

A homework assignment is given to each family member to "Catch a Person Pleasing You" (see Figure 9-3). This involves recording daily on a structured sheet at least one behavior performed by another family member that the subject experienced as pleasing. In addition, the subject is asked to record his or her own response to the specific positive behavior. Here is a further example of training communication of positive feelings:

THERAPIST: Mr. James, I'd like you to tell your wife about something she's done this week that pleased you.

MR. JAMES: She's been doing pretty good. She's a good wife, I guess.

THERAPIST: Would you be a little more specific and tell her about some particular thing you liked?

MR. JAMES: I like her cooking. Yeah, I like her cooking. Real good.

DAY	PERSON WHO PLEASED YOU	WHAT EXACTLY DID THE PERSON DO THAT PLEASED YOU?	WHAT DID YOU SAY TO THE PERSON?
MON			
TUES			
WED			
THURS			
FRI			
SAT			
SUN			

Examples:

Looking good	Work in yard	Being considerate	Attending treatment
Being on time	Being pleasant	Going out	Making phone call
Helping at home	Having chat	Showing interest	
Cooking meals	Making a suggestion	Taking medicine	
	Going to work		
	Offering to help		
	Tidying up		
	Making bed		

FIGURE 9-3. *Catch a person pleasing you.*

220

THERAPIST: That's good. That's getting much more specific. Is there a special dish she's cooked in the last few days? I'd like you to speak directly to her.

MR. JAMES: She cooked a chicken yesterday. Very nice.

THERAPIST: Good. Did you say anything to her when she did that.

MR. JAMES: No. She knows I like it. I always like the way she does chicken.

THERAPIST: OK. Well, let's imagine you're back having dinner yesterday, and you're eating the chicken. Where were you sitting?

MRS. JAMES: We was both at the table with Susan and Jimmy.

THERAPIST: OK. Let's sit down where you were last night. Now I'd like you to imagine you are eating the delicious chicken your wife has cooked. I would like you to tell her exactly what you like and how you feel about it.

MR. JAMES: OK, I'll try. Mom, I don't need to tell you how much I'm enjoying this chicken. You know it's my favorite and I like it when you cook it. I really like you doing this for me.

THERAPIST: That's great. What did you like about the way your husband did that?

MRS. JAMES: He hasn't done that for years. You know, give me a compliment like that. I feel real good.

THERAPIST: It's nice to get complimented. What about his communication skills, Jimmy? What did he do that's on that sheet you've got?

JIMMY: He looked at Mom and smiled. He said exactly what he was pleased about, and he said he liked it when she cooked it.

THERAPIST: Right. He was specific about what he was pleased about and said how it made him feel. What do you think are his chances you'll fix chicken again, Mrs. James?

MRS. JAMES: I'd say they're very good right now!

In this example, we see the therapist shape a relatively poor expression of positive feelings into a rather touching exchange between a man and his wife. The emphasis was on increasing the specificity of the target behavior and the associated good feelings. A further issue in this case was to generalize this response to the everyday setting where this rather withdrawn husband would spontaneously praise his wife. The homework assignment to "Catch a Person Pleasing You" assisted somewhat in this case, and Mr. James reported noticing a specific behavior he found pleasing performed by a family member on each day of the week. On several occasions he expressed his positive feelings about these behaviors. He complained that it was not his style to verbalize his feelings, and the therapist later shaped him into responding with a pat on his wife's hand, a smile, and a "Thank you, darling," which they found mutually rewarding.

MAKING POSITIVE REQUESTS

Rationale

When using the term "positive request," we are referring to a specific way of communicating to another person that some specific behavior change is desired. It is self-evident that people living together are always going to be engaging in some behaviors that bother other individuals (e.g., playing music too loudly, driving too fast, smoking cigarettes), while at the same time, not engaging enough in other desired behaviors (e.g., helping out with the dishes, conversing, going out to dinner). We can all think of many things we would like other people to do *differently*. How a person communicates these desires may have far-reaching effects, not only on whether people comply with the requests, but also on the general level of tension in the home.

All too often, requests for behavior change are conveyed in the form of demanding or guilt-inducing remarks ("Why don't you ever buy me flowers? You never buy me anything anymore"). To be fair, it must be admitted that coercion, in the hands of an "expert," can be effectively used to negatively reinforce a desired behavior. ("All right, all right. I'll clean up my room—just stop bugging me about it already"). Despite occasional successes, however, coercion tends to be counterproductive, eliciting stubbornness and resistance, and even where compliance eventually ensues, it may be accompanied by resentment and deterioration in the quality of the relationship.

It is possible to ask for a change in behavior in a way that effectively communicates what change is being sought, and why, without having to demand, threaten, or manipulate. We refer to this as "making a positive request," because it involves making a positive communication about the behavior that is being requested, rather than a demand or emotional manipulation. The elements that make up a positive request are straightforward and easily taught to families.

Training Families to Make Positive Requests

The first step in introducing the notion of positive requests is to discuss with the family how each of them goes about asking other family members to do something he or she desires. An ideal time for the therapist to bring up this topic is after observing an ineffectual attempt by one family member to influence another, particularly if the other was obviously put off or annoyed by a coercive exchange.

While discussing how people communicate their wishes to one another, the therapist can elicit different approaches that have varying degrees of effectiveness. Most individuals do not like hearing demands or being told what they "ought to," "should," "must," "need to," or "have to" be doing differently, so it is usually a simple matter to get everyone to acknowledge that certain communication styles put them off and make them less likely to comply with the request.

From this basis, the therapist can then introduce the notion of a positive request. There are three fundamental elements that go into making a positive request: (1) nonverbal aspects of communication such as physical proximity, eye contact, voice tone, and facial expression; (2) being very specific about exactly what it is that is being requested; and (3) stating how it would make the requesting person feel if the person were to comply with the request. If a blackboard is handy, it might he helpful to write these steps down for reference during behavioral rehearsal. We have also used handout sheets (see Figure 9-4). Phases such as "I would like it if you . . ." or "I would be very pleased if you . . ." may be useful to note. Stereotyped requests of this sort seldom reflect spontaneous expressions of feelings, but nonetheless may be preferred to coercive demands.

Example:

JEAN: He came home and said he had a bust-up with his boss. I was busy putting the children to bed and he shouted at me to stop and come and have a drink with him.

THERAPIST: (*to George*) Do you remember where you were standing when you asked your wife to come and have a drink? Let's go to those positions and then I would like you to say exactly what you said to Jean.

FIGURE 9-4. *Making a positive request.*

- LOOK AT THE PERSON
- SAY EXACTLY WHAT YOU WOULD LIKE THAT PERSON TO DO
- TELL HOW IT WOULD MAKE YOU FEEL

IN MAKING POSITIVE REQUESTS, USE PHRASES LIKE:
- "I WOULD LIKE YOU TO _____"
- "I WOULD REALLY APPRECIATE IT IF YOU WOULD _____"
- "IT'S VERY IMPORTANT TO ME THAT YOU HELP ME WITH THE _____"

GEORGE: I was here and she was over in the bathroom with Gretchen. Shall I say what I said?

THERAPIST: Yes.

GEORGE: Well, I said something like, "Jean, I need you to come and talk with me. Put the children to bed and come right now.

THERAPIST: What did you like about the way George made that request of you?

JEAN: He made it pretty clear that he wanted to talk to me.

THERAPIST: Yes. That's good. Is there any way we could suggest that George might improve his positive requests?

JEAN: He could follow the steps on the handout sheet, like looking at me or saying how he would feel if I did talk to him.

THERAPIST: That's right. He could do that. Let's try it again, George, but this time I'd like you to tell Jean how you would feel if she did come and talk with you.

GEORGE: Fine. Jean, I want you to come and sit down and talk about some of the bad things that happened at work. I'd feel good if you did.

THERAPIST: That seemed much better. Jean, what did you notice that George improved?

JEAN: He seemed calmer and he was more precise.

THERAPIST: I also liked the way he said he would feel good if you sat down and talked with him.

The point may be made that there are no guarantees that even a brilliantly phrased positive request will be honored every time. A person can attempt only to communicate his or her feelings in as direct, specific, and competent manner as possible and hope that the other person complies with the request. If the other person does not comply, he or she at least does so knowing full well how the requesting person feels. To begin nagging or to lapse into a stream of inappropriate hostile comments will serve only to increase family tension levels and may further entrench the noncomplier's stubborn refusal.

Alternatively, the request itself may seem unreasonable, in which case it simply becomes an effective communication of thoughts and feelings even if the person does not comply: "I believe that drinking any alcohol at all is sinful and I'd like you to stop drinking beer." The therapist monitors the quality of requests that are made in family discussions. Positive requests are praised and coercive, guilt-inducing statements are restated in a positive manner. Excessive advice giving, particularly when done in a guilt-inducing fashion, is at best ineffective but more often tends to be annoying and counterproductive. Thus, the parent who is prone to tell the daughter what she should, ought, must, or has to do is unlikely to get a consistently satisfactory response. A more effective approach is to express the same feelings in a positive request.

Example:

MRS. SAND: Judy, why don't you go to bed at a reasonable hour? You have to get a decent night's sleep. You know you should be going to bed earlier than you have been.

JUDY: Yeah. Right.

THERAPIST: I noticed that Judy was looking out the window while you were telling her what she should be doing. Usually, people do not like to be told what they should or ought to be doing, even if the advice is reasonable and sound. I would like you to try again to communicate the exact same concerns, but this time put it in terms of a positive request of what exactly you would like Judy to do differently, and how it would make you feel if she did.

MRS. SAND: OK. Judy, I would like it if you would try to get to bed a bit earlier at night. I think that it's important to get plenty of rest, especially now that you're working, and I would be very pleased if you did.

THERAPIST: Very nicely put. Judy, was there any difference in the two ways your mother expressed her feelings as far as how they made you feel?

JUDY: Yes. The first time it seemed like she was nagging me and treating me like a little kid, but the second time I liked it better. She just said what she would like me to do.

THERAPIST: Yes. I think that's right. (*to Mrs. Sand*) The second time you communicated very clearly how you felt without telling Judy what she *should* be doing, and I think she would be more likely to consider your request when it is put that way.

JUDY: Yeah, I would. But the reason I stay up is that I can't sleep if I go to bed early. I suppose I could get some more sleeping pills from the doctor.

The therapist coaches the mother to restructure her communication into a direct, constructive request for change in her daughter's behavior that avoids the coercive message implied in the original comments. The issue is not resolved, but Judy appears receptive to a discussion about her sleep difficulty, and the power struggle between an overconcerned, intrusive mother and her strong-willed daughter is avoided. Here is a further example of the same mother talking to her daughter after she walked out of her job.

MRS. SAND: I feel very disappointed. I thought you were really keen on getting a job and getting it all together. You kept saying, "I must get a job. I must work. I have to get a job for myself." You never told me this. Why didn't you tell me you were worried? You don't talk to me. You just walk around saying nothing, and I'm your mother. You should talk to me. If you can't talk to me, who can you talk to?

THERAPIST: I like the way you are expressing your concerns to Judy. But you began to get a little demanding when you asked her why she didn't talk to you. How did you feel, Judy?

JUDY: I switched off when she started laying her guilt trip on me. I'll talk to her when I want to.

THERAPIST: This is a difficult issue. Let me show you how I might talk to my daughter if I were a concerned mom like you. Can I change seats with you Mrs. Sand? I want you to notice how I make a positive request that Judy talks about her worries with me. (*modeling for Mrs. Sand*) Judy, I'm sorry to hear that you were worried about starting the job. I thought you would be pleased. I would like it very much if you would tell me when you are worried, rather than trying to cover it up. I like it when you sit down and we discuss some problem or other. It makes me feel good when I know what's on your mind and when I can give you some advice or help.

In this example, the therapist chooses to model a positive request as well as a more empathic style of discussion. It is important for therapists to recognize that they serve as models to the family throughout the course of treatment, not merely at times when they specifically demonstrate a communication skill. For this reason, the therapist must use the same communication skills he or she hopes to teach others to use. It is crucial that the therapists themselves avoid coercion and, instead, make positive requests of family members. A therapist who tells families what they "should" or "ought to" do can hardly expect them to avoid such remarks in their own unsupervised family interaction.

COMMUNICATION OF NEGATIVE FEELINGS

The structured learning involved in the relatively easy task of expressing positive feelings serves as a template for the more difficult expression of negative feelings. These include anger, frustration, disappointment, sadness, envy, and fear. Once again the three major factors are (1) to specify the *behavior* associated with the negative feeling; (2) to state clearly the feelings evoked by that behavior; and (3) to express nonverbal emotions congruent with the verbal communication.

The need for specificity that draws attention to those *precise behaviors* of the target person that engender negative emotions reduces the tendency toward overgeneralized *ad hominen* attacks—for example, "I don't like the way you cleaned your room" compared to "You're the most untidy, lazy boy in the world." Specificity of criticism is considered a major component in the "benign" criticism codings of family interaction employed by several researchers (Vaughn & Leff, 1976a; Doane, 1978) which offer some validation for this approach.

A rationale for the expression of specific negative feelings that may be presented to families makes the following points:

- Everyday expression of negative feelings provides feedback to others and may lead to changes in their behavior.
- Expression of specific negative feelings soon after unpleasant behavior avoids "bottled up" emotions that may burst forth in violent expression on later occasions, or lead to inappropriate covert expression.
- Expression of specific negative feelings may precede (1) a request for behavior change: "I'm not enjoying this steak, Beverly. It's a little too rare for my liking. I'd prefer it done a little more next time"; or (2) a problem-solving discussion: "It irritates me to see the mess your bedroom has been in for the past few weeks. I have asked you to tidy it many times now, but I don't seem to have succeeded and I'm getting rather frustrated about it. I'd like to hear your side of the story and see if we can get a plan organized to deal with this problem."

In addition to generalized, hostile criticism, other common inappropriate expressions of negative feelings are coercion or threats and nagging. Coercion involves attempting to shape behavior to a desired goal through constant threats: "If you don't tidy up your room, I'll put you out on the street." Nagging is somewhat less clearly defined, but usually involves a high-frequency expression of dissatisfaction with rather trivial shortcomings, often phrased in a querulous manner: "How many times have I told you I don't like my steak too rare?" It may be difficult for many family members to differentiate between appropriate expression of negative feelings and less effective coercion or nagging, which clearly lacks specificity and induces angry responses that further reduce the specificity of the desired behavior change. The boy who is threatened with eviction unless he tidies his room may respond: "Well, I think I'd be better off if I did move out. At least I'll get you off my back."

Again the training of each family member to proficiency in this skill is aided through the behavior rehearsal, coaching, and reinforcement sequence. During training everyday negative feelings are used, with care taken to avoid opening up expression of major wounds and issues until family members demonstrate competency in the specific expression of negative emotion. Even then it is questionable that major grievances should be aired unless it is clear that such issues constitute an ongoing family stress that may be resolved. However, expression of progressively more substantial negative issues may be encouraged as the family's problem-solving skill develops, so that ultimately the family members are encouraged to discuss any issue they choose, either during the sessions or during family discussions at home between sessions. A cue sheet is provided to each family member to serve as a reminder of the steps of expressing negative feelings (Figure 9-5).

In many families, any expression of negative emotions is considered bad, especially admitting to one's own feelings of sadness, insecurity, apprehension, jealousy, or frustration. Therapist modeling through self-disclosure of his or her own negative emotions toward displeasing behavior of family members during the sessions may facilitate the open, appropriate expression of unpleasant feelings by family members—for example, "I'm disappointed you didn't complete your homework assignment, Paul." Therapist modeling during structured behavior rehearsal may similarly enhance the expression of negative feelings.

The expression of unpleasant feelings in a clear and specific manner is an important component of effective problem solving. It is often the initial step in communicating to others that a problem exists, and in addition serves as a medium for expressing the negative aspects of each proposed solution to a problem. Expression of negative feelings outside a problem-solving context is probably of limited value. Getting it off one's chest is most effective when the issue of concern can be resolved subsequently in a speedy fashion. Families are taught to follow up any expression of negative feelings with a positive request for appropriate behavior change or, where the issue is more complex, by initiating a problem-solving discussion.

Examples: (1) "Jerry, it bothers me to see you pacing about like that. I'd like you to come and sit down with Mom and I so we can find out what's upsetting you."

(2) "Mom, I'm annoyed about all the fattening food you're cooking us when I'm trying to lose weight. Could we discuss this later and see if we can work something out?"

It is advisable that family members have established competence in making positive requests and have rudimentary problem-solving skills before they are encouraged to express negative feelings.

- LOOK AT THE PERSON: SPEAK FIRMLY
- SAY EXACTLY WHAT THE PERSON DID THAT UPSET YOU
- TELL THE PERSON HOW IT MADE YOU FEEL
- SUGGEST HOW THE PERSON MIGHT PREVENT THIS FROM HAPPENING IN THE FUTURE

FIGURE 9-5. *Expressing negative feelings.*

A structured homework exercise on "Expressing Unpleasant Feelings" (see Figure 9-6) may be employed to prompt and evaluate the effectiveness of each family member's attempts to express negative feelings. The format is very similar to the homework exercise on the expression of positive feelings, and involves compiling a daily record of unpleasant interpersonal episodes and the manner in which they were expressed and resolved.

LISTENING SKILLS

Attentive listening skills are a complex set of skills that we attempt to teach families. The components of this training are:

- to sit near a person and invite him or her to discuss a problem.
- to use nonverbal eye gaze, posture, head nods, grunts, and so on to indicate attentiveness.
- to ask clarifying questions about the topic to check the accuracy of what the speaker has said: for example, "I heard you say . . . ; is that right?"
- to clarify the emotions and attitudes you have observed being expressed by the other person: for example, "You seem a little angry with your mother. Is that right?"

Families are told that attentive listening not only facilitates communication within the family, but also is an important skill in dealing with crises. It is mentioned that much of the work of a therapist consists of using active listening skills in the facilitation of problem solving with his or her patients. The handout given to family members is rather simplistic, but serves as a reminder of the core ingredients of listening (Figure 9-7).

- SAY EXACTLY WHAT DISPLEASED YOU.
- TELL THE PERSON HOW IT MADE YOU FEEL.
- SUGGEST A WAY THIS COULD BE AVOIDED IN FUTURE.

DAY	PERSON WHO DISPLEASED YOU	WHAT EXACTLY DID THE PERSON DO THAT DISPLEASED YOU?	HOW DID YOU FEEL? (angry, sad, etc.)	WHAT DID YOU ASK THE PERSON TO DO IN THE FUTURE?
MON				
TUES				
WED				
THURS				
FRI				
SAT				
SUN				

Examples:

I feel angry that you shouted at me, Tom. I'd like it better if you spoke quieter next time.

I'm very sad that you did not get that job. I'd like to sit down and discuss some other possibilities with you after dinner.

I feel very anxious when you tell me I should get a job, it would help me a lot if you didn't nag me about it.

FIGURE 9-6. *Expressing unpleasant feelings.*

- LOOK AT THE SPEAKER
- ATTEND TO WHAT IS SAID
- NOD HEAD, SAY "UH-HUH"
- ASK CLARIFYING QUESTIONS
- CHECK OUT WHAT YOU HEARD

FIGURE 9-7. *Active listening.*

Enhancing Attentional Deficits

Perhaps the most common deficit of listening is a lack of attention to the speaker. Attentional deficits have been consistently shown to contribute to the poor performance of persons suffering from schizophrenia on psychological tests. Complex theories have been developed to explain this dysfunction (Asarnow & Asarnow, 1982).

In families, attention is often reduced for various straightforward reasons such as attempting to discuss issues while the television is on, communicating while working in the kitchen, talking about important issues while eating a meal or driving on a busy street. To maximize attention, such extraneous activity should be minimized, and the people involved should be in a comfortable posture, near one another, so that the nonverbal components of eye contact, vocal and facial expression, and touch can be fully utilized. This usually involves sitting together facing one another at a table or in a living area; the former is preferable when taking notes might be usefully employed, as in planning a goal or problem solution. The therapist's office setting or the circle of chairs employed by group and family therapy or the round conference table is not an incidental arrangement, but one found to maximize effective communication and problem solving. Such arrangements may need to be structured into the family living environment, whether it is sitting at the dining table or switching off the television and rearranging the chairs in the living room. Mother may need to wait until she has completed her chores in the kitchen, or father until after the baseball game on the television, before attempting to communicate about an important matter. In many family settings, the telephone is the greatest source of distraction and families may consider taking their phones off the hook when an important family matter is to be discussed. Once the family members are comfortably seated together, without distracting stimuli, the major problems of attention are usually eased considerably.

A second common source of inattention is boredom. This occurs when family discussions are lengthy and irrelevant issues are brought up frequently. We suggest that such discussions be kept to a minimal length and one person chair the discussion to keep it flowing briskly. Often a request for positive behavior change may take only a minute or two; seldom does a problem-solving discussion require more than 15 or 20 minutes to reach a tentative plan. Families are instructed not to exceed half an hour in any discussions, but are encouraged to have briefer, more frequent discussions about major ongoing problems rather than tension-producing marathon sessions.

For anyone who has attempted to convene a meeting with a disparate group of colleagues in a work setting, the logistics of scheduling meetings at convenient times for more than two people presents many headaches. Active families have similar scheduling difficulties, and are encouraged to set aside a brief period each day for important communications and a longer period once a week for more difficult issues. Immediately before or after mealtime is the most commonly suggested time for convening the family group. Attempts to provide reinforcement for attendance such as going out for dinner or a movie have had limited success. Meeting while eating a meal has been discouraged, owing to the competing activity, although snacking or drinking may be effective reinforcers for the longer problem-solving meetings. It is preferable that these reinforcers be provided before (to promote prompt attendance) or after (to reward problem solving) the meeting. However, these arrangements will depend on the attentional difficulties of individual family members, which when severe should probably lead to strict exclusion of all possible distractions.

Nonverbal Feedback of Attentiveness

Although eye contact and an alert facial expression are perhaps the best indicators of attentive listening, head nods and grunts—"uh-huh," "yeah," "I see"—provide additional feedback to the speaker. This skill is promoted by coaching and modeling. Therapists or family members demonstrate the impact of this nonverbal feedback mode and reinforce its performance. The neuromuscular effects of neuroleptic drugs may reduce this gestural activity in some persons, but they can usually correct this with minimal coaching.

Clarifying Questions

A simple, yet effective intervention to enhance listening skills is to increase the use of clarifying questions. In order to ask relevant questions, the subject must receive and process information from the speaker and identify areas where his or her understanding of the information being communicated is incomplete. This aspect of communication has been termed "receiver skills" by Charles Wallace and his colleagues at Camarillo, who have effectively trained inpatients suffering from schizophrenia to identify appropriate clarifying questions (Wallace *et al.*, 1980). The extensive training provided in individual "receiver-skills training" is not feasible in the family setting where prompting family members to ask clarifying questions is a major component of active listening.

Example:

THERAPIST: Mrs. Hooper, I would like you to tell your husband about the difficulty you've been having with your supervisor. (*Turns to Mr. Hooper.*) I would like you to listen closely to what your wife says and to ask her as many questions as you can to make the situation as clear as possible to you. Sarah, I would like you to help us by counting the number of questions you hear your dad ask. (*to Mrs. Hooper*) OK, so you tell him about your supervisor for 2 or 3 minutes; you ask as many questions as you can, even silly ones; and you, Sarah, help me count exactly how many questions your father asks. OK?

MRS. HOOPER: Well, Frank, you know Mr. Edwards, don't you?

MR. HOOPER: The fellow with the bald head?

MRS. HOOPER: Yes, that's him. Well he started in on me today about my filing.

MR. HOOPER: What was wrong with your filing?

MRS. HOOPER: Nothing, of course. But that didn't stop him picking on me. He brought a big pile of folders and dumped them on my desk after lunch and told me I'd better get them finished in an hour.

MR. HOOPER: Why did he do that?

MRS. HOOPER: Search me. Probably trying to stir up trouble.

MR. HOOPER: Were you mad at him?

MRS. HOOPER: I certainly was.

MR. HOOPER: Did you say anything to him?

MRS. HOOPER: No, I just worked frantically and got them finished in just less than an hour.

MR. HOOPER: That must have exhausted you.

MRS. HOOPER: It surely did. But it made me so mad.

MR. HOOPER: What did you do then?

MRS. HOOPER: I told Marjorie, and she told me I should stand up to him more.

THERAPIST: Let's stop there for a moment. How many questions did you count your father making, Sarah?

SARAH: Four, I think.

THERAPIST: Very good. How did you feel your husband was listening to you?

MRS. HOOPER: He seemed to want to find out what was going on, and he didn't interrupt what I was talking about.

THERAPIST: Are you saying that he seemed interested in the problem at work?

MRS. HOOPER: Yes. He did seem to want to help me sort it out.

THERAPIST: Apart from the questions, Sarah, did you notice any other aspects of attentive listening that your father demonstrated?

SARAH: He looked at Mother when she was talking and sort of leaned toward her a bit.

THERAPIST: Excellent. I thought you looked very interested in your wife, and you gave me the impression that you were eager to find out about the situation so that you could help support her.

Note that the therapist provides precise instructions and involves each family member in the exercise. The daughter becomes the cotherapist in this instance, providing specific feedback to her father, the struggling student!

Paraphrasing, Checking, and Empathy

The final elements of attentive listening involve a more sophisticated level of information processing not characteristic of the less well educated, lower socioeconomic families that predominate in our clinics. These are paraphrasing and summarizing the information transmitted in order to verify its accuracy; this may include checking out the emotional content expressed in the message. Paraphrasing is particularly useful when instructions are being communicated.

Example:

MOTHER: Roger, I would like you to put out the trash tomorrow morning before you go off to work.

ROGER: You want me to put out the trash tomorrow, Mom?

MOTHER: Yes. But it is important that you do it before 9 o'clock before you go to work, because it's collected around 10 to 11.

ROGER: Well, if you say the trash collection is at 10, I'll put it out before 9 o'clock, OK?

MOTHER: Good. That'll be a big help to me, dear.

Family members may assist in prompting paraphrasing in one another. For example, the mother in the previous example might have asked her son to repeat her instructions had he not done so spontaneously. Paraphrasing the content of emotional expression is somewhat more difficult and is usually reserved for instances in which gross deficits of misinterpretation are evident. One hypersensitive paranoid son frequently accused his mother of being hostile toward him. He specified her tone of voice and avoidance of eye contact as the cues that led to this assumption. He was encouraged to give her feedback at the exact times he felt she was expressing hostility toward him. He did so, and on many occasions his mother was able to correct his perception and tell him that she was angry about other events, or often merely tense and nervous when she had been thinking about her sister, who had died recently.

Difficulty seeing the other person's point of view is a common issue. Reversal of roles is a useful strategy that may assist in the resolution of such conflict. The two participants are asked to reverse their identities, to repeat a communication sequence, and to act in the manner they would expect the other person to behave in the situation.

Example:

THERAPIST: You seem to be having difficulties seeing any reason why Jean might like to stay out later on Saturday nights other than to have sex with men, Mr. Jeffs. Is that right?

MR. JEFFS: Yeah. I can't think of anything, can you?

THERAPIST: I would like us to try something a little different. I would like the two of you to change roles. Jean, I would like you to imagine you are your father, and, Mr. Jeffs, I would like you to play Jean for a moment. Let's change seats too. Now I would like you to tell each other what you feel about staying out later on Saturdays as if you were speaking for the other person.

MR. JEFFS: Well, Daddy, I'm 22 years old and I'm a grown woman. I want you to trust me. I just want to be able to stay at a party till a reasonable hour so that I don't have to feel embarrassed. The parties don't start till late, and I'd rather not go rather than have to leave almost as soon as it starts.

JEAN: I worry a lot about you. I hear so much about women getting raped and murdered. I'd hate anything to happen to you. I don't like your being out past midnight. I can't get to sleep, nor can your mother.

THERAPIST: OK. That's great. What did you hear your father say when he took your part, Jean?

JEAN: Well, he seemed to understand where I'm coming from. You know, the embarrassment and how the parties always start so late. I don't like them that much anyway, but my friends all go and I don't want to be left out.

Father was subsequently asked for feedback. He agreed that he was worrying excessively and that he would try to trust Jean's judgment, which had been excellent in the past. The use of role reversal forces participants to consider the alternative perspective, and breaks down the fixed positions often held by family members.

The Behavioral Family Therapist as a Model
for Good Communication

An obvious but sometimes overlooked principle of behavioral therapy is that the therapist should always model the communication skills he or she is hoping to teach the family. This simple point has several important implications. First, therapists must keep their wits about them when dealing with very disturbed families that are doing or saying unpleasant things to one another. If the therapist, under duress, becomes critical or judgmental, or makes excessive guilt-inducing statements to family members, he or she will be an ineffective teacher. This is not to say that the therapist must never express negative feelings—in fact, at times it may be necessary to interrupt a family member and give some very specific negative feedback about how they are communicating if they are, in fact, doing so in a very destructive fashion. Here the key is to be very specific. The therapist wants to model how to express negative feelings regarding specific behaviors without condemning the person globally.

In a similar vein, communications between cotherapists should be direct, clear, and specific. This can be difficult, particularly in a training situation where the trainee might be likely to waffle a bit when expressing feelings or ideas with which he or she isn't sure that the primary therapist concurs.

Another way in which therapist modeling is important is at times when a family is in crisis. When family members feel certain that everything is falling apart and tension levels increase and communication and problem-solving skills begin to deteriorate, the therapist's maintenance of a calm, low-key manner can ultimately lead to other family members' adopting a similar attitude during future family crises as a result of this modeling. We have often been impressed by the extent to which family attitudes and communication styles have improved over a period of 6 to 12 months, even in families that initially seemed slow to acquire these same skills via behavioral rehearsal and other structured behavioral interventions.

Emphasis on Process versus Content

Behavioral family therapy emphasizes the process of communication rather than the semantic content of messages observed during sessions. The treatment session is seen as an exercise, a dress rehearsal, where new modes of communication can be tried out without fear of failure or recrimination. To this end, the therapist plays the role of coach and facilitator, who creates and controls the collaborative team spirit. Clearly, when family members attend a therapy session preoccupied with current family tensions, the therapist will need to postpone any specific agenda (e.g., training in problem solving) until the family crisis can be resolved. However, the therapist will attempt to orchestrate the crisis intervention in such a manner that the family can practice and receive feedback and reinforcement for effective use of communication and problem-solving skills. Although the therapist may need to take a more directive and personal role in the session at such times, he or she carefully demonstrates effective use of the skills being taught the family. The therapist may draw attention to his or her behavior and solicit specific feedback—for example, "Joe, what steps did you notice me take when I responded to your wife's negative feelings just now?" This enables the family to see the therapist as a person who has acquired a relatively simple set of skills, not as a masterful god-like creature they can only admire from a distance.

Content is not entirely ignored, but questions such as "Why did you say that?" or "What made you do that?" are avoided. Many family discussions become bogged down with these issues, which seldom lead to effective problem resolution. A father who tells his son he "cannot stand having him around anymore" may be making a very hostile comment. The therapist may solicit feedback that indicates that the statement was over generalized, that he avoided citing specific behavior that upset him, but that his angry feeling was clearly expressed. The therapist might invite the father to repeat his communication and coach him to state the specific behavior of his son that annoys him so greatly. Inevitably this focus on process serves to de-escalate expression of raw emotions and to provide a structure for more effective communication of feelings.

Use of the Home Environment

The effectiveness of behavior rehearsal is probably enhanced by the degree to which the rehearsal resembles the real-life interaction. *In vivo* procedures have proved superior to those that employ fantasy in the treatment of anxiety disorders, and a similar *in vivo* approach to behavior rehearsal might be expected to have similar benefits. However, there is one important difference when the rehearsal is conducted in a marital or family setting—any interaction between family members may be considered *in vivo*, whether it occurs in the clinic or in the family living room. Although the therapist may function as a facilitator of improved communication between family members, he or she is not usually essential to this process. One exception was a mother and son who found that communication between them was almost impossible and agreed not to communicate any important feelings outside of therapy sessions, when they employed the therapist as a mediator to help them communicate in a less destructive manner.

The therapist provides a structure to guide family members in their expression of feelings, but throughout sessions family members perform in a real interaction, expressing spontaneous feelings. This is contrasted with the expression of feelings in a social-skills training group, where role rehearsal is conducted within a contrived setting and transfer of skills to the natural environment must be carefully orchestrated.

At times, communication skills that involve persons outside the family group, or family members who are not at the session, are rehearsed. On these occasions, family members may engage in role playing in the traditional manner.

CONCLUSIONS

Behavioral family therapy employs a skills-training method to enhance the interpersonal communication skills of family members in the family group. Major deficits in the accurate expression and reception of information and feelings are remedied through repeated behavior rehearsal accompanied by coaching, modeling, feedback, and reinforcement, followed by homework practice between sessions.

The value of clear communication is considered primarily in terms of the manner in which problem-solving discussions may be facilitated. To this end, families are trained to competence in expressing specific positive and negative feelings, making requests in a positive way, and listening attentively.

However, a wide range of more specific communication problems may be found in families. Some of the more common are described in the next chapter along with specific strategies that have been employed to deal with them.

CHAPTER 10

SPECIFIC COMMUNICATION PROBLEMS AND STRATEGIES

The methods of interpersonal communication training that were outlined in the previous chapter serve as a template upon which to assemble a range of specific strategies for dealing with specific communication problems. In this chapter, we will endeavor to illustrate the way in which many common family communication difficulties may be restructured. These problems include deficiencies and inappropriateness of nonverbal and verbal communications. Many of these issues (e.g., vague communication) have been associated with family theories of the etiology of schizophrenia that have linked disordered family communication to the onset of the florid illness. Although we have concluded in Chapter 1 that these communication problems are not specific to schizophrenia, they are common in families with a son or daughter suffering from this disorder. All of these difficulties detract from effective and efficient family problem solving, and therefore contribute to the persistence of the high stress levels in these families, which appear to contribute to symptom exacerbations of schizophrenia in the vulnerable family member (see Figure 3-1).

NONVERBAL INADEQUACY

Emotional messages are most readily expressed without words: love and affection through proximity, eye gaze, smiling, touch, and intimate sexual contact; anger through body posture, eye gaze, frowning, clenched jaw, fist shaking, punching, and slapping; disgust through head shaking, shoulder shrugging, turning, and walking away. It is therefore not surprising that in distressed families deficiencies of nonverbal expression are frequently prominent. These difficulties in families with a member who has schizophrenia are often major contributors to the lack of clear communication noted in these households.

The deficits in nonverbal communication skills can be classified in two major categories. First, there may be family members who show gross inadequacy of nonverbal expression, such as minimal eye contact or expressionless facial or vocal features. Second, there is the problem of inappropriate nonverbal communication, the most widely publicized variant of which is the "double bind," where incongruity of simultaneous verbal and nonverbal expression is observed. Both these forms of non-verbal inadequacy are seen as characteristic behavioral features of schizophrenia when markedly displayed (blunting of affect, and incongruity of affect), but are seen quite frequently in "normal" family members. The lack of specificity of these nonverbal features has led to their diminished significance in the diagnostic classification of schizophrenia (DSM-III, 1980; Wing et al., 1974.)

DEFICIENCIES OF NONVERBAL EXPRESSION

Specific deficits in nonverbal components of emotional communication are readily detected in the pretreatment observations of family interaction. Most severe deficits are also noted during individual interviews with therapists. One young man made no eye contact at all in a series of interviews, while his father spoke in a very rapid soft voice that was almost inaudible. Where such deficits are specific to certain situations (e.g., an assessment interview or a family discussion) and are less prominent or absent in other situations, the problem is one of determining the contingencies that surround this differential performance and dealing with them in a specific manner. However, where the communication skill appears to be totally lacking from a person's repertory, some basic skill training may be required. This is seldom feasible in a family group and additional individual coaching may be required. This may be difficult where the deficient person is a family member other than the index patient. In either case, the skill training model is employed with repeated rehearsal of the deficient skill followed by feedback, coaching, modeling by the therapist and other family members, and social reinforcement for gradual progress. Some specific deficits include the following.

Eye Gaze

A lack of eye contact has profound consequences for an individual. This deficit reduces the input of perceptual cues enormously and the person may be prone to misconstrue much interpersonal communication in a similar manner to a deaf or blind individual. In addition, people are less likely to approach a person whose eyes are downcast than they are a person who looks them in the eye in an open, receptive fashion. On the other hand, a person who tends to look piercingly at people is usually perceived by others as hostile and threatening. Others sometimes make furtive glances about when feeling persecuted. Such gazes tend to make observers feel somewhat uneasy.

A mother and her daughter tended to sit on opposite ends of a sofa and when they spoke to one another looked directly ahead. It was often difficult to know to whom they were talking. The therapist prompted them both to look at the person to whom they were talking. With a little shaping, they were able to improve over several weeks.

Body Posture and Gesture

Body language, as conveyed by posture and gesture, on occasions creates false impressions. A mother who slumped into a chair was often mistaken as unhappy and not interested in participating in family discussions. A twin brother, who usually joined sessions without a shirt, revealed a tanned, well-muscled torso that contrasted strikingly with his "sick" twin. A young woman patient tended to wave her hands about in exaggerated, awkward gestures that drew attention to herself. These postures and gestures were readily modified with feedback and social reinforcement.

Facial and Vocal Expression

A lack of variation in facial expression, or a vocal monotone is observed quite frequently in persons with schizophrenia and their families. A wider range of nonverbal emotional expression may be shaped through persistent coaching with social reinforcement.

Example:

MRS. SANDERS: (*smiling and speaking in a matter-of-fact tone*) It is annoying when Herb comes in late sometimes.

THERAPIST: Mrs. Sanders, would you tell your husband how you feel when he comes home late without calling you? I would like you to sound as if you mean it. It's something that annoys you, so try to sound and look annoyed.

MRS. SANDERS: Herb, you upset me on Friday when you didn't come home. Please don't do that, honey.

MR. SANDERS: OK. I get carried away and don't notice the time. I'm sorry.

THERAPIST: That's very good, Mrs. Sanders. How did she come across to you [Mr. Sanders]?

Mr. Sanders: She sounded rather ticked off, all right.

Therapist: What did you like about the way your mother did that, Janet?

Janet: Mom usually smiles a lot when she's angry. But she didn't do that at all. I could see she was annoyed a bit too.

Therapist: So sounding annoyed and looking stern helped communicate that feeling more clearly. Janet, I'd like you to notice when your mom tells somebody she's angry and to give her some encouragement for looking and sounding angry.

Janet: OK. But I hope she doesn't go around getting mad at all of us. (*Laughs.*)

One son complained that his father spoke in a loud voice frequently and it sounded as if he was angry. The father said it was his usual voice and he was not angry, but agreed that his loud voice might come across that way. He rehearsed speaking in a softer tone when discussing everyday matters and his wife and son reported gradual improvement and gave him appropriate reinforcement for his efforts.

Another father spoke in a babyish tone with an inappropriate grin when talking to his 30-year-old daughter, who responded to him in a matching baby-like fashion. This speech pattern was pointed out and the father readily adopted a style of communication appropriate to talking with an adult woman. The daughter had a moderately severe speech impediment that had been present since childhood. She worked with the parents in practicing clearer speech. They arranged for her to read interesting passages from the newspaper to them after dinner and reinforced her gradual improvement. They encouraged her to record passages into a portable tape recorder and to play them to herself to identify words she found particularly difficult and could practice herself. A definite improvement was noted in her speech fluency over a period of 3 months. This was accompanied by less inappropriate giggling, which appeared to camouflage her speech problems.

Reciprocity

The intermeshing of nonverbal behavior is considered an important facilitator of emotional communication. At the most basic level, this involves persons engaging in a discussion to all assume a similar posture— all standing, or all sitting. At a more complex level, this involves assuming similar gestures and body movements, such as crossing legs, and matching facial and vocal expressions. A film of close friends conversing, when played at high speed, makes them look as if they were dancing in unison.

In one family, members attempted to communicate important information or to establish a problem-solving discussion when one person was in the kitchen, another watching television, and the third pacing around the room. They were instructed to avoid communication in such situations and to arrange a family meeting where they could all sit comfortably together without distraction and discuss the issue. Mealtimes, when the family sat around the table, were considered potential meeting times, particularly when all had completed their meal and were not distracted by their eating behavior. Even when less substantive issues were to be discussed, the family members were encouraged to choose an appropriate time and place to communicate their feelings—preferably when all concerned with the issues were sitting or standing together without distractions. In several families, achieving this basic structure proved surprisingly difficult, but once achieved, it substantially enhanced the effectiveness of their communication behavior.

VERBAL COMMUNICATION PROBLEMS

Poverty of Content

While the deleterious effects of certain types of communication have been well documented in the literature, less has been said about lack of meaningful verbal interaction. We have noted that in many families there is a pattern of noncommunication, particularly where one parent has limited verbal skills. Initially, this may appear somewhat benign, or may be confused with low-key affective expression. In fact, it may lead to a great deal of intrafamilial stress and tension as stresses are ignored and basic routines of daily living are seldom discussed, thus making constructive change unlikely.

The challenge to the clinician is a formidable one, because the participants may have had marked deficits in communication over a lifetime and may not see this as a problem. Often the therapist is met with silence, passivity, the "I don't know" response to questions, or resistance to exercises in communication training. The therapist needs to reinforce even the most marginal or inadequate attempts at direct communication. Often other, more competent family members or persons outside the household can lend support. Shaping may be a slow and tedious process, and can be expedited by having family members repeatedly role-play basic family interactions. The therapist may choose to model and take an active role in such rehearsal, without appearing to be overly competent in his attempts.

Example:

THERAPIST: Mrs. Bean, I would like you to tell John how you felt about his recent job interview.

MRS. BEAN: Well, uh, I don't know.

THERAPIST: Were you pleased that he went to look for a job? What did you like about the way he went about it?

MRS. BEAN: Well, uh, yes.

THERAPIST: Can you tell him how it made you feel?

MRS. BEAN: I felt good.

THERAPIST: I liked the way you told him how you felt, and you smiled at him. That was very well done. I wonder whether you can tell him exactly what it was that you liked.

MRS. BEAN: I liked the way he combed his hair and looked nice.

THERAPIST: Oh, I see, you liked the way he prepared himself for the interview. John, is it clear to you what your mom liked?

JOHN: Yeah. She liked the way I looked.

THERAPIST: How do you feel about that, John?

JOHN: Good.

THERAPIST: I'm very pleased with the way both of you expressed your positive feelings directly and tried to be specific about what you liked. I wonder if you did that when John came home from the interview?

MRS. BEAN: No, We didn't.

THERAPIST: Well, I'd like you to replay what happened when John walked in, and this time I'd like you both to talk about the job interview without me interrupting. OK?

Over several sessions of prompting and reinforcement, this mother and son gradually increased their verbal competence and began to discuss some long-standing family problems. Excessive praise for such small increments of behavior may seem insincere, but the therapist must accept lower expectations for change and demonstrate patient, genuine support for these tiny steps toward competence.

Unclear Communication

Vague, unfocused, generalized, and confused communication is a commonly found deficit of family interaction. Singer and Wynne (1963) have extensively explored these deficits in their studies of "communication deviance" that were reviewed in Chapter 1 (pp. 21–22). While mild degrees of unclear communication are found in all family discussions, a severe disturbance substantially reduces the effectiveness of problem solving and may contribute to increased family tension. Several examples of unclear communication are discussed in this section.

Vague Communication

A very prevalent communication deficit is lack of specificity in the content of verbal communications. Vague statements that are not anchored to specific behavior are not as effective in communicating feelings as statements that specify the behavior with its associated feelings. This is true whether the speaker is attempting to communicate positive or negative feelings, or merely providing information. For example, if a man tells his son that he is "very proud" of him, that is an expression of feelings that would be likely to make his son feel pleased. However, a more specific communication about the exact behavior that pleased the father would provide even more effective feedback. Thus, he might say, "It made me very proud this morning to see you going out on a job interview, wearing a clean suit, and with your hair looking neat."

Vague statements not only detract from clarity but, in addition, particularly when expressing negative feelings, can contribute to increased tension and feelings of frustration or resentment. The expression of nonspecific negative feelings is rarely helpful and is frequently distressing.

Example:

MR. CANDY: (*to his son Bill*) You'd better shape up and shape up fast, because we aren't going to put up with this crap much longer!

THERAPIST: It sounds like you are pretty angry with Bill, but I'm not sure exactly what it is that he is doing that is bothering you. I would like you to tell him again how you feel, but this time I would like you to specify exactly what he is doing that you don't like, and exactly how it makes you feel.

MR. CANDY: Bill, I am mad as hell with you, because you lie in bed until the middle of the afternoon nearly every day. I want you to get up and help clean up the house.

BILL: I feel so tired in the mornings, Dad. But I could help about the house, I guess.

THERAPIST: That was a splendid effort to tell Bill how you felt about his sleeping late. There was no doubt in my mind what you were so mad about. What did you hear your Dad say, Bill?

It is noticeable how the effort to specify the exact behaviors and feelings provides greater structure to a highly emotive outburst and tends to reduce the hostility expressed. Consequently, the potential for constructive resolution of the conflict is much greater than where the only alternative to "shaping up" is rejection from the household. Whenever a vague statement is made, family members are prompted to ask for clarification and the speaker is requested to repeat his or her comment in a more precise manner until it is clear to every family member.

Mixed Messages

Mixed messages take many forms. The classic "double bind" refers to a discrepancy between what is said verbally and what is communicated nonverbally. The verbal message is contradicted by the nonverbal message. At other times family members may communicate their feelings in a rambling, indirect fashion that similarly confuses the person for whom the message is targeted.

Example:

MR. CANDY: (*speaking pedantically, with no anger in his voice, in the general direction of his older son, Bill*) It's not that I'm bothered or upset that Bill isn't working or doing anything else constructive with his life. In fact, it would be nice if everybody could sleep to noon and go out and party all night. That doesn't bother me at all. I'm just worried to death about the welfare of Jerry [the younger son]. I'm worried that his mind might start to rot from lack of stimulation under this kind of environmental influence.

In this confusing, long-winded narrative, the father appears to deny that he has any negative feelings about Bill's lack of constructive behavior. At the same time, he appears to attribute the understimulation of the environment as emanating from Bill's behavior. Instead of expressing his negative feelings directly, he expresses some highly critical feelings in a confusing, indirect manner. The session continued:

THERAPIST: Bill, what did you hear your father say to you?
BILL: I don't know. He was going on about my life-style I guess. That I sleep too much and party too much, or something.
THERAPIST: I was a little confused too, Mr. Candy. I would like you to tell Bill exactly what he does that concerns you, and to look him in the eye when you talk to him.
MR. CANDY: OK. (*Looks at Bill.*) I'm not sure what to say, but I guess I'm a bit concerned about the way your laid-back life-style may influence Jerry. You know, if you set the tone for the family your younger brothers may do the same.
THERAPIST: Good. That seemed much clearer to me. Would you tell your dad what you heard him say that time?

BILL: Dad, I think you were trying to tell me that I might be a bad influence on my brothers and that upsets you.

MR. CANDY: That's right. You see, if you were in your own place, it wouldn't matter, but with Jerry I think it could be harmful.

BILL: I see what you're getting at, but I don't agree with you.

THERAPIST: OK. That was excellent. You don't have to agree with your dad, Bill, but at least it is clearer what his concerns are.

The importance of simplifying ideas and expressing feelings directly, with good eye contact and nonverbal expression, is illustrated by this sequence.

Paradoxical Communication

The use of paradoxical interventions, such as "prescribing the symptom," have become fashionable in family therapy in recent years (Selvini-Palazzoli *et al.*, 1978). We have tended to avoid the use of such interventions with families where a person has had schizophrenia. Our model of simple, direct, specific communication is incompatible with paradoxical communication. Indeed, the double-bind hypothesis has implicated naturally occurring paradoxical messages as a potential factor in the pathogenesis of schizophrenia.

One situation in which paradoxical communications may be effective is in reducing the tension during the session where a comment by the therapist or a family member may provide humor. However, even in these instances, the humorous intent of the comment should be made highly explicit.

Overgeneralized Statements

Another common defect in communication is the tendency to make overgeneralized statements, particularly when expressing feelings of hurt, anger, disappointment, or resentment. Thus, a 20-year-old daughter who has just been scolded for staying out too late at night told her mother, "You're *always* sticking your nose into other people's business." Or a father said to his unemployed 25-year-old son, "The reason you don't have a job is because you're lazy. You've *always* been lazy and preferred sleeping and watching TV to going out and finding a job."

In both of these cases, there is an element of truth to the statement, but they are delivered in such a global, all-inclusive manner that they obviously represent distortions of the actual facts. Overgeneralized statements like these are often accompanied by much negative affect such as anger, criticism, dislike—but can just as well be made with little or no affect. In the second example above, the statement was made very matter-of-factly, with no overt display of emotion.

Overgeneralized negative statements can be very harmful, particularly when they are critical or rejecting in tone. In such instances, the therapist is advised to intervene immediately, before overgeneralized criticism adds to family tension and distresses the criticized person. Even less malignant examples of overgeneralization are nevertheless inaccurate and exaggerated and can lead to feelings of being picked on unfairly.

In dealing with overgeneralized statements, the therapist's tasks are twofold: First, family members are taught to recognize such statements; second, they are once again instructed to substitute specific statements for generalized ones. The therapist is very directive in this regard, as was illustrated in the following family discussion involving a 70-year-old woman and her son:

MRS. JAMES: He's been just terrible. I don't know what got into him yesterday, but he was terrible. I don't know if I can stand this much longer. Can you give him a shot or something? Everytime he . . .

THERAPIST: (*interrupting*) Well, it sounds like you're feeling upset all right, but I'm feeling concerned about the way you were communicating your feelings just now. I think if I were Bob I'd be feeling pretty put upon and feeling pretty badly right now. Bob, how did you feel when you heard your mother say you were "terrible"?

BOB: I don't feel very good. I feel like I should run out of the house.

THERAPIST: I think that when a person is feeling upset or angry it is especially important to be as specific as possible about exactly what is making you angry. Now I know that no one is totally terrible 24 hours per day, even on a particularly bad day. So I would like it if you could say again what it was that bothered you about yesterday, and try to be as specific as possible.

MRS. JAMES: Well, we were driving to lunch and Bob suddenly started turning pale and he began to sweat and get shaky. I ended up having to drive us all back home. I've never seen him that bad before.

THERAPIST: Good. That was very specific and communicated exactly what happened that was upsetting to you yesterday.

From this point, the therapist may have chosen to continue discussing issues involved in the communication of negative feelings, dealing more with the process than the content. Repeated behavior rehearsal could be used to give the family members a chance to practice these skills. In this instance the therapist chose to have the family work on problem solving how to cope with Bob's anxiety attacks in the future (see Chapter 12, pp. 301–303).

INAPPROPRIATE COMMUNICATION

Deficiencies in verbal and nonverbal communication occur to some extent in all families. Thus, there is no family in which some communication training would not prove beneficial. However, for reasons of efficiency of therapy, only major communication deficits are addressed. These deficits clearly interfere with the problem-solving functions of the family. But there is another group of communication problems that are addressed routinely when such problems are present. These patterns of family communication not only detract from problem resolution, but contribute to family tension. They include intrusiveness, invalidation, threats, violence, and an emphasis on negative behavior.

Invalidating the Thoughts and Feelings of Others

The open, direct expression of feelings and ideas is a central goal of family communication training. Patterns of expression that run counter to this goal are dealt with immediately in family sessions. One striking example of this inappropriate communication involves statements that invalidate another person's direct expression of thoughts or feelings. A person may say he or she is feeling depressed, bored or lonely and have another family member turn around and say, "Don't be ridiculous, you haven't been feeling that bad, you are really quite happy most of the time." A similar invalidating may follow expression of an idea. When Mrs. White suggested to her husband that he might consider joining a bowling league, he responded, "That's impossible! That is the most insane idea you've come up with yet. You know I hate bowling alleys."

When responses that deny the thoughts and feelings of others are elicited, the therapist intervenes immediately and takes a strong advocacy role for the person who is attempting to express himself or herself. The person who made the invalidating statement is told that his or her comments are inappropriate and destructive. Feedback is sought from the recipient of the remarks to elicit feelings of rejection, frustration, and aversion to subsequent open communication. If the recipient cannot readily articulate these feelings, an empathic statement by the therapist may be employed. The therapist may say, "You know, if I felt depressed and my mother told me I didin't, that would make me feel confused and frustrated, like she didn't really want to understand me. And I wouldn't want to talk to her about my true feelings in the future." The need for further training in empathic listening behavior is clear in such cases and the session might proceed by working on this issue, or the therapist might consider it better to postpone such training to a later convenient time, especially if such inappropriate communication is relatively infrequent and not seriously compromising current problem solving.

An important variation of this problem is the usual response of family members when a person expresses a delusion. The patently false belief is generally met by an invalidating statement such as, "That's not true. You're just imagining things." Alternatively, family members may attempt to talk the person out of the belief through logical arguments. The therapist points out that although the idea may sound improbable to other people, it is very real to the patient, and that acknowledging the validity of the experience for him or her is an essential first step before the family member may state his or her own contradictory opinions. For example:

You believe that the neighbors are trying to kill you and that seems scary, but I don't agree with you. They don't seem too friendly, but I'm sure they don't mean any harm to you.

It is evident that empathic communication such as this will not have any immediate profound effects on a fixed delusional belief. It may allow a problem-solving discussion to ensue without invalidating the deluded person's current life experience. Good communication is very helpful in dealing with a person with florid symptoms of schizophrenia. Further discussion of methods of coping with delusions and other symptoms is included in Chapter 12 (pp. 300–301).

Intrusiveness

Let us examine a transcript of a session with a mother and her anxious, withdrawn daughter.

THERAPIST: Sally, I'd like you to tell me about your vacation.

MRS. GERARD: She is too nervous to speak. She gets like that at times. She thinks that we are against her when all we're trying to do is help. Don't you think I should give her more medicine when she's like this? Wouldn't a shot help her, Doctor? I'd do anything if it would help my Sally.

During this interchange, Sally became restless and began looking around the room. She did not appear to be attending to her mother's speech about her.

Mrs. Gerard displays several of the common communication deficits considered intrusive. These include (1) speaking on behalf of the person when that person is present; (2) describing that person's own thoughts and feelings without checking them with the person for accuracy; (3) excessive worrying about the person; and (4) assuming the role of an expert adviser to professional consultants.

Intrusive persons may interrupt family members and therapists in an irritating fashion. They appear to watch the minute behavior of the patient and the other, waiting for any small sign that something might be amiss. One woman sat up every night at her son's bedside for fear that he might commit suicide while she slept. During the day she had her husband watch over him while she had a short nap.

Overconcerned, intrusive behavior such as this is very difficult to counter. However, it has the effect of smothering the self-expression of its recipients. The therapist acknowledges the concern that is expressed, but encourages the intrusive person to provide support in a more effective manner. In the example above, the therapist continued:

THERAPIST: You seem very, very concerned about Sally and seem to want to help her so much. But unfortunately you can't make her better yourself. You can help tremendously, though. One way you can do that is to encourage Sally to speak up for herself and tell doctors and other people what she feels is going on. I'd like you to ask Sally how she feels right now and what she's been thinking about while we've been talking.

MRS. GERARD: What have you been thinking about?

SALLY: Oh, nothing.

MRS. GERARD: You see, Doctor, she won't tell me anything.

THERAPIST: It takes time and patience. Let's try again.

MRS. GERARD: What are you worried about, my dear?

SALLY: Nothing. Nothing, really.

MRS. GERARD: You look very nervous.

SALLY: Do I? I guess I'm a bit nervous.

THERAPIST: (softly) Good. Very good.

MRS. GERARD: Do you think a shot might help you?

SALLY: No way. It might help you. Yeah, why don't you get a shot?

MRS. GERARD: Maybe I need one (Laughs.)

THERAPIST: Very good. I really liked the way you asked Sally some questions about how she was feeling and what might help her. I felt you were trying to understand what she was feeling and thinking about. How did you feel about it, Sally?

SALLY: She let me get a word in occasionally!

THERAPIST: Perhaps we can continue this discussion. I'd like you to ask Sally some more questions, Mrs. Gerard, as many as you can think of.

The session continues with training in active listening skills.

The insightful comment that Sally made about her mother's possibly benefiting from an injection points out the excessive anxiety often expressed by highly intrusive persons. Methods that foster relaxation of their overactive cognitions are helpful. Tranquilizing drugs are not particularly effective at relieving this constant worrying. Refocusing concerns and thoughts into more constructive activities, especially hobbies and interests outside the home, may be more successful.

Pseudomutuality

"Everything is fine" is a customary response to the inquiry, "How are things?" Several families persistently employed such a response throughout therapy and thereby made the task of resolving ongoing problems or enhancing communication effectiveness appear less relevant to the immediate family situation. "Well, things have been bad in the past, and I'll grant you they could get bad again in the future, but just now we're doing OK, thank you."

Lyman Wynne and his colleagues likened this family response to a "rubber fence" from which the therapist bounced back each time he or she attempted to probe the suspected areas of difficulty (Wynne *et al.*, 1958). In most families in which we have noted this response style, serious marital discord has been apparent, but the parents have been unwilling to discuss this issue in the family sessions.

The behavioral approach attempts to deal with this response style by accepting the response at face value and emphasizing the learning potential of the situation. The therapist responded to "We're doing OK, thank you" in the following manner:

THERAPIST: That's good to hear. I am pleased that everything is going fine right now. I wonder why everything is going well at this time. I suspect it may have something to do with the way you are working together or handling problems. What do you think people are doing that is different from times that are not so good? Jim, I'd like you to tell me about something you've noticed that is different.

JIM: I don't know that anything has changed really.

THERAPIST: Has you father or mother or brother been doing anything differently that you've noticed?

JIM: I suppose. My father hasn't been on my case so much. Yeah, and sometimes he sits down and asks me how things are going.

THERAPIST: Are those things he used to do?

JIM: No. He's never been that friendly before. The only time he would talk to me was to blast me for something.

THERAPIST: How does that make you feel when your father sits down and chats with you?

JIM: I like it. It makes me feel he cares about me.

THERAPIST: I would like you to tell your father that.

JIM: Dad, I feel you are concerned about me when you come and talk to me now. I enjoy our conversations.

MR. KASPER: I've been enjoying talking with you, Jim. I've always tried to talk with you like that.

THERAPIST: That's very good. I liked the way you expressed your positive feelings to your father. What did you notice about the way Jim expressed himself, Mrs. Kasper?

MRS. KASPER: He was very direct about what he felt.

THERAPIST: Did he say exactly what it was he was pleased about?

MRS. KASPER: Yes. He said it was the conversations.

THERAPIST: So James expressed his good feelings about his father's different approach to him appropriately, using both the ingredients of expressing feelings we discussed 2 weeks ago. What were they, Mrs. Kasper?

MRS. KASPER: To be precise, and to say how it made him feel.

THERAPIST: That's right. He said exactly what it was that pleased him and told his father exactly how it made him feel.

The therapist takes advantage of the "We're doing fine" routine to demonstrate a specific change in family behavior that may have contributed to the shared positive feelings. Confrontation of the possible lack of validity of the initial response is avoided through the educative mode. Later in the same session several family problems were spontaneously divulged by this family and led to teaching the family to express unpleasant feelings appropriately. The behavioral family therapist attempt to roll with the punches and to avoid confrontation with the family. He or she attempts to gain the trust of the family, and allows them to dictate the level of disclosure of problems. It is possible that some families may retain their pseudomutual responses indefinitely, but this has not been our experience to date where most families have been eager to discuss their problems after some initial reticence.

Discounting Attempts to Achieve Competence

One of the important ways to foster a supportive atmosphere in the family is to encourage family members periodically to share feelings of pleasure or appreciation for specific things other members have said, to ask a family member to give another person some positive feedback and have him or her reply, "But he hasn't done *anything* positive lately." This devastating comment is frequently directed at the person with persistent psychotic symptoms and consequent considerable handicap, or to a person who formerly functioned very well and seems by contrast to be doing very poorly at present. In response to this, the therapist follows two general strategies: first, he or she works with the parents to lower their expectations regarding the level of performance they require in order to give positive feedback; and second, he or she works with the family to give positive feedback for all *efforts* to achieve competence even if the end result falls short of the expected goal.

The issue of the handicapped patient is addressed in the early stages of treatment while educating the family about the nature of schizophrenia. Patients who are suffering from florid symptoms such as thinking disturbances and auditory hallucinations are likely to be very handicapped in their general level of performance. Even where florid symptoms are absent, the so-called "negative" symptoms of schizophrenia—apathy, anhedonia, blunted affect, and so on—may produce handicaps of their own. Finally, neuroleptic medications can produce side effects such as sedation and akinesia which may affect the level of daily functioning.

The most important thing the therapist can do, however, is to teach the family to reinforce the handicapped person positively for all his or her *efforts*, even if the level of performance is less than adequate. Thus, when such a person is unsuccessful at getting hired for a job he or she should nevertheless be praised for going out and turning in job applications. Or a person who is very apathetic and prone to lying around in bed much of the time might be praised for spending the afternoon in the living room and keeping company of family members even if he or she doesn't say or do much. The therapist may frequently have to demonstrate to parents how to observe and reinforce low-level behaviors such as these. Often families will require too great a behavioral change before they consider it worthy of comment or praise.

In some cases of schizophrenia, the patient may never again be able to function at premorbid levels, particularly with respect to employment and some aspects of interpersonal functioning. In many cases where premorbid levels can be approximated, it may nevertheless require many months or even years of gradual progress to achieve. Most patients are well aware of their handicaps and often become quite depressed and discouraged over their inability to function in the manner they had formerly. Family members who focus on the patient's accomplishments in the past may unwittingly contribute to his or her sense of failure and hopelessness in the present.

This problem is illustrated in the James family. Bob, age 45, had been very athletic in high school and college, earned a master's degree in education, got married and had a son, taught high school, and was in line to become assistant principal at the time he began having psychiatric problems at age 35. Over the next few years he was divorced by his wife, had difficulties at work that led ultimately to his resignation, and finally developed florid symptoms of schizophrenia at age 40. He was placed on neuroleptics and rapidly gained 50 pounds. His florid symptoms were fairly well controlled; however, he continued to suffer from apathy, anhedonia, emotional blunting, and occasional auditory hallucinations.

In one session, his mother said, "Bobby used to be so athletic and trim—he could run like the wind. And he used to have boundless energy— you always had lots of projects going, didn't you, Bob?" The therapist, noting Bobby's restlessness during this, inquired, "Bob, how were you feeling while your mother was talking about the past just now?" Bob replied that he was feeling "bad—like a failure." This came as a surprise to his mother, who thought she had been quite complimentary. The therapist went on to note that things that might formerly have been quite easy to accomplish might later be difficult for anyone who is trying to cope with an illness like schizophrenia, and that talking about the past in this way can be quite discouraging. Following this exchange, the mother was encouraged to give specific praise for her son's present accomplishments, and behavioral rehearsal was employed to give the son a chance to practice expressing his feelings of disappointment and frustration more openly to his mother.

Another way efforts to improve performance are discounted is the "good . . . but" response. A positive remark is followed immediately by a negative remark that serves to minimize the effectiveness of the praise and to focus on remaining problems. One father frequently employed this response pattern:

MR. WARREN: Everything has been going really well lately. Sam has been helping me with the yard and talking about looking for a job. I'm very pleased about that. *But* he still interrupts all the time. When I sit down to watch television he keeps asking me silly questions. Always silly questions, about his car or girls.

Note how the very positive communication is soon forgotten in the latter criticisms of Sam. To modify this communication pattern, it is important not merely to suppress the expression of negative feelings, but to encourage independent statements of both negative and positive feelings. The session continued:

THERAPIST: I liked the way you praise Sam's efforts at helping you. You also mentioned a specific behavior that you were unhappy about. I suspect that was the main thing Sam recalls about what you said to him right now. Is that right, Sam?

SAM: Yeah. I didn't think talking to him was wrong.

THERAPIST: I would like you to repeat your praise for Sam's helpfulness and this time I would like you to bite your lip and leave the criticism for another time.

MR. WARREN: Sam, thanks for all the help you've given me in the yard. We have appreciated that a lot. . . . But Doctor, he still interrupts all the time.

SAM: I liked it better. I didn't feel so discouraged that time.

THERAPIST: Now, Mr. Warren, I'd like you to tell Sam about what bothers you about him.

MR. WARREN: Sam, I don't like you coming and interrupting me all the time when I'm watching television. I wish you could wait till I've finished watching it before we had a conversation.

SAM: OK, Dad. I'll try not to be a nuisance.

Emphasis on Negatives

When families focus predominantly on negative behaviors in the therapy session, it is usually a reflection of a high level of family tension. While it is important to discuss specific negative events or behaviors in an effort to effect change, it is equally important not to allow families to dredge up and dwell on exclusively negative material, particularly if it is all directed at the same person. It is incumbent on the therapist to "stop the action" in a direct manner and to restructure the content to either more neutral or positive topics rather than to allow family members to go on and on in a critical fashion. The way in which a therapist intervenes is illustrated in the following vignette:

MR. BARON: Jack's behavior has been terrible all week. First, there were the threatening phone calls with messages left on the answering machine, then someone came up to my wife saying he wanted something from Jack. Then there were messages about scoring dope and requests for money. Later he had the audacity to borrow 20 bucks from his brother-in-law to buy a guitar. His mother discovered that initials had been carved in her new rocking chair and that a statue had been broken. He busted up his pillow and made a hell of a mess. He also had his radio stolen. I've had it up to here. (*The father spoke as he moved about the living room gesticulating wildly. The son was visibly upset by his father's tirade and kept his eyes riveted to the floor.*)

THERAPIST: Mr. Baron, I can see you are very upset and irritated by Jack's behavior. You've given a very clear account of the exact things he's done that have really bothered you recently. I wonder whether you can make some requests for change of those behaviors which upset you the most. Jack, I want you to listen to how your father comes across to see if there is any difference this time. OK?

MR. BARON: Jack, I want you to show respect for family property and for our well-being. I don't want any more telephone threats, or strangers coming to the door. I do not want you borrowing money from family members or buying dope, and I would like you to attend a workshop regularly.

THERAPIST: That was much better. Jack, what did you notice about the way your father spoke to you that time?

JACK: Well, just what he said, you know, that I should keep away from the house and not borrow money or buy dope.

THERAPIST: I noticed that you were looking at him when he spoke to you. What did you like about the way he spoke with you?

JACK: Well, he wasn't yelling and I could understand him.

THERAPIST: How do you feel when your father yells at you?

JACK: Bad, real bad. Makes me feel I'm rotten and can't do anything good.

MR. BARON: That's exactly the way I feel about you at times.

THERAPIST: What about at other times? What has Jack done this week that's pleased you? Would you tell him?

MR. BARON: I was pleased you took the trash out without my asking you. And I was also pleased you told me how you got the 20 bucks.

THERAPIST: Very good. So Jack's done some things to please you. How does it make you feel, Jack?

JACK: Well, I have been trying to shape up. I'm glad you notice some things, Dad.

The behavioral approach assists in slowing up the flow of invective and in restructuring the negative feelings into a more constructive framework. The emphasis on the process of communication further assists in controlling the level of tension to the point where healthy problem solving becomes feasible. The therapist switched the content of the session to a review of the family's problem solving efforts to obtain SSI benefits, a bus pass, and other prerequisites for Jack's planned workshop attendance. By the end of the session, the father was able to thank his son for helping him paint the bathroom the preceding day.

Hostile Threats and Violence

In times of high tension, families may resort to making unrealistic demands or threats, and physical violence may ensue. These forms of emotional expression are always destructive and lead to a heightening of stress. Often the person with schizophrenia will become the focus of family frustration. He or she is particularly vulnerable to such scape-goating because the rising family tension may begin to provoke an ex-acerbation of his or her florid symptoms—a situation that threatens to overwhelm the family already in crisis. At such a point, the most obvious coping effort appears to be ejection of the patient from the household, usually by means of admission to a hospital.

In these instances, the therapist takes a highly directive role in resolving the crisis by leading the problem-solving efforts. In a firm, low-keyed manner, the therapist encourages each family member to express hostile feelings in a specific, direct way, and facilitates the behavioral analysis of the issues that precipitated the crisis. When tensions begin to boil over in the session, the therapist terminates the discussion and attempts to restructure the hostile expression into a constructive com-munication of dissatisfaction with the behavior of other family members.

Example:

MR. CANDY: I'm going to ignore him. I don't care what he does. I give up on him. I want him out of here.

THERAPIST: What aspects of Bill's behavior are you especially mad about?

MR. CANDY: Everything. He does everything he can to upset me and his mother. I'll kill him if I have to spend another day with him around.

MRS. CANDY: Oh, George, you know you don't mean that.

THERAPIST: Mrs. Candy, you seem to see things differently from your hus-band. Can you tell me what Bill has done that has upset you and George?

MRS. CANDY: I think George is fed up with bad behavior. Bill is so rude and won't listen to us.

THERAPIST: Is that accurate, George? How do you see things?

MR. CANDY: I've just had it up to here with . . .

THERAPIST: Can you tell him what he has done that is bothering you?

MR. CANDY: I already have.

THERAPIST: Well, I'd appreciate it if you'd do it again for me because I'm confused about what's been going on.

BILL: He's mad about the other night.

THERAPIST: I'd like you to tell me what happened the other night, George.

MR. CANDY: Bill went out Tuesday night and bought a tape deck after we told him not to.

THERAPIST: So what did you do when he did that?

MR. CANDY: I got mad and shouted at him and he sassed me and walked out, so I locked him out for the night.

THERAPIST: I'm very pleased you've told me about it. Sounds like you had reason to be pretty angry. Have you discussed the problem since?

MR. CANDY: I talked with Faye and told her that we plan to return the tape deck and get the money back.

BILL: I didn't know you were returning it, Dad.

THERAPIST: Well, this sounds like an issue we could do some problem solving on.

Another example of a threat and a common rejecting theme seen in many families goes along the lines of "If you get sick again and need to go to the hospital, you can't live at home anymore. You'll have to live elsewhere." This and other examples of "you'd better behave or else" puts needless pressure on the person who is threatened and often masks discussion of the current displeasing situation. Any threat needs further exploration by the therapist to determine whether additional problem solving is indicated. Often exploration of family members' feelings in response to being threatened will have a profound impact on the person making the threat:

THERAPIST: Fred, how do you feel when your mother threatens to put you out?

FRED: It makes me feel awful.

THERAPIST: I would like you to tell her exactly how you feel when she says that to you.

FRED: Mom, I feel that you don't care for me at all when you say you'll throw me out if I get sick again. It puts a lot of pressure on me, so I'd rather you didn't say that anymore. OK?

THERAPIST: Very good.

MRS. SAMUEL: I'm sorry, Fred, it's just that I don't think I could stand to go through all that again. I'm an old woman and when I see you like that I get to feel very frightened.

THERAPIST: What are you frightened about?

MRS. SAMUEL: He looks wild-eyed, and I'm scared he might beat me up like the boy across the road.

FRED: I've never laid a finger on you. He [the neighbor boy] drinks, he doesn't get schizophrenia. I'll never fight anyone, least of all you.

MRS. SAMUEL: That's easy for you to say, but how can I be sure?

FRED: Just trust me, Mom. I promise. You don't trust me enough.

THERAPIST: I liked the way you both communicated your feelings about that problem. Fred, you did an excellent job of telling your mother exactly what she did that upset you and how it made you feel. Mrs. Samuel, you expressed your feelings that you felt frightened by Fred very clearly. Did it come across clearly to you, Fred?

FRED: Yeah. But I can't help it.

THERAPIST: No, you can't. And your mother can't help feeling frightened. So let's see if we can work out some plan of what we can do if that situation happens in the future.

The subsequent discussion led to a plan whereby Mrs. Samuel would tell Fred when she was frightened and would phone the therapist for support and advice. The therapist agreed to make an emergency visit to the home if indicated. Mrs. Samuel agreed that under no circumstances would she call the police to deal with this situation. Fred reiterated that he would never lay a finger on his mother. A written plan was made and filed in the dossier in which the family kept notes on their family problem-solving sessions.

CONCLUSIONS

In this chapter, we have discussed several specific patterns of communication difficulties that occur in some families. Although the communication problems cover a broad range of interaction patterns, the main thrust of the intervention is similar in each situation. Behavioral family therapy attempts to promote the direct expression of thoughts and feelings and to link this expression to the specific behavior of family members.

The therapist functions as a model of these effective communication skills while prompting, coaching, and reinforcing the efforts and competent performance of each family member. During family problem-solving discussions, he or she continuously monitors the communication process to assess specific assets and deficits that enhance or detract from effective problem resolution. The deficiencies become the focus of specific communication training only when it is clear that they represent a significant source of impairment for family problem solving. This ongoing functional analysis of the family system prevents undue attention to imperfections of interpersonal communication that have only limited functional relevance and which may prove time-consuming to correct. Certain patterns of inappropriate communication such as intrusiveness, invalidation, or hostile threats are considered invariably to interfere with problem resolution and to contribute to family stress. They are dealt with at the time they arise during the family discussion. Interventions to deal with less serious deficits may be scheduled by the therapist at what appears an appropriate point in the family therapy process.

CHAPTER 11

PROBLEM-SOLVING TRAINING

INTRODUCTION

The manner in which families go about coping with difficulties is important both in terms of managing stress and in developing social effectiveness. Effective coping behavior is crucial for households in which one or more persons suffer from a chronic illness, particularly when that illness is stress-related. Schizophrenia is an illness, like peptic ulceration, diabetes, asthma, and rheumatoid arthritis, that is made worse by environmental stress. The two major sources of this stress are life events and family tension. Critical, hostile, or rejecting attitudes, or emotionally overinvolved and intrusive behaviors have been implicated as having a particularly deleterious effect on persons with schizophrenia. These patterns of family interaction tend to mediate against effective problem resolution during times of family crisis, whether the source of stress is related to external factors (financial problems, trouble with the law, dispute with friends) or family factors (arguments, marital discord, behavioral disturbance).

Families vary widely in their sophistication and skill at coping with problems. Some show exceptional tolerance and resourcefulness that enables them to cope with the most severe problems of schizophrenia with little distress, and others tend to be deficient in this regard. In some cases, this appears to be related to general deficiencies in communication skills of some or all members of the family. In other cases, the problem is not clearly related to communication skills *per se*, but has more to do with ineffective strategies adopted by the families. For example, some families are run by "benevolent despots," who unilaterally decide the nature and extent of the family response to most family problems. In such a case, creative efforts to seek solutions to problems by other family members are discouraged. Other families have excellent ideas on how to solve their problems, but fail to follow through; that is, there is a failure at the stage of implementing an agreed-upon solution. Some families never structure family discussions, and in others, efforts to conduct a family discussion escalate into emotional exchanges that merely raise everybody's tension levels without effectively resolving the problems.

For these reasons, we have found it extremely helpful to train families to utilize a structured problem-solving method to facilitate their coping efforts. The approach comprises six steps and has been derived from the behavioral problem-solving method of Spivack (Spivack, Platt, & Shure, 1976). The first step is to discuss the problem and to reach an agreement on what exactly the problem is. Second, the family is taught to generate a list of possible solutions. This step is a no-holds-barred brainstorming exercise in which *all* ideas are acknowledged without judging their merits as of yet. Third, the family systematically discusses the pros and cons of each of the proposed solutions. Fourth, the "best" solution or combination of solutions is selected. Next, the family makes specific plans on how to implement the solution. This may involve several steps with specific assignments to family members. Finally, progress toward solving the original problem is reviewed at some later point. Legitimate efforts toward implementing the solution should be praised, even when they prove unsuccessful. Where the problem is unresolved, a further problem-solving discussion is instituted.

To aid families in their problem-solving efforts, we provide them with a form on which to jot down notes while conducting a problem-solving session (see Figure 11-1). This form lists the six steps and has blanks to fill in the description of the problem, the list of alternative solutions, the selected solution, and the specific steps involved in implementing the solution. Filling out the form helps to structure the family's efforts and provides a written record for future reference. Families save these forms in a loose-leaf binder so they have a convenient record of problems encountered and the ways in which they have coped with them for future reference.

This problem-solving method has many advantages. It encourages everyone to participate in seeking a greater diversity of proposed coping strategies. In fact we set a rule that each family member has to come up with at least one solution, even if it is a "bad" one. This counters the tendency that some families have for unilateral decision making by one family member. Moreover, the structured nature of the approach enables families to discuss emotionally charged issues in a relatively calm and productive manner. By requiring families to generate a list of at least five or six alternative solutions, one can be assured that proper consideration has been given to several possibilities, rather than acting on the first thought that pops into someone's mind.

Step 1: What is the problem?
Talk about the problem, listen carefully, ask questions, get everybody's opinion. Then write down *exactly* what the problem is.

_____

_____

Step 2: List all possible solutions.
Put down *all* ideas, even bad ones. Get everybody to come up with at least one possible solution.
1. _____
2. _____
3. _____
4. _____
5. _____
6. _____

Step 3: Discuss each possible solution.
Go down the list of possible solutions and discuss the advantages and disadvantages of each one.

Step 4: Choose the best solution or combination of solutions.

_____

_____

Step 5: Plan how to carry out the best solution.
Step 1. _____
Step 2. _____
Step 3. _____
Step 4. _____

Step 6: Review implementation and praise *all* efforts.

FIGURE 11-1. *Solving problems.*

The problem-solving approach is useful for coping with a wide range of situations. It is obviously well suited for working on problems involving the entire family. However, it is equally effective for helping an individual family member cope with a personal problem (problems at work, trying to get a date, coping with boredom). In addition, the problem-solving approach can be readily applied to planning goals of any kind. These might include financial planning, recreation and leisure planning, and a wide range of social activities. Thus, the approach not only is a means of reducing environmental stress, but also offers a framework for enhancing the social functioning of all family members. In the initial stages of training families to use this approach, it is often advantageous to work on attaining goals rather than solving problems, particularly with families that tend to focus on the index patient as the "family problem." This helps to maintain a positive orientation and avoids the defensiveness that may interfere with the task of teaching families to use the problem-solving method competently. A summary of the content of issues addressed in problem solving in behavioral family therapy sessions with schizophrenic patients is provided in Table 11-1.

Although this approach is basically straightforward, there are many issues that arise when attempting to teach it to families. It is not sufficient that families can effectively employ problem-solving methods in sessions with guidance from the therapist. The aim of the behavioral family therapy approach is that the same methods can be executed by the family itself outside of therapy sessions and without prompting by the therapist. The remainder of this chapter will examine each of the six steps in detail and explore the issues that commonly arise when teaching the approach to families.

STEP 1: DEFINING THE PROBLEM

The first step in family problem solving is to discuss the nature of the problem and reach a consensus on exactly what the problem is. This is accomplished best in an open-ended, though not excessively lengthy, family discussion. The first prerequisite for this step is clear, direct communication of thoughts and feelings. The effectiveness of communication training can be assessed by the ability of family members to structure a family meeting and to discuss openly their views on the problem at hand. The importance of being specific and being able to reach an agreement about the nature of the problem cannot be overemphasized. In many cases where the problem solving proves unsatisfactory, the failure can be traced to deficiencies in defining the problem.

In essence, families are required to perform a behavioral analysis that aims to elucidate the specific factors that are contributing to a current problem. This is no simple task. Often it is very difficult to pinpoint exactly what the problem is, and it is important to avoid premature closure on the problem's definition. For example, one family session began with Joe, the 22-year-old, eldest son, who had his first and only episode of schizophrenia a year earlier, stating that he felt the family therapy sessions were no longer helping him and should therefore be discontinued. His father and two brothers were invited to discuss their feelings about Joe's problem. They revealed that they thought Joe was worried about being considered ill and a "schizophrenic." Joe admitted that this was indeed part of his concern. He had been feeling particularly uneasy over the fact that he had avoided disclosing anything about his illness to his steady girl friend of 4 months. On several occasions he had

TABLE 11-1. *Content of Problem Solving within Family Therapy Sessions: Patient versus Family Focus over 2 Years*

	Percent of total[a]	Distribution over 24 months		
		0–3 months	4–9 months	10–24 months
Patient focus				
Coping with illness	17%	32%	36%	32%
Symptoms, medication, weight gain, drug abuse, grooming				
Rehabilitation planning	12	19	36	45
Job seeking, training, school				
Individuation/independence	12	14	24	52
Moving away, coping with relationships, marriage plans				
Social activity	11	28	53	19
Developing friendships and activities, dating, social-skills training, neighbors, relatives				
	52%			
Family focus				
Family problems	16	24	40	36
Siblings, parent employment, marital conflict, illness, death in family				
Financial matters	9	17	51	32
Budgeting, bills, disability, purchases				
Household	9	36	39	15
Housing, repairs, chores, garden				
Family meetings	6	46	35	19
Schedules, homework, tasks				
Family leisure activity	6	32	32	36
Vacations, visitors, weekends, parent socialization				
Transportation	2	11	33	56
Cars, buses				
	48%			

[a]443 problem-solving sessions were analyzed.

had to make excuses for leaving her to attend his clinic appointments and family therapy sessions and was feeling guilty that he had not been more open with her. His "best option" off the top of his head was to drop out of treatment, thereby ceasing to carry the stigma of a "psychiatric outpatient" and "schizophrenic," and to unburden himself of the need to remain secretive about his medication and family therapy sessions.

After clarifying the nature of the problem in this fashion, it was clear to the family that the original statement that the therapy sessions were not helping any more did not really capture the true nature of the problem. After redefining the problem of the son's uneasiness over being in treatment and not disclosing this to his girl friend, the family then went on to generate a list of alternative ways of dealing with the situation, including his original solution to drop out of treatment. He rehearsed the anticipated conversation with his girl friend with his brother, Jim.

At the next family session, Joe reported that he had had a very good talk with his girl friend about these matters, and that she had told him about some past difficulties of her own for which she had sought psychological help. He no longer desired to drop out of treatment or to stop his medication.

Another communication skill that aids in this problem-definition step of family problem solving is attentive listening. This includes asking clarifying questions, paraphrasing, not jumping to quick conclusions, and attending to the nonverbal aspects of communication. It is explained to families that are impatient to seek obvious solutions that most problems are not easy to solve—otherwise they would have been solved already. With difficult, long-standing interpersonal problems, rapid resolution is unlikely despite expert problem solving. In these instances, it may be more helpful to be simply an empathic listener than to respond immediately with stereotyped suggestions and advice. We have often told families that we are training them to function in a very similar manner to psychotherapists. A major feature of psychotherapeutic interviewing, both behavioral and psychodynamic, is attentive, empathic listening. Most of the time, families can solve their own problems when they occur in the context of a supportive environment with people to help clarify the issues, and can facilitate the development and implementation of creative, yet realistic solutions.

One of the common pitfalls that lessens the effectiveness of problem solving attempts is lack of specificity in defining the problem. The need for operational descriptions of the problem or goal is evident when families attempt to find solutions for problems such as "improving Sally's attitude," "having more friends," "being bored," "socializing more," or "feeling nervous." These rather global problem definitions tend to generate broad-based solutions and protracted discussions that inevitably return to the question, "What exactly is the problem?" Families are told to return to the problem definition on several occasions if necessary, until a clear description can be written on their note sheets. Many individuals have vague verbal communication styles that mediate against specific pinpointing of problems. Communication training continues throughout the family therapy so that over a period of weeks or months improved speech clarity and improved efficiency of problem definition can be achieved.

A problem of anxiety in Bob, the 45-year-old divorced man, illustrates the value of clear problem definition. Bob described a problem of fearfulness and "pressure building up inside" that he experienced while driving his 12-year-old son back to his ex-wife's house after weekend visits. These episodes would sometimes escalate into full-blown panic attacks that he coped with by pulling over onto the shoulder of the road. He had difficulty remembering any other specific contingencies surrounding these episodes, and initial problem-solving efforts proved ineffective. After several sessions of empathic discussion with his mother and aunt (who lived in the household), it became clear that the bouts of anxiety were preceded by thoughts and fears about his inadequacy as a parent. In particular, he was concerned about his son's apparent disinterest in the Catholic religion (Bob was a devout believer). This prompted fears that his son would go to hell because he had insufficient faith, and that it would be his fault for not having provided more spiritual guidance. Having thus defined an initial problem of anxiety that might have been considered to be associated with thoughts about a failed marriage, it was now much clearer what the problem actually involved. It was now possible for the family to generate several suggestions for coping with the precipitants of his anxiety attacks. These included strategies for increasing his son's interest in religion—having him join a church-affiliated youth group, for example—as well as cognitive interventions that Bob could use to control his negative thoughts. For example, his aunt told him that his concern might be premature because most 13-year-olds are not as interested in religion as their parents, and that he might remind himself that his son was currently immersed in football and school activities and there would be ample opportunity for him to become involved in church activities as he grew older. Bob's mother reminded him that he did take his son to Mass every visit, which was more than most parents did.

Another important aspect of problem definition is to make certain that everyone is in reasonable agreement about the description of the problem. This seems obvious, yet many problem-solving efforts founder in the later stages because different family members have formulated the problem in quite different terms. Thus, when one family was solving how to find the mother a job, it became evident that the three family members had each implicitly defined the problem in very different ways. The father was assuming that his wife did not really want to work because the pay was poor. Daughter Sally was assuming that the problem was trying to determine what sort of work her mother would find satisfying and enjoyable. Meanwhile, the mother was actually feeling very insecure about how she would cope with work after 20 years at home, and whether Sally would be able to cope without her. With so many different agendas, it was little wonder that they seemed to be working at cross purposes.

One way to reduce this problem is to teach families to designate a "leader" each time they arrange a problem-solving discussion. The leader has the responsibility of chairing the discussion and at some point getting each family member to define the problem explicitly as he or she sees it. Where differences of opinion are elicited, the problem description should be explored further. Hopefully, the entire family will be able to agree at some point on a relatively explicit statement of the problem, which can then be noted on the worksheet. It is often better to have several problems to solve than to spend long periods of time attempting to define the *real* problem. In the example above several problems may be defined: (1) finding a constructive activity for mother outside the home; (2) finding a satisfying paid job for mother; (3) coping with starting a job after 20 years. Each of these problems might be solved in turn.

It is evident that the skills required to elicit, explore, and specify a difficult personal or familial problem are considerable. Even skillful therapists will at times be unable to specify accurately the relevant parameters of a problem. Fortunately, many problems are more straightforward. For the more difficult ones, any progress made toward clarifying the nature of the problem is bound to be helpful, and the therapist and family may have to be content with simply trying to make progress toward defining the problem. In any event, reaching some consensus on definition of the problem at hand provides the necessary closure to continue on to the next task of the problem-solving process.

Example:

THERAPIST: Now I'm going to ask you to have a family discussion for the next 5 minutes or so in order to give each of you a chance to describe the problem as you see it. At the end of that time, I'll want to see whether you have reached any agreement on what the problem is before you tackle solving it. Try to be as specific as possible, and ask each other questions if things aren't clear.

JIM: Well, I don't know what the problem is. I'm never around.

MR. KASPER: Well, that's part of the problem. You're never around and things don't get done around the house. Nothing gets put away or straightened up, and I come home from work tired, and your mother can't do it all.

MRS. KASPER: Your father is right. You two just haven't been pulling your weight around the house.

GREG: Well, what do you want us to do?

THERAPIST: It sounds like you need to set up some plans for delegating household chores. I wonder what has worked in the past and who does what around the house.

MRS. KASPER: Well, I do everything.

THERAPIST: How would you like that to be different? What changes would you like to see?

MRS. KASPER: Well, I'd like both boys to do more.

THERAPIST: Can you be more specific about what you want them to do?

MRS. KASPER: I'd like them to clean up their mess.

THERAPIST: I'm unclear about what you mean. What about you, Greg and Jim?

JIM: Well, I think she means to clean up the dishes and put the food away after we eat.

THERAPIST: Is that what you meant, Mrs. Kasper?

MRS. KASPER: Yes, it is. I also meant cleaning up their bedrooms, not leaving piles of dirty clothes and towels around and picking up the bathroom.

MR. KASPER: I'm concerned about the yard work and putting out the garbage and watering as well.

GREG: I'm sure that my food is contaminated, and the water is bad, and the FBI is checking our mailbox, so I won't spend time in the yard.

JIM: There he goes again about those plots. You know the FBI isn't after you.

THERAPIST: Let's get back to the discussion of the problem. What have you agreed on?

MRS. KASPER: Well, I think we were discussing how to get the chores done.

THERAPIST: Mr. Kasper, would you agree this is the problem?

MR. KASPER: Yes, I agree it's a major problem.

THERAPIST: What about you, Jim and Greg—what do you think?

GREG: I agree.

JIM: I'm not here, but I guess it's a problem for them.

THERAPIST: OK. I'd like for one of you to write down the problem and let's see whether you can come up with some solutions.

In initial sessions the therapist may provide considerable modeling of active listening as he or she assists the family to pinpoint the problem in operational terms. However, the therapist attempts to face his or her interventions as quickly as possible and to hand over the leadership responsibility to the family members, while providing coaching and reinforcement from the sidelines.

STEP 2: GENERATING ALTERNATIVE SOLUTIONS

Once family members have reached a consensus on the problem definition and it has been recorded on the worksheet, the next step is to generate a list of possible solutions. A brainstorming approach is employed to encourage creativity and to maximize the participation of every family member. Every member is invited to suggest a possible solution, and every alternative is welcomed at this stage. The immediate objective is to obtain a list of at least five or six alternative solutions to the problem. The family member who has been designated the leader may guide this process of soliciting suggestions as well as recapitulating previously mentioned ideas.

Any attempt to judge or comment on the relative merits of any suggestion proffered is discouraged by the therapist until the next step of problem solving. Statements such as "I've got a great idea . . ."; "This is the best solution . . ."; "That's a crazy idea . . ." are either specifically ignored or responded to with a statement to the effect that both good and bad ideas are equally important at this stage. To this end, the therapist briefly acknowledges *every suggestion offered* and instructs the leader to write each idea down on the list. The therapist avoids making suggestions until it seems evident that no further solutions are forthcoming from the family. However, he or she may model for more reticent families in the early stages of problem solving training. The therapist may find it beneficial to make outlandish or seemingly impractical suggestions in an effort to promote divergent thinking and to reduce stereotyped problem solutions.

Example: Mark, age 22, and his parents and sister Janet agreed to explore the problem of how to increase social activity, particularly in the area of meeting female acquaintances for dating opportunities.

THERAPIST: Now I would like all of you to put your heads together and try to come up with some ideas of how Mark might go about meeting new friends, particularly women. Remember, no suggestion is too outrageous to consider. We'll write them all down first and discuss them later on.

MARK: Well, I could join Photodate. It would be terrific.

THERAPIST: OK. Good. Write that down, Janet, and we'll discuss what we like about it in a few minutes. What other suggestions do you have?

MRS. SANDERS: What about a course at the community college?

THERAPIST: Another idea well worth considering. What about other suggestions?

MARK: I could go up to strangers in bars or on the street.

MRS. SANDERS: That sounds pretty stupid to me.

THERAPIST: Janet, I would like you to write that suggestion down. Right now we don't want to rule out any options. We'll discuss their relative merits *after* we come up with a few more suggestions. How many do you have so far? Would you like to review what we have?

JANET: Number 1: Photodate. Number 2: Community college course. Number 3: Go up to strangers in bars.

THERAPIST: I'd like you folks to come up with at least two more possibilities. Janet, do you have any suggestions?

JANET: Well, what about going to a church group or to the arcade at the beach?

THERAPIST: Very good. Those are two more ideas. Have you thought of joining a health club or spa?

JANET: OK. We have six possible solutions written down.

THERAPIST: Great. You all did a good job of thinking creatively, and I like the fact that each person contributed something. What's the next step in the problem solving, Janet?

JANET: We discuss each solution and say what the pros and cons are.

The structured problem-solving format ensures that closure is reached on each step before moving to the next. The natural tendency to short-circuit this process and follow the lead of a seemingly "good" idea is averted, and full consideration is given to solutions that at first sight may appear improbable, even absurd. There are several pitfalls that may be encountered during the brainstorming step. Families that show a poverty of verbal responses are especially difficult in the early stages of training. Very few responses may be generated, and these are almost always stereotyped solutions to the problem that offer little creative potential.

An example of such a family was Mr. and Mrs. Bean, Rita (age 25), and John (age 23). They defined a problem of cleaning up the lawns and the garden. After the therapist encouraged them to make a list of suggestions on how the work could be achieved, Mr. Bean suggested that he could mow the lawn. However, no further suggestion was offered and the four family members lapsed into a tense silence.

THERAPIST: Father has said he could mow the lawns. Has anyone got any other suggestions about what could be done? Rita, what do you think?

RITA: I can help with the watering if Mom shows me how to do it.

MRS. BEAN: We can do it together for a while. Also the pruning needs to be done.

MR. BEAN: What about the weeding?

MRS. BEAN: And the drain spout needs fixing.

THERAPIST: I like the way you asked each other questions about what needs to be done. You have broken down the big problem of cleaning the yard into a number of smaller specific tasks. Let's continue listing all the jobs to be done; then we can decide how each one will get done.

One reason for this family's initial difficulty generating alternatives was the lack of specificity of the problem description. The problems of cleaning the yard involved many tasks that could not be solved by any one strategy. However, the therapist took care to reframe the problem solving in a constructive manner, taking care not to appear critical of the deficiency in the earlier step.

A surfeit of solutions can also present problems. However, all suggestions must be recorded, and at the next step a quick screening of unlikely solutions can be conducted so that no more than six or seven possibilities are discussed in detail.

When families come up with poor-quality suggestions, the therapist may feel impelled to make several more imaginative suggestions. It should be remembered that it is the *process* of problem solving that is being trained, not the content. Clever solutions from the therapist may inhibit the family from creating their own solutions and risk setting up a dependence on the therapist for the "best answers." This defeats the purpose of the training. However, when a major crisis is being resolved, the therapist's expertise may be freely employed, but even then there may be beneficial effects from inducing effective solutions from family members wherever feasible.

Dominance of one family member over the others may occur despite the structure imposed by the brainstorming approach. One individual may come up with most of the ideas or may aggressively proclaim his or her suggestion as being "the best," "the right one," "the only thing we can do." The therapist assertively confronts such railroading and prompts other family members to volunteer their suggestions.

One final difficulty encountered in generating alternative solutions occurs when there are only two family members performing the problem solving. This is a particular problem when one member of the pair is severely disturbed and has difficulty performing the problem-solving task. Whenever possible, a third person—friend, relative—may be invited to participate, but where that does not occur the therapist may have to take a more active participant role in the brainstorming process at times.

STEP 3: EVALUATION OF ALTERNATIVE SOLUTIONS

Once the list of potential solutions to the specified problem has been generated, each alternative is discussed briefly. Once again, the approach aims to maximize participation of every family member. The democratic structure employed gives every person an opportunity to have his or her opinion heard. Each potential solution to the problem has both positive and negative aspects which need to be examined by the family group. There are no right or wrong solutions to problems, only ones that seem to fit best the particular circumstances of the problem and the available family resources. Even seemingly absurd solutions have some merits relative to their drawbacks. By insisting on this pluralism, the decision-making process is somewhat prolonged and more time is devoted to an objective evaluation of the solutions. We do not insist that families record their discussion of the pros and cons, although some may find this useful. It is important that lengthy debates are avoided.

Example:

THERAPIST: Mrs. Kasper, I would like you to go through the list of alternatives now and to discuss the pros and cons of each possible solution.

MRS. KASPER: Well, the first suggestion was that Jim might go to the church social group Friday evenings.

MR. KASPER: Well, it's free and it's a nice group of Christian, single people.

JIM: Yeah, I'd get to meet some people. Probably girls go there.

MRS. KASPER: They plan a lot of different activities that are interesting.

THERAPIST: What do you see as possible drawbacks?

JIM: It's a religious group. I'm not into religion myself. But you probably see it differently, Mom.

MRS. KASPER: It might not have a lot of people your age. You know it might be older folks.

THERAPIST: I'd like you to summarize the advantages and drawbacks of that solution, Jim.

JIM: The good points in favor are its cheapness and there may be girls there. Against that is the religion, and maybe its for older people.

Families are taught to proceed in this manner until they have discussed all the options originally enumerated. Some clearly unsuitable solutions may be crossed of the list of options at this stage, in order to expedite further discussion.

Several problems may emerge that interfere with this problem-solving step. The tendency to jump immediately to the obvious solution to the problem occurs quite commonly. Even when the best solution appears obvious, it is crucial to explore every other suggested possibility. Not only does this present the opportunity for creative solutions, but at a more basic level it reinforces the confidence of the person who made the suggestion.

> MR. BARON: Well, I think Arizona is the best place for us to go. Yeah, I vote that we go to Arizona. All right with you guys?
>
> THERAPIST: Hey, wait a minute, Mr. Baron. I'd like you to discuss all five of the suggestions, one at a time, to see what everybody likes and dislikes about each one. Once we've heard everyone's opinion, we can choose the one we all like the best.

At times one family member may dominate the discussion of the solution to the problem so that other persons are excluded. The problem becomes that person's special mission rather than a shared family issue. The therapist may redirect the discussion by inviting other family members to contribute their own assessments of the merit of the proposed solutions. Further structuring of this aspect of the problem-solving discussion may be necessary when family members jump from topic to topic without reaching closure on any point.

Example:

> BILL: Well, I think having a list of chores is a good idea.
>
> JERRY: I'd rather change chores every week. You do the yard one week, dishes the next.
>
> MRS. CANDY: But then who would take out the garbage?
>
> MR. CANDY: How will we work out the allowances?
>
> THERAPIST: We're getting off the track. I would like you to discuss the list of plans that were suggested to get the chores done. Let's take them one at a time and say what we like and don't like about each one, before we start planning the details. OK? Try to stick to the task.

STEP 4: SELECTING THE "BEST" SOLUTION OR STRATEGY

After each proposed solution has been reviewed, the family is instructed to reach a group consensus on the best solution. This negotiation phase may be very straightforward when one solution appears clearly superior to all others. Very often this is not the case, however, and discussion of the *relative merits* of the various possible solutions is needed. Once again, effective communication skills facilitate this process. Clear expression of feelings, attentive listening, and statements of acknowledgments assist in reaching a compromise that may be deemed acceptable by the majority of family members. In the early stages of problem-solving training, the therapist may need to structure this activity and act as ombudsman in the discussion.

Example:

THERAPIST: Now I would like each of you to pick one or two solutions, or even a combination, that you like. Mr. Baron, what do you think would be best?

MR. BARON: Well, I like the idea of going to San Diego or La Jolla for the weekend.

THERAPIST: Mrs. Baron, how do you feel about that? What's your choice?

MRS. BARON: I like La Jolla, but I think Santa Barbara would be nice this time of year.

THERAPIST: What about you, Sam?

SAM: I like the desert or Death Valley best for fun.

THERAPIST: It seems you all prefer different places to go. Now I want you to tell one another why you feel the way you do and try to arrive at a compromise.

The therapist remains neutral in the decision making and provides a structure and additional clarification to the discussion. The therapist stresses that planning is not feasible until agreement can be reached. The agreed solution need not be the "ideal," but should be realistic and practical. Often the optimal solution involves a combination of several alternatives. Constraints of material and emotional resources may determine the pragmatic choice of a solution. The attempt to reach a consensus continued:

MRS. BARON: Al and I agree on La Jolla, but, Sam, you're still keen to get out to the desert.

SAM: Well, I could go along with La Jolla if we could go to the Safari Park that's near there.

MR. BARON: I like that idea too. We could go to dinner in San Diego after that.

MRS. BARON: That might be a bit too expensive.

MR. BARON: So we're all agreed on La Jolla for the weekend with a trip to the Safari Park?

SAM AND MRS. BARON: Uh-huh.

THERAPIST: You all contributed very well to the discussion. I was very pleased to see the three of you working together as a team.

Many problem-solving methods are considered to have been completed once there is consensus about the solution to the problem. Our methods recognize that translating a proposed solution into a successful plan is a crucial aspect of problem solving that cannot be overlooked.

STEP 5: PLANNING

After the relief at reaching agreement on the best solution for resolving a problem issue, it is tempting to believe that the problem is now resolved. Covert rehearsal of the successful implementation of a solution may lead to premature closure of the discussion. However, to achieve successful overt performance of the best solution, careful planning is essential. It is at this stage that many families tend to fail in their problem-solving efforts.

For many persons, it is sufficient to have the reassuring knowledge that they believe they could effectively achieve resolution of the problem or attain the goal *if they wanted to*. This approach may be reasonable where the problem is one that might be expected to occur in the future and where the family, therefore, cannot provide a solution at the present time. However, this is not usually the case. In most instances, the implementation of a potential solution needs to occur as soon as possible to reduce ongoing stress associated with the often long-standing difficulty.

Planning involves a series of steps that vary considerably with the nature of the problem. However, some general issues can be delineated:

- *Elect a coordinator*: Who will coordinate the plan—give the orders, monitor progress, provide prompting?
- *Review resources*: What resources will be required? Money, time, personnel, special equipment, and skill.
- *Allocate resources*: How can personal resources be best utilized? Who will do what?
- *Anticipate consequences*: What negative consequences are likely? How can they be coped with? What positive consequences are possible? How can they be coped with?
- *Set a date*: When is the best time to implement the plan?
- *Rehearsal*: What is the step-by-step plan? Family members may find it helpful to rehearse aspects of the plan either covertly (in their imaginations), or overtly in role-played practice.

Once the family has considered these issues, a step-by-step plan is written down in detail. This approach may appear overdetailed, but experience has shown that unless plans are made in this clearly delineated fashion, full family participation is unlikely and one or two family members are burdened with the issue, which frequently remains only partially resolved.

One family, experts at devising solutions to their problem of obtaining Social Security benefits for their handicapped son, were unable to implement the plans they had developed. These plans tended to be rather vague, and relied heavily on the young son's carrying out the major part of the plan without much assistance from other family members. After several failures, when the son forgot to go to the Social Security office, the therapist conducted a more detailed planning session. The parents revealed their ambivalence toward the idea of their 18-year-old son's receiving large sums of money that he could use to buy drugs. They were greatly relieved when they learned that they themselves could be made the recipients of his checks and monitor his expenditures. After this perceived consequence was dealt with, the parents worked together with their son to secure the benefits.

Coordination

Plans that involve more than one family member may need to be carefully coordinated. A team leader or coordinator is elected from the family members for this express purpose. This need not be a parent, and need not be selected from the main protagonists of the problem-solving plan. The family members as a group are invited to choose the most appropriate person. The elected coordinator then takes an authoritative role in the execution of the plan. This involves supervising the setting up of the plan, securing appropriate resources, prompting and encouraging the problem resolution, and monitoring the progress of the problem-solving steps.

It is very important that the coordinator be clearly delineated. Where this is not done, family members may blame one another for not executing the proposed plan, or a dominant family member may inappropriately assume the coordinator's role. More often than not the family will elect the more dominant parent, but at times children may be given this responsibility.

Review of Resources

Very often a seemingly perfect solution cannot be carried out because the family lacks the resources to execute the plan. Although the most crucial resource is usually the interpersonal skill of family members, more mundane matters such as family finances, availability of time, or specialized skills or equipment may be essential for the effective implementation of the problem resolution. A careful check on resources is essential. Many families commit themselves to courses of action that are very costly, and create tension as a result of financial pressures. One woman decided to help her son buy a new car while he was receiving welfare. After 3 months, his welfare was discontinued and the car repossessed when she found she could not help him with the payments. Interpersonal skills can be readily tested through role play of the anticipated problem solution. A 25-year-old man rehearsed initiating a conversation with a girl at a doughnut shop. It was clear that his lack of fluency and awkward posture would guarantee failure in his quest. Social-skills training was instituted to enhance his conversation effectiveness.

Anticipation of Consequences

Earlier in the problem-solving sequence, the pros and cons of each potential solution have been evaluated briefly. During the planning phase, a more detailed review is advocated. This involves a discussion of the most likely consequences, both good and bad. It is not sufficient to examine merely the negative consequences and to consider potential coping strategies; it is also important to evaluate ways of dealing with the most optimistic consequences.

One young man fretted over the way he could cope with anticipated rejection from a girl he planned to ask for a date. When she told him she would be delighted to go out with him, and wondered why he hadn't asked sooner, he panicked, abruptly ended the conversation, and went home in despair, thinking that he could never handle women. In a subsequent family discussion, his parents suggested alternative ways he might have coped with this overwhelming success. Had such a consequence been considered during planning, the outcome of this venture might have been more positive.

More frequently, however, planning involves considering ways of coping with anticipated negative consequences. A cognitive "safety net" is constructed to provide the participant with strategies to prevent a catastrophic reaction when the best-laid plans prove unsuccessful. Family members are trained to employ behavioral, affective, and cognitive methods to cope with disappointment. These include:

Behavioral
• Leave the situation.
• Approach the situation again as soon as possible.

- Review the attempt with family member(s) to assess what went right and what went wrong.
- Consider alternative strategies.
- Family members praise for *all efforts*, no matter how ineffective or inept.
- Engage in an enjoyable activity to provide distraction.

Affective
- Express feelings of disappointment, frustration, hopelessness, and so on to family member(s).

Cognitive
- Note self-reinforcement for *all efforts*, no matter how ineffective or inept they appear.
- Label any attempt as *"partial success"* rather than failure.
- Blame failure on poorly planned strategy rather than personal inadequacy.
- Avoid ruminating about failed attempt by revising strategies for future attempts.
- Consider a "partially successful" attempt as practice and as a useful learning experience.

Many persons avoid dealing with issues that they have a more than adequate repertoire of interpersonal skills to handle. Anticipating fear of failure (or success) is a powerful inhibitory factor. Much avoidance behavior appears to stem from a lack of a sense of security that the worst (and best) consequences can be dealt with. A few minutes spent developing a safety net may greatly enhance the probability that the participants will attempt to implement the plan. Once this initial reluctance can be overcome, the result is often surprisingly good.

A 20-year-old moderately retarded girl feared her parents leaving her alone at home. When psychotic, she had heard voices outside her window that she believed were her neighbors plotting to assault her. During a planning session focusing on this problem, her parents outlined the various strategies she could employ if she suspected somebody was breaking into their very secure house: (1) She could call the police—the number was on the telephone; (2) she could call a friendly neighbor; (3) her parents would leave a forwarding number whenever possible, and call her at specified times; (4) she could lock herself in a bathroom and escape through the window if an intruder did indeed enter the house; (5) the family labrador would bark loudly and scare off any intruder; (6) she could watch television in her bedroom and try not to think about burglars; (7) she could leave most of the lights on in other rooms.

Once this plan was discussed, she agreed to stay alone for gradually increasing periods, and after 6 months she was able to cope for 2 weeks while her parents took an overseas vacation.

Setting a Date

Procrastination is another factor that reduces the effective implementation of well-considered plans: "I'm going to start next week . . . next month . . . tomorrow . . . give me a few minutes to chew it over. . . ." The procrastinator may feel that his or her performance may be inadequate, or that there are deficiencies in the plan. If this is the case, there are two obvious alternatives: (1) revise the plan and counter these potential weaknesses; or (2) go ahead as planned and see what happens—the experience will prove more valuable than further brooding.

A valuable component of any plan is the decision of when the plan will be implemented. In some simple cases (e.g., a phone call to a job agency), an exact time can be specified. In more complex plans, a deadline may be set, before which the planned steps will have been attempted. Failure to implement the plan after the appointed time necessitates a review to evaluate the lack of effort. At times the deficiency may be obvious and require minimal further planning; in other circumstances the entire problem-solving process may need to be repeated. As we have continually emphasized, the behavioral approach demands the *implementation* of strategies, not merely the comforting knowledge that an effective solution is possible. A failure to generalize problem solving to the real-life problem is considered a total failure of the intervention. For this reason these rather mundane aspects of problem solving are accorded a high priority in the therapy process.

Rehearsal

The final step in the planning phase of problem solving involves rehearsing the strategy. This may be likened to the pregame preparation of a football team, where the coach checks that each player is prepared for his part in each specific move, that the sequence of steps is clear to the team, and that in the event of a failure to execute the strategy backup safety moves have been developed. This rehearsal may take the form of a step-by-step discussion (covert rehearsal) of the procedure, or in some instances a role-played practice run (overt rehearsal). Where practical skills are involved, overt rehearsal of the behavioral skills may prove more effective, especially when a role play can closely replicate the real-life situation. If it is not possible to conduct a realistic role rehearsal, or where cognitive strategies are emphasized (e.g., taking a written test), then family members may be instructed in *covert rehearsal*. This involves visualizing oneself attending to each step of the procedure, envisaging the potential hazards and the means to be used to cope with them, and then following the plan through to a successful completion. Many persons begin to visualize the planned strategies, but when a potentially difficult situation confronts them, they frequently terminate their covert rehearsal and begin a sequence of negative, self-doubting thoughts. The ability to envisage coping behavior despite fantasies of the worst possible consequences appears to assist in overcoming anxiety-provoking situations (Kazdin, 1975). As mentioned before, consideration of coping with the best possible consequences may be similarly important, yet readily overlooked.

Example: Melvyn, a 20-year-old living with his mother, brother and sister, had missed several appointments to attend a sheltered workshop program on account of his sleeping in. It became clear that although he was eager to attend so that he could get a job in the near future, he did little preparation for these appointments. His family provided minimal prompting or support. A detailed plan was worked out that involved his phoning the intake worker the day before his appointment to confirm the arrangement and to get details on what he should bring, appropriate dress, and so on. The evening before his appointment he would get his clothes ready, set the alarm clock, take his medicine, and then retire by 10:00 P.M. Prior to this, he would check that his clothes were clean, and check the bus schedules. Finally, on the morning of the appointment, he would get up when the alarm rang, eat some cereal and toast for breakfast, and get to the bus stop 10 minutes before the bus departure. This schedule was considered step by step, and all suspected hitches were pinpointed. Several potential problems were defined and appropriate coping strategies suggested. They included:

Problem: What if Melvyn forgets any of the steps? *Coping strategy*—have a person prompt him to carry out each step. Niece Samantha (11 years) is chosen because she has the best memory and will be around that evening and morning. (Mother works the night shift.)

Problem: How will Melvyn react to Samantha's prompting? Melvyn indicated that he wouldn't mind, but appeared somewhat uncomfortable. An overt rehearsal of Samantha telling Melvyn that it was the time he had set to go to bed was conducted. Her prompt was changed from "Melvyn, it's your bedtime now" to "You asked me to remind you when it's 10:00 so you could go to bed early tonight. It's just 10:00 now."

Problem: What to do if the plan goes wrong and Melvyn is delayed so that he will be late for his appointment? *Coping strategy*—call the intake worker and explain the problem solution.

Both overt and covert rehearsal are employed. In addition to the procedures described in this example, a flow-chart checklist was devised (at Melvyn's suggestion) and posted on the refrigerator door, so that he could receive frequent nonintrusive reminders of the plan. Good management procedures are as important in the home setting as they are in the boardroom.

STEP 6: REVIEW IMPLEMENTATION EFFORTS

The final step of problem solving is to implement the planned strategy and to review the results. Solving problems is an ongoing process, with complete success rare on the first attempt. This is an important principle to disseminate to patients and their families, who may believe that with the special assistance they are receiving from the therapy they could expect to achieve instant and total success, even when tackling long-standing, seemingly intractable issues. Of course, it is probably not wise to encourage them to tackle such difficult problems at first, but to suggest they choose smaller everyday problems that may be successfully resolved despite relatively inefficient deployment of the approach. As proficiency in problem solving accrues, progressively more difficult issues may be the focus of family problem-solving efforts.

Review of the efforts made to effectively implement the specific strategies planned in the problem-solving discussion is a crucial component of the method. A cleverly devised plan may provide a certain degree of aesthetic or intellectual satisfaction, but is of little real value until it has been implemented. Once this has been attempted, a family discussion is recommended to discuss both the successful steps, as well as those that were less effective. It is as helpful for families to clearly define those actions that enable certain specific goals to be achieved, as it is to discern the strategies that failed. The concept of failure, however, is invoked sparingly during this review process. An attempt is considered a failure only when the family does not make any effort to implement the plan. Any attempt is considered at least a "partial" success, in that at the very least the family will have acquired some potentially useful feedback concerning the effectiveness of the plan. Failure to initiate the strategy provides no such opportunity to modify subsequent attempts. Thus, the family is encouraged to pinpoint the strengths and weaknesses of their efforts, and where the goal has not been achieved, to immediately set about further problem solving to seek a more effective plan for subsequent implementation. This constructive problem-solving framework helps motivate family members to continue working day by day on the major problems in their lives until satisfactory goals have been achieved.

Example: Despite careful planning with his family, Melvyn was 20 minutes late for his sheltered workshop appointment. All the steps were carried out as planned. Unfortunately, the bus routes had been changed the previous week, and after waiting at the former bus stop for a half hour, Melvyn decided to walk to the workshop. Because he had planned to catch an early bus he was not excessively late. Upon arriving at his destination, he explained the difficulty he had encountered to the receptionist, who advised him of the new bus route and reassured him he was not too late to be seen. However, the assessor told him that although he was suitable for the program he would have a 6-week wait before he could start. He had previously thought he would enter the program immediately, and returned home feeling dispirited. His mother and sister reviewed the situation with him that evening. They praised him for his efforts in making the appointment, including his decision to walk when the bus failed to arrive, as well as the manner in which he explained his lateness to the receptionist. They briefly reviewed alternative ways of getting the up-to-date bus information and concluded that on future occasions phoning the bus information service might be the preferred strategy. Thus, the goal of making the appointment on time was a partial, yet functional success. But the broader goal of achieving constructive daily activity was unresolved, at least in the short term. A further problem-solving discussion was devoted to planning activities for Melvyn while he awaited starting the workshop program.

CONCLUSIONS

Effective family problem solving is the cornerstone of behavioral family therapy. The six-step process is a seemingly straightforward procedure that can be mastered by many families in a few sessions. This structured approach to coping with stressful situations that emerge in everyday family living can also be deployed to assist family members in coping with stress outside the family as well as to promote their social effectiveness and to achieve personal life goals.

The topics families dealt with during the 2 years of treatment sessions are summarized in Table 11-1. It is important to note that the issues are evenly distributed between those that focus on the well-being of the patient, his or her illness and community functioning, and the family as a whole. Almost half the families in the program consisted of only two persons—the index patient and one parent. Thus, this analysis provides evidence that this approach involves systematic stress reduction encompassing the entire family, and is not merely focused on the management of the patient and schizophrenia. In most families the index patient's illness and associated disability was at times the major stress in the family.

However, in many families even greater problems were not infrequent. These ranged from issues such as severe poverty or inadequate housing to family violence, drug abuse, and severely discordant relationships among family members other than the index patient. In many instances the index patient was a tower of strength in assisting the family to work out solutions to these major problems. It may be noted that many of the problems were not major interpersonal issues, but rather mundane everyday problems. Such day-to-day problems, left unresolved, can readily emerge as a considerable source of ambient tension, and should not be considered inconsequential. The behavioral family therapy approach allows the family to prioritize their own perceived stresses to a great extent, and attempts to avoid value judgments about the significance of the wide variety of problems observed in family relationships.

The relative simplicity of this problem-solving procedure belies the complexities of family transactions that are essential for effective problem resolution. These include an adequate repertoire of communication skills essential before a family can conduct an open, directive problem-solving discussion. Perhaps the most crucial skill is the ability to pinpoint the specific problem clearly. Once the exact nature of the problem has been defined in operational terms, the brainstorming process to generate potential solutions leading to the eventual choice of an optimal solution is relatively straightforward. However, this approach emphasizes that successful implementation of the solution is only achieved after careful, detailed planning.

The final step of the training program involves family problem solving without therapist involvement, and efforts to promote this generalization are applied continually throughout the therapy program. Although at times of crisis the therapist may become an active participant in the problem-solving process, at other times he or she functions more in the role of a teacher or coach while the family learns to employ the model to cope more effectively with their perceived problems.

For purposes of clarity of description of the specific components of behavioral family therapy, we have arbitrarily separated communication and problem-solving training. In practice the training of both is closely integrated with coaching in deficient functional communication skills being conducted within the broader problem-solving framework. The continual emphasis on specificity of communication of ideas and feelings is a persistent theme that contributes to all aspects of the behavioral family therapy approach.

CHAPTER 12

SPECIFIC STRATEGIES FOR
FAMILY MANAGEMENT

INTRODUCTION

The structure of behavioral family therapy tends to focus intervention on the *process* of family communication and problem solving rather than on the *content* of the issues. Families are taught a framework for effective problem solving which they are encouraged to use unaided to solve the various problems they face in their everyday lives. This approach can be applied effectively to families regardless of the nature of the illness in the index patients. In the present study, the population was defined as having an adult child suffering from schizophrenia. However, the authors have treated families with identified problems ranging from having disturbed adolescents to marital discord, agoraphobia, obsessive–compulsive disorders, generalized anxiety states, obesity, and major affective disorders. The family therapy component, although the central unifying therapeutic intervention, was one of several in the family case management approach. Family education about schizophrenia, communication training, and problem solving has already been described. Ancillary interventions that are consistent with the basic behavioral psychotherapy paradigm include (1) additional behavioral interventions, (2) symptom-management strategies, and (3) community management issues.

ADDITIONAL BEHAVIORAL INTERVENTIONS

We have outlined such techniques as behavior rehearsal, feedback, and homework tasks in an earlier chapter. In this section, we will discuss the application of some of these strategies to deal with some of the specific problems commonly encountered in the long-term management of schizophrenia in a family setting. Six interventions are particularly germane in working with such families: (1) contingency contracting; (2) shaping, successive approximation; (3) token economy; (4) social-skills training; (5) time out and setting limits; and (6) homework problems. A review of these will follow.

Contingency Contracting

The notion that interaction between two or more individuals is governed by a set of rules that reflects a balance between mutual rewards and costs forms the basis of the contingency contract. Richard Stuart (1969) and Patterson and Reid (1970) applied these reciprocity concepts to family interaction where conflicts resulted from excessive use of aversive control to solicit rewards, cooperation, and compliance from a family member. Such nagging, demanding, coercive behavior was frequently reciprocated by the recipient, who returned unpleasant responses in kind. The goal of the contingency contract is to reverse the exchange of unpleasant interaction behaviors. A written agreement between the warring factions is negotiated on the basis that each person is expected to give as much as he or she gets out of the contract. The written contract is then signed by both parties and compliance with the agreement is reviewed at subsequent sessions. A written contract may be unnecessary in many instances but has the advantage of precisely defining the agreed responses and representing a firm commitment to behavior change. The contract frequently may require amendment, and serves as an excellent focus for further data collection. The challenge for the therapist and the family is to negotiate a highly specific exchange of pleasing behaviors. Whenever possible, high-frequency everyday behaviors are preferred to behaviors that may only occur in special circumstances.

Example: Mr. and Mrs. V expected their 15-year-old son, James, to spend most of his leisure time with them and their 9-year-old daughter. He refused to go out on family visits to friends and relatives. The parents accused him of being lazy about the house, doing nothing to help, and lounging about in disgusting clothes watching rubbish on television. At times he lost his temper with both parents, swearing and calling them names.

James felt that his parents were always picking on him, showed no interest in him or his friends, and when they did talk to his friends, his mother embarrassed him by ridiculing him in front of them. He avoided family outings because his mother always told stories about how bad he was at home. He had pestered his father to help him with his math homework, but his father always said he was too busy.

In the course of five meetings with the family, several contracts were negotiated. These included:

Responsibilities	Privileges
James	
Complete one major household chore to Mother's satisfaction—clearing kitchen, taking out trash, watering plants	Payment of 50 cents upon completion of chore
Wear clean jeans when watching TV	Watch 30 minutes of TV of own choice
Go on one family outing each week	An ice cream treat of own choice
Mr. V	
Help James with math for 2 hours in evening	A cup of tea in bed in morning
Watch James play football	Car washed
Mrs. V	
Make two positive statements about James to his friends or relatives	James tells Mother one thing he likes about her

It may be noticed that these contracted behaviors are highly specific and that a specific reward is contingent upon completion of a clearly agreed upon behavior. Another form of contract known as the *quid pro quo* strategy has been criticized in some circles. This variant makes the positive behavior of one person contingent upon the positive behavior of the other. For example, Mr. V would help James with his homework only *after* James carried out a household chore. If James did not first achieve his desired behavior, his father would not carry out his part of the contract.

The contracts negotiated by James and his parents were carried out reasonably well by all three. James had great difficulty expressing positive feelings toward his mother as a reward for her praising him to other people. He rehearsed this in the sessions on several occasions, and, although it was evident that he had considered affection for his mother, he found it hard to express these positive feelings verbally. He was able to hug his mother without difficulty, although he expressed some embarrassment that a 15-year-old boy should be doing this.

Contingency contracting has been widely employed in behavioral marital therapy and has considered application in enhancing marital satisfaction within the family system. We have employed this strategy within the problem-solving framework of family sessions.

Shaping

Shaping involves the step-by-step prompting and positive reinforcement, usually with praise, for successive approximations to a specific desired response. This is a particularly useful strategy for dealing with the more severely handicapped individual who tends to learn new responses over an extended period. One man who had a 20-year history of schizophrenia was praised and paid one dollar by his parents for mowing progressively larger segments of the front lawn without a break.

The effect of breaking down goals into micro segments enables a family member to achieve progress that can be readily observed and reinforced by other family members. The tendency to push a person who is rehabilitating from schizophrenia to quickly regain his or her former performance level has precipitated many a relapse. Structuring the rehabilitation program to a self-paced series of small incremental steps with contingent reinforcement is considered the most effective strategy. Family members and community supporters often require considerable training to enable them to show pleasure with modest short-term improvements, and to forego comparisons with premorbid performance, goals, and expectations. This is a major concern with patients who have suffered their first episode of schizophrenia and have recovered with expectations of a rapid return to previous functional levels upon discharge from the hospital.

Token Economy

A refinement of operant reinforcement strategies is occasionally used to enhance the motivation of one or more family members to perform more desirable behavior by awarding points or tokens for the performance of these behaviors. The tokens are exchanged for tangible reinforcers such as food, drink, entertainment, personal attention, or activities. This approach was one of the earliest behavioral interventions to be applied to the natural setting when Ayllon and Azrin (1968) devised a "token economy" for an entire long-stay ward of a state hospital. While it is difficult to apply this approach in its original form in a family setting, we have found it especially useful when adapted to more discrete issues within the family system. As Lamb and Goertzel (1971) have pointed out, the risk of the institutional understimulation, with resultant secondary handicaps, is as great in the family home as in the much maligned long-stay hospital wards. For maximum success, all household members need to be involved in the problem in order to provide consistent allocation of reinforcers. More than one family member can be the target of this intervention at any one time. One family adopted this approach while all four members were on weight-reduction programs.

Example: A 25-year-old man who had a chronic schizophrenic illness made constant demands on his parents for attention and food. His behavior was often inappropriate and the parents could do very little to please him. A list of behaviors the parents desired was drawn up together with a list of reinforcing food and activities chosen by the son. Points were accorded to each desired behavior observed by the parents, which could then be exchanged for any of the reinforcers listed. In a matter of days, the parents were praising their son for his pleasant behavior, and he was delighted to be receiving an abundant supply of food and cigarettes without having his "parents on his case all the time."

Social-Skills Training

We have discussed the skill-training module for enhancing the communication skills of family members. One specific application of this model is in assisting family members in their interpersonal skills in social settings outside the family. The same basic model of repeated behavior rehearsal with constructive feedback, modeling, and reinforcement of alternative performance is employed. Family members are taught to function as trainers who can apply the skill-training modality in real-life situations. This approach has been successfully employed in a group setting (Falloon *et al.*, 1981) and has proved a valuable asset for families where individuals with a limited repertory of social skills for handling friendships, work, dating, and so on can be taught improved social behavior over an extended period.

Time Out and Setting Limits

Both these procedures have been discussed in detail earlier (pp. 172–173). However, they are of particular value in dealing with the more impaired schizophrenic patients and will be briefly mentioned again.

Time out is a procedure taught to most families to enable members to excuse themselves from stressful situations politely when they feel under pressure. This enables patients and family members to escape from an overstimulating setting that might lead to an exacerbation of florid symptoms.

A firm statement of the acceptable limits of a family member's behavior often plays a crucial role in curbing disturbed or potentially destructive behavior. One boy kept telling his sister that she had never had a mental illness and would be cleansed by attending a faith-healing cult session with him. The parents firmly instructed the boy to stop this harassment of his sister, saying that they understood his concern that she be restored to her former state as soon as possible, but that taking her to a highly dramatic faith-healing session was potentially harmful and totally unacceptable to them.

Homework Problems

The performance of specified tasks between therapy sessions in a crucial component of behavioral interventions (see Figure 12-1). The real-life performance of behavior change is the goal of this approach. Thus, failure to complete the homework tasks is an important issue in determining the effectiveness of the intervention.

There are two aspects of the unsuccessful homework problem: First, there is failure to complete the homework goal successfully despite adequate effort. Second, there is the problem of a lack of reasonable effort to attempt the specified task. The evaluation of both situations differs substantially.

Homework Unsuccessful: Adequate Effort

The specific tasks assigned to a family for homework are those relevant to the problem solving during the session, usually the identical issues that have been discussed and rehearsed during the family session. Before moving to a different issue, the therapist must be assured that the family can indeed perform the tasks specified in the previous session. These may involve communication skills or problem-resolution plans. At the beginning of the next session, the family is invited to discuss their successful efforts to resolve the issue.

All efforts are warmly praised provided they are perceived as being task-relevant. Frequently the "ideal solution" is not totally effective. Family members are inclined to write off such attempts as futile failures. Negative cognitions are reassessed by the therapist, who endeavors to relabel these failure experiences as "partial" successes. A detailed behavioral analysis of the planned steps that were undertaken by family members is conducted with the family, and deficits in the strategies as employed are discussed. Major hitches may require further problem solving or behavior rehearsal. Minor hitches may be resolved through specific discussions. A frequent cause of lack of success is that the goal is somewhat unrealistic.

One family planned to increase the daughter's participation in household chores so that she would cook the family meal every night. When she cooked three meals the first week, they complained about her lack of cooperation on the other four nights. She felt discouraged and stubbornly refused to continue as formerly agreed. The family was redirected toward reinforcing her performance on the nights she cooked for them and eventually she agreed to alternate cooking with her mother. A structured program of rewards that were contingent upon her cooking was also instituted to reinforce her efforts.

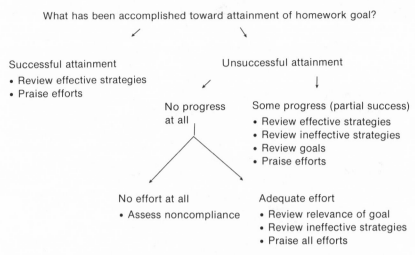

FIGURE 12-1. *Evaluating homework performance.*

Homework Unsuccessful: Inadequate Effort

"Well, we had so many things on our minds, problems and the like, we just couldn't spare the minute or two for our homework." This excuse is a frequent one that illustrates the paradox of many families: "We are too involved with our problems with one another to communicate."

Of course there are weeks when family life is so hectic that very little time can be found to organize a family meeting. However, people always manage to find time for the activities they find rewarding—meals, TV shows, collecting paychecks, going to a movie. Thus, reluctance to make adequate attempts to complete an agreed-upon homework task should be treated with the same firmness as a reluctance to ingest important medication.

Repeated failures to attempt homework leads to therapist frustration and becomes a therapy problem. The therapist is expected to take a lead in problem solving this issue. This usually involves a detailed behavioral analysis that goes beyond the acceptance of the usual excuses and examines the family's responses to the task in detail. There are a variety of explanations for failure to complete homework tasks, as any school-teacher knows. We will discuss a few of the common roadblocks and some of the strategies used to overcome them.

Task Too Difficult. In this situation, family members feel overwhelmed by the homework task and want the therapist to help them with it. During therapy sessions, they may feel more confident of their abilities, but once the therapist leaves, they quickly regress to a helpless state. In such instances, it is crucial to induce the family to take small steps initially and then gradually shape successive changes through repeated rehearsal in the sessions, setting tasks the family members appear to have mastered in the sessions, and praising each small increment of behavior change reported outside the sessions. Such a family is highly sensitive to criticism, and confrontation or coercion should be avoided.

Too Busy. The disorganized family that appears to lurch from crisis to crisis is a particularly difficult therapy problem. Their perception that they constantly have more important issues to deal with is often accurate. However, decision making and planning are usually ineffective and result in inadequate problem solving with repeated failures that escalate rather than resolve tensions. Therapeutic strategies must address the lack of structured planning in such families. A major focus for such coordinated family efforts is the family discussion meeting. A brief 5- to 10-minute meeting at least once a week, preferably daily, can lead to substantial changes in such a family. Setting up this meeting time is likely to prove exceedingly difficult as resistances to communication, hidden agendas, and power struggles between family members are confronted. It is important to stress the importance of the meeting *per se* and not to overvalue the significance of the homework task for which the meeting is to be convened. The latter may appear too trivial to warrant the changes necessary to achieve the family summit.

In order to enhance the reinforcing potential of the meeting, several families have found it useful to schedule the meeting at a mealtime or to provide food that is enjoyed by all family members (e.g., a cake) as a reinforcer. A chairman is elected for each meeting to prompt each family member to attend, introduce the "agenda" and take the "minutes." This business-like approach is preferred by many families to the psychotherapeutic group therapy model.

A further difficulty encountered is the one family member who refuses to cooperate. Families often choose not to meet unless everyone is present and give up after several attempts to persuade or coerce the "black sheep" to attend. Another business meeting paradigm—the quorum—is usefully employed here. This is usually two members in the smaller family groups with which we have worked, but the number is worked out by each family. Other strategies to deal with the reluctant participant have included choosing household chores at this meeting, thereby leaving the nonattender with the least desirable jobs.

Something Important Always Comes Up. Families that appear earnest in their desire to participate fully in behavioral family therapy but frequently complain that they are distracted by unexpected events may respond to a strategy described by Birchler and Spinks (1980) as the "antisabotage procedure." This involves a covert rehearsal of all the potential "roadblocks" that might prevent completion of the homework task. Each block is systematically removed through careful problem solving. Families may find it useful to role-play anticipated problems and to rehearse antisabotage strategies in the therapy sessions. At times, families may complete their homework tasks during the course of a session; the therapist is able in this case to observe their behavior without interruption. At other times, families may decide to complete their homework immediately after the therapist leaves. This avoids the sometimes difficult scheduling problems of families with members who have shift-work jobs and enables a clear link between family therapy and natural family interactions.

We Do It Our Way. A final note concerns the families that find the behavioral model difficult to accept into their mode of functioning. They may resist the highly specific and egalitarian structured approach with notions that sex roles and generation differences are of paramount value in their family system. In families acculturated in strong matriarchal or patriarchal models, such conflicts may be more common. We have attempted to adapt to the family rules in these instances by forming a clear alliance with the culturally dominant parent, with whom the therapist consults. The therapist and the parent negotiate the homework task and his or her role as the chairman is clearly designated. Attempts at changing a hierarchical system to the more democratic model favored by systems-theory proponents have not been effective. The structure of the family in these instances is supported as an important asset. This has enabled us to work successfully with families of black, Hispanic, and oriental backgrounds.

SYMPTOM-MANAGEMENT STRATEGIES

In contrast to several recent developments in the family treatment of schizophrenia, the primary focus of family therapy is clearly the family system. On the other hand, we do not agree with the philosophical position that treating the patient's illness is potentially damaging because schizophrenia *is* disordered family communication, not a medical illness. Our approach is pragmatic: We attempt to maximize the health and social functioning of every member of the family through stress reduction and enhanced coping skills. At times this necessitates reducing the stress caused by symptoms of schizophrenia or problems associated with treatment such as side effects of medication, and noncompliance. The person exhibiting symptoms (usually the index patient) is often the focus of these efforts, although problem-solving strategies may be indirect and primarily involve the responses of other family members or direct involvement of the patient (e.g., increased medication). This section outlines some of the problems commonly seen in families with persons who suffer from schizophrenia and the specific strategies we have employed within the behavioral family therapy framework.

Medication Compliance

The cornerstone of the community management of schizophrenia is the continued ingestion of low doses of neuroleptic medication. Until recently it was believed that poor compliance with medication was the only reason patients suffered relapses of the acute illness, and that providing medication in long-acting injectable form was thought to provide a simple, cost-effective answer to this dilemma. However, despite the advent of the depot neuroleptics, which many unwilling customers rejected as painful, intrusive, and with bothersome side effects, a substantial proportion of relapses persisted (Falloon *et al.*, 1978; Hogarty *et al.*, 1979).

Tablets have the advantage of providing the patient and psychiatrist with the potential to vary the dosage in order to increase therapeutic potency or reduce unpleasant side effects as indicated. In addition, they appear to have less severe side effects when applied in low dosages. For these reasons, we have advocated the use of tablets whenever possible. To sustain high levels of medication compliance and thereby maximize therapeutic potency, minimize risk of side effects associated with irregular ingestion, and aid in establishing optimal doses at the lowest possible levels, we have taken great care to establish regular tablet-taking behavior. The specifics of this strategy include the following, as outlined in Table 12-1.

Educate the Patient and the Family

The patient is provided detailed information concerning the nature of the illness; the expected benefits from medication; the nature of the medication and its mode of action; and the potential risks associated with the medication. The goal is to establish the patient and his or her family as informed consumers with a sufficient knowledge base to participate actively in monitoring the effects of the medication themselves. These goals are analogous to those employed in teaching diabetics about insulin. The educational approach is described in detail in Chapter 8.

Train Coping Strategies

Part of the education process details several effective coping strategies to minimize the unwanted effects of the medication. These strategies include:

TABLE 12-1. *Strategies for Maintaining Medication Compliance*

1. Educate the patient and his or her family about medication and its benefits and risks.
2. Train patients in strategies to cope with unwanted side effects.
3. Ensure prescribing physician's empathic responses to reported side effects.
4. Develop prompting strategies.
5. Operant procedures: shaping, incentives.
6. Cognitive restructuring.
7. Monitoring plasma levels of neuroleptics and providing therapist, patient, and family feedback.

(1) waiting until side effects diminish; (2) reducing dosage on physician's advice; (3) changing to different drug with different, hopefully less troublesome, side effects; and (4) taking an additional drug to counter side effects.

These strategies require clear communication between doctor and patient. The patient may benefit from rehearsing his or her approach to the physician. For some physicians, a very assertive approach might be required to impress upon him or her that the patient believes the drug is producing an extremely bothersome effect. It is important to remind the patient that the prescribing physician is the expert on the effects of the drug and that if the physician seems certain that a given symptom is not likely to be associated with the drug, the physician is probably right. Nevertheless, whatever the cause of the bothersome effect, the doctor should be expected to provide effective treatment of the disturbance and an acceptable explanation.

Some of the side effects that have been identified as leading to poor compliance, such as akinesia and akathisia, are quite subtle and difficult to differentiate from the symptoms of schizophrenia, or secondary affective disorder (Van Putten, 1978). For this reason, the patient may be encouraged to give the physician a detailed description of the symptoms.

Further specific coping strategies are described in Chapter 2 and may be effective in assisting patients to minimize the unpleasantness of the drugs when it persists, despite the best efforts of the physician.

Ensure Physician Empathy

A careful, concerned approach to side effects of long-term drug therapy is a critical element in effective management. Neuroleptics have an extraordinary range of effects involving every organ system of the body. In Europe, chlorpromazine, the most widely used of the early phenothiazines, was called "Largactil" by the drug company marketing it because it had a "large (range of) actions." It was originally developed to lower body temperature for hypothermia in early open-heart surgery procedures.

If the patient says he or she believes the drug is causing an effect, the physician should take care to listen attentively. If the physician neglects to do this, the patient is likely to lose confidence and take control of his or her own treatment—usually by deciding to reduce or stop the medication. The use of checklists of common side effects at each medication visit, as well as examination for neuromuscular effects (e.g., extrapyramidal or dyskinesias), assists in demonstrating concern for the patient's well-being while at the same time helping to educate the patient about the type of effects most likely to be associated with the drug.

Develop Prompting Strategies

Not all poor compliance results from resistance to the medication. Perhaps the most common reason people do not continue to take their tablets regularly is the age-old problem of forgetfulness. This problem is magnified with schizophrenia, when conceptual disorganization is present. One woman patient frequently forgot whether she had taken her tablets, and at other times a hallucinatory voice would tell her not to take the tablet. She developed a system whereby she placed a tablet next to her toothbrush every morning and took the tablet when she brushed her teeth before retiring every night. She never missed brushing her teeth and quite soon she took her tablets regularly. Her mother was able to check in a nonintrusive fashion whether her daughter had put the tablet out, and then whether she had taken it. When necessary, she prompted her daughter supportively.

Other patients have used plastic containers that hold the daily dosage of medication for an entire week. This provides a simple monitoring device that can be put in a purse or pocket for people who need to take medication at work or away from home.

Reduction of irritating nagging by the parents is an extremely important feature of these prompting procedures.

Operant Procedures: Shaping and Incentives

On occasions, despite attempts at prompting, educating the patient and family, and minimizing undesirable side effects, poor compliance persists. A specific incentive program may be developed that rewards tablet taking in a systematic fashion. Parents of young children often employ this strategy when they give their child a piece of candy after the child takes the medicine. Drug manufacturers have now developed pleasant-tasting medicines for children that have inherent reinforcing properties.

One patient improved his compliance when he received a chocolate bar or ice cream treat immediately after he had taken his tablets. This reinforcement was coupled with praise for his tablet taking, and when the primary reinforcer (food) was withdrawn, the secondary social reinforcement (praise) was sufficient to maintain excellent compliance. Tablet taking became a positive emotional experience for the patient and his family, instead of an unpleasant event.

In other cases, the mere use of praise contingent upon tablet taking was effective in shaping improved compliance. Focus on failure to take tablets with coercion and nagging was seldom effective in inducing sustained increases of compliance.

Cognitive Restructuring

The patient, family, and therapist may all enhance tablet-taking behavior through repeatedly reviewing the rationale for continued drug therapy. This is outlined in the earlier educational sessions with the patient and family, but needs to be firmly instilled in the minds of all concerned. In addition to the therapist frequently reiterating the reasons for long-term medication, the family may go over these principles with the patient. Patients may also review this rationale themselves each time they take their tablets. In one case, we instructed a patient who smoked to make a card that fit into his cigarette pack and to write on it three reasons for taking regular medication. He wrote: "I take regular medication because (1) it makes me calm; (2) it stops me from hearing voices; (3) it helps me to sleep." He was instructed to read this card to himself three times before lighting a cigarette.

A simple rationale for long-term medication that was frequently employed involved the "insurance policy" analogy. Patients are instructed to think of the regular taking of neuroleptics as an insurance policy against the risk of relapse and rehospitalization. A small, regular "investment" will provide a cushion in the advent of an accident or disaster: without it, the worst accident is bound to occur and overwhelm all coping resources.

Plasma Level Feedback

We have been measuring the plasma levels of neuroleptics throughout our program. To our surprise, very few patients have complained about the monthly venipuncture procedures. Two patients have requested that their blood tests be discontinued after 1 year and reported that their fear of venipuncture had made them reluctant to attend their medication appointments. The provision of feedback about the levels of medication in their bodies has provided patients and their families with a greater awareness of the treatment rationale. Surprisingly, very few tests have shown the absence of medication. Therapists' and families' concerns that the patients were not taking their medication have usually proved groundless, and a greater sense of mutual trust has developed. Where suspicions of poor compliance have been supported by evidence of low or absent plasma levels, the therapist has been able to deal with this issue with greater confidence than in the case where evidence of poor compliance is circumstantial. Also, the prescribing physicians have been able to titrate doses to very low levels where evidence of adequate plasma levels has minimized the risk of excessive reduction. Patients are supported by this increased therapeutic confidence and improved compliance may result. A routine assay of neuroleptics is not yet available, but hopefully is not too far away. It will undoubtedly add a major dimension to the community management of schizophrenia.

Coping with Persistent Symptoms of Schizophrenia

With good drug and supportive therapy, 75-80% of persons suffering from an acute episode of schizophrenia can achieve an almost total remission of their florid symptoms such as thinking disturbances, delusions, and hallucinations. This estimate is probably a little high because it is based on clinical reviews rather than detailed research assessment of mental status. However, this means that one in four or five patients may suffer from persistent symptomatology. Although hope that a complete remission may yet occur must not be abandoned, the symptoms will necessitate coping responses if the patient is going to be able to restore a modicum of his or her premorbid social functioning. The two most common persisting symptoms are delusions and auditory hallucinations. We teach patients and their families some strategies to improve their skills at coping with these symptoms.

Auditory Hallucinations

The methods employed by patients to cope with persistent voices have been studied in detail (Falloon & Talbot, 1981). They include a wide range of cognitive and behavioral strategies. Three coping strategies were chosen by the majority of patients: relaxation or going to sleep, reduced attention to the voices, and seeking people to talk to, or with whom they can spend time. Engaging in leisure activities, and increasing physical and mental activity including work, when possible, appeared to help divert attention from the voices. Thus, socioenvironmental manipulations appeared to prove effective in coping with persistent hallucinations. Many chronic patients will have learned their own self-control methods, but patients with recent onset may benefit from the collective experiences of fellow sufferers and be instructed to test out a variety strategies to find which one, or what combination, is most effective, and at the same time is socially appropriate.

Strategies that did not appear very effective in controlling the voices were attempts to reason and debate with the them, and attempts to suppress them by telling them to be quiet or to stop. Many patients resorted to such strategies when in despair but agreed that they were not helpful. Patients who were prepared to accept the fact that, despite the best medical treatment and social support, the voices were likely to persist, appeared to mobilize their coping strategies more effectively than those who constantly battled the symptoms and refused to accept that there was no immediate treatment that could rid them of the hallucinatory experiences.

Some patients enjoy their voices and are reluctant to lose them, particularly when they are pleasant and reinforcing. In these cases, an aversive conditioning paradigm has proved a useful strategy. Patients are given a thin rubber band to wear on their wrist. Each time a voice is heard the patient snaps the band against his or her wrist. The sharp pain of the band serves to counter the reinforcing properties of the pleasant voices.

Because every patient is different, a detailed behavioral analysis of the contingencies surrounding the persistent phenomenon is of vital importance in the development of the specific coping strategies to be employed by each patient. Family members can be most helpful when they readily avail themselves as persons with whom the index patient can chat about everyday affairs in order to distract himself or herself from the voices. In addition they can reinforce constructive work and leisure activities. A heightened awareness of signs that the patient is hearing voices may help a family member to prompt effective coping. In some patients, increased motor activity (e.g., pacing), increased social withdrawal or sleeping, or attempts to interact more may signal the presence of hallucinations. If patients and families are clearly aware of the usual outward manifestations of their hallucinations, they can work toward developing a mutually supportive coping plan.

Delusions

Persistent delusions are a more difficult problem with which patients and their families must cope. The process of delusional thinking appears to involve a constriction of cognitive awareness so that alternative explanations for an observable event are not seriously considered. Family members are encouraged to avoid debate about the truth or falsity of the patient's beliefs, but to acknowledge calmly the patient's own convictions and distress about same and simply state their differing interpretations.

An example of this was a young woman who believed the Hollywood film industry owed her $6 million for scripts they had taken from her mind. Her mother listened to her patiently and laughed, saying: "Jenny, I do hope you'll think of your old momma when you get all that money. I could sure use a million! I'm glad you've got your dreams, but praise the Lord you be so lucky to get paid for your thoughts!"

Where patients have become more concerned about delusions and have begun acting on them, family members have been told to use their problem-solving skills to get the patients to examine other possible explanations for their experience of the world.

Example:

MRS. MASTERS: Bill, you think that there are people out there who want to kill you, right?

BILL: Yeah, they are after me alright.

MRS. MASTERS: What makes you think that, Bill?

BILL: Well, I went to the store to get Mary some cigarettes this morning and I heard this woman say "He's going to die."

MRS. MASTERS: You thought she was talking about you, did you?

BILL: Yeah, she was talking about me.

MRS. MASTERS: Do you think she could've been talking about somebody else?

BILL: No. It was definitely me.

MRS. MASTERS: What else was she saying? Did you hear?

BILL: No. I wasn't listening.

MRS. MASTERS: You weren't listening, you say. So perhaps you didn't hear her real clear.

BILL: It was clear enough. I'm pretty sure of what she said. She said her husband was in the hospital.

MRS. MASTERS: Was she talking about him then?

BILL: She could've been.

MRS. MASTERS: If he was in the hospital, he might have been going to die.

BILL: No. Look, Mom, I've told you she was talking about me when she said that. I don't want to talk about it anymore, OK?

MRS. MASTERS: OK. I was just worried you might have been a bit confused and didn't hear real clear.

At other times, family members may choose to ignore patient's comments that appear absurd and to distract the patient by introducing another topic of conversation. They are discouraged from colluding with the patient's irrational thinking and from attempting to understand the meaning of the delusion.

Anxiety Management

Little attention has been devoted to one of the major problems in the community care of schizophrenia—reducing high levels of anxiety. Although anxiety has been described as being commonly associated with schizophrenia, and theories developed that consider an inability to cope effectively with overwhelming anxiety a crucial component of the pathogenesis (Mednick, 1959; Kretschmer, 1927), there is little mention of effective anxiety management in the existing psychiatric literature on the treatment of schizophrenia. Indeed psychophysiological research has suggested that persons with schizophrenia tend to habituate more slowly than others to a variety of stimuli, a characteristic that might cause an attenuation of conditioning processes, thereby interfering with the usual deconditioning to anxiety-provoking stimuli through repeated exposure (i.e., getting used to new situations). Recent biochemical findings that suggest dysfunction of opiate receptors in the brain may further support this lack of habituation through the usual reward–punishment learning paradigm. We and other clinically oriented researchers (Mendel, 1976) have observed that anxiety management differs somewhat in schizophrenia from the neurotic conditions, although the phenomena are qualitatively similar.

How then do we manage anxiety symptoms in persons with schizophrenia? Essentially we have employed methods similar to those used in the treatment of anxiety in other persons. This involves the graduated exposure of the patient to the feared object or situation. This may be accompanied by concomitant deep muscle relaxation, as in systematic desensitization (Wolpe, 1969), or with therapist-supported real-life exposure as in the *in vivo* exposure approach of Isaac Marks (1978). The one crucial difference is that with schizophrenia sufferers, even when in remission, the duration of exposure and the overall time span of the treatment program is attenuated considerably. The short-term intensive anxiety-management programs commonly used for phobic persons are probably relatively ineffective, but an approach that continues over months or even years may finally prove effective.

A further difference is that the person with schizophrenia may develop irrational fears associated with delusions or hallucinations. One young black man was fearful of leaving his house because he believed people were following him. He stayed in his room with the shades drawn while his family were at work during the day. He lived in a dangerous neighborhood and had been knocked down by police while walking with a friend in the street. His fear of leaving the house persisted after his persecutory delusions were no longer evident. He then presented features more characteristic of agoraphobia.

Treatment in this case involved an *in vivo* desensitization paradigm whereby the patient and his mother and sister constructed a hierarchy of feared situations and accompanied the patient to these places and stayed with him until he felt calm. This often took an hour or more, during which time the family members had some difficulty helping him to relax. On one occasion, they visited the bank and waited in a long line. Larry became agitated when the man behind him in the line kept complaining and cursing about the wait. He thought the comments were directed toward him and rushed out of the bank. His mother followed and explained that she believed the man was upset about the long wait. She persuaded him to return to the line, where the same man offered them their place again. The mother struck up a conversation with the man and Larry relaxed.

Understimulating settings, such as waiting in lines or sitting in sparse clinic waiting rooms, tend to increase the delusional thinking or hallucinatory interference of persons with schizophrenia as well as the unwanted ruminations of anxiety. Efforts to provide distracting stimuli, to foster a relaxed atmosphere, and to avoid long waits may enhance clinic attendance of anxious and paranoid patients.

The utilization of family members in the *in vivo* management of anxiety has been pioneered by Andrew Mathews in Oxford, and this approach is readily adapted to the family management structure we have employed (Mathews, Gelder, & Johnston, 1981). It is necessary to emphasize the need for the patient to remain in the feared situation until he or she feels calm, and to mention that this may take at least an hour.

Another approach to anxiety management employs a cognitive paradigm. This has been termed the "safety net" technique. The anxious person is invited to imagine carrying out a feared sequence. At each anticipated anxiety-arousing step the person is invited to stop and consider the worst possible scenario. Then, he or she is asked to problem-solve that worst consequence and define a plan for coping with it effectively, all before moving on to the next anticipated disaster. This rehearsal of coping with catastrophe often assists in overcoming excessive anticipatory anxiety: "If the worst I can imagine happens, I have a plan to cope with it." Patients may write down the plan on a card to carry as a portable safety net for "emergencies." This approach has also been used for paranoid patients to enable them to cope with their irrational fears.

The "Amotivational Syndrome"

"He's just bone lazy. He lies about all day on the living room sofa. He should get out and get a job or go to school, or, hell, anything, just do anything but lie around!" This woman was describing the exasperation she felt at the apathetic, listless behavior of her son, who prior to becoming ill had been a hard-working clerk who led an active social life and played a guitar in a rock and roll band. The discrepancy in his present performance level was striking and engendered a strongly critical response. Initially, Robert and his mother attributed his anergia to the 200 mg of chlorpromazine he had been given, but when this state persisted after the dosage had been reduced to 50 mg daily and other less sedating neuroleptics had made no change, they concluded that he was lazy.

This state has been given a variety of names in recent years—amotivational syndrome, akinesia, negative symptoms. None are particularly apposite. Patients are often surprisingly eager to get out and about, to get jobs, and to become more socially active. But, despite good intentions, they just cannot seem to get themselves started. At times they may appear to suffer from motor retardation and the parkinsonian side effects of neuroleptics, but a similar problem is seen on low doses of medication. At other times, the picture may mimic depression, and undoubtedly the lack of constructive activity and the contingent positive reinforcement from self and others may result in a depressed mood state. Nonresponse to antidepressant drugs is common. A closer analysis of this state often reveals a combination of all these factors, along with a thinking disturbance that appears to impair the decision-making process, so that the person cannot readily decide to get up and take a particular course of action.

What treatment can be offered for this poorly understood problem? The answer to this question is not clear. Obvious suggestions include lowering the dosage of medication to the minimally sufficient level, helping the person to establish specific daily goals and plans so that his or her decision making is minimized, and providing a stimulating home environment. Drug interventions may include the addition of an anti-parkinsonian or antidepressant if parkinsonian or depressive features can be isolated. Apart from these management strategies, the use of operant reinforcement behavioral strategies such as shaping constructive activity, or the development of a token economy program has been used effectively to enhance the motivational contingencies in the family environment (see p. 288).

Depression Management

Symptoms of depression are common during the course of schizophrenia. Although episodes of severe depression are not often observed, feelings of unhappiness, hopelessness, guilt, and worthlessness, accompanied by sleep and appetite disturbance with slowing of motor and cognitive processes, are seen at times in the vast majority of persons who suffer an episode of schizophrenia. Clearly there is an overlap with the "amotivational syndrome" and the parkinsonian flattening of expression associated with neuroleptic drug therapy.

These depressive symptoms have been observed most frequently in the period of social readjustment after recovery from an acute episode of schizophrenia. It is assumed that depression is an understandable response to feelings of despair about the future, loss of social effectiveness, and the stigmatization of mental illness (McGlashan & Carpenter, 1976). However, depression is present during the acute episode in a majority of patients and it can be argued that its appearance in the postpsychotic phase is due to the "unmasking" of depressive symptoms when the psychotic symptoms become less prominent (Hirsch, 1982).

However, regardless of whether the depressive symptoms are considered primarily existential or biological in origin, the treatment of these features is very important. There is a relatively high risk of suicide in these cases. Rather than adopt any general theoretical posture about the origins of the disturbance, we advocate a behavioral analysis of each case to determine the specific strategies that may be employed in the treatment of the symptoms. Drug therapy with antidepressants is not generally helpful in such cases, and runs the risk of precipitating a relapse of schizophrenia through excessive stimulation. However, a reduction in the dosage of the neuroleptic medication or the addition of an antiparkinsonian drug may be of some value (Johnson, 1981). Pharmacological intervention is always accompanied by psychosocial techniques that attempt to counteract the depressive thoughts and behaviors. (Beck, Rush, Shaw, & Emery, 1979; Falloon, 1975; Lewinsohn, Biglan, & Zeiss, 1975). These strategies include:

- Informing the patient that feelings of depression are a *usual* feature in the recovery from schizophrenia; they are time-limited, and often indicative of a good outcome from a severe illness.
- Restructuring thoughts comparing past achievements with present deficits to a focus on *achievements since the onset of the illness.*
- Focusing on taking small steps toward *realistic short-term goals*, with less attention to long-term goals.
- Increasing positive reinforcement from the environment through *engaging in pleasant everyday events* and interaction, with encouragement, praise, and attention for these efforts from family members and friends. At the same time *minimizing aversive events* and interaction—for example, criticism from family members, experiences of failure, major life changes.
- Increasing reinforcement through strategies that *prompt positive thoughts about oneself,* such as repeatedly reading cue cards that describe positive attributes about oneself.

Bleuler (1911) observed that "the most serious of all schizophrenic symptoms is the suicidal drive. . . . People are being forced to continue to live a life that has become unbearable for them for valid reasons" (p. 488). The risk of suicide needs to be carefully evaluated and measures undertaken to minimize this risk. At times this may include hospital admission for skilled nursing care and medication adjustments. Families need to be involved in the supervision of oral medication particularly if more than 1–2 weeks' supply is dispensed. Dispensing physicians should assess the risks and benefits of *all* medications prescribed, and ascertain from the family what additional medications are accessible in the home. When ideation about weapons such as guns and knives is present the therapist must take an active stance and enlist the family's cooperation to ensure that dangerous weapons are adequately secured.

With expert tailoring of the interventions to each patient the management of depressive episodes in the course of schizophrenia is usually effective and recovery is complete.

Sexual Problems

Although data are lacking it would appear that sexual difficulties are common in persons who have suffered an episode of schizophrenia. Some of these problems are associated with the neuroleptic drug therapy, which appears to diminish sexual dirve and responsiveness in males and females and to contribute to impotence and failure to ejaculate in men. These problems, often considered beneficial in the hospital setting, where sexual behavior tends to be suppressed, are a major handicap in community functioning. Such difficulties tend to persist and contribute to marital discord in married patients, and tension or avoidance of intimate sexual relationships in single persons. For these reasons reports of sexual difficulty necessitate immediate attention.

The evaluation of sexual inadequacy includes a full sexual history and often a physical examination. One male patient reported concern about the shape of his penis and was assumed to be suffering from Peyronie's disease—a condition that produces bending of the penis and painful erections. After several appointments to a genitourinary clinic and discussion of probable plastic surgery operations his penis was examined and found to be quite normal. His initial concern had centered on worries that his particular method of masturbation *might* affect the shape of his penis.

The treatment of sexual difficulties in schizophrenia is similar to sexual therapy in other people. As with other problems, a behavioral analysis that pinpoints the problem and evaluates the environmental and interpersonal contingencies specific to the problem is the basis for intervention. Neuroleptic drugs are one specific factor that may contribute to sexual problems in some cases. If a particular drug is thought to be a possible cause of the difficulty, lowering the dose or changing to a drug considered less likely to cause the dysfunction may be considered.

A difficulty encountered in family therapy is whether such issues should be discussed in the family session. This decision is the prerogative of the patient. In most cases individual consultation for evaluation is more appropriate and can be conducted on clinic visits to obtain medication from the psychiatrist. Issues related to sexual functioning—sexual activity, pregnancy, venereal disease—should be kept in confidence from the family unless the patient expresses a desire to obtain assistance from family problem solving of the issue.

COMMUNITY SUPPORT FOR THE FAMILY

The focus of the previous part of this chapter was on the family member who was recovering from schizophrenia and its complications. In this part, we will be discussing some of the specific strategies employed to enhance the functioning of other family members and the family as a whole. Again, it is important to recognize that throughout the program, the interventions are all directed toward maximizing the social functioning of all family members in the most efficient manner. Continuous assessment of the behavioral performance of all family members is conducted with careful analysis of the overall impact of each specific intervention strategy on the interrelationships of all family members. Problems are initially identified by the family, and the therapist then takes care to deal with problems such as scapegoating or triangulation by directing communication or problem-solving exercises to deal specifically with these issues. When the family seems reluctant to resolve problems of this nature, the therapist is encouraged to express his or her own feelings in an assertive manner, clearly identifying the issue as the *therapist's* own problem (e.g., "I am bothered by the way you all seem to pick on George. I would like to do some problem solving on this"). The therapist then leads this problem-solving rehearsal. Behavioral family therapy is an approach that employs a systems-theory orientation, which uses strategies that are highly specific and are for the most part, but not exclusively, based on learning-theory principles.

Several areas of concern have involved enhancing the community involvement and support of the family. These include issues such as the single-parent household, effective use of social network support, and establishing the independent roles of parents and children as functioning individuals in the community.

The Single Parent

The breakdown of the traditional nuclear family unit through death or divorce has been a major concern of family therapists who have developed many theoretical constructs on the notion of a family group having a mother–father–son–daughter constellation. Almost half the families we have worked with have had only one parent in the household, and in a large proportion of those, only one child (the person with schizophrenia) has been living in the home. Because the behavioral model is pragmatic and essentially atheoretical, we have merely taken into account the specific advantages and disadvantages of the family group, independent of issues of size and composition. However, while this feature has not been a major concern that might necessitate major therapy revisions, it has led to some specific problems that appear common to this subgroup of families.

The first problem concerns the lack of support for the parent in coping with household difficulties. Even where other siblings are living in the home, the single mother or father often shoulders all the responsibility for the household; from payment of bills to provision of food, household chores, and support and care for all the offspring. This self-sacrificing behavior is a major component of the emotional overinvolvement factor of expressed emotion (Vaughn & Leff, 1976) and as such is considered a potential source of family tension.

Example: Mrs. Roberts was a 52-year-old woman who lived in a three-bedroom rented house with her two sons (19 and 23 years), a divorced daughter (26 years), and the daughter's two children (8 and 10 years). She slept on a living room sofa, bought the food, cooked for the household, and paid all the bills from her two janitorial jobs (14 hours a day). She suffered from gastritis and severe tension headaches, but did not obtain treatment because she had to save all her money to pay the bills.

Her youngest son had developed schizophrenia at the age of 15, but despite considerable behavior disturbance, she had supported him for nearly 5 years before she sought medical assistance. She had no time for social or leisure activities and had lost contact with her family and friends.

The strategy in this and other similar cases was to establish a more equitable sharing of family responsibilities and resources. Family members were instructed to attend the family therapy sessions, which were carefully scheduled to make this feasible, as well as family meetings that were organized by the family themselves. During these sessions, the mother was encouraged to communicate her angry and depressed feelings about the perceived lack of concern and commitment from her children, and they in turn described their frustration and guilt that she seemed to actively discourage their taking more responsibility and helping her out. After problem-solving the issue of household finances, the family agreed that the mother would give up her second job and that each person living in the home would contribute a similar amount to the household budget each month. Immediate funds were found for the mother to attend her doctor. In later sessions, problem solving concerned sharing household chores, resocialization activities for the mother, and planning a trip to visit her family in the South. The mother found that the son who had schizophrenia was a great source of emotional support. He prompted others to play their roles as contracted and introduced her to a friend's mother, with whom she shared several common interests and soon became a close friend.

A further problem that this woman and many other single parents have involves dealing with behavioral disturbance in more than one family member. This is most prominent when the son or daughter with schizophrenia is the only other supportive person in the household, and is either persistently ill or shows signs of an exacerbation with impaired communication and judgment. In these instances, family problem solving between parent and child becomes very difficult, as does the ability to enforce any appropriate limits. A third party is a great asset at this time. A friend or relative living outside the household may be drawn into the family system at such a point. The therapist may need to become more actively involved as a supporter of the parent in problem-solving efforts. The presence of the third party helps diffuse the intense emotions that may be present between parent and patient at that time.

Example: Mrs. Green lived with her daughter Sandy in a small apartment. Sandy heard voices persistently, but had been showing signs of increased social functioning recently. She went out with some old friends over the weekend and came home the next morning in a very disturbed, disoriented state. She denied taking any drugs but her mother felt otherwise and was sure her daughter had been in contact with PCP. She was furious but did not say anything to Sandy for fear that the resulting argument would make her daughter's schizophrenia worse. At a family therapy session later in the week, she discussed this episode with the therapist and was strongly supported in her expression of strong criticism of drug-taking behavior. A contract was made that any future episode of this nature would result in Sandy's not being permitted to return to live at home. Two brothers who lived nearby were persuaded to join the family sessions. One later admitted that he too heard voices and experienced delusions of external control, but had never sought treatment and had managed to cope with them. This revelation stunned the other family members, but served as a coping model for Sandy—unfortunately a model that did not involve taking medication!

In addition to maximizing the shared coping potential of the family, it is crucial to enhance the social network support to the single parent. Initially, the therapist may provide a vital supportive role, but the transition to community support is essential as contact with the therapist is gradually reduced. Confidants outside the immediate family are often difficult to develop. Where a divorce or death has occurred recently, a major readjustment for the parent is provoked. Without a close friend, parental coping capacity is readily exceeded by only moderate stressors. The patient with schizophrenia often becomes the parent's only source of support, and this presents a very precarious situation. Single parents are themselves vulnerable to depression and psychosomatic disorders and problem solving often focuses more on their problems than those of their sons or daughters.

Marital Discord

Two-parent families are not without their difficulties. Clearly, where both parents have effective communication of feelings and needs, and where joint problem solving is performed, tension within the household is minimized. However, this is frequently not the case. Major parental conflict that was considered of etiological significance in the earlier family therapy literature on schizophrenia can be as stressful as coping with single parenthood. Thus, specific strategies may be employed to enhance marital consensus.

Behavioral methods of marital therapy are very similar to those outlined for the nuclear family group. They are well described by Jacobson and Margolin (1979). The major difference is that more use is made of contingency contracting as the framework for communication and problem-solving training. This procedure is described earlier in this chapter and will not be further discussed at this point. However, one frequent question is how to focus on the marital relationship in *family* therapy. This may prove difficult where the major deficits of communication or problem solving have been between parents and children, especially when a child is severely handicapped by schizophrenia. The role-rehearsal methods allow the therapist to focus on the marital relationship from the start of family therapy in a variety of ways. These include:

1. Having the parents practice communication of positive and negative feelings toward one another through a round robin of rehearsals that involve each family member taking a turn expressing feelings to every other member. Where problems in parental communication are identified in these rehearsals, repeated practice with constructive feedback and reinforcement from the therapist and other family members is provided. Homework tasks may involve promoting generalization of improved expression of feelings outside the therapy sessions.

2. A similar enhancement of marital communication may occur from parental rehearsal of empathic listening behaviors.

3. The problem-solving approach is a further vehicle for attempted resolution of parental conflicts. Many sources of marital discord are played out in everyday family situations, and parents are seldom reluctant to practice their problem-solving techniques with target situations that they perceive as relatively innocuous. However, in pinpointing the source of the problem, brainstorming potential solutions, and deriving effective plans, more substantial relationship issues are uncovered in a structured, low-key setting. Adult and adolescent children, who frequently find themselves caught up in the ineffective bickering between the parents, find it easier to sit on the sidelines and make constructive suggestions while the parents struggle with their relationship difficulties. Problem solving within the sessions is frequently framed as "practice" for the "real" thing, which occurs outside the therapist-supervised sessions. This further reduces the emotional level of such exchanges, which, although structured, are indeed real communications between individuals who share a continuing relationship—unlike behavior rehearsal in nonfamily groups.

4. Contingency contracting may be introduced by the therapist in the planning phase of problem solving. No specific modifications are needed when the technique is used in this fashion. However, the level of intimacy of suggested rewards and requests for change may be impaired by the presence of other family members. Few parents appear comfortable discussing issues such as their sexual activities in a group with their children. However, that decision is one that is in the hands of the parents, who have sometimes been surprisingly open in family therapy sessions. When an unresolved intimate problem that parents have been unwilling to discuss in front of their children persists, marital therapy has been provided independently. The need for this has been minimal.

We have felt the need to respect parents' wishes not to disclose marital secrets in the course of family therapy. In some families, marital discord is clearly evident, but the parents have established a coping pattern that allows them to function competently in their other family roles. The therapist may wish to discuss this issue with the parents to clarify their mutual desire to change or maintain the *status quo*. Where parents express a desire to perpetuate their less-than-optimal patterns, we avoid any direct confrontation. However, the indirect effect of communication and problem-solving procedures may go some small way to enhancing the marital relationship. In one such case, the parents worked together on a major problem and announced in a family session that they had attained their goal: The father, to that point a covert alcoholic, had not had a drink for 3 months! The behavioral family therapy provides the family with the tools for change; we leave it up to them to carve out the changes they wish to make. These independent efforts receive the greatest applause from the therapist, much in the way the school teacher applauds a student for achieving a successful career through the application of principles taught in the classroom.

Social Network Support

A major source of support in the community is derived from contact with other people. Support is traditionally obtained from the extended family or tribal network, but with the increased mobility of city dwellers, non-kinship relationships with friends, neighbors, and co-workers have become important sources of support at times of crisis. The finding that families with persons who have schizophrenia have contact with fewer individuals in the community is probably similar to that of other families where a member has a chronic illness associated with social impairment. Ross Speck and his colleagues in Philadelphia have reported considerable improvement in the crisis management of isolated families through facilitation of social network support in large group sessions (Speck &

Attneave, 1973). Furthermore, it is apparent that enmeshed, overinvolved parents tend to attempt to cover up family stress and to shun support from people outside the nuclear family. This self-imposed quarantining of the family reduces their potential to cope with stress and may be a factor in the link between high overinvolvement in family members and exacerbation of schizophrenia.

Mrs. Roberts was the 52-year-old woman we described earlier who lived with two sons, a divorced daughter, and two grandchildren. She worked at two jobs and supported them all single-handedly and was an example of a person who minimized supportive contact with her social network. Although she came into contact with around 20 people on a frequent basis, she never disclosed her household problems to anyone. Instead, she put on a smiling face, joked with them, and listened to *their* complaints and provided *them* with support. She had no friends or confidants and became very dependent on the family therapist and other project staff.

A major problem addressed by the therapist was the mother's goal to develop a relaxed, confiding relationship with a person in the community. Initially, she was very reluctant to risk discussing her problems with another person. However, with persistent encouragement from the therapist and the family members, she did begin to discuss her difficulties with several people she felt she could trust. These included her work partner, her landlady, and the mother of her son's best friend. She rehearsed responding to the "How are you doing?" inquiry from her friends with alternatives to "just fine," until she felt comfortable replying that she was feeling "pretty bad" on those occasions when she was especially bothered by a crisis in the home.

The Multifamily Group

Another method of increasing social network support is through the multifamily group, a format that has several staunch advocates (see pp. 94–96). This approach has proved useful as an adjunct to intensive individual behavior therapy (Falloon *et al.*, 1981) and during the follow-up phase of home-based family therapy. The most valuable feature of the multifamily group appears to be in educating patients and families about schizophrenia and its management. This sharing of the experiences of the illness and its management by both patients and parents can have a striking impact on families that feel socially isolated from people with whom they can openly discuss their experiences without fear of ostracism. One woman who was severely handicapped by persistent hallucinations and delusions of control was so impressed by two recovered schizophrenic patients' reports of the benefits of medication that she vowed to take her tablets without fail. Poor compliance was rapidly resolved, despite the lack of success from considerable previous problem solving by the therapist.

Parents appear to derive substantial support from sharing their disappointment and frustration with the burden of schizophrenia on themselves and other family members. Contact outside sessions is advocated by therapists to provide mutual support with crises, and also for pure social activities. However, there are several limitations to the family group, such as the following:

1. Difficulties conducting problem solving and communication training in the group format. This training is specified for each family and there is seldom substantial overlap in the specific problems of different families.
2. Generalizing issues to group themes tends to encourage dealing with relatively superficial problems. Few families chose to disclose their more crucial difficulties. This can tend to focus more on the patient as the "problem" with associated "scapegoating."
3. Poor attendance by fathers and nonschizophrenic siblings and relatives—often the nonattenders with the source of major family tensions.
4. Reduced compliance with homework procedures.
5. Disruption by disorganized patients with limited attention spans.
6. Limited ability to provide adequate ongoing behavioral analysis of family problems.

Although none of these difficulties have been effectively overcome, a compromise that allows families some individualized time reviewing of their between-sessions problem-solving efforts has enabled the group to focus on the specific difficulties of each family in addition to working on issues common to several families.

There are only limited data on the comparative effectiveness of multifamily groups and individual family therapy. Multifamily groups do appear to provide some tangible benefits that outweigh many of the disadvantages. They are specifically of assistance with very socially withdrawn patients and their parents.

One common problem identified by parents and patients in one multifamily group was that of discussing the patient's illness with people outside the family. The stigma they perceived to be associated with having a person with schizophrenia in the family was profound and led to withdrawal from social contacts. Formerly sociable families reported never inviting people to their homes since the patient became ill.

In the group, family members and patients were invited to describe the responses they gave to the question "What's been wrong with you (your son, daughter, etc.)?" A wide range of responses were provided. Some preferred to remain purposefully vague and to politely limit the conversation to the fact that they had been ill, but had pretty much fully recovered. Others found a straightforward response more comfortable: "I've got a problem with the chemistry in my body that's a bit like diabetes. I have to take some tablets every day to keep things in synch. The doctor told me to take things easy and not get under too much stress . . ." was the way one patient had explained his illness to a good friend. This explanation was considered an excellent explanation of the illness without detailing the symptoms. The emphasis on having a medical illness, affecting biochemistry, that at times produces concentration and thinking difficulties, and is treated with medication by physicians with assistance from therapists who teach stress management, appeared to be an explanation that satisfied most inquiries. Families decided that talking about the nature of delusions and hallucinations tended to mystify other people. The open use of the term "schizophrenia" was generally avoided. Therapists supported this avoidance of labeling on account of the high level of misinformation concerning schizophrenia in the community. However, encouragement was given for patients and families to discuss their diagnosis with intimate friends and family members in an attempt to reeducate at least a small support network.

During the multifamily group, several members role-played scenes in which an inquisitive friend or acquaintance probed for information about the illness. They were coached by other group members in assertive methods of handling such situations. The therapists facilitated this process and avoided imposing their personal responses upon the family members.

REHABILITATION COUNSELING

In addition to the psychosocial interventions designed to minimize the morbidity of schizophrenia, a crucial aim of our approach is to maximize the role functioning of both the patient and his or her family members. The importance of work as a rehabilitation tool has been widely recognized (Wing, 1978; Strauss & Carpenter, 1977; Morgan, 1974; Mendel, 1976; Paul, 1969). During times of economic prosperity, obtaining a job is a realistic goal for all patients who have attained a social remission of their schizophrenia. However, alternatives to competitive work may be preferable for patients with limited vocational skills at times of high unemployment and economic austerity. Thus, the thrust of rehabilitation in our program is to attempt to meet the needs of fully or partially recovered patients to help them engage in a fulfilling structured daily activity, not necessarily a full-time paid job.

Gordon Paul (1969) pointed out the importance of full collaboration with the patient's family in the development and implementation of an effective rehabilitation plan. For these reasons, we chose to have the rehabilitation counselor function as a consultant to the patient and his or her family in order to facilitate their problem solving in this area. Detailed planning and implementation of the rehabilitation program were left in the hands of the patient and family with ongoing assistance from the therapist.

No more than four 1-hour sessions were employed in the time-limited rehabilitation counseling. During these sessions the counselor sought to achieve the following specific goals: (1) conduct a behavioral analysis of vocational and leisure functioning; (2) define the person's goals for (a) work, and (b) leisure activities; (3) develop a list of potential sources of assistance in achieving maximal role performance in these areas; and (4) complete a typewritten report to the therapist, patient, and family.

Behavioral Analysis of Role Functioning

This involved an abbreviated behavioral analysis that sought to elucidate the person's strengths and weaknesses in the limited areas of work and leisure activities. Past levels of functioning were examined. Difficulties within these areas were pinpointed to specific deficits, such as lack of assertive behavior with supervisors, problems in conversing with work mates, short attention span, insufficient positive reinforcement from self and others for competent performance. In some instances, the deficits had been present only under certain contingencies—for example, overde-manding supervisor, noisy work station, or after an unpleasant life event. In others, a repetitive pattern of difficulties was evident. The detective work of the counselor sought to clarify the areas where either new behaviors were likely to be necessary and/or where environmental con-tingencies needed to be carefully considered to maximize role performance. The ideal work environment is a dream few persons ever realize. However, successful rehabilitation of the mentally impaired is largely determined by a close matching of skills and deficits with the demands of the work situation.

An example of this is James, a 25-year-old man who worked as a security guard at a trucking yard. He enjoyed his job despite the changing shifts and the unreliable co-workers, who teased him. The one thing he did not like was the 10 miles he had to travel to work, and he frequently asked his supervisor if he could transfer to a yard nearer his home. When a vacancy finally arose and he was transferred, he found the new situation less to his liking. The supervisor was abrasive and unapproachable, and the other workers were even more likely to arrive late to change shifts, and often not to arrive at all, necessitating that James work a double shift. The biggest disappointment was that the trucks were loaded with uninteresting containers in the new job, whereas they were loaded with the latest-model cars at the former—a major interest that made the long, lonely hours pass more quickly and provided plenty of interesting discussion with the truck drivers. James coped by taking a radio to work with him, but after several days of consecutive double shifts he approached his supervisor to ask if he could be spared the extra work. The supervisor shouted at him, and James walked off his job and was fired.

A month or two later James found a job in a yard where aerospace components were delivered. His supervisor was easygoing, and he again enjoyed talking about the merchandise with the drivers. However, the unreliability of co-workers persisted and he found himself working double shifts several nights a week. Assertiveness training in two family sessions enabled him to discuss this problem with his boss, who gave him a week off and subsequently did not ask him to work more than one double shift per week.

CRISIS INTERVENTION

The importance of crisis intervention (see Table 12-2), often in the context of telephone contact, is illustrated in the following vignette.

Mr. Gerard phoned his family therapist at 2 PM one Tuesday.

MR. GERARD: David is very upset and is refusing to go to work. He won't talk to his mother and me, and says he is going to kill himself.

THERAPIST: What led up to this?

MR. GERARD: He's been very moody lately. He's been working double shifts for the past week and has been pretty irritable.

THERAPIST: I see. Did anything happen today that upset him?

MR. GERARD: Well, he went for a walk with me earlier and he saw some couples walking arm in arm in the park. He started getting mad that he didn't have a girlfriend and started going on about it.

THERAPIST: What did you do?

MR. GERARD: I tried to talk to him and told him not to worry. One day he will get married, but he wouldn't listen. He said no girls like him and he wants to die. So I just left him alone.

THERAPIST: What is he doing now?

MR. GERARD: He's on his bed. Would you like to talk to him and tell him to go to work?

THERAPIST: Yes, in a moment, but I would like you and Mrs. Gerard to sit down with David and do some problem solving about the problem of his lack of a

TABLE 12-2. *Components of Family Crisis Intervention*

1. Early detection: 24-hour availability of therapist; encourage early contact; identify potential stress and plan early intervention strategies.
2. Assist family to identify precipitating problem—seldom the "presenting" problem.
3. Prompt family problem-solving efforts.
4. Consult on family plans for crisis resolution.
5. Offer expert suggestions when crisis involves symptom exacerbation, or when family coping potential is exhausted—may include increased medication or hospital admission.
6. Provide outreach support, home visits.
7. Reinforce all crisis-resolution *efforts*.
8. Review successful strategies so that family learns to cope more effectively with future crises.

girlfriend. I'd appreciate your doing that right away, and then ask David to give me a call and tell me what you have planned.

Mr. GERARD: OK. I'll try that. Well, thanks very much. I'll call you back then.

This conversation between a father and a therapist is representative of the approach we have employed in handling family crises. When family problem solving has proved ineffective, the therapist provides consultative support and attempts to redirect the family toward further efforts.

Less than an hour later, David phoned the therapist to report that they had discussed his girlfriend problem and had planned that he would go to the beach over the weekend and start up a conversation with a girl; the next week he would join a bowling league in the neighborhood where many single girls bowled. He said he felt too tired and was going to take the evening off work and go in tomorrow. His therapist praised him warmly and suggested that he might consider talking to at least five girls because if he only chose one the chances would be high that she would tell him to "push off." He agreed to try to talk to as many girls as possible, and thanked his therapist. The therapist phoned David the following Monday and was told that he had spoken to two girls at the beach. He had a brief but pleasant conversation with each, had spent a further half hour problem-solving this issue, and had been attending work regularly. He was warmly praised, as were his parents.

While this may appear to be a relatively minor crisis, one might speculate that without the combined responses of parents, therapist, and patient, a more serious situation (e.g., loss of job or suicide attempt) may have transpired. Many crises develop from relatively trivial precipitants.

Thus, adequate initial problem solving by parents, the immediate and concerned support of the therapist, the need for the patient and family to assume continued responsibility for the problem, and follow-up contact to review the outcome of the planned solutions are all essential components of crisis management.

Another specific problem encountered with the management of schizophrenia is the crisis of how to deal with the paranoid patient.

Example: Gary was a 23-year-old man who lived with his mother in her downtown apartment. He had been very well until the previous month when his chlorpromazine was lowered from 200 mg daily to 100 mg. At that time, he began to develop a wide range of somatic complaints, such as chest pain and headaches. When he found he was unable to gain relief of these pains, he began to attribute them to external forces that were controlling his body. He was fearful to leave the house and refused to attend the clinic. He said there was nothing wrong with him and refused all medication. He refused all food because he believed it was poisoned. He would not trust anybody, including his mother, his family therapist, or the psychiatrist who prescribed his medication. He refused to take oral medication and was unwilling to discuss his treatment.

A critical problem for this family and others is how to maintain a healthy relationship with the patient while effectively treating his paranoid symptoms. The personal rejection experienced is particularly difficult for the family, who are likely to become frustrated and respond with hostility and rejection. Therapists similarly may reduce their support and have the patient admitted to the hospital. This may be necessary if the patient threatens violence or his or her physical state deteriorates owing to improper nutrition. However, crisis management can usually provide effective support to the patient and family in their own home. The steps suggested include:

1. Maintain a concerned, consistent approach to the patient. Empathize with his or her feelings of fear: "You seem terrified by what you believe is going on!"

2. Reinforce all observable coping behavior: "I like the way you have been listening to music to take your mind off your unpleasant thoughts."

3. Express negative feelings in a firm manner, without overt or covert rejection or threats: "It is very upsetting to me when you refuse to talk about things with me. I would like to discuss your problems with you because I believe I can help you to sort them out a little."

4. Insist that the patient continue to take regular medication. This may entail intramuscular medication, and if the patient refuses to attend the clinic this will necessitate a home visit by a nurse or psychiatrist. Paranoid patients may often accept intramuscular injections quite readily, although care should be taken to ensure that side effects are minimized. This may necessitate giving a somewhat lower initial dose than might be recommended in other situations.

5. Avoid lengthy discussion with the patient about his or her delusions. Make it clear that you do not share the patient's beliefs, but avoid arguing over the validity of his or her conclusions. In this case, if you want to keep a friend don't discuss politics, religion, or *delusions*!

6. Explain to the family that the patient is experiencing an exacerbation of schizophrenia and train them in the management skills described above. Observing the therapist handling the patient is a most efficient method of teaching family members management skills. To maximize learning, this modeling must be accompained by a clear explanation of the salient features of the therapist's behavior. Rehearsal with therapist coaching is also used in such instances.

These communication skills are similar to those recommended for effective communication in everyday family interaction. The only difference is that with the paranoid individual, a high standard of communication is required, often under extremely burdensome circumstances. The exquisite sensitivity of such a person to criticism (either verbally or nonverbally expressed) makes this one of the most testing crises encountered in the course of schizophrenia. A tremendous burden is placed on the families, which have to cope with these disturbed patients 24 hours a day.

Home visiting from skilled nurses on a daily basis is seldom available for the home care of the mentally ill. During a crisis this support may greatly relieve the burden, particularly when accompanied by training in nursing management skills. With the provision of such services, the need for hospital care may be substantially reduced. Family members are often willing and able to assist as "nursing aides," but cannot be expected to function as "charge nurses"!

CONCLUSIONS

It can be seen that the management of schizophrenia entails much more than the treatment of thought interference, delusions, and hallucinations. A holistic approach that involves all aspects of the life of the index patient and his or her family members is advocated. Behavioral family therapy, with its emphasis on continual analysis of functional problems, provides a framework upon which solving problems associated with a wide range of issues can be attempted. At times it may be necessary for the family to seek consultation from experts other than the treating therapist and physician. However, such consultation is agreed upon only after all other alternative solutions have been evaluated in the problem-solving manner, and always remains a family decision. At all times new, creative solutions to problems are sought to provide the optimal, humanistic coping with the myriad of issues that face families in their care-giving roles.

SECTION THREE

CLINICAL EFFICACY

CHAPTER 13

RESULTS FROM
A CONTROLLED OUTCOME STUDY

In order to establish the effectiveness of the behavioral family therapy approach we chose to compare it with individual supportive therapy in the community management of a population of adult patients who had experienced a recent episode of florid schizophrenia and were continuing to live with their parents. The individual case management approach combined optimal neuroleptic drug therapy, rehabilitation counseling, problem-solving psychotherapy, crisis intervention, and practical assistance with problems such as seeking financial resources and housing. In contrast to the home-based family management, therapy sessions took place primarily at the clinic and family problem-solving training was not undertaken in any systematic fashion. That is not to say that family members were excluded from the management or not informed about the nature of the patient's illness and its management. Involvement of all family members was encouraged, but the families of the individual-management cases were not routinely seen in conjoint family therapy sessions. To conduct an objective comparison between the two treatments, patients were randomly assigned to the two treatment conditions and assessments were made by reliable raters, who were unaware of the treatment patients were receiving.

The period of treatment for patients in both treatment groups was 2 years. Patients were selected on the basis of a high risk for relapse associated with living in stressful family environments. Patients with a definite diagnosis of schizophrenia who were living with their families were referred, after discharge, to the Family Aftercare Program, of which the Family Therapy Research Project was a part. After a while, the existence of the project became known around Los Angeles and a handful of families from other parts of the city were referred to us. To be considered for participation in the project, patients and their families had to meet specific criteria relating to age, diagnosis, living arrangements, and ambient family stress.

Age. This was a study of adult schizophrenic patients who lived with their parents. Consequently, there was a requirement that the index patient be between 18 and 45 years of age.

Diagnosis. All patients had to have a diagnosis of "definite" for schizophrenia based on the Present State Examination (PSE; Wing *et al.,* 1974). Although not originally a selection criterion, all study patients met DSM-III criteria for schizophrenia.

Living Arrangements. In order to be included, index patients had to be either living with one or both biological parents, or in close physical proximity with considerable daily contact. Of the 39 patients, 35 lived with their families in a single household. Two index patients maintained separate apartments in the same buildings as their parents, and two others lived within two blocks of their parents.

Language. Although entry criteria did not include ethnicity, because the therapists were all English-speaking, families entering the study were required to employ English as the primary language in the home.

Family Stress. All patients entering the study were chosen on the basis of evidence of high family tension. This was assessed through the Camberwell Family Interview (see pp. 42–43). Of the 39 families selected for the study, 36 were rated high on the index of expressed emotion (EE), and the remaining three showed evidence of extreme family burden or tension, despite low EE ratings.

Twice as many male as female patients entered the study and there was a rich diversity of ethnic backgrounds in those selected. Forty-two percent were Caucasian, 36% black, and 17% Hispanic. Although most were young and had completed high school, a few patients were in their late 30s and early 40s, four had earned college degrees, but five had not completed high school. Most families were in the lower socioeconomic categories, and nearly 40% were headed by a single parent, usually a mother.

Almost all patients showed evidence of nuclear schizophrenia (82%) on PSE examination during their index episode. One-quarter were experiencing their first episode of schizophrenia. On average, they had been ill for 4 years, with three hospital admissions. After random assignment to the two treatment modalities there was close matching on sociodemographic and clinical variables.

THERAPISTS

The three authors were the principal therapists for all patients and families included in the study. Thus the disciplines of clinical social work, psychiatry, and psychology were all represented in a truly interdisciplinary effort. Although all three therapists had at least 5 years of clinical experience at the time the program began, there was considerable diversity in theoretical orientations and range of experience in working with the chronically mentally ill and in doing family therapy.

The first author and principal investigator of the project, Ian Falloon, MD, first developed an interest in family interventions while working as a family doctor in the late 1960s. His formal training in behavior therapy and family therapy began in 1970 during residency training at the Maudsley Hospital, London, where he began working with families under the supervision of Drs. Isaac Marks and Robin Skynner. Dr. Falloon was a founding faculty member of the Family Therapy Institute of London and taught behavioral family therapy in the family therapy course. His interests turned to home-based family therapy for depression and schizophrenia in 1972, and he has been developing the model of behavioral family therapy used in the present study ever since.

The second author, Jeffrey Boyd, PhD, received an eclectic training background at Florida State University, from which he received his PhD in clinical psychology in 1979. Coming into the project with a family systems orientation to family therapy, Dr. Boyd was trained in the specific behavioral interventions used in this study. He worked from 1978 to 1982 at the Los Angeles County/University of Southern California Medical Center in various clinical research projects involving chronically mentally ill patients. Dr. Boyd currently works at the Hennepin County Mental Health Center in Minneapolis.

The third author, Christine McGill, MSW, began as a caseworker in Baltimore in 1969, where she provided home-based services to high-risk pregnant adolescents. Ms. McGill later worked in emergency services at Johns Hopkins Hospital, where she developed an interest in working with persons with major mental illness. While completing her MSW degree at the University of Southern California in 1977, she joined Dr. Falloon and was trained in the behavioral family model. She is currently completing her PhD in social policy and administration.

Throughout the intensive treatment phase of the study, the clinical staff of the project had weekly case conferences, wherein treatment issues and strategies were discussed. These meetings were structured as problem-solving case discussions with role plays of difficult individual and family situations to stimulate development of alternative intervention strategies. The three authors worked very closely for the entire 3 years of the project and consulted informally with one another on virtually a daily basis about a wide range of clinical issues, involving both individual and family therapy cases. This not only served to clinical advantage, but was a source of mutual support for the therapists.

TREATMENTS

Behavioral Family Therapy

The family therapy followed the method outlined in Chapters 7 to 12. All sessions were conducted at home. Family therapy sessions were conducted on a weekly basis during the first 3 months of treatment, on a biweekly basis for the next 6 months, and monthly for the final 15 months of the 2-year study. Each session began with a review of the daily journals kept by every family member that described family and personal life experiences from each individual's perspective. A brief meeting with the index patient allowed the therapist an opportunity to conduct a brief mental-status examination and to pinpoint any illness-related issues. Following these 5- to 10-minute interviews, the therapist met with the entire family for 45 minutes.

Individual Treatment

Virtually all individual sessions took place at the clinic. There were occasions when patients stopped coming into the clinic for various reasons (lack of transportation, exacerbations, ambivalence about continuing in treatment, etc.). At these times, home visits were made to get them coming to the clinic regularly. The majority of individual therapy patients kept their scheduled clinic appointments on a regular basis. Scheduling of sessions was identical to that for family treatment cases: weekly for 3 months, biweekly for the next 6 months, and monthly thereafter.

The model of treatment was that of supportive case management. The focus was on practical aspects of everyday living. Vocational goals, family relationships, other interpersonal relationships, leisure activities, and coping with symptoms were all commonly addressed. Psychodynamic approaches to developmental material were not employed, although identity issues *vis-à-vis* social role functioning and having a major psychotic mental illness were frequently explored. Behavioral methods were used to treat depression and anxiety disorders where they contributed to the patient's overall difficulties.

Although we generally tried to avoid having family sessions among this group of patients (in order, obviously, to guarantee a significant contrast between the treatment approaches being compared), certainly no effort was made to exclude key relatives from treatment. Thus, if, as often was the case, a patient was regularly brought to the clinic by a parent, the therapist would typically have a brief visit with that relative alone. Here, we simply tried to follow standard clinical practice regarding the desirability or need to meet with the relative. In a few instances (generally surrounding a crisis of some kind), sessions were conducted including the patient as well as the family. Although the therapist in these cases may have attempted to facilitate the family's coping with an emergent problem, this was done without formally training relatives in communication or problem-solving skills or using behavior rehearsal or other specific behavioral methods.

Medication

Neuroleptic maintenance is clearly a cornerstone of treatment for patients with schizophrenia. The goal throughout this project was to ensure that all patients were regularly taking optimal dosages of neuroleptics so that any significant differences in outcome would have to be attributed to factors other than medication. This was, as might be guessed, a difficult goal to achieve in some cases.

Because there is some evidence that intramuscular injections of fluphenazine decanoate are associated with more side effects and possibly worse "negative" symptoms (social withdrawal, affective blunting) than orally administered medications, patients were initially treated with the latter. Chlorpromazine was used in a majority of cases, though high-potency drugs such as fluphenazine, haloperidol, and thiothixene were also employed. When erratic compliance with oral medications emerged as a treatment problem, various steps, depending on the circumstances, were taken to remedy the situation. If such steps failed, the patient was then switched to long-acting injections. We were fortunate to have available the services of Thomas Cooper, MS, of Rockland State Hospital in New York, who performed periodic assays of chlorpromazine, haloperidol, and fluphenazine blood levels on all patients being prescribed those drugs. Although the results from these assays were generally delayed for several weeks, they were still very useful in assessing compliance in some of the more difficult cases. Naturally, in most cases information from the patient, and occasionally, from the patient's relatives was sufficient to make these determinations. Also available to the treatment team were monthly blood prolactin levels performed on campus. Since neuroleptic drugs increase the blood levels of the hypothalamic hormone, prolactin, these assays provided feedback about neuroleptic effects in a much more immediate (1–3 days) way.

Pharmacological aspects of treatment were managed somewhat differently from standard clinical practice. Regardless of treatment conditions, all patients were scheduled for monthly clinic visits to see their prescribing doctors (Javad Razani, MD; Howard Moss, MD; and Alex Gilderman, PharmD) and the research nurse (Ruby Palmer, RN). These visits accomplished several purposes: Medication response and side effects were monitored and changes in drug regimen prescribed whenever appropriate; a standardized set of ratings scales were administered to assess general psychiatric symptomatology, specific "target" symptoms of schizophrenia, and medication side effects; and patients were seen by the research nurse, who weighed them, took their blood pressure, withdrew blood specimens, and administered injections when appropriate. For methodological reasons, every effort was made to keep these raters blind to the patient's treatment condition. As much as possible, however, patients did continue to see the same doctor for these monthly visits throughout the 2 years of the study.

Rehabilitation Counseling

Services of a rehabilitation counselor (Robert Miles, MS; James Gleisinger, MS) were made available to all patients participating in the program. These services included vocational counseling and leisure activity planning. The counselor was often helpful in assisting the patient to discover programs and resources available in the community. In those instances where patients failed to get into the program desired, obtain the job they had applied for, and so forth, the counselor helped to analyze what went wrong and to actively apply remedial measures (e.g., role-play a job interview, assist with application forms). At the time of this study, community resources for the chronically ill were being eroded or curtailed in the Los Angeles area. Thus, for those individuals not ready or able to compete in the open job market, finding appropriate programs was very difficult.

To standardize this aspect of treatment, 4 hours with the rehabilitation counselor were made available to all patients in both treatment conditions. This does not, of course, represent the total extent of rehabilitation efforts. In working with chronically ill psychiatric outpatients, principal therapists also must do rehabilitative work if they are to be maximally effective. One of the advantages we found with the family treatment approach was that it facilitated these rehabilitation efforts. Many of the families were quite ingenius at discovering programs of which we were unaware, or developing their own intermediate steps aimed at preparing their son or daughter for eventual employment in the competitive market or for participation in social and leisure activities.

Crisis Management

Effective management of crises can contribute substantially to a more benign course of the illness when treating schizophrenia. Crisis interventions that reduce the stress associated with an unfortunate life circumstance and point the way toward effective coping can drastically reduce the chances of a major relapse into psychosis. Alternatively, emergent situations that are poorly dealt with, or chronic problems that are an ongoing source of aggravation or distress, can add significant amounts of stress and tension to the person with schizophrenia, who may already be poorly equipped to withstand relatively low levels of stress. Therefore, the delivery of psychiatric and psychological services at crisis points is critical, and we tailored our program accordingly. All patients and families knew how to reach their principal therapist at all times. This was usually accomplished by providing them the therapist's home telephone number. In addition, most patients had permission to contact either of the other primary therapists in the program, in the event they were unable to reach their regular therapist. This 24-hour availability was felt by the therapists to be very important. Although many mental health professionals might quake at the thought of freely giving out their home telephone number (and there are certainly some patients for whom such practice might raise problems), we were generally pleased with the success of this policy. There were a few instances when patients or their parents called inappropriately, but there were many instances in which brief, timely telephone interventions were instrumental in short-circuiting incipient family crises. Perhaps even more significantly, many families reported that simply being *able* to get hold of their therapist (and having permission to do so) was a source of comfort and sense of support to them, enabling them to feel more confident in tackling problems on their own, knowing they had a backup if things took a turn for the worse. Again, with a few exceptions, we did not find that our patients or their family members became overly dependent on the therapists as a result of this somewhat liberal policy regarding home telephone calls.

In the family treatment condition the model for crisis management was identical to that for dealing with everyday issues: problem-solving sessions conducted by and for the family members. If a family member called and it became apparent that no family efforts to systematically attempt to cope with a problem had taken place, the therapist would encourage the family to convene a family meeting, identify precisely and consensually the problem, discuss alternative strategies for coping with the problem, and so forth. If these problem-solving efforts proved ineffective, they were then instructed to call the therapist back. Frequently, families were able to make considerable headway on tackling their problems with this kind of encouragement.

Continuity of Care

A strong argument can be made that in order to provide optimal aftercare treatment, one must also make provisions for continuity of care. Schizophrenia for most patients is a recurring illness characterized by partial or complete remissions interspersed with periods of symptomatic exacerbation, possibly leading to hospital admissions. Consequently, one hindrance to effective long-term management is the comings and goings of numerous mental health professionals in the patient's life. In many settings, when a patient is returned to outpatient treatment following discharge, he or she will be assigned to a new therapist. Thus, many of the patient's therapeutic relationships may turn out to be short-lived and unstable. An additional factor is the slowness with which the therapeutic alliance often develops. Many schizophrenic patients are guarded and distrustful, and a maximally effective therapeutic relationship may take many months or even years to develop.

In our program, we attempted to provide good continuity of therapeutic care. Each patient and family were assured that their primary therapist would continue to work with them for at least 2 years. The advantage of this became apparent in the second year of treatment. Despite decreasing the frequency of therapy sessions to one per month (from an average of more than two per month during the first year of treatment), most patients continued making clinical progress. This was true, moreover, for patients in both treatment conditions. Not only did the patients and families become more effective "consumers" of pharmacologic and therapeutic services, but the therapists also became more skilled at knowing how much stress a given patient could tolerate, what specific sorts of issues were most distressing, how best to elicit the support and cooperation of the family, and so forth.

Another aspect of continuity of care has to do with the degree of involvement of outpatient treatment staff during periods of inpatient treatment. Particularly with the recent trend in public policy to separate inpatient and outpatient mental health programs into nonoverlapping administrative frameworks, there is frequently little or no communication between mental health professionals involved with a patient's treatment at different points in time. It is not uncommon to find hospital staff formulating a diagnosis and instituting a treatment plan without benefit of the information that outpatient clinic staff could provide regarding the patient's functioning and treatment during the preceding months or even years. Similarly, outpatient care givers frequently fail to make optimal use of consultation with the inpatient treatment team.

In our program the primary therapist was, as a general rule, actively involved in all phases of inpatient treatment including consulting with emergency room staff at the time of admission, working with the treatment team on the ward, and participating in the process of discharge planning. The therapist's involvement was greater for those patients admitted to the psychiatric unit at the Los Angeles County/USC Medical Center (roughly 75% of all admissions during the study) than for those patients admitted elsewhere. All in all, it was our feeling that this involvement in a consultative role facilitated the inpatient management of acute psychiatric episodes and resulted in speedier return of the patient to the community.

RESEARCH DESIGN

Following completion of baseline assessments, index patients were randomly assigned to receive either family or individual management. The last of the baseline assessments to be completed was usually the family interaction tasks, which were not attempted until the index patient was relatively stable in his or her recovery from the precipitating episode of schizophrenia. This meant that we had been following most of the patients for 4–8 weeks following discharge from the hospital. Provided the patient and his or her parent(s) were willing to give informed consent to participate in the study (acknowledging that they had an equal chance to receive either treatment), the random assignment was made at this final family assessment session. The family was immediately informed of the determination, and the first therapy session was scheduled for the following week. The assignment of cases to therapists was not randomized. Each therapist was assigned equal numbers of patients in each condition.

Figure 13-1 summarizes the basic research design. All index patients were scheduled to receive 40 therapy sessions over a 2-year period. For the first 3 months, sessions took place at weekly intervals. For the next 6 months, sessions were biweekly. At the 9-month point, sessions were tapered to monthly maintenance visits. Although this was the general scheme, extra sessions were scheduled when indicated or requested by patients or families in either treatment condition.

Months 9 and 24 represented major assessment points, at which a variety of self-report and clinical interview assessment procedures evaluated each patient's mental status, as well as social adjustment, burden on the family, and attitudes toward the illness, treatment approach,

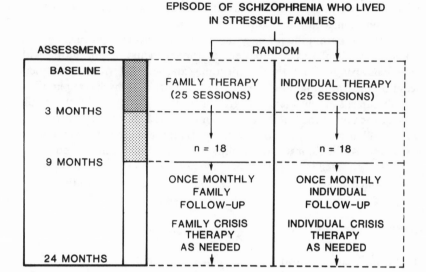

FIGURE 13-1. *Summary of the design.*

and so forth. In addition, a series of behavioral laboratory assessments of family interaction patterns was conducted at the 24-month point. These family interaction assessments had also been performed at baseline and at the end of the third month of treatment, by which time those who had been receiving the family treatment would have already been taught the basic skills of the structured problem-solving method.

Assessments

We endeavored to perform a broad spectrum of assessments. Much prior outcome research involving treatment for schizophrenia can be criticized for placing too much emphasis on rehospitalization rates and giving short shrift to other aspects of outcome. Certainly, reducing the number and duration of psychiatric admissions is a major objective in the community treatment of schizophrenia. Yet even this could be argued. There are clearly instances—particularly with behaviorally disturbed, persistently psychotic patients—when an elective hospitalization of 1 or 2 weeks would provide temporary relief from the family's extreme burden and might better enable them to continue as primary care givers. At other times brief hospital admission might be helpful in restabilizing medication.

The severity of schizophrenia is not readily measured. There are no rating scales that specifically measure this syndrome in a quantitative fashion. Relapses and exacerbations have been defined predominantly according to qualitative clinical changes (e.g., reappearance of florid symptoms) or severity of social dysfunction (Falloon *et al.*, 1983). Thus, it was necessary to fashion a battery of assessments of psychopathology from existing measures, as well as to develop some new measures.

In addition to measuring the impact of treatment on the illness we were interested in measuring the psychosocial functioning of the patient and his or her family members. Although few family members appeared to have significant psychopathology or social handicaps themselves, we assessed these functions in order to establish whether family therapy might effectively diminish the problems of all family members.

Measures of the process of treatment were also employed to assess the efficacy of specific components of treatment, and to measure some of the variables (e.g., life events) that could not be controlled by the experimental design but which might contribute to the outcome. A brief description of the major assessment procedures will be provided. A detailed assessment manual is available from the authors.

Severity of Schizophrenia

The course of schizophrenia is most typically one of remission and exacerbation. But many other courses are common, including partial remission with gradual deterioration or improvement. In order to measure the varied courses of this condition it is important not only to measure episodes of acute exacerbation, but to measure symptoms continuously over time. While the florid symptoms of hallucinations, delusions, and thought interference are most dramatic and are associated with social crisis and hospital admission, the "negative" symptoms of social withdrawal, apathy, and flattened affect may contribute substantially to deficient social functioning. Thus, several measures of psychopathology were employed in the study. They included:

Clinical Exacerbations. These were measured by the therapists, who noted all major and minor exacerbations of schizophrenia throughout the study. Episodes of depression and anxiety were noted in addition. No attempt was made to standardize these clinical ratings, although there was excellent consensus among the three therapists concerning major exacerbations of schizophrenia.

Target Symptom Ratings. Blind ratings of the two or three florid symptoms that were characteristic of the presentation of an acute exacerbation of schizophrenia were selected for each patient prior to beginning the study and were rated on a 7-point scale of severity at each monthly clinic visit and at the time of crisis or hospital admission.

   Brief Psychiatric Rating Scale (BPRS). Blind ratings on the BPRS were made monthly. Four factors derived from this scale measured thought disorder, withdrawal ("negative" symptoms), hostile–suspiciousness, and depression–anxiety (Overall & Gorham, 1962; Goldstein *et al.*, 1978).

Social Functioning

The social functioning of patients was measured in an interview with the parent most involved in his or her care. An abbreviated version of the Social Behaviour Assessment Schedule (SBAS; Platt, Weyman, Hirsch, & Hewett, 1980) was employed. This semistructured interview contained scales measuring the patient's social role performance, behavior disturbance, and disruption on the family system. In addition, ratings of the relative's distress and dissatisfaction with the patient's behavior were made by the blind assessor.

   A self-report measure of social functioning, the Social Adjustment Scale (SAS), was administered to patients and their family members before treatment and at 3, 9, and 24 months. This included ratings of work; leisure activities; relationships with parents, spouse, and children; and financial status (Weissman, Prusoff, Thompson, Harding, & Myers, 1978).

Family Functioning

Family functioning was measured in terms of (1) the adjustment of individual family members, (2) the subjective burden attributed to caring for the index patient, and (3) the family as a problem-solving unit. Changes in family problem solving, communication, and coping with life stresses will be discussed in the first part of Chapter 15, which is devoted to the process of therapeutic change. In this chapter family members' personal adjustment and burden will be discussed.

   Each family member completed the 64-item Hopkins Symptom Checklist (HSCL) at baseline and at 9 and 24 months to assess clinical symptom changes. In addition, family members completed the social adjustment questionnaires (SAS) at baseline and at 9 and 24 months.

   Family burden was assessed during the SBAS interview with the key family informant. After seeking information about the manner in which the index patient's behavioral disturbance interfered with the day-to-day functions of other family members, the informant was invited to describe his or her subjective feelings of burden attributed to patient care. This was rated on a 4-point scale by the blind rater.

Results

An effective therapy for schizophrenia aims not merely to reduce the severity and duration of acute exacerbations, but also to minimize overall morbidity for the patient and his or her family and thereby enhance their quality of life. In the best of all possible worlds these benefits would be achieved in a cost-effective manner. The remainder of this chapter will compare the outcome of family and individual management approaches on these parameters, with an aim to translate these research findings into everyday clinical practice.

CLINICAL OUTCOME

Perhaps the most central clinical question addressed in this study is whether the family therapy approach improved the general course of the patient's disorder. The course of schizophrenia, of course, is difficult to measure in an objective, quantitative fashion. Much of the current literature focuses on acute relapse of florid symptoms as the major outcome variable in assessing the effectiveness of various treatment approaches. Unfortunately, there is little agreement regarding what constitutes a relapse, so we have chosen to examine several aspects of the clinical course: (1) exacerbations of all psychiatric symptoms, regardless of type; (2) exacerbations of specific schizophrenic symptoms; and (3) hospital admissions.

Exacerbation of All Psychiatric Symptoms (Figure 13-2)

Schizophrenia is a complex syndrome characterized by certain symptoms, including specific types of delusions, hallucinations, and thought disturbances. These well-delineated psychotic symptoms do not represent the full range of psychopathology that can afflict the patient; they simply constitute the criteria for establishing the diagnosis. Depression, anxiety reactions, relationship problems, apathy, withdrawal, and loss of confidence are some of the accompanying problems that may, in fact, often be more debilitating and less readily treated than the primary symptoms of schizophrenia.

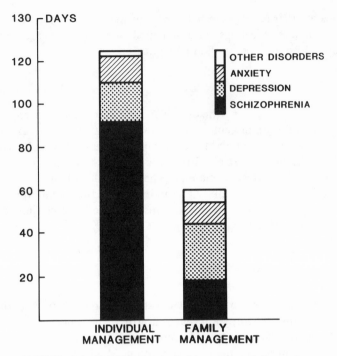

FIGURE 13-2. *Exacerbations of all symptoms: 0-9 months.*

In the present study, all acute episodes of clinical significance occurring during the first 9 months of treatment were tabulated from a detailed chart review. The total number of clinical episodes (major and minor) was similar for both treatment groups (40 for the family treatment and 43 for the individual treatment groups). However, patients who received family treatment tended to have episodes of briefer duration and lesser severity. Family patients averaged 2 months of clinical instability during the first 9 months of treatment, whereas individual patients spent 4 months in an unstable state that required active therapeutic intervention. This represented a considerable burden for both the treatment team and the families.

Closer scrutiny of Figure 13-2 reveals that there were no clear differences between the two treatment groups with respect to the frequency and severity of *nonschizophrenic* episodes. Patients in both groups were more or less equally likely to experience episodes of depression or to have anxiety or other management problems (although it must be remembered that depression and anxiety were commonly present when schizophrenic symptoms predominated). There were, however, clear differences with respect to exacerbations of schizophrenic symptoms. Individual therapy patients were far more likely than family therapy patients to experience a major episode (21 vs. 3 episodes, respectively), and these episodes tended to be of greater duration (69 vs. 21 days). Although the family treatment group was somewhat more likely to experience minor exacerbations, the total time spent in either major or minor episodes of schizophrenia was far greater for the individual therapy group.

These clinical data have not been subjected to statistical analysis owing to their lack of rigorous, objective measurement. They are presented to provide a clinician's view of the impact of the therapy. They would suggest that the effects of the family intervention were specific to the prevention of major exacerbations of schizophrenic symptoms, and made limited clinical impact on the less prominent affective and neurotic episodes experienced by the patients. Further support for these clinical findings was found in the analysis of data obtained from more objective assessment methods.

One such objective measure was the Brief Psychiatric Rating Scale (BPRS). This 18-item scale was administered on a monthly basis by clinicians blind to the treatment condition of their patients. Item scores were broken down into four factor scores (Goldstein et al., 1978) that were examined separately. In addition, the total score was examined for its variability from month to month for each patient (providing a measure of stability–instability of symptoms over time).

Factor 1 is termed "hostile–suspiciousness" and consists of the items "uncooperativeness," "hostility," and "suspiciousness." An analysis of covariance, with the score at the beginning of the first month of the study as the covariant, showed no significant changes over time or between the treatment groups.

Factor 2 is termed "anxious–depression." It is made up of "guilt," "depression," "anxiety," and "tension." Again, the analysis of covariance showed no changes over time, or in relation to the type of treatment provided.

Factor 3 is termed "withdrawal," and comprises "motor retardation," "blunted affect," "emotional withdrawal," and "grandiosity" (scaled negatively). As such, this factor could be considered to measure some of the negative or deficit symptoms often associated with schizophrenia. While there was no significant change over time, there was a trend suggesting that the family therapy group was less withdrawn over the 9-month period.

Factor 4 is termed "schizophrenic thought" and comprises the items "conceptual disorganization," "unusual thought content," and "hallucinations." Although not a measure of specifically schizophrenic symptoms, this factor provides some measure of florid schizophrenia. The analysis of covariance showed a significant difference between the treatment groups that favored the family-treated patients.

Although there were no statistically significant differences between treatment groups on BPRS total score over the 9 months, the stability of these scores was greater for the family treatment.

Exacerbations of Specific Schizophrenic Symptoms

On several indices of specific symptoms of schizophrenia, the family treatment appeared to be superior. One way of examining this was simply to ask the therapists to rate whether or not each of his or her patients had suffered a major relapse of schizophrenia during the first 9 months. Relapse was defined as a significant exacerbation of schizophrenic symptomatology necessitating a major change in treatment, such as hospital admission or significant increases in the patient's medication, in order to reestablish clinical stability. By this measure, one of the 18 family-treated patients relapsed (6%), compared to eight of the 18 individual-treated patients (44%).

Although the difference in relapse rates between the two treatment conditions is statistically significant, it should be noted that this was a therapist rating and that the definition of relapse fell somewhat short of being an objective measure. Still, these figures are offered for purposes of comparison with other studies that have defined relapse in a similar fashion.

Perhaps even more convincing were the results obtained with the target-symptoms ratings. These ratings of specific schizophrenic symptomatology made by clinicians who were blind to the treatment condition of the patients strongly supported the therapist's observations.

Figure 13-3 shows the maximum level of target ratings attained by patients during the 9-month aftercare period. These scores represent the worst that each patient fared with respect to florid schizophrenic symptoms. As can be seen, for family therapy patients the scores were considerably lower than for individual therapy patients, although relatively few were completely free of schizophrenic symptoms throughout the entire 9 months. The tendency for fewer family-treated patients to experience major exacerbations noted by the therapists was also noted by these independent raters. In addition to the maximum levels attained, an analysis of the month-to-month target ratings indicated that family therapy was superior at maintaining stability over the entire 9 months. Indeed many family-treated patients became less symptomatic than they had been at baseline, so that during the ninth month ten of the 18 were in full

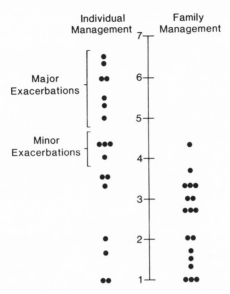

FIGURE 13-3. *Maximum target rating (blind) during the 9 months of treatment.*

remission of schizophrenia. The compelling conclusion is that family therapy reduced the risk of severe exacerbations of schizophrenia, and possibly enhanced the likelihood of remission of the illness.

Hospital Admissions

Because the major aim of our study was to examine changes of schizophrenic symptoms in patients receiving behavioral family therapy, community tenure was of secondary importance as a research issue. However, factors related to health-care delivery and cost-effectiveness make this an important matter in its own right.

Table 13-1 depicts the breakdown for study patients of time spent in hospital, in jail, and in residential facilities during the first 9 months. It is clear that relatively brief periods were spent in hospital when compared with the time spent in major exacerbations (see Figure 13-2). This is a reflection of the extensive amount of crisis support provided to patients and their families in *both* treatment conditions.

However, the most striking effect is the remarkably low admission rate of the family therapy patients. Indeed, neither of the two patients who received family therapy and were hospitalized were admitted for exacerbations of schizophrenia: One took an overdose in a depressed,

TABLE 13-1. *Community Tenure at 9 months*

	Family ($n = 18$)	Individual ($n = 18$)
Hospital days (mean)	.83	8.39
Patients admitted	2 (11%)	9 (50%)
Jail days (mean)	.06	.50
Patients admitted	1 (6%)	2 (11%)
Residential placement (mean)	.11	3.33
Patients admitted	1 (6%)	2 (11%)
Total days out of home (mean)	1.00	12.22

suicidal state; the other became a management problem after his parents went on an out-of-state vacation for 2 weeks, entrusting his care to a special residential care home whose professionally trained workers found him to be a behavior-management problem. Suicidal and threatening gestures are common precipitants of hospital admissions; exacerbations of delusions, hallucinations, and thought interference are less likely to precipitate hospital admission unless they are accompanied by severe behavior disturbance. Several hospital admissions of the individually treated patients were also more closely linked to behavior difficulty than to exacerbations of schizophrenia, which on most occasions were effectively managed in the community setting with assertive support to the patient and his or her family.

The hospital is only one form of institution to which disturbed persons are admitted. Others include jails, nursing homes, board-and-care homes, and halfway houses. Four patients were jailed for brief periods as a result of behavior disturbance.

To conclude this section concerning the clinical findings, the results revealed substantial benefits for those who received family therapy in addition to optimal doses of neuroleptic medication and comprehensive case management. These included fewer major episodes of florid schizophrenia, and a reduced need for hospital care in the family-treated cases. These benefits appeared soon after the start of family therapy and continued throughout the 9-month period. However, there was little evidence that the treatment was altering the underlying vulnerability of the patient to further episodes of schizophrenia; treatment merely tended to blunt the severity of episodes when they occurred.

Clinical remissions of schizophrenia were more prominent in the family group, and the negative, withdrawal symptoms were less prominent.

There was little impact noted with respect to depressive and anxiety symptoms. These symptoms were evident at intake to the study and remained a management issue throughout.

PATIENT SOCIAL ADJUSTMENT

A strong argument can be made that the most important criterion for treatment outcome of a mental illness is the restoration or development of competent social role behavior. The aim of the family treatment was not merely to reduce stress through enhanced problem solving, but also to promote development of social competence. A similar goal was shared by those persons who received individual treatment.

Social functioning was assessed in three ways: (1) *clinical reports* of patient's work, study, and leisure activities; (2) *patient's self-report* of his or her work, leisure, interpersonal, and family functioning on a standardized questionnaire (SAS; Weissman *et al.*, 1978); and (3) *report of family informant* on index patient's social performance and behavioral disturbance (SBAS; Platt *et al.*, 1980).

During the first 6 months of the study, social rehabilitation was difficult for many patients, particularly those with long-standing illness and persisting disability. First-episode patients with histories of good premorbid role functioning often were able to reestablish themselves in their previous jobs, but found themselves having more difficulty reintergrating with their friends and social activities. Much of this difficulty appeared to stem from concern about how they could explain the nature of their condition to their friends. They feared the stigma of the "schizophrenia" label.

Success in obtaining jobs appeared to be closely related to whether the person had held a job immediately before the onset of the index schizophrenic episode. All persons who obtained work during the 9 months had been working at the onset of their schizophrenic symptoms. Overall, family-treated patients spent one-third of the follow-up period in regular work activity, including daily volunteer and part-time work. Individual patients spent slightly less time engaged in work activity, although eight patients in each condition (44%) were employed for some part of the first 9 months.

Persons who were not working were encouraged to participate in educational programs to improve their potential to eventually obtain gainful employment. Others, whose rehabilitative needs were greater, were encouraged to participate in sheltered workshops. When these additional data are considered, the family therapy patients spent about half of the 9 months engaged in work or educational pursuits, compared to approximately one-third of the time for individual therapy patients. Much of this difference probably stems from the longer periods spent in various states of symptomatic exacerbation on the part of the individually treated patients. It was also our impression that the family therapy was more effective in harnessing the resources of the family and getting them to assist in some of the practical matters essential to obtaining and sustaining constructive daily activities. These included ensuring that patients were prepared for their activities and got to work or classes on time, motivating them to participate in household activities and social functions, practicing job-seeking skills (such as interviewing), and helping to solve difficulties associated with these activities.

Figure 13-4 compares the work and educational activity of patients in the two treatment conditions during the first and second years of the study. It is evident that whereas family treatment appeared to enhance these activities substantially beyond the level noted in the 2-year period prior to the study, there was no increase in the activity level of individual patients in the course of the study. Furthermore, it may be noted that during the second year of the study family patients showed substantial gains in their work activity.

The self-repoted levels of social functioning of patients suggested that during the 9 months of active treatment, small but significant gains in social adjustment occurred in patients who received family treatment, whereas the group receiving individual treatment showed no overall improvement and perhaps experienced some slight decline in their adjustment from their baseline at the start of treatment. Several patients had difficulty completing the questionnaire (SAS) in a valid manner, so the reader should be cautioned against too literal an interpretation of these data. However, the consistent trend favoring the family approach supports the clinical view that family-treated patients were making positive gains in their social adjustment, whereas individual patients were more likely to be maintaining their level of adjustment, and in some cases falling back.

An analysis of covariance of the difference between the two treatments at 9 months when the baseline assessment was the covariate showed significant differences on the scales measuring interpersonal functioning, family relationships, and the total score. So few patients were engaged in work or study at *both* assessments that the covariance analysis of that scale was of limited meaning. The one item that assessed satisfaction with financial situation favored the individual treatment group, but is difficult to interpret. Increased need for financial resources may be contingent upon improved social functioning, particularly when the patient is unable

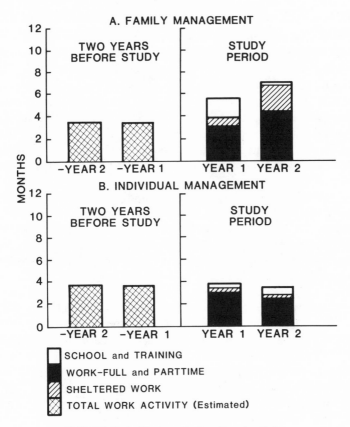

FIGURE 13-4. *Work and educational activity.*

to get a well-paid job. All other scales favored the family treatment condition.

The primary measures of patient social performance and behavior distrubance were derived from the SBAS. The parent most involved with caring for the patient was the subject for this structured interview. Audio tapes of the interviews were rated by a research assistant who was blind to the patient's treatment condition.

The first set of these measures, *behavioral disturbance*, reflects the degree to which the patient displayed a variety of behavior disturbances. Patients in the individual therapy group tended to show little positive change in their degree of behavior disturbance at the 9-month assessment, when compared to the pretreatment assessment. On most items, a greater number of patients were reported impaired at 9 months. On the other hand, fewer family-treated patients tended to show behavioral impairment at 9 months than at baseline. Significantly fewer family-treated patients displayed bodily complaints, problems of medication compliance, odd or unusual behavior, or miscellaneous other disturbances at 9 months than at baseline. At 9 months, significantly fewer family patients displayed self-neglect, medication compliance problems, or odd or unusual behavior than individual patients. More family-treated patients showed bodily complaints at baseline than individual patients. This suggested that the family-treated patients showed less behavior disturbance than the individual cohort at 9 months, although in some instances they had been more impaired at baseline.

This trend favoring improved behavioral functioning was somewhat more prominent when the informant's distress concerning patient behavior was measured. Significantly fewer informants of family-treated patients were distressed by social withdrawal, slowness or underactivity, worry, self-neglect, and medication compliance than informants of individually treated patients. Thus, not only were fewer family therapy patients behaviorally impaired, but those who were proved less distressing to their relatives. The former observation is consistent with a reduction in florid symptomatology in family-treated persons, and the latter may suggest improved tolerance toward deviant behavior in informants receiving behavioral family therapy.

Improvements in the family-treated patients appeared most prominent in behavior associated with the social impairments of schizophrenia, such as withdrawal, bizarre behavior, and self-neglect. Less change was noted in areas associated with affective disturbance—misery, agitation, suicidal behavior, and sleep disturbance. These findings support the pattern of symptom change noted in the clinician's ratings described earlier. One very striking finding was a lack of reported problems with medication compliance in the family-treated group. This compared with compliance problems reported in nearly 40% of individual patients—a figure consistent with levels of poor compliance found in several community studies of drug-taking behavior.

The second set of SBAS-derived measures, *social performance*, represents the parent's description of each patient's level of performance on a variety of role-performance items. Results on these items add further support to the observation that more family-treated patients appeared to improve their social functioning over the 9 months of treatment than did individually treated patients. At baseline, two-thirds of the family-treated patients were considered to have impairments in their relationships outside of the family, whereas at 9 months only five of the 18 (28%) patients were reported impaired by their relatives. This level of unimpaired sociability was significantly greater than for the individually treated patients, as was the functioning in household tasks.

However, at least half the family-treated patients remained impaired in the areas of household tasks, leisure activities, and work or study. A reduction in the number of family-treated patients who were considered severely impaired in work or study performance appeared to reflect an increased effort to explore job and educational opportunities, although at the 9-month assessment few had succeeded in establishing themselves in employment or courses.

Despite only slight gains in social performance, relatives of family-treated patients reported substantially less distress than relatives of individually treated patients concerning the impaired social performance of their schizophrenic family members at the 9-month assessment. This was statistically significant on six of the seven social-performance items. This pattern was even more striking when the ratings of the informants' satisfaction with social performance were examined. These data suggest that family therapy may have contributed to a reduction in the level of expectations of relatives for unimpaired social functioning in their sons and daughters during the first year.

ADJUSTMENT OF OTHER FAMILY MEMBERS

While the major thrust of our study was to measure the impact of family therapy on the established schizophrenic illness of one of the family members, the functioning of other persons in the family was also an important consideration. It has been suggested that families with schizo-phrenic members have a tendency to resist change through homeostatic mechanisms, so that when the person suffering from schizophrenia im-proves, other family members deteriorate in a reciprocal fashion. The behavioral method of family therapy involves a careful analysis of recipro-cal behavior patterns *prior to intervention* so that negative changes are predicted and avoided through careful structuring of the interventions. Thus every member of the family is expected to benefit from changes in the family system. To test the effectiveness of this approach, it was necessary to evaluate the adjustment of each family member as well as the index patient.

The measures of family adjustment included questionnaire ratings of symptoms and social adjustment. In addition, the burden on the family of caring for the index patient was assessed on the SBAS interview.

At the beginning of treatment half the parents had ratings considered abnormal on one or more scales of the Hopkins Symptom Checklist.

After 9 months fewer family-treated parents tended to report symptoms of depression, anxiety, obsessive–compulsive, interpersonal sensitivity, or bodily complaints. There was a slight tendency for individually treated parents to report more symptoms, but their initial levels were low, suggesting that they may have been underreporting their distress at the baseline assessment. No parents or other family members showed evidence for the emergence of schizophrenic symptoms during the study. Many parents reported feeling that the support they derived from the program may have prevented them from breaking down. Siblings who participated in the program appeared to benefit in a similar manner.

The Social Adjustment Scale (SAS) was completed by 50 family members before and after 9 months of treatment. Few reported significant adjustment problems on this self-report measure, and there was no difference between family and individual family members at either assessment. Many family members who received family therapy achieved considerable changes in their lives over this period. Parents felt less bound to caring for their sons and daughters with schizophrenia, took jobs, and engaged in increasing social and leisure activities outside the home. Several families left their index patients at home for a week or two while they went on vacations, often the first trips they had made for many years. At the beginning of treatment in the study, the family problems most frequently attributed to the index patient and his or her illness were emotional problems in another family member (47% of all families), tension in family relationships (44%), the impaired physical health of another family member (28%), interference with the household routine (25%), and financial stress (25%). Problems with leisure activities, work performance, and social activities were reported in many families, but tended to be attributed to factors other than the index patient.

At 9 months, the problems attributed to the patient had substantially diminished in the family-treated condition, whereas little change was reported in the individually treated families. Significant improvements were noted in the emotional problems of other family members and financial stressors that were considered patient-related. Significantly fewer family-treated patients were considered to interfere with the household routine than their individually treated counterparts. Indeed, very few families that had received family therapy considered the index patient to be a factor in the family difficulties. However, despite less blame being accorded the index patient, relatively small improvements in family functioning were reported. Fewer families receiving family therapy reported social and leisure activity problems, and family relationships were reported as tense in eight of the 18 families at 9 months compared to 12 families before treatment.

This trend toward reduced attribution of adverse effects to the index patients may have been the result of their improved social behavior, or possibly to a reduction in "scapegoating" of the patient for family difficulties. The same tendency was not observed in the individual condition, where family difficulties remained and continued to be attributed to the patient. These data are consistent with the reports of continued distress and dissatisfaction associated with the social functioning of the individual patients. Family-therapy relatives reported minimal distress and dissatisfaction after 9 months of treatment despite only partial amelioration of the index patient's functional impairment.

A global rating of family burden associated with living with the index patient indicated that significantly fewer families that had received family therapy experienced moderate or severe burden after 9 months (17%) than had reported this level of burden before treatment (78%) (see Figure 13-5). Eleven individual families reported moderate or severe burden at 9 months (61%).

These data strongly suggest that the family management program reduced family burden associated with having a family member who had suffered schizophrenia, and that the adverse effects and negative attitudes

FIGURE 13-5. *Subjective burden.*

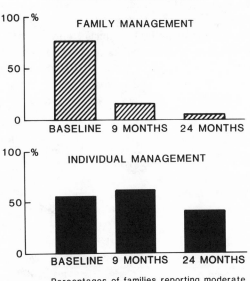

Percentages of families reporting moderate or severe burden attributed to caring for the index patient.

associated with this index patient were greatly diminished. Moreover, there was no indication that any family member suffered an increase in emotional or physical health problems or a decrease in social functioning as a result of the family-based approach. On the other hand, several family members spent substantially more time out of the home, left index patients and went on vacations, and expanded their social and leisure activities and their network of community contacts. A few persistently symptomatic patients continued to present a major management problem for family care givers, who expressed their gratitude for the support provided by the family therapists, but who shared the therapists' frustrations at the lack of day-care centers, sheltered workshops, and facilities for short-term care of patients when the families wanted a brief respite from their care-giving roles.

CONSUMER SATISFACTION

To establish a new treatment modality, objective evidence of its effectiveness must be accompanied by a high level of consumer satisfaction with the service provided. It is evident from Figure 13-6 that almost all patients and their family members considered both the individual and family management approaches very satisfactory. Somewhat surprising was the finding that most individual patients and their family members regarded the support their families received as "good" or "very good." This attested to the considerable effort made by therapists to involve all families in the treatment, not just those receiving behavioral family therapy. These positive responses on a rating scale were accompanied by unsolicited statements of gratitude by patients and family members of both conditions throughout the 2-year program. Very few expressed dissatisfaction with their management at any time.

THE COST OF FAMILY TREATMENT

Another crucial factor that determines the deployment of a new therapy is its cost. Innovative treatments, although often effective, are usually more expensive than traditional approaches (Weisbrod et al., 1980). We have demonstrated that behavioral family therapy is an effective approach for community management of schizophrenia. However, at what cost were these gains achieved? An extensive analysis of the comparative costs of every aspect of family and individual management was conducted (Cardin, McGill, & Falloon, in preparation). Despite account-

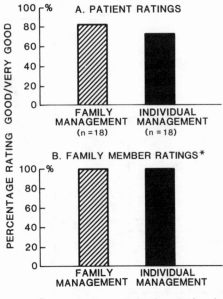

FIGURE 13-6. *Consumer satisfaction: global.*

ing for the additional cost of conducting family therapy in the home, the overall costs for family treatment were less than for the individual method (Figure 13-7). A greater number of extra appointments, emergency visits, days in hospital, and visits to a nurse for intramuscular neuroleptics contributed to the additional costs accrued by individual patients. During the second year of treatment these differences were even more pronounced. The economic benefits that accrued from salaried employment did not appear as a substantial factor until the second year of the program, when several family-treated patients obtained paying jobs. Thus, family management appeared to be substantially less expensive than the more traditional individual clinic-based approach, and to offer promise of diminishing costs with time.

TWO-YEAR OUTCOME

Treatment was continued for all patients in the study for at least 2 years. One individually treated patient withdrew from the study during that period, making a total of four dropouts overall (two from each treatment

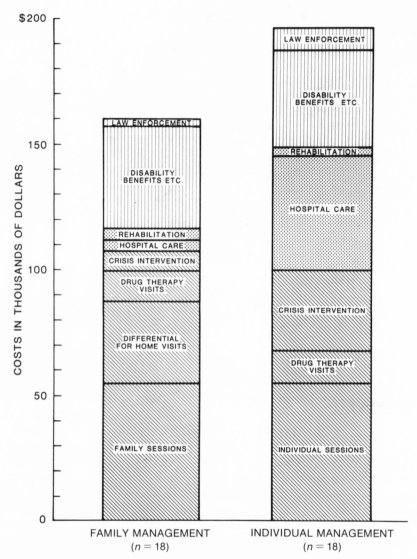

FIGURE 13-7. *The cost of treatment.*

condition). The remaining 35 index patients and their families completed assessment at the 2-year point. One-third of the patients in the family-treated group received predominantly individual psychotherapy during the second year, and a similar proportion of individually treated patients received family-based treatment over much of this period. This compromises somewhat the validity of the controlled comparison of the two treatment approaches.

The clinical data continued to support the long-term efficacy of the family model. Two further major exacerbations occurred in the family condition, although one of these was a patient who elected to have individual psychotherapy and refused drug therapy after the 9-month assessment. The other was the patient who relapsed during the first 9 months. Seven additional individual treatment cases had major exacerbations after 9 months, making a total of 15 (83%) over the entire 2 years. Six other individual patients who had relapsed during the first 9 months had further major exacerbations of schizophrenia subsequently. Thus, while the course of individual patients was characterized by continued relapses, often accompanied by hospitalization, family-treated persons tended to remain stable despite substantially reduced therapist contact. In several cases, families met in multifamily groups on a monthly basis. Other families were seen in the clinic, and a few continued to receive family therapy at home. Social functioning continued to improve in family-treated patients and in those individual patients who remained clinically stable. Twelve (67%) of these family patients were employed in full-time jobs or training throughout much of the second year of treatment. For eight of these this was paid, competitive employment. Gains in interpersonal functioning were evident. Two patients married, one giving birth to a son. Another had the music and lyrics of a song he had written produced by a record company. Patients with persistent symptoms tended to make less progress, but nevertheless showed little tendency toward social deterioration. Progress in individual patients was evident, but less dramatic, with deterioration apparent in several cases.

Family burden appeared to be associated with the severity of the index patient's disability, and many family therapy relatives reported no burden at all at the 2-year assessment. Where major functional disability remained, however, family members remained distressed, regardless of the type of treatment provided.

Enhanced clinical and social status in the index patients was usually accompanied by enhanced functioning of other family members. In no instance did other family members show deterioration in their clinical or social adjustment when the index patient improved. Several parents of individually treated patients sought treatment for emotional difficulties they attributed to the stress of caring for the patient. In these cases, family therapy was offered, although a supportive casework approach was employed that offered a problem-solving approach that was less structured than the behavioral family therapy model.

CONCLUSIONS

The results of this controlled study of behavioral family therapy in the context of a comprehensive community management program for adults suffering from schizophrenia strongly support the efficacy of this approach. Family therapy proved more effective than individual supportive psychotherapy in preventing exacerbations of the florid symptoms of schizophrenia and subsequent hospital admissions. Exacerbations did occur in family-treated patients, but these tended to be less severe and relatively short-lived, seldom leading to major disruptions in the lives of patients of their families. Depression did not seem to be affected by the treatment approach. In addition to reducing exacerbations of schizophrenia, the family therapy seemed to contribute to a tendency for further improvement of schizophrenia symptoms from baseline, leading in many cases to total remission.

This enhanced clinical status was not achieved at the expense of social functioning. While it is possible to reduce stress and stimulation in an environment until the florid symptoms of schizophrenia diminish, in such a milieu, perhaps best illustrated by the back wards of the old mental asylums, persons suffering from schizophrenia tend to become apathetic and expressionless, and to lack the inclination to engage in constructive activities. Patients in this study seldom showed these negative features of schizophrenia, and those who received family therapy showed greater improvements in their social performance than the individual therapy cases.

These increments in social status did not readily lead to new jobs and relationships. A lack of rehabilitation resources made the transition to full functioning slower than might have been expected. However, during the second year of the study, these gains became more evident.

The care-giving potential of the family was harnessed to assist in the management of the index patient. This placed considerable stress on the family unit. Surprisingly few reported feelings overburdened by this rather onerous task. There was little evidence that the families suffered as a result of providing care for the index patients. On the contrary, family therapy appeared to relieve the burden associated with the index patient, whereas individual therapy was not accompanied by any such benefits.

The most notable change was a substantial reduction in the distress and dissatisfaction family members expressed about the index patients' social deficits. A more tolerant, supportive attitude with lowered, but realistic, expectations probably contributed to a lowering of family tension in families that participated in family therapy.

These benefits of the family approach remained clearly evident during the second year of treatment. Clinical stability was maintained, social functioning continued to improve, and families remained supportive. Major gains involved many patients' obtaining paid jobs, developing new relationships, leaving home, and participating as active, functional individuals in the community.

Behavioral family therapy appeared to represent a major advance in the community care of schizophrenia when combined with optimal drug therapy and effective case management. Furthermore, these benefits were achieved at a cost lower than the more traditional methods, and with an excellent level of consumer acceptance. The mechanisms for effectiveness are discussed in Chapter 15 in the hope that future refinements of the methods can be developed.

CHAPTER 14

CASE STUDIES

The data from the controlled study of family therapy presented in the previous chapter offered evidence that the family approach to treatment is highly effective. However, statistical tables cannot present a picture of the course of treatment of each family. In this chapter, we have selected several cases that illustrate both the benefits and the limitations that typify this therapeutic approach. To date, we have not seen any clear contraindications for this family therapy approach with adult schizophrenics who are living with their parents. However, some families undoubtedly benefit more than others and in no instance was the family therapy conducted without problems. We do not know precisely which aspects of the total intervention were major contributors to successful outcome and which were redundant. These few case reports may provide a more comprehensive presentation of the clinical efficacy of the approach.

CASE STUDY 1: MELVYN FRANCIS

This is a case report of a young black male who was living with his mother and two disturbed older siblings. It illustrates the limitations of the family approach where individuals who are the source of substantial family stress cannot be adequately involved in family problem solving. As a result the index patient continued to suffer exacerbations of his condition.

Melvyn Francis was a 19-year-old youngest son of black parents. He was born in Mississippi and came to Los Angeles after his father deserted the family when he was 4 years old. Since that time he had lived with his mother except for a few months when he shared an apartment with a friend.

He was referred from the Psychiatric Emergency Unit after his mother had taken him for treatment when he told her that there were people out about the neighborhood who were "confusing his mind" and making him do "crazy things." He had been locking himself in his room, not eating, and making threatening gestures to his mother's grandchildren and to passersby on the street. He believed that this presecution was led by a supervisor he did not like at a janitorial job he had held 3 years ago. He experienced "crazy" thoughts being placed in his mind, and believed that his thoughts were broadcast on radio and television, that the police would read his thoughts. He thought that his sister's two young children were part of the plot because they stared at him and made him "act crazy." He heard voices talking about him when there was nobody around. These experiences had come on over the past 2 years, and although his mother was aware that something was not right, she thought it best not to say anything to him, but to help him as much as she could.

Melvyn had been a slow learner throughout his schooling and had attended classes for the educationally handicapped. He had learned the rudiments of reading and writing upon leaving school, and was keen to continue his basic education subsequently. His IQ tests supported this observed intellectual deficit (Wechsler Adult Intelligence Scale: full scale = 63; verbal = 61; performance = 64). His persistent complaints of frontal headaches led to comprehensive neurological assessment, including EEGs, that failed to reveal any evidence of organic pathology.

Despite his limited intelligence, Melvyn got along well with people. He had a warm and friendly disposition, was polite and helpful, and shared a love of rock music with several friends. During high school, he had played guitar in a band and he enjoyed arranging and singing his own versions of hit tunes. He shared this interest with his mother and a 10-year-old niece.

Family Assessment

Mrs. Francis was a 49-year-old woman who had separated from her husband 16 years earlier. She had not maintained contact with her relatives in Mississippi, and had only one friend in Los Angeles—an alcoholic woman living across town. She accompanied Melvyn and her two grandchildren (10 and 6 years) to each clinic appointment during the stabilization phase, and appeared eager to speak for him. She referred to her children as "he" or "she," seldom using their first names, and often confusing the interviewer as to whom she was discussing.

Mrs. Francis spoke with a southern accent, and dressed in clean but shabby clothes with broken-down shoes. She addressed staff deferentially and smiled profusely. She expressed considerable gratitude for all assistance provided. Her 25-year-old daughter, Christy, and 23-year-old son,

Samuel, completed the six-person household. (Another brother, Jimmy, age 20, lived in his own apartment in Los Angeles.) They lived in a three-bedroom house in downtown Hollywood. The house was in poor repair with a gaping hole in the kitchen roof through which rain entered; tattered curtains were tacked across the windows, and furniture was stacked in corners in the living room. The house appeared clean. Mrs. Francis explained that the landlady had refused to repair the kitchen, and that Christy's boyfriend had "gone berserk" one night and had broken all the windows and ripped all the drapes, when under the influence of PCP.

The Camberwell Family Interview (CFI) with Mrs. Francis was characterized by an excessively dramatic presentation of the development of Melvyn's problems over the past 2 years. She was tearful and distraught as she recounted the gradual deterioration of his social functioning. She made three critical remarks regarding his symptomatic behavior, and several positive comments about his previous functioning. She appeared devoted to Melvyn and described many examples of her sacrifice for him. These included sitting up all night watching over him, rushing home from work when he complained of mild side effects of medication, and paying for all his support without seeking financial assistance: "I'm not the kind of mother that would just throw my kids aside"; "I just keep asking myself why? Why me?" "I've been going from doctor to doctor [to seek help for Melvyn], I've been all about town. You name the hospital—I've been to them. All times of night, my off days." This excessive maternal concern was considered inappropriate in the case of a 22-year-old man, who appeared capable of playing a greater role in the management of his condition, and was rated as 4 (marked) on the overinvolvement scale (0–5) of the CFI.

Although CFIs were not conducted with the other adult members of the Francis household, informal interviews revealed that they were highly critical of Melvyn and had considered him "crazy" since he was a child. They strongly disapproved of their mother's excessive concern and thought that he should be "sent to a home." Christy and Sam both worked full time. They paid no rent to Mrs. Francis and contributed little to the upkeep of the house.

Preliminary Behavioral Analysis

This family unit appeared to revolve around the mother. She considered all her children to be somewhat inadequate and to need her help to solve their problems. They, in turn, accepted this state of affairs and appeared to take advantage of her offers of assistance. So the mother, in the limited time she had a home, took on a constant round of cooking, cleaning, baby-sitting, taking people to doctors' appointments, and finding ways to pay the bills.

The assets of the family included the following: the mother's concern and loyalty to her children, her willingness to work hard to support the family, her good humor, and her ability to provide appropriate reinforcement for expected behavior; Melvyn's pleasant personality and willingness to help others; Christy's intelligence and concern for reducing family tension; Sam's physical strength and preference to keep to himself; the grandchildren provided company for family members who were not at work.

The most notable deficits appeared to be an almost total breakdown in family communication. People living under the same roof showed almost total disregard for one another. Problem issues were solved by the mother alone, with no problem-solving discussions with others. Very little mutual sharing was conducted on the emotional level either. The result of this lack of effective problem solving was inefficient and stressful handling of family finances and household chores. No family member had an adequate understanding of the nature of schizophrenia and its treatment. They all believed that if Melvyn could behave appropriately, he would get well. Most family members appeared to have competent social-skills repertoires, but did not display these skills within the family context.

Treatment Goals

The initial treatment goals included (1) to educate the family about schizophrenia; (2) to increase problem-solving discussions in the family; (3) to relieve the mother from the burden of sole responsibility for the well-being of all family members; (4) to establish shared responsibility for household management including rent payment and chores; (5) to increase the mother's social network; (6) to improve the mother's physical condition; and (7) to increase Melvyn's social activities outside the home.

Intensive Treatment Phase: 0-9 Months

At the beginning of family treatment Melvyn's mental status had improved. He was mildly guarded and suspicious but denied hallucinations, delusions, or thought interference. He complained of feeling low-spirited and was concerned about persistent frontal headaches and back pain. His mother had slipped at work and had twisted her neck. She had been off work for several weeks and complained that she was unable to eat. Melvyn was stabilized on 200 mg of chlorpromazine daily, which he took 75% of the time.

Although Christy and Sam were invited to attend the family sessions, they both refused to attend the morning sessions. They were both in bed, but not sleeping.

Melvyn described how schizophrenia had made it difficult for him to get along with his friends because he "couldn't understand what was going on." He said, "like when I wake up, I start dreaming. Like a nightmare." Mother complained that she couldn't cope any longer and would have to throw Melvyn and the "other ones" out. She appeared hostile and commented, "From now on, I'll care for Number One!" It was apparent that her major concern was Sam, who had been smoking PCP recently and behaving in a threatening manner. The therapist assisted in problem-solving this issue, and Mother told Sam that she would not permit him to stay in the home if he came home intoxicated.

Melvyn and his mother were attentive throughout the education sessions, but it was apparent they both absorbed only a small portion of the material presented. They appeared preoccupied by more pressing concerns. Mother returned to work, and shortly thereafter obtained a second job as a household cleaner. This left Melvyn alone for much of the day and evening. Family problem solving focused on increasing his social contacts through (a) a dating agency, (b) basic education courses, and (c) an activities center. He implemented plans concerning (a) and (b) competently and began attending classes in reading and math. It was evident that Melvyn and Mrs. Francis had excellent communication skills, but required prompting to use them appropriately. Mrs. Francis explained strategies she might use to get her landlady to fix the kitchen. Among the alternatives she and Melvyn considered were: make a direct request; seek legal aid; refuse to pay the rent; do it themselves and bill the landlady; do nothing and move out. They planned to ask the landlady, and if unsuccessful, to petition for legal assistance. Melvyn continued to progress. His symptoms were in complete remission and he was renewing aquaintance with several old friends. Mother prompted and praised him for these efforts. However, tension with his sister and brother continued. Attempts to schedule family meetings proved fruitless, but Mother attempted to discuss issues raised in family sessions with them both. Sam told his mother that he could not meet with a therapist because he would be sent to a drug program and lose his job. On one occasion, Melvyn and Sam had a fight after Sam had accused Melvyn of being crazy. Mother told him he would have to leave the house immediately. He refused to go and she did not attempt to enforce this plan. This illustrates the dilemma of the single mother when she attempts to set limits with adult children.

Melvyn and his mother both complained of tension headaches and other muscular pains. One session was devoted to strategies for relieving such aches through deep muscular relaxation. Both were pleased to find that some improvement accrued from this strategy.

After 3 months of family sessions, Melvyn was enjoying a modest social life, attending school, and suffering only occasional headaches. The kitchen roof had been repaired and Sam had paid some rent. Family problem solving continued to revolve about Mother, but communication had improved somewhat. On a few occasions Sam and Christy had joined Mother and Melvyn in brief family discussions, and had eaten meals together. Mother was able to express her displeasure about the lack of support she received from her children in managing the household and to make positive requests for their assistance. Unfortunately, even with the most assertive requests, compliance cannot be assured.

Melvyn had never dated before so several sessions focused on problem-solving issues such as arranging a date, conversations, planning transportation, and what to tell people about his illness. In addition to examining a variety of alternative strategies for dating behavior, Melvyn and his mother practiced a series of conversations in which Mother played the role of a date, and was able to give him excellent coaching from a woman's perspective. He made outstanding progress and was soon dating two attractive girls. However, Mrs. Francis had found that managing two jobs and a family was very stressful and she complained of increasing muscle aches and stomach pains. Arrangements for Melvyn to assist with chores were moderately successful, but he objected to having to bear the brunt of the work when his brother and sister contributed nothing. Mother was inconsistent in rewarding Melvyn for his efforts, and tended to focus on the occasions he forgot to take out the trash or wash the dishes. She was shown how to reinforce him every time he completed a task and to prompt him in a noncritical manner to comply with tasks. Melvyn paid for food and some utility bills from his SSI check. Now that he was dating he complained more bitterly that his brother and sister were not assisting in the household expenses and were eating his food. He nevertheless offered to paint the interior of the house.

The therapist arranged a special meeting that both Christy and Sam (belatedly) attended. Christy described her concerns about the family and the lack of cohesiveness; "Everybody goes his own way." She complained that Mother was "doing too much, worrying too much, and nagging too much." Sam agreed that she was working too hard. A plan was developed that called for Mother's stopping her second job, and for each household member to contribute an equal share of the rent and household expenses and to share the household chores. Mother gave up her second job and for 2 or 3 months the family finances were satisfactorily resolved. Family tension, which had been extremely high, was slightly reduced with each family member contributing to the expenses, although little headway was made in securing assistance with the chores. Mother found herself continuing to complete tasks that others had agreed to do.

In the seventh month of treatment, Melvyn began to experience difficulties with one of the girls he was dating. She became too demanding of his attention and began to ask more intimate questions about his illness. He decided that he would terminate the relationship and planned and rehearsed the way that he would go about this in the family session. He subsequently carried out this delicate social maneuver with panache. His mental status was clear of all symptoms at this time, but he had been complaining of some neuromuscular spasms and muscle stiffness thought to be related to the chlorpromazine, which had been reduced to 100 mg daily. However, 2 months prior to this it had been noted that his plasma level of chlorpromazine and serum prolactin had dropped dramatically, and reduced compliance was suspected. Two weeks later he complained that people seemed to be looking at him in the street and that people may be plotting against him. He stopped eating food at fast-food restaurants and had some difficulty getting to sleep. His medication was increased to 300 mg daily, and his symptoms had greatly decreased within 2 weeks. He stopped going to his classes at this point.

Follow-Up: 10-24 Months

The 9-month assessment overlapped this exacerbation period, at which time Melvyn had some mild florid symptoms and his social functioning was concomitantly reduced. This relapse caused little change in family behavior. Mrs. Francis treated Melvyn in a calm, understanding manner and prompted other members of the household to do likewise. Through family problem solving they found ways of distracting him from his thoughts. They encouraged him in his interest in music and going out to visit museums. When he began discussing his irrational fears of persecution, they listened to him and then changed the subject.

Melvyn's full remission was slow. His compliance with medication had continued to be poor throughout this episode. He later said that he had thought it might be poison and took very little. However, he did return to a full remission, and picked up his social activities where he had left off. Three months later he again reduced his medication intake and appeared headed for a further relapse. At that point, fluphenazine decanoate injections were instituted on a monthly basis and he again became asymptomatic. Throughout this period, family tension was high. Brother Sam had been smoking PCP regularly and stalked the house without speaking to anyone, like a time bomb about to explode. The room he shared with Melvyn reeked of the ethereal odor of angel dust. Melvyn showed signs of having been affected by this close contact. He was irritable, at times appeared confused, and his behavior was somewhat unpredictable. Sam spent all his money on drugs and ceased to pay his share of the rent. When Mrs. Francis attempted to speak to him, he became angry and she backed away fearing he may have become violent. Family sessions were devoted to planning ways of dealing with Sam and it was decided to tell him that he would have to leave. Upon receiving this ultimatum, he vowed to shape up and for a month he behaved more appropriately and payed some rent. However, this improvement proved short-lived. Attempts by family members and the therapist to engage him in therapy were met by the response, "He's [Melvyn] crazy, not me, I don't need no psychiatrist. It's not my problem."

Mrs. Francis was showing increasing signs of wear and tear. She complained of tension headaches, poor sleep, and appetite loss. Family therapy involved planning involvement and support for her outside the home. She described "putting on a brave face" in public and always listening to workmates' problems without sharing her own. She agreed to renew contact with an old friend whom, although an alcoholic, she could relax with and talk about problems. She made some effort to enhance her social-network support. She called her sister in Mississippi to discuss her troubles and began arranging a vacation there later in the year.

A few weeks later Melvyn learned that his SSI payments would be cut off. Within a week he became increasingly disturbed; he believed this event had been perpetrated by a group that was plotting his destruction and interfering with his mind. He believed that comments on television referred to him and that his thoughts were being controlled. He withdrew and spent much of his time lying on his bed, avoiding communication with anyone. He became more animated when friends visited and occasionally went out with them as if nothing were wrong. He explained that, like his mother, he too could "put on a happy face" despite feeling very miserable, and that he didn't like being alone. He refused oral medication, believing it to be poison. He continued to accept biweekly intramuscular fluphenazine (25 mg per dose). For the final 4 months of the study, Melvyn remained very suspicious and tense. He denied experiencing anything more than some ideation that people in the streets might be against him, but he was reluctant to leave the house and withdrew from his friends and former social activities.

During this time, family tension was extreme. For reasons that were never clarified, Melvyn's SSI was not reinstated and he was refused all welfare payments. He appealed these decisions but serious inefficiencies delayed the hearing for several months. His sister Christy moved out of the house without warning, taking her two children, and not paying any of the rent for the month. Sam began taking PCP again and refused rent payment. Without sufficient income to cover expenses, Mrs. Francis asked her landlady if she could postpone one month's rent payment. The landlady refused and took her to court to serve an eviction notice. Mrs. Francis sought legal assistance and won a claim against her landlady for irregularities in rental practices. Melvyn managed to stay calm during this stormy period, and helped his mother solve these difficult issues. However, in the few days after he and his mother moved out of the house into temporary accommodation in a run-down hotel, he became agitated and fearful. He described persecutory delusions and began receiving unpleasant messages from the TV. He was admitted to the hospital where he quickly and fully compensated. Two weeks prior to this he and his mother accompanied his therapist to a court hearing regarding his SSI, which resulted in subsequent reinstatement of his benefits.

At the 24-month assessment, Melvyn was in the hospital. His mother remained intrusive and overprotective, but was aware of this fault and attempted to correct her behavior and to prompt Melvyn to take the floor. She was able to express constructive criticism of his behavior, and the two showed competence in problem solving. During his hospital stay and after discharge, Melvyn returned to the excellent level of social functioning that had been seen during the early months of the program. Free of the two irresponsible siblings, Melvyn and his mother appear to cope very effectively.

This case illustrates the limitations of the behavioral family therapy approach in cases of massive family and environmental stress. The inability to involve the two major stress-producing family members in problem-solving discussions greatly limited the effectiveness of the treatment. The patient's low intelligence also contributed to less effective treatment and necessitated the mother's taking a somewhat more intrusive role than might have been ideal. It also reduced the impact of the education about schizophrenia. Melvyn never clearly understood the nature of his illness or the rationale for medication. He thus became prey to the problem of poor compliance that clearly contributed to the severity of two of his exacerbations. Together with the overwhelming stressors encountered, it was not surprising that the outcome was less than optimal. However, Mrs. Francis and Melvyn agreed that without the family intervention, the situation would have been much worse for them both. Mrs. Francis believed that she would have undoubtedly suffered a major mental illness herself and that the family therapy prevented serious deterioration in her health.

It could be argued that this situation might have been resolved by sending this patient to a residential care home outside of the family. However, during most of the time he spent at home, Melvyn was a tower of strength to his mother and she was grateful for his assistance. During the 2 years, Mrs. Francis gradually reduced her intrusiveness and prompted Melvyn's independent decision making. Emotional separation was already in progress, and physical separation was planned in the future. Substantial progress had been achieved on all the treatment goals, despite several setbacks. The changes in target symptoms, drug therapy, family tension, and life events are portrayed graphically on the life chart (Figure 14-1). This method of charting progress is recommended for the clinical therapist attempting to follow the patient's progress on several dimensions at the same time.

CASE STUDY 2: LAURA GUSTAVSON

This case illustrates the effectiveness of behavioral family therapy in a single-parent family where the index patient is a well-educated mature woman, with good premorbid personality traits. The major deficits appear to be her mother's lack of problem-solving skills, need for emotional support, and difficulty in expressing her feelings. (See Figure 14-2, pp. 372-373.)

Laura Gustavson was a 36-year-old only child, born in Los Angeles of Norwegian parentage. Both parents had immigrated from rural Norway as adults and had met in the United States during the Depression and married. The father, who had been a civil engineer and was deceased for 8 years, was by history shy and withdrawn as Laura had been during her childhood. Laura had been living with her elderly mother since 1976 when she was divorced by her Norwegian-American husband of 6 years. He had remarried and they maintained no contact. Laura expressed a continued desire for childbearing, and despaired at having no children. Following the separation, she moved back home with her mother. Although she continued to maintain an apartment, she in fact spent the majority of her time with her mother in a close relationship in the house where she had been reared.

Laura was first hospitalized in 1968 in a private general hospital at age 25 by the family internist for acute onset of catatonic mutism, bizarre posturing, and somatic delusions. Hospitalization was brief (1 week) and she responded quickly to neuroleptics and was discharged home to her family.

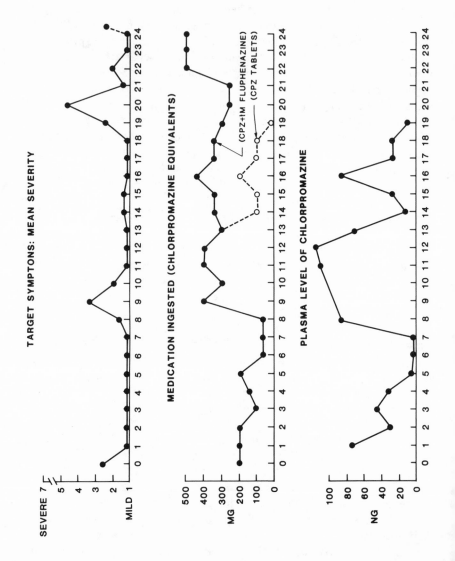

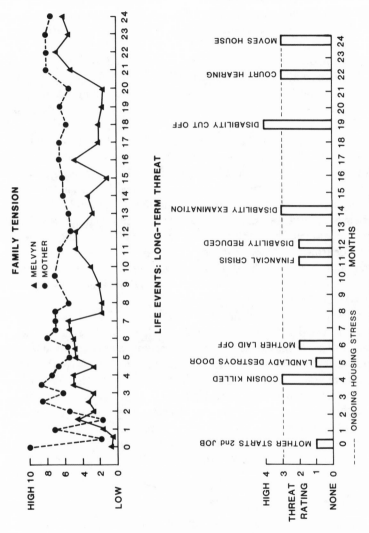

FIGURE 14-1. *Life chart: Melvyn Francis.*

FAMILY TENSION

▲ MELVYN
● MOTHER

HIGH 10
8
6
4
2
LOW 0

0 1 2 3 4 5 6 7 8 9 10 11 12 13 14 15 16 17 18 19 20 21 22 23 24

LIFE EVENTS: LONG-TERM THREAT

MOTHER STARTS 2nd JOB
COUSIN KILLED
LANDLADY DESTROYS DOOR
MOTHER LAID OFF
FINANCIAL CRISIS
DISABILITY REDUCED
DISABILITY EXAMINATION
DISABILITY CUT OFF
COURT HEARING
MOVES HOUSE

HIGH 4
THREAT 3
RATING 2
1
NONE 0

0 1 2 3 4 5 6 7 8 9 10 11 12 13 14 15 16 17 18 19 20 21 22 23 24
MONTHS

---- ONGOING HOUSING STRESS

365

Laura graduated from a prestigious private university with a BA in psychology and went on to obtain teaching credentials in elementary education. She was employed as a substitute teacher and later taught nursery school. However, for the past 10 years she has been employed in a secretarial capacity and she has maintained a positive work history although usually quitting jobs at the point she became symptomatic.

She is of middle socioeconomic status, has traveled to Europe many times, and has the highest premorbid adjustment of those in our study cohort. In the period 1978–1979 before entering our program, Laura was admitted five times to Los Angeles County/USC Psychiatric Hospital. Prior admissions were characteristically marked by agitation and sleep disturbance, delusions of persecution and grandeur, bizarre behavior, thought blocking and broadcast. Laura's florid symptoms responded quickly to neuroleptics after hospital admission. She then became depressed with flat affect. Once settled in the ward she expressed a desire to remain in the ward and be taken care of indefinitely. On several occasions she experienced distressing muscular spasms, including oculogyric crises that appeared associated with the drug therapy. This resulted in an aversion to neuroleptic drugs that led to her premature termination of medication shortly after each admission. On several occasions this had been followed abruptly by another exacerbation and readmission within a month or two of discharge.

Laura associated all of her hospital admissions with the stress of her job. She would usually develop ideas that people were talking about her or scrutinizing her behavior. She would become overly aroused and unable to concentrate or tend to task and would impulsively leave the job. Generally, there would be several days of interrupted sleep. Her last florid episode of schizophrenia was characterized by bizarre ideas about the need for breast feeding, the powers of "Amazon women," people resembling apples, and matters of her own sexuality. Thought derailment was marked, her speech was incoherent, and she postured in a prayer position. Her therapist guided her to the hospital for her index admission.

Family Assessment

Mrs. Gustavson was a 75-year-old widow who spoke with a Norwegian accent and was involved in Norwegian-American social activities. She lived comfortably in a house built in the 1940s for her husband and herself and appeared to have more than adequate financial resources left by her husband. She had always been a homemaker and particularly enjoyed gardening on the lakefront property. She was in remarkably good health despite episodic bouts of flu and viruses which were quite debilitating.

She had a good social support system and was involved in senior citizen activities including excursions and trips. Mrs. Gustavson had stopped driving and was thus dependent on Laura or others for transportation. This made it extremely difficult for her to get to the clinic or hospital at times of crises, and thus staff had had limited contact with Mrs. Gustavson prior to assessment for the project.

On the Camberwell Family Interview Mrs. Gustavson showed little criticism but much evidence of overinvolved, enmeshed behavior with her daughter, with marked distress during the interview. She was rated 4 (marked) on the rating of emotional overinvolvement. She broke down and cried several times during the interview and said she had no idea what her daughter's problem might be. She stated that she had never been told anything at all about the illness and she thought Laura was "just plain oversensitive." She knew nothing about medication or treatment despite Laura's multiple hospital admissions. She was bent on maintaining social appropriateness and was somewhat reluctant to describe some overinvolved behaviors which later became evident. Three months into treatment it was revealed that at times of stress Mother and Laura shared the same bed. Mrs. Gustavson showed marked lack of objectivity in attributing the problem to Laura's divorce of several years back. There was some evidence of dissatisfaction with Laura's functioning on household tasks, but Mrs. Gustavson seemed reluctant to make specific critical comments.

Preliminary Behavioral Analysis

This family unit seemed very concerned with creating an impression of having no substantial problems. In particular, they both went to considerable pains to minimize the significance of Laura's illness. Mother and daughter appeared very dependent on one another for support, but seemed frustrated by their mutual inability to adequately satisfy their independent emotional needs. In many ways Mrs. Gustavson seemed to expect Laura to replace her lost husband—as a companion, driver, person to provide structure, to accept her doting affection, and at times to share her bed. While Laura wanted her mother to help more constructively to regain the independence that she had lost after her divorce, she found comfort in her mother's overinvolved behavior, and avoided expressing this desire for independence. Thus their enmeshment was mutually reinforcing, and served as a means of coping with their respective fears and interpersonal deficits.

Laura demonstrated excellent conversation skills. Her speech was expressive and fluent, and she appeared graceful and poised. She had several close relationships, including a steady boyfriend. Her job skills were good, but she frequently worried excessively about her performance, fearing that she had made mistakes unless she received praise for each assignment completed. She was extremely sensitive to criticism in her social relationships as well. She avoided social contact with her workmates and worried that they gossiped about her. Because they generally came from a lower socioeconomic and educational background, she claimed they had few interests in common. She tended to lack confidence in her friendships and responded to relatively mild stress with tension and sleep difficulties. She constantly sought reassurance from her mother. She preferred structured work and social settings. Laura tended to take the first job that she was offered, regardless of its suitability. When she found she was unable to tolerate the situation any longer she would abruptly leave.

Mrs. Gustavson's assets included being a very attractive, gracious hostess, who kept her home and garden immaculately. She spent her days homemaking or shopping. She had a wide circle of friends she met regularly, and engaged in a busy schedule of social activities. Her mobility was restricted by arthritis and by her unwillingness to drive her car. Her ability to express both positive and negative feelings was deficient. She expressed feelings in a vague, circumstantial manner with poor eye contact and limited facial expressiveness. She frequently spoke for Laura in an intrusive manner. She tended to find fault with Laura's friends. While she intimated that she wanted Laura to do more household chores, she never asked Laura for help, and left little for her daughter to do, despite Laura's eagerness to assist. Mrs. Gustavson had negligible skills to cope with Laura's episodes of illness, and avoided contact with professional care givers.

Mother and daughter avoided problem-solving discussions and seldom collaborated on plans. They chatted freely about everyday matters. At times of crisis they both tended to panic and to call friends for help. As the crisis developed they avoided discussion in the face of obvious mounting difficulties.

Treatment Goals

The initial treatment goals included the following: (1) to ensure medication compliance and educate the patient and mother about how to cope with side effects; (2) to teach them about schizophrenia and the importance of medication; (3) to facilitate communication between mother and daughter about symptoms and warning signals of impending relapse; (4) to enhance communication with particular emphasis on mother's expression of all feelings and Laura's assertiveness with her mother and her friends; (5) to enhance Laura's job-seeking skills, especially her ability to gather specific information about potential jobs during a job interview and to be able to say "no" appropriately; (6) to structure family problem solving for day-to-day decision making; and (7) to continue to reinforce Laura's outside social and work activities and Mother's social life.

Intensive Treatment Phase: 0–9 Months

Laura was devoid of florid symptoms of schizophrenia when she began treatment although she had some definite symptoms of depression and anxiety. She had started a new full-time clerical job at the family's Norwegian Lutheran Church during the first week of the family treatment, and she was experiencing considerable stress on the job and was having difficulties learning new tasks and following instructions.

The first family education session was held in the home a week before Christmas. Both Laura and her mother asked thoughtful questions about theories of etiology. Laura was particularly interested in further explanations of dopamine pathways. Mrs. Gustavson seemed particularly relieved to be told something about the disorder. Laura tended to relate her condition to "insomnia" and was still experiencing some sleep disturbance. The second session about medication was particularly important, as Mrs. Gustavson did not have any grasp of the importance of medication and the relation of compliance to relapse. Laura was still having some side effects and we were able to discuss ways of minimizing them. She considered that some of her current depression and anxiety might be associated with the fluphenazine and at her next medication appointment she requested her doctor to change her to chlorpromazine. Mother and daughter were better able to understand the muscular spasms Laura had previously experienced. Mother had perceived these episodes as factitious disorders and had not been supportive of Laura's need for relief. Laura began to talk more openly about previous schizophrenic symptoms, and Mother agreed to become more involved in her medication regimen. The therapist did respond to a call from Laura on a Sunday afternoon within the first month of treatment, when she was experiencing side effects. She was instructed to take additional benzotropine which relieved the problem. Mother encouraged Laura to call the therapist which she did once or twice over the next 2 years when in crisis. Mother and daughter learned to identify the relationship of precipitating stress to onset of symptoms or prodromal warning signs of relapse.

In the sessions dealing with communication, Mother would make a lot of responses stating, "We feel . . ." or "I know Laura feels. . . ." Mother responded well to restructuring and was able to specify positive statements, requests, and some feeling statements very competently. Laura did an excellent job of demonstrating good, positive communication skills and was able to tell her mother that she liked positive feedback and wanted more of it. There was little evidence of family tension, and much generation of mutual affection and admiration in sessions. Both smiled and laughed as they mastered better skills. Laura was able to be appropriately assertive with her mother but was having some difficulties doing likewise with her boss. We took the opportunity to role-play such work-related situations in sessions. Mrs. Gustavson had some difficulties expressing negative feelings although Laura was able to do so easily. Mrs. Gustavson had a tendency to make guilt-inducing "should" statements, which was pointed out to her. She also would make statements that were mildly critical or denying Laura's feelings, such as "Oh, that's ridiculous. You shouldn't feel that way." These were likewise redirected.

A stressful life event with which Laura had to cope was her mother's 3-day holiday to Las Vegas. She was extremely apprehensive about her mother's departure and being alone in the house. Contingency contracting between mother and daugther problem-solved this issue prior to Mrs. Gustavson's departure. Every possible disaster that could befall Laura was listed and she described the coping steps she would use to respond to each contingency. Laura then planned her own 3-day schedule, and her mother agreed to call her from Las Vegas and to prepare food that could be readily served when Laura arrived home from work. Laura made evening plans during her mother's absence. Following Mrs. Gustavson's return, the therapist was invited to dinner after a session and reviewed positive coping efforts. During dinner Mrs. Gustavson and Laura expressed much interest in the therapist's background and personal life, a feature noted frequently during home visits to many families.

By the sixth session, Laura was stable on chlorpromazine, had successfully endured a brief separation from mother, and was accepting her diagnosis of schizophrenia and talking openly about it.

The following week, the therapist found Mrs. Gustavson bedridden and Laura in considerable distress about her mother's health. Two topics were elicited for potential resolution—ongoing maintenance for yard and garden, which had become too great a burden on Mrs. Gustavson even in good health; and the problem of feeding 16 black feral cats which had taken over the yard like the birds in the Hitchcock movie. Mother and daughter were able to resolve how to get rid of the cats by using the model to come up with possible solutions and then implementing a step-by-step plan which took 3 weeks to complete. The task called for contracting two community agencies to enlist cooperation in trapping the cats and removing them to a shelter.

Laura was able to express her concern about her mother's health and her fear of what would happen when her mother died. She was also able to express negative feelings about her mother's not getting to the doctor for treatment of an ear infection.

The family was generally coping with day-to-day events very well, with efforts at problem solving between sessions. They worked on the yardwork problem themselves and at the 3-month assessment were able to demonstrate excellent problem-solving abilities and greatly improved communication.

Around the time of the 3-month assessment, Laura lost her job, stopped sleeping, and after her chlorpromazine was increased to 300 mg reported more side effects. She quickly got a new job in a probate office and stabilized once again on 200 mg chlorpromazine.

From 3 to 9 months, the family situation remained stable and supportive with good problem-solving efforts. They had regular family meetings to practice problem solving between sessions. Laura adjusted well to the new job and began to lead a more active social life: dating, attending a church group, going to social clubs and dances. During this time, her mother went away several more times and Laura coped quite well. The home was burglarized twice and they decided to have an alarm system installed for protection.

An interesting aspect of Laura's psychiatric presentation was that she began to disclose symptoms that she had never divulged before. These included delusions of being the Virgin Mary, experiencing the Immaculate Conception, thought insertion, and auditory hallucinations. Laura also described current experiences of transient psychotic symptoms, particularly on the job, which included persecutory ideas and thought control. She also had periods of sleep disturbance usually attributed to overstimulation, or social stress with her boyfriend or on the job. Another major stress occurred when Laura had to deal with the arrival of houseguests from Norway who would come and stay at her home for extended periods of time. This situation was perhaps even more stressful on Mrs. Gustavson, who had difficulty setting limits on their stays. A major focus of treatment was to help Mrs. Gustavson cope with the visiting relatives, whom she became highly critical of in her distress.

Another area that emerged in the family sessions was the dating behavior of both mother and daughter. Mrs. Gustavson had several male acquaintances who seemed to be actively showing interest in seeing her. Laura seemed to be somewhat threatened by her mother's suitors. On the other hand, Mrs. Gustavson appeared critical of Laura's boyfriends. They resolved this issue with guidance from the therapist. A contingency contract was established where mother agreed to allow Laura to cook dinner

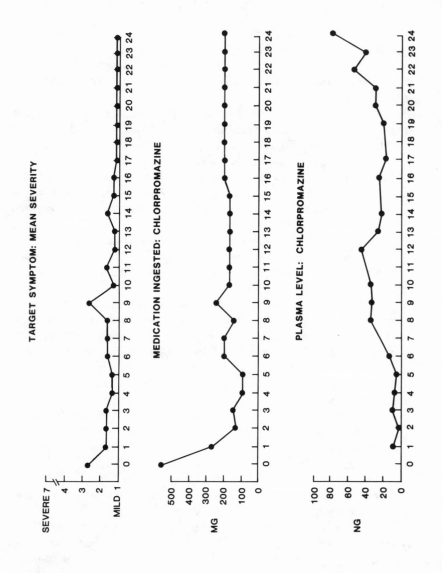

TARGET SYMPTOM: MEAN SEVERITY

MEDICATION INGESTED: CHLORPROMAZINE

PLASMA LEVEL: CHLORPROMAZINE

372

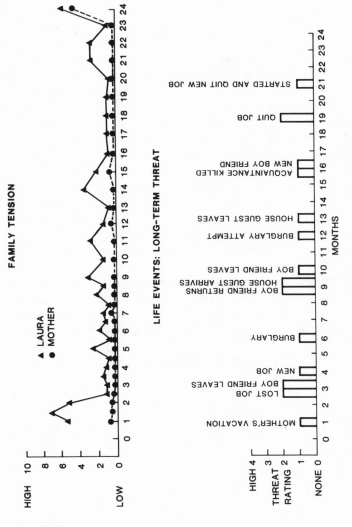

FAMILY TENSION

HIGH 10

8

6

4

2

LOW 0

0 1 2 3 4 5 6 7 8 9 10 11 12 13 14 15 16 17 18 19 20 21 22 23 24

▲ LAURA
● MOTHER

LIFE EVENTS: LONG-TERM THREAT

HIGH 4

THREAT 3
RATING 2

1

NONE 0

0 1 2 3 4 5 6 7 8 9 10 11 12 13 14 15 16 17 18 19 20 21 22 23 24

MONTHS

MOTHER'S VACATION

LOST JOB
BOY FRIEND LEAVES
NEW JOB

BURGLARY

BOY FRIEND RETURNS
HOUSE GUEST ARRIVES
BOY FRIEND LEAVES

BURGLARY ATTEMPT
HOUSE GUEST LEAVES

ACQUAINTANCE KILLED
NEW BOY FRIEND

QUIT JOB

STARTED AND QUIT NEW JOB

FIGURE 14-2. *Life chart: Laura Gustavson.*

373

and entertain her friends without hovering over her, and Laura would excuse herself after dinner when her mother had men friends visit. This arrangement worked well for both parties.

Follow-Up: 10–24 Months

Laura and Mrs. Gustavson continued to function well during the follow-up phase. Laura continued to lead an active social life. When her boyfriend departed for a long trip to Europe she spent more time with her girlfriends, dated other men, and engaged in a wide range of interests. She had several close female friends, some of whom had mental illnesses. One of these friends stopped her medication and was readmitted. Laura had difficulty talking about her illness with others. She was quick to recognize that several of her friends were on medication and had psychiatric illnesses, but was reluctant to reveal her situation even when queried by a boyfriend who she knew was on lithium. The educational material was reviewed on several occasions and Laura continued to describe occasional symptoms in the family sessions. At one point after a year of treatment, Mrs. Gustavson asked whether Laura could stop medication. Laura told her mother in no uncertain terms that she knew that she needed the medication, and further review of the handouts on neuroleptic maintenance helped Mrs. Gustavson understand Laura's reasoning. Laura experienced bouts of depression from time to time which were usually related to her job or personal relationships. Mrs. Gustavson remained supportive in helping Laura cope with her feelings of emptiness and sadness at these times.

After 1½ years in the program, Laura and her mother took a vacation together and shortly thereafter Laura left the job which she had held in the probate office for over a year. They had planned that she would take the rest of the summer off to be able to enjoy yet another distant relative visiting from Norway. This time, Mrs. Gustavson was able to set a limit of 1 month on the stay, and they both planned activities to entertain their visitor. This proved to be far less stressful and more enjoyable than previous experiences, and Laura was extremely supportive of her mother's needs.

Soon after the departure of the cousin, Laura took a series of temporary jobs, several of which she left abruptly. Mrs. Gustavson remained low-key and supportive of Laura's difficulty in finding permanent employment. She no longer associated Laura's termination of employment with relapse or need for hospitalization. They continued to develop strategies for seeking employment. Laura continued to maintain an active social life which included dating, seeing friends, attending classes and singles groups, as well as church and recreational activities. The boyfriend of long standing returned to Los Angeles and they resumed their relationship. At the end of 2 years, the therapist had dinner with Laura and Mrs. Gustavson over the Christmas holidays. They expressed great appreciation for the program. Mrs. Gustavson was particularly effusive about the importance of the home visits because that demonstrated to them how much we cared.

CASE STUDY 3: PAMELA KURIHARA

This is a case report of a young Japanese-American woman who had been floridly psychotic for over a year before finally obtaining effective treatment. Her recovery was complicated by a severe postpsychotic depression that eventuated in a suicide attempt by drug overdose. This case also illustrates the need to explore and understand the cultural factors that might bear on family coping under very stressful circumstances. (See Figure 14-3, pp. 380–381.)

Pamela Kurihara was a 22-year-old, single Japanese-American woman who was referred to the Family Aftercare Program following discharge from the psychiatric unit at the Los Angeles County/ USC Medical Center. Her life had been psychiatrically uneventful until about 18 months prior to admission. At about that time, a 2-year-long romantic relationship ended which left Pamela with pervasive feelings of anger, guilt, and despair that she would never be successful in love. Over the next few months she became increasingly withdrawn from her family and friends, sinking steadily into frank psychosis. She became very paranoid, saw significance in patterns of variously colored cars passing by her house, and came to feel that an "experiment" was being conducted to see "what it would take" to drive her crazy. She began believing that the television and radio were giving her special messages instructing her on how to become more "spiritually pure." By 6 months prior to admission, her parents had persuaded her to see a psychiatrist, who elected to treat Pamela with psychotherapy alone. She continued to deteriorate, eventually coming to believe that her grandmother, who lived at home, had "healing powers" and that she should stop eating in order to become "spiritually healed." She lost 20 pounds and was finally brought to the hospital by her parents in a cachectic, disheveled state, markedly hypoactive, staring, and unresponsive to questioning.

In the hospital Pamela was started on neuroleptic medication and gradually became less withdrawn and more responsive to her surroundings.

She was discharged on 40 mg per day of haloperidol. When first seen in the Family Aftercare Program, she was still quite floridly psychotic. She complained of feeling like she was "floating" and "not well grounded to reality." She was experiencing both auditory and visual hallucinations, thought broadcasting, and thought blocking. She was preoccupied with notions regarding the "spiritual realm" and "spiritually correct" ways to talk (certain words were good to use, other words were bad to use, and so forth). She displayed severe rigidity and akathisia from her neuroleptic medication.

Pamela the youngest of three children. Her father was born in Japan and was employed as a truck mechanic. Pamela's mother was born in the United States to immigrant parents from Japan. Her oldest brother died in an automobile accident at the age of 14 (when Pamela was 8). The other brother, in the wake of this tragedy, vowed that the family would never mourn his death. For the next 10 years, he was involved in gang activities, had many contacts with the police, and ultimately died of a drug overdose at the age of 22 in an apparent suicide.

Pamela's premorbid adjustment had been good. She was a good student in high school, had attended one semester of college, and had been quite active in extracurricular activities. With the exception of the months immediately preceding her hospital admission, Pamela had always had an adequate number of close friends.

Family Assessment

During the pretreatment family assessments, it became clear that the entire family was quite dysfunctional. Mr. Kurihara was anxious and quite emotionally distant from Pamela and her mother. He put in long hours at work and spent most evenings reading or watching television. He was unhappy with his job and seemed generally somewhat depressed. It was difficult to interview him and to engage him during family sessions owing to his taciturn nature.

Pamela's mother was much more animated and engaging. Not surprisingly, in light of the tragic family history, she tended to be somewhat overprotective and emotionally overinvolved with respect to Pamela. There was a strong sense of this being a "doomed" family. A certain fatalism prevailed in the family: the two sons had died tragically, and then the final surviving offspring developed a debilitating, seemingly unrelenting, psychotic mental illness. The initial passivity in coping with this floridly psychotic member bore testimony that this was in a very real sense a "dying family."

Results on the pretreatment Camberwell Family Interview (CFI) with Mr. Kurihara revealed that he had little apparent understanding of the effects of Pamela's schizophrenic illness on her overall adjustment. He was critical of her for not continuing her college studies and for quitting a job she had had as a cashier. He was also critical of her for being up all hours of the night, clanging pots and pans, and so forth. In general, when asked to talk about Pamela's recent, at that time, behaviors and symptoms, he was reserved and uncommunicative, made no positive remarks, and conveyed a sense of being emotionally quite cut off and distant from her.

Mrs. Kurihara's CFI revealed her to be highly distressed and concerned over the welfare of her daughter. She was moderately overinvolved and overprotective of Pamela, but obviously not without cause. She expressed significant critical feelings, primarily directed at her daughter's symptomatic behaviors. It bothered her greatly that Pamela was up all night and seemingly never slept. She shared her husband's concern over Pamela's declining social and work adjustment. As Pamela became increasingly negativistic and mute in the months prior to admission, her mother became increasingly distressed. Pamela eventually stopped talking altogether and would sit motionless for long periods of time. Mrs. Kurihara found and read Pamela's abnormal psychology textbook in order to learn what was the matter and what to do about it. In addition to these illness-related problems, she had long been critical of Pamela for leaving doors unlocked and drinking wine in the house. She was also critical of her general "messiness."

It further emerged during the mother's CFI that there were certain family prohibitions that affected the family's ability to cope with their daughter's illness. The father had always disliked arguments, so there was a family rule against arguing or quarreling in front of him. He also did not like to hear about problems from his wife, and when she did bring things up he did not have much to say. The net result was a family constellation characterized by an emotionally distant father/husband and a mildly overinvolved mother–daughter relationship.

Preliminary Behavioral Analysis

Analysis of the family's style of interaction during the pretreatment behavioral assessments and during the early family therapy sessions indicated several possible areas for intervention. The family members were generally uncommunicative, especially Pamela and her father. Negative feelings, in particular, were not communicated very frequently or very well. Pamela's parents led a pretty austere existence, with few pleasant activities and little socializing with friends and relatives. Pamela's mother, while easily the most engaging and talkative member of the family, was inclined toward a rather guilt-inducing style of communication with Pamela (e.g., "Pam, don't you think it is bad to drink alone in your apartment?"). On the positive side, there was much genuine concern, especially on the part of the mother, for Pamela's well-being, and there was a sense of a large reservoir of good will and openness to whatever recommendations might arise out of participation in family therapy. Theirs was a respectable and respecting, upright, middle-class family that was quite at a loss over how to cope with this family crisis.

Treatment Goals

The goals of treatment, as initially formulated, were: (1) educate the family regarding the nature, course, and treatment of schizophrenia; (2) increase the amount of conversation in general; (3) reduce the frequency of guilt-inducing remarks and teach the family more effective ways to communicate negative feelings; (4) overcome the family's passivity and get them activated in coping with their individual and collective problems; (5) get the parents more involved in activities outside of the family (especially Pamela's mother); and (6) improve the family's ability to identify sources of stress and cope more effectively with them.

Intensive Treatment Phase: 0–9 Months

The early family therapy sessions proceeded smoothly and productively. In the initial educational sessions, Pamela was able to describe her psychotic experience clearly to her parents, who responded with understanding, sympathy, and decreased critical attitudes. All three were very interested in the didactic materials and rapidly assimilated them. There was an initial assumption on all of their parts that Pamela's having developed schizophrenia meant there was something wrong with her deep down inside—some defect in her personality—a weakness that caused her to become psychotic. This notion was refuted vigorously. The therapist told them that the only defect she had was to have been unlucky enough to have been born with a biological vulnerability to develop schizophrenic symptoms under high levels of stress. The point was made repeatedly that schizophrenia is an illness that Pamela *has*, not something that she is.

By the second month of family therapy, Pamela was free of psychotic symptoms for the first time in 2 years. She still believed in the existence of the "spiritual realm" and believed her psychotic experiences to have been real, but these experiences had stopped and she was happy about that because she was much more relaxed and able to converse with other people more freely. The family made some progress in communicating their feelings more effectively, at least during the sessions. They were quick to pick up the structured problem-solving method and, on several occasions, had spontaneous family meetings between sessions to do problem solving on emergent issues.

After 3 months of treatment a new problem emerged—a rather severe postpsychotic depression. Although free of psychotic symptoms, Pamela felt that her mind did not "work as well any more." She complained that her head felt "half dead." Whether this was mild thinking problems related to schizophrenia or a side effect of her medication (which, by this time, had been decreased to 200 mg of chlorpromazine) was unclear. She also felt that she was unattractive, had little to offer anyone, and despaired of ever again being able to work or find someone that she might love and eventually marry. As Pamela became more depressed, her parents seemed to become more passive. Problem-solving discussions in sessions focused on coping with side effects, scheduling pleasant activities, and coping generally with depression.

Things continued to get worse and Pamela eventually overdosed on her chlorpromazine and over-the-counter sleeping pills. She stated that life was a struggle and she simply did not want to make as much of an effort as would be required to straighten it out. The attempt was unsuccessful owing to her vomiting up all of the pills. Hospitalization was not required. There was a family session the next day, during which both parents were angry at Pamela for "taking the easy way out." It became clear that in one sense, she was acting out the entire family's depression. When asked his feelings, Mr. Kurihara stated simply, "She's the last one." When asked what it would be like if Pamela were dead, the mother stated, "We're already half dead." It became clear that life was somewhat of a struggle for all three of them and had been since the death of the first son 14 years previously. Everyone agreed that the family had never been the same after that tragedy.

Two weeks later, Pamela's mother phoned the therapist and told him that Pamela had purchased a quantity of sleeping pills. The therapist, recognizing that the family was having a very difficult time mobilizing, told her to find the pills and get rid of them. Although she initially felt constrained about searching through Pamela's things, with the therapist's admonition, she waited until her daughter left and then virtually took her room apart looking for the pills. She eventually found them and flushed them down the toilet. This constituted the first strong action that communicated to Pamela that her mother did not want to see her die and would fight against that outcome. Upon learning of this, Pamela became

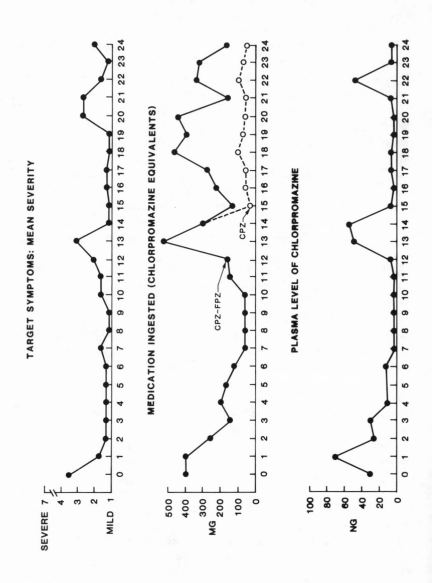

TARGET SYMPTOMS: MEAN SEVERITY

MEDICATION INGESTED (CHLORPROMAZINE EQUIVALENTS)

PLASMA LEVEL OF CHLORPROMAZINE

380

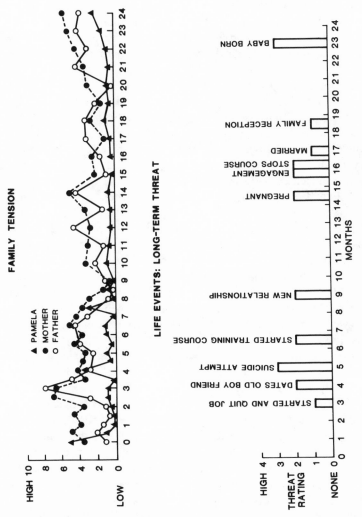

FIGURE 14-3. *Life chart: Pamela Kurihara.*

381

very angry at her mother, declaring, "Now I'll just have to do it sooner. I can't risk having you discover where I hide the pills from now on." Attempts to mobilize the father at the next family session were fruitless. When asked how he would feel if Pamela killed herself, he replied, "In some cultures they sacrificed their best people and it was an honor to die young." He seemed quite resigned to her demise and there was a quality of already beginning to do his grief work prior to her death. Pamela's reaction to this was to say, "Well, at least I don't have to feel guilty about doing this."

At this point, the prognosis did not look good at all, and, when Pamela soon thereafter acquired more contraband sleeping pills, the therapist directed the parents to bring her to the hospital against her wishes. She then bolted into her bedroom, grabbed about half of her pills (15 Quaaludes), and swallowed them. Her parents then drove her to the emergency room where she had her stomach lavaged and was shortly thereafter transferred to the psychiatric unit.

During Pamela's 9 days in the hospital several therapeutic strategies were undertaken. Therapy sessions with her parents were aimed at mobilizing them as a resource for Pamela. Distinctions were drawn between the deaths of her brothers and her situation. The therapist emphasized that the current problem was depression, not schizophrenia, that this depression would be time-limited, and that there was no reason that Pamela could not recover from this and lead a normal, fulfilling life. Meanwhile, cognitive behavioral interventions were being employed with Pamela, as well as starting her on antidepressant medication (imipramine, 150 mg/day).

The weeks following discharge proved to be a turning point. Pamela was still significantly depressed, and the therapist used the family sessions to get the family to manage the daughter much as if she were still in the hospital. Medications were kept and administered by Mrs. Kurihara. Each evening Pamela and her parents planned out the next day's activities. Pamela ate all of her meals with her parents, as well as having morning coffee with her mother. Pamela agreed to permit her mother to check on her in her room at periodic intervals. At the same time, family sessions focused on the problems and feelings of hopelessness that all three of them were experiencing. Problem-solving sessions addressed issues such as planning a weekend family vacation, the father's dissatisfaction with his job, the mother's desire for the parents to get out to visit friends more often, and Pamela's efforts to reestablish some of her old friendships. Pamela's father became somewhat more open to his wife and daughter bringing up problem areas for discussion. Her mother decided to go back to work part time.

As Pamela's parents began to function somewhat more effectively, Pamela began to feel her energy level and willingness to cope return to normal. She began seeing her old friends and enrolled in a 2-year college program to learn to become a dental hygienist. At the 9-month point in treatment she met a man she began dating regularly. During these months, Pamela occasionally experienced mild exacerbations of her schizophrenic illness. She would feel as though the radio were talking to her and giving her messages aimed at promoting her spiritual growth. Interestingly, when psychotic symptoms returned, she always informed the therapist. At these times, she professed belief in the reality of the "spiritual realm," but stated that she knew the therapist believed these experiences to be symptoms, so she would let him know.

Follow-Up: 10–24 Months

At the 1-year point, Pamela had a minor relapse of schizophrenia. Over a period of a few days, she became increasingly preoccupied with her delusional system. One day in class she felt that it was "spiritually correct" to sit perfectly still in silence. Eventually paramedics were called, who took her to a nearby hospital emergency room from which she eloped. She walked to her car, drove over to the clinic, and told her therapist what had happened. She was willing to increase her medication and a family meeting was convened to problem-solve the matter. The family again structured things so that the home was essentially like a day treatment program for the next 2 or 3 days and the symptoms quickly remitted without hospitalization. Pamela's boyfriend stuck with her throughout this episode and continued to be very supportive. She returned to college classes (where people had assumed she had suffered some kind of seizure) and completed the semester.

Despite some ups and downs, Pamela generally did quite well during the second year of treatment. Her boyfriend joined the family sessions and the family conducted their own problem-solving discussions effectively. She and her boyfriend got married and eventually had a baby boy. Pamela decided not to continue into the second year of the dental hygienist training program. Her parents became proud grandparents. Her father left the job he didn't like and went into semiretirement, bought a used diesel truck, and made plans to develop a part-time trucking business. Pamela's mother continued her job, which she greatly enjoyed. Pamela and her husband, who had a well-paying full-time job, began a home-based part-time business selling Amway products. Although Pamela continued to have episodic problems with medication side effects, feelings of depression, and transient psychotic symptoms, she continued to maintain the considerable gains she had made in her social, educational, and marital adjustment. The baby son was named after the family therapist.

CASE STUDY 4: GEOFFREY DANNER

This case concerns a mother and son who had a long history of poor communication and limited collaborative problem solving. These stressful conflicts were heightened by the father's recent death. The benefits of family management were evident in the improved course of the index patient's illness and the enhanced effectiveness of family coping. (See Figure 14-4, pp. 390–391.)

Geoffrey Danner was a 30-year-old younger son of Mexican-American parents. His mother was of Hispanic descent and his father was proudly German. Both parents spoke fluent Spanish and German, but discouraged Geoffrey from using either language.

He was admitted to the hospital 2 months after his father died from chronic emphysema and heart failure. Geoffrey became sullen and depressed after his father's death. He felt sure that his father could have been saved by better medical care, and threatened to sue the doctors. He lost faith in the family's Jehovah's Witness religion because he could not reconcile his father's death with a "good" God. He began to hear voices accusing him of being a Nazi criminal and he was convinced that the police were going to arrest him and put him on trial. It appeared to him that World War II was still in progress and that everyone in the United States wanted to kill him. He felt he was a special person, one of the original settlers of Los Angeles, and that his father had probably been one of the oldest persons in the country. He thought the United Nations was part of a Bible prophecy and had completely fallen to Satan. Most of the voices came from inside his head—"It was like my head was an amplifier." He experienced thoughts being placed in his mind through television that were not his own thoughts. At times he felt very depressed with what was happening to him, but this mood was not persistent. He stayed in the hospital for a 17-day compulsory stay after which he left against medical advice, somewhat improved, but still floridly symptomatic. He was receiving both oral and intramuscular fluphenazine medications.

Geoffrey had suffered from episodic schizophrenia since the age of 20 and had been admitted to the hospital prior to the present admission. All episodes had been characterized by auditory hallucinations and paranoid ideation. Although medication had been prescribed his compliance with aftercare treatment had been very poor. In the 2 years prior to the index episode he had been grossly impaired with persistent auditory hallucinations and paranoid ideation, and he spent most of his time in his room sleeping and listening to music. He had worked for 4 months 2 years earlier as a casual delivery driver for a Cadillac car merchant.

Although the index episode was the only exacerbation that had been precipitated by a major life event, Geoffrey associated all of his hospital admissions with family pressures. His early development had been unremarkable until early adolescence when he developed a severe renal disease at age 11. He changed from being a cheerful, friendly child to a moody, irritable adolescent. He missed long periods of school and withdrew from his friends because he was unable to join in physical activities. On one occasion his mother refused to consent to a blood transfusion for him; a court order was obtained, without which he would have died. He never forgave his mother "for leaving me to die."

His initial episode of schizophrenia began when he was 19. He had graduated from high school, and was attempting to get a job and to reenter social activities with his peers. They were all experienced sexually, and he had had very limited contact with girls. He became very anxious and confused. He began to masturbate regularly but felt guilty. When he had intercourse with a girl he felt that was wrong also. He believed his religious parents would be horrified by sexual activities and could not talk to them. He felt extreme pressure, and after abandoning his girlfriend he began to hear accusatory voices inside his head. After barricading himself in his room he was taken to the hospital by the police where he responded rapidly to neuroleptic treatment and was discharged in 3 weeks. He found that the drugs he was prescribed either made him very nervous and unable to sleep or knocked him out, so he did not take any medication. He had four further episodes that were very similar. In the 2 years prior to the study he was hospitalized once, but had persistent auditory hallucinations and paranoid symptoms throughout. He spent most of his time in his room and seldom conversed with his parents.

Family Assessment

Mrs. Danner was a 51-year-old woman who spoke with a Spanish accent. She attended each clinic appointment with her son during the period immediately after his hospital discharge and appeared very concerned about the side effects of his medication. During the 6 weeks of stabilization she made two emergency visits herself to express her fears about how dangerous he was, and that he would not take his medication and subsequently might kill her. He had never threatened her or anyone in the past. When she was interviewed on scheduled clinic visits she spoke in a whisper so that he would not overhear her conversations and "get violent."

Mrs. Danner spoke in a similarly guarded fashion during her Camberwell Family Interview (CFI). Her interview was remarkable for the number of positive comments (13) she made about Geoffrey. They were mixed with fearful comments, many of which were hostile and rejecting. On the one hand she described him as smart, loving, honorable, talented, witty, artistic, kind, and cheerful, and on the other as irritable, bad-tempered, violent, domineering, frightening, noncommunicative, resentful, and dangerous. She described her sense of inadequacy in dealing with Geoffrey now that her husband had died, and her own difficulties in coping. She made numerous threats to leave Geoffrey if he began to get ill again. For the week after her husband's death she had left the house and gone to stay with friends, without letting Geoffrey know where she was. She made several remarks about his "dangerous illness." Mrs. Danner indicated that she frequently lost her temper, that she was "a nagger" but "tried not to be." She complained that Geoffrey did not communicate his feelings with her, that he tended to withdraw and did not converse with her.

She made five critical remarks and was rated as moderately overinvolved (3) on the scale of emotional overinvolvement (0–5).

Preliminary Behavioral Analysis

This family unit was in a state of transition at the time of initial assessment. The father had been dead for less than 3 months and the mother appeared overwhelmed by the responsibility of Geoffrey's care. The assets observed included Geoffrey's intelligence, creative ability, sensitivity, and verbal ability; his mother's ability to see his positive qualities, her close involvement with her church, awareness of her temper and nagging behavior, and her close and regular contact with family and friends. Both Geoffrey and his mother appeared to recognize that he had an illness that required careful treatment. Both appeared to be able to communicate their needs to others, and both were articulate.

Their observed deficits included Geoffrey's irritability, long-standing feelings of rejection, poor compliance with long-term medical treatment, stubbornness, withdrawal when ill, and lack of social skills—particularly the ability to express both positive and negative feelings in close relationships.

Geoffrey and his mother spent a large amount of time together. Their main activities outside the home involved attending several hours of church functions together. Neither had worked for almost 10 years. Geoffrey spent considerable periods of the day and night listening to music, and had attempted to write songs on the piano his mother had bought for him 2 years ago.

Mrs. Danner's observed deficits included her irritability and nagging, intrusive behavior, tendency to infantilize her son, lack of understanding of schizophrenia with a tendency to lable all undesirable behavior as illness-related, and her rigidly held religious beliefs.

Together they seldom attempted any joint problem solving, and everyday conversation was strained. The father's recent death highlighted these difficulties and the family atmosphere was extremely tense.

The Danners lived in a small two-bedroom bungalow in the East Los Angeles barrio. Two old trucks in the yard were reminders of the father's small fruit-selling business. Neighbors peered at visitors from across the street and police patrolled the streets frequently. The house was neat and pleasantly decorated. Geoffrey had chosen the decor and the furnishings, and although his mother was pleased, he expressed some dissatisfaction that the colors were not quite those he had intended.

Treatment Goals

The initial treatment goals were as follows: (1) ensure patient's compliance with medication; (2) allay Mother's fears about schizophrenia through education; (3) increase appropriate communication of feelings between mother and son; (4) reduce Mother's intrusive behavior and redirect her attention to interests other than the index patient's, perhaps encouraging her to take a job; (5) establish family problem-solving discussions; and (6) increase Geoffrey's independent activities outside the home, both vocational and social.

Intensive Treatment Phase: 0–9 Months

Geoffrey was free of most florid symptoms when he began family treatment. He was taking 150 mg of chlorpromazine before bed on 50% of occasions. He had some feelings of sadness and guilt about his father's death. His thoughts frequently turned to memories of his father and questioning why he had died. He was disillusioned with religious explanations of the rationale for death, particularly the fundamentalist Adam and Eve story. Mrs. Danner appeared to have more fully resolved her grief and derived support from her church and her unquestioned beliefs.

Both mother and son were highly attentive and interested in the educational sessions. They were amazed at how well the description of symptoms and the relationship between stress and relapses fitted their own experiences. The distinction between the illness and personality variables was partially grasped by the mother, who learned to recognize the warning signals of potential relapse. Geoffrey accepted the importance of continued medication and asked his mother to assist him by putting out his tablets every evening and prompting him should he forget. His compliance became 100% and remained excellent for the next 2 years. Although her fears were somewhat reduced she continued to worry about the potential of violence if Geoffrey were to relapse. Geoffrey feared that she would call the police if he lost his temper, and the therapist problem-solved this issue with them. It was planned that if Geoffrey appeared threatening or seemed to be relapsing that his mother would call the therapist and discuss the best solution. Subsequently Geoffrey agreed to call himself if he experienced any difficulties. His mother made three calls during the first 9 months at times when she and Geoffrey had argued. She was reassured that these episodes were not illness-related, and proceeded to treat them as family problems.

Geoffrey expressed his gratitude at learning the nature of his illness, read over the handout materials several times, and referred back to them on several subsequent occasions. He was fascinated with the proposed relationship between stress and symptoms, and carefully monitored his stress levels throughout.

The serious disturbance in communication between mother and son presented a considerable challenge. Both avoided discussing their feelings. Geoffrey intially refused to communicate positive feelings toward his mother, citing his Hispanic acculturation as a reason. When it was pointed out that communication skills are relevant in a wide range of interpersonal relationships including work, friendships, and heterosexual relationships, he became a little more interested. Both demonstrated good communication skills so that the task became one of increasing the frequency of this behavior. Mrs. Danner completed standard homework assignments conscientiously, but Geoffrey refused to comply. The therapist problem-solved this issue and mother and son planned to meet for 10 minutes every day to "practice" their communication skills. This plan did not work initially. Both made excuses for why they could not find time to meet, and sabotaged the agreement. The therapist again addressed the problem and focused on the planning phase. He elicited every possible reason that might prevent them from meeting. In the midst of making the list of potential excuses Geoffrey announced that he would meet with his mother every day between 3:00 and 3:10 PM sharp! He subsequently kept to this agreement whenever possible. Mother and son began to discuss long-standing problems and to plan their mutual future. They demonstrated excellent and creative problem solving of a range of situations that varied from Geoffrey's music writing to family financial affairs.

At the 3-month assessment of problem-solving ability Geoffrey and Mrs. Danner were both very anxious and felt somewhat guarded about expressing their personal feelings on a tape recording. Their clinic assessment showed poor communication and problem solving although the naturalistic survey of coping behavior showed some improvement in their coping behavior at home.

At 9 months Geoffrey's condition remained stable. On two occasions he had brief episodes of depressed mood. He had felt tht life was unjust and questioned why good people, like his father, had to die when there were so many people living in the world. One of the episodes followed the death of an elderly aunt. On another occasion he described feelings that the police might be spying on him because he might have appeared somewhat odd. He had heard news reports of police brutality and was worried that they might attack him for no apparent reason. This period of persecutory feelings occurred when he was dating a girl and beginning to get emotionally involved with her. He recognized that this relationship might prove too stress ful for him and might lead to a relapse and he decided to terminate the affair, after which his symptoms dissipated. His medication had been reduced to 100 mg chlorpromazine daily. When further reduced to 50 mg he found he was unable to sleep, so 100 mg appeared the optimal dose. He very seldom missed a dose. He explored several job opportunities and vocational training programs but could not find a suitable job or training program near his home. He and his mother decided to save to buy him a car so that he could find work or training in less deprived areas. Meanwhile, Mrs. Danner found herself a part-time housekeeping job and continued to keep busy with her church group. Geoffrey spent several hours each day composing songs on the piano and working with some contacts, who assisted him in transcribing the musical scores and having a professional group perform the songs on demonstration tapes. He sent several arrangements to music companies and received considerable encouragement but no contracts. His mother was extremely proud of his efforts and encouraged him to perform his new songs for visitors. When Geoffrey did not want to play a version of a song that he wasn't completely satisfied with, this caused some friction. Geoffrey explained his reluctance to perform at these times and suggested that she not insist when he told her that he did not wish to perform for her guests.

In addition to his composing, Geoffrey and his married brother, who lived nearby, completely remodeled a small house at the rear of the property. When this was completed they moved into this smaller but

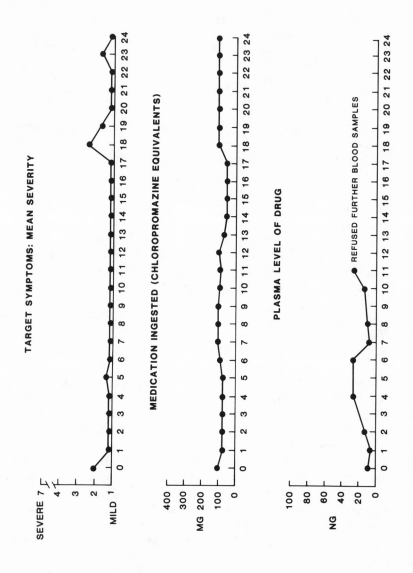

TARGET SYMPTOMS: MEAN SEVERITY

MEDICATION INGESTED (CHLOROPROMAZINE EQUIVALENTS)

PLASMA LEVEL OF DRUG

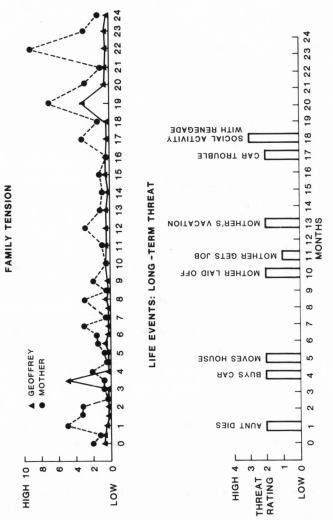

FAMILY TENSION

HIGH 10

▲ GEOFFREY
● MOTHER

LIFE EVENTS: LONG-TERM THREAT

FIGURE 14-4. *Life chart: Geoffrey Danner.*

391

comfortable house, and rented the larger house. Geoffrey continued to work on the decor and yard of the "new" house. His talents in design were evident and his mother expressed considerable gratitude for his efforts.

Follow-Up: 10–24 Months

The family remained relatively stable over this period with a tendency to more relaxed communication and continued good problem solving. His mother appeared less concerned about Geoffrey and more confident in his ability to care for himself. He became more active socially and developed several friends. Although her religious beliefs strongly opposed alcohol or extramarital sex, and she expressed her disapproval clearly, she was tolerant of his social activities. She became very concerned when she heard that a cousin with whom he was associating used street drugs. Geoffrey reassured her that these drugs would make his schizophrenia worse and that he would not touch them.

Geoffrey and his mother began to make plans for his eventually living away from home, and began to look for suitable accommodation. He placed his name on the subsidized housing waiting list for a single apartment. At times his mother expressed inappropriate overprotectiveness. Geoffrey was able to tell his mother that he did not like being babied and that he preferred to make his own decisions.

On the second anniversary of his father's death Geoffrey became somewhat despondent. During the previous month he had bought a car that he had had checked by a mechanic and the next day it had broken down on the freeway and he resold it at a loss. This had upset his plans to start a training program and to earn some extra money. He reported to his psychiatrist that he had been depressed and had heard a few "voices." The psychiatrist suggested he increase his chlorpromazine to 200 mg. The following day he decided to get out of his "rut" and went out with some friends and felt much more cheerful. He did not increase his medication and the next week denied that he had really experienced auditory hallucinations.

His mother continued to work part time and to remain socially active. She took two week-long vacations to visit relatives and was delighted at how well Geoffrey coped in her absence. On two occasions she complained of feeling anxious and depressed for a week or two. At these times she said she missed her husband's support and expressed regret that Geoffrey wasn't a more affectionate and supportive companion.

After 2 years most of the treatment objectives had been achieved. Mother and son were leading productive lives. Mother's overinvolvement was substantially reduced and she was coping well with her life problems.

Geoffrey had a steady girlfriend and was working steadily toward his goals of independent living and social and vocational functioning. He was very compliant with his treatment, with excellent insight into the nature of his illness and its optimal management. Both continued to have difficulties communicating their feelings calmly, but were able to resolve significant family problems effectively.

As the therapist was leaving the house after the last treatment session a postman delivered a parcel containing a record album that included a song for which Geoffrey had composed both the music and lyrics. After excitedly playing it on his record player he told the therapist, "You know, I started this song when you first came here 2 years ago, and I owe it all to you. You've helped me to become quite a normal person again. . . . I know I have schizophrenia but I can cope with it now. . . . I'm planning to move in with my girlfriend soon and I'm sure I can handle that. . . . I wonder if I could help you with your program. You know, teaching other poeple how to handle schizophrenia." His mother smiled proudly.

CHAPTER 15

CONCLUSIONS AND FUTURE DIRECTIONS

Schizophrenia remains the most perplexing of psychiatric disorders. Its cause is poorly understood, its course variable and relatively unpredictable, and its management exceedingly difficult. The clinician walks a tightrope between inadequate doses of neuroleptic medication and excessive amounts that produce debilitating side effects; social stimulation presents a similar dilemma in rehabilitation. This latter problem is shared by the community care givers, usually the index patient's family, who find that even minor excesses of social stimulation, life changes, or stress may induce flare-ups of florid symptoms, and that a lack of social pressure seems to induce increasingly inappropriate social behavior, apathy, and withdrawal. Thus, the optimal balance between biological, psychological, and social systems has seldom been met by current programs of drug and psychosocial management. In light of this daunting background the success of the family management program that is described in this volume is remarkable.

Three possible explanations for the highly successful results of an intervention program based on the family support system might be proffered. First, the program may have provided the mix of already recognized therapeutic ingredients in optimal proportions. Second, the program may have included a vital new ingredient of substantial therapeutic power. Third, the results may have been spurious, merely artifacts of the research design, and unlikely to be replicable. Each of these possibilities deserves further discussion.

RESEARCH VALIDITY

The cold figures of research data often obscure clinical reality. In this study the data obtained from standardized rating scales appeared to closely parallel the clinical status of index patients and their family

394

members over the course of the study. There were no surprises for the clinicians to puzzle over. Indeed, at times the improvements of patients at the clinical level seemed more dramatic than was reflected on rating scales that were designed for a higher functioning population with norms considerably higher than the severely disabled and socially deprived persons who entered our clinic in the heart of East Los Angeles. The significant advantages of the family approach were abundantly evident not only in terms of symptomatic stability and continued improvement, but also in gains of social functioning. Many of the more tangible social gains, such as paid employment, development of close relationships, and normality of social contact, were clearly apparent only after a year of treatment. But these changes were highly stable and continued throughout follow-up into the third and fourth years of our contact with the patients and their families. Few family therapy patients did not share this sustained enhancement in the quality of their lives.

Individually treated patients were not immune to enhancement of their social functioning and several rapidly returned to excellent levels of attainment, particularly those who had experienced their first episodes of schizophrenia and had good premorbid work and social skills. However, despite return to competent social role performance these individuals carried on aura of vulnerability, a brittleness that one sensed would lead to rapid breakdown in functioning under relatively minor stress. The index patients and their family members reported this sense of potential vulnerability. Comments such as "I must be wary," "I'm not ready for that yet," "She's very sensitive, not sure of herself like she was before" expressed the mutual sense of concern. These patients seemed most handicapped in their interpersonal relationships. They avoided forming intimate relationships; they tended to withdraw from peer-group activities, and to remain somewhat peripheral in family functioning. Indeed, this vulnerability led to florid relapse in almost all individual cases at some point in the 2-year study. This relapse of symptoms was usually preceded by a life event that, while often quite minor, nevertheless overwhelmed the person's coping mechanisms. Although the family members were aware of the stress, they lacked the ability to communicate with and assist the index patient in coping effectively with the problem. By the time the patient or family contacted the therapist for assistance, the florid episode of schizophrenia was established and prevention of a breakdown in social functioning through crisis intervention was not feasible. Such crises tended to further reduce the patient's and family's confidence and to result in greater holding back and loss of social role performance.

Individually treated patients who began at a less competent level of functioning were usually maintained at that level, but tended to relapse more rapidly and more frequently, so that little enhancement of the quality of their lives, even of a transient nature, was observed, and some deterioration was common. However, the support provided by the program served to reduce the severity of their episodes and to provide greater stability than previous community treatment, so that patients and their families were well satisfied with the results.

Therefore, the clinical superiority of the family approach was clearly recognized as an increased stability of symptomatic state and a gradual, but sustained, improvement of social role functioning. This appeared to be achieved through a decrease in the vulnerability to life stressors and a subsequent ability to cope with social situations and relationships without major difficulty. Family members were able to treat the index patients in a more matter-of-fact way, thereby freeing themselves to return to more usual routines.

The design of the study enabled most major biases to be controlled successfully. It seemed unlikely that these observed effects were mere artifacts of the research. However, before we can confidently report these findings as valid, a crucial component of the scientific method remains to be applied. The study must be *fully replicated*. While it is unlikely that the study will be repeated in exactly the same manner, plans are already under way to conduct a larger-scale study of the method with more carefully controlled drug therapy. However, in support of the findings in favor of behavioral family therapy, two similar studies of family approaches have shown excellent results (Leff, Kuipers, Berkowitz, Eberlein-Vries, & Sturgeon, 1982; Hogarty, personal communication). The Pittsburgh study of Anderson and Hogarty (see pp. 108–112) is still in progress. The preliminary results suggest that family intervention that aims at stress reduction is highly effective in preventing major clinical exacerbations over a 1-year period, but is not substantially superior than a behavioral social-skills training method where the focus is on individual treatment. The London study of the Leff group (see pp. 112–114) aimed to reduce expressed emotion and close contact with relatives in 11 index patients. The intervention program included education about schizophrenia, a group for family members, and a small number of conjoint family sessions. This low-intensity family intervention succeeded in preventing relapse in ten of the 11 patients. Six of 12 patients randomly assigned to standard aftercare relapsed. These results suggest that our findings are not an isolated occurrence, but that a growing body of controlled research supports the basic clinical data concerning the prevention of symptom exacerbation. While far from indisputable, the evidence for the validity of this method of family therapy in the management of schizophrenia is growing.

A VITAL THERAPEUTIC INGREDIENT?

Psychotherapy research operates at two levels. First, one compares the outcome of two or more therapy methods while attempting to minimize the impact of interpersonal and nonspecific variables that may confound the results. Second, one attempts to define the process by which differences in the outcome of the therapies are achieved. The former enables the validation of the efficacy of a new approach; the latter serves to refine the approach so that ingredients that contribute to its efficacy are defined and redundant components can be disregarded, thereby improving the efficiency of the method.

The present study was designed primarily to define outcome parameters, but we were interested in exploring some aspects of the process of therapy. To this end several process measures were included. These included medication, life events, changes in family problem solving, and family education.

Medication

The investigators designed this study so that every patient would receive the optimal dosage of neuroleptic medication throughout the 2 years of the program. In order to avoid discrimination, the prescribing physicians were not informed of the treatment condition to which each patient was assigned. They were instructed to evaluate the patient's mental status each month (or more frequently as necessary) and to prescribe the amount of neuroleptic sufficient to control florid symptoms of schizophrenia. Although any drug was permitted, the ability to obtain plasma level assays of the drugs restricted the prescribing to chlorpromazine, fluphenazine hydrochloride, and haloperidol wherever feasible. Evidence of noncompliance or poor compliance as gauged by patient and family reports and plasma level assays led to the use of intramuscular fluphenazine decanoate in several cases. At all times the drugs were titrated to the minimal sufficient dosage to avoid side effects and maximize social functioning.

In all cases included in the 9-month assessment medication was ingested over the entire 9 months. However, in some cases suboptimal dosages were ingested as a result of partial compliance. Excellent compliance was noted in two-thirds of family treatment cases and over half the individually treated patients. However, the average dosage prescribed over the 9 months was somewhat higher in the individual group. As a result of this the dose that appeared to have been ingested by this group remained higher than that of the family-treated patients (Figure 15-1).

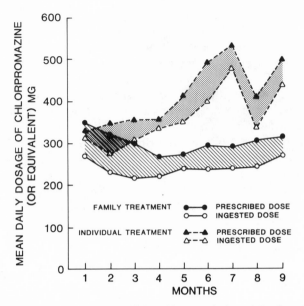

FIGURE 15-1. *Neuroleptic dosage.* (*Printed by permission of the American Medical Association.*)

There was considerable variability in these dosages, and as a result the differences were not significantly different.

These data refute the suggestion that the effect of the family management of schizophrenia was achieved through better medication compliance, and subsequently a larger ingested dosage of neuroleptic drugs. On the contrary, the trend suggests that the family approach may have contributed to a reduction in the need for continued high doses of medication. In the light of recent reports of the harmful effects of high doses of neuroleptic maintenance drugs, this may suggest an important advantage for behavioral family therapy.

Life Events

The slings and arrows of outrageous fortune must be accounted for in the treatment of a stress-related disorder lest one group find themselves beset by an excess of unfortunate events unrelated to their illness or its treatment. This might lead to a worse course for the illness. Throughout the study trained research assistants (Cathy Wood-Siverio, BA; Grant Marshall, AB; and Robert Miles, MS) conducted telephone interviews with household members to inquire about changes and stressors that had occurred to any member of the family in the past 2 weeks. The reports transcribed from these interviews were later rated by a blind assessor (Jean Pederson, MS), who determined the severity of stressful events. It was concluded that a wide range of events occurred in both conditions. However, a greater proportion of the events that could be expected to produce long-term stress were found in the individual treatment condition. But when those events that appeared to be the consequences of the patient's illness or behavior were excluded, there were equal proportions of "independent" life events in both conditions. Thus the excess of "dependent" events in the individual treatment patients probably resulted from the poorer control of their schizophrenia that landed them in stressful circumstances from time to time. An example of this was a man who lost his job when he began expressing beliefs that his supervisor was plotting to kill him and that his thoughts were controlled by the devil.

It can be concluded that there was no evidence that an excess of major or minor life events in either group contributed to the differing outcome of the two treatment methods. Any difference in the distribution of major and minor events appeared to result from stresses that were probably brought about by the patient's illness and consequent behavior, not by misfortunes independent of his condition.

Changes in Family Problem Solving

The most crucial question to answer is whether the behavioral family therapy induced lasting changes in the manner in which the family responded to stress. In particular, it is important to know how many families that received family therapy used the specific problem-solving methods they were taught in the treatment sessions to handle problems as they arose outside the sessions. Families were evaluated (1) by the therapist; (2) by structured family assessments; and (3) by naturalistic assessments of family coping.

Therapist Assessment

Throughout treatment the therapist observed the problem-solving behavior of the family. This ongoing behavioral assessment formed the basis for subsequent intervention and was a vital part of the therapy process. In addition to the therapist's observations of problem-solving attempts during the sessions, each family member completed a daily journal that detailed efforts to cope with everyday problems. With the aid of a simple checklist (see Figure 15-2) the therapist was able to report whether specific elements of communication and problem-solving behavior were apparent. As well

COMMUNICATION TRAINING

1. Family members able to receive and process verbal communication.
2. Family members and patient able to identify specific positive behavior
3. Family members able to give positive feedback for specific positive behavior
4. Family members able to identify specific negative behavior
5. Family members able to ask for for specific behavior change in a positive way
6. Family members able to express negative feelings.
7. Family members able to listen actively
   – non verbal reinforcement

   – reflect content

PROBLEM SOLVING TRAINING

1. Family members able to identify specific problem issues
2. Family members able to generate 5 or more alternative solutions
3. Family members able to acknowledge all suggested alternatives
4. Family members able to evaluate all alternatives
5. Family members able to agree on "best solution"
6. Family members able to plan strategy for implementing "best solution"
7. Family members able to implement "best solution"
8. Family members able to review outcome of "problem"

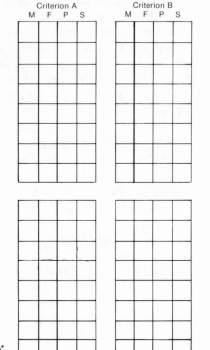

Criterion A — Spontaneous evidence in session/diary
Criterion B — Prompted within session

FIGURE 15-2. *Communication and problem-solving training checklist.*

as recording spontaneous problem-solving behaviors in family members the therapist recorded those functions that he or she observed family members perform competently with prompting during the session. The aim of the behavioral family therapy approach is to develop effective problem-solving behavior in the natural environment in the absence of the therapist. Thus, it was not sufficient that families be able to carry out adequate problem solving under the guidance of the therapist. Considerable effort was expended to promote generalization of these skills to everyday family living.

Thirteen families (72%) demonstrated generalized problem-solving competence after 9 months of treatment, and a similar proportion showed good interpersonal communication skills. Fathers tended to be less competent than mothers or index patients and were often less involved in effectively structuring family meetings or other problem-solving efforts.

Marital discord between parents appeared to be a factor in families in which there was less generalization of problem solving. This issue proved difficult to confront during family sessions and was seldom raised as a topic for problem solving in the sessions. Where such tension was evident the therapist would encourage communication between spouses during the sessions and promote problem solving of marital issues outside the family sessions. However, it was considered important to view the therapy sessions as training workshops that built the skills that family members could then deploy on a multiplicity of issues they felt important. One mother proudly disclosed that her husband was an alcoholic, and that after several sessions of problem solving together he had stopped drinking for the past 3 months.

Training did not cease after 9 months. Almost every family that continued in family therapy after that time acquired competency in problem solving and was able to use it spontaneously whenever problems arose. Crises became minimal in these families, in marked contrast to continued difficulties and emergencies in many individually treated family units.

Structured Family Assessment

The assessment of family functioning under standardized conditions in the clinic enabled changes in communication and problem-solving behavior to be compared between family therapy and individual therapy conditions. Such assessments lack the validity of naturalistic observations of spontaneous interaction patterns, but are more readily recorded and rated. Two types of task were employed. The first aimed to measure family communication and problem solving while engaged in a neutral task, such as examining a Rorschach card in the family group. The second assessed family interaction while attempting to resolve a "hot issue" in the family— the "confrontation" task.

The data on the family Rorschach await analysis. However, the preliminary analysis of the confrontation task revealed a substantial increase in problem-solving behavior after 3 months of family therapy (Figure 15-3). No change in problem solving was noted in the individual therapy families, but they tended to make more criticisms in their discussion of the family issues. Family therapy appeared to lead to some overall changes in the amount of criticism, and in guilt-inducing and intrusive statements family members employed. Where the problem-solving methods that had been trained in therapy were not employed in the family discussion, increased criticism was noted in a manner similar to the individual group. It appeared that effective problem solving tended

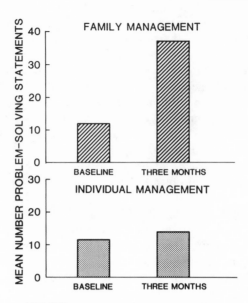

FIGURE 15-3. *Problem-solving behavior.*

to dampen criticism in family discussions of current problem issues, without totally eliminating the expression of negative feelings. A close correlation was noted between therapist observations of effective problem solving at home and observation of similar behavior in the clinic. At the 2-year follow-up further enhancement of family problem solving was observed in the clinic tests, suggesting that this was a relatively stable pattern of family interaction. Families continued to use their problem-solving agenda sheets (see p. 263) to record their problem-solving family discussions at home throughout the 2-year program.

Family Coping

A further assessment of family problem solving in the home environment was conducted on an ongoing basis during the biweekly interviews concerning family stressors. Family members were interviewed about their responses to stressful situations and events involving any member of the household. A rater who was unaware of the therapy the index patients were receiving rated the coping behavior on an 11-point scale. Most families had ten or more situations that were rated. A mean rating of coping over 3-month intervals indicated that coping improved over the 9-month active family treatment period, but that no such change was observed in the individual families (see Figure 15-4). Moreover, this coping rating correlated highly with both clinical and social outcome variables. This measure appeared to provide an excellent guide to progress toward the primary goal of the family therapy—effective problem solving of everyday stressors in the natural environment.

Family Education

A final family measure involved the acquisition of knowledge about schizophrenia and its management. A questionnaire was given before and after the family education portion of the program and repeated at 3 months and 9 months. This combined open-ended questions with a series of multiple-choice questions. After family education, both parents and index patients scored 50% higher on the questionnaire and retained this knowledge 9 months later. Indeed, their knowledge about schizophrenia after these sessions approached that of mental health professionals!

This increased understanding of the illness as a stress-related condition and the importance of low-dose drug therapy may have contributed

FIGURE 15-4. *Mean coping ratings during year 1.*

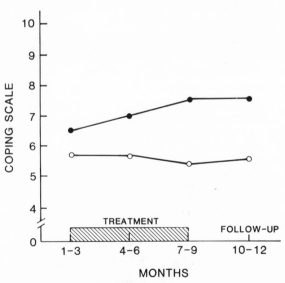

O INDIVIDUAL TREATMENT
● FAMILY TREATMENT

to improved compliance with medication and to application of common-sense coping methods based on stress-reduction rationales. Many families and patients expressed considerable gratitude and relief for the straight-forward education material. For many it was the first time that they had discussed the disorder as a family, and the first time the index patient had openly expressed his or her psychotic experiences. This disclosure usually provoked an outpouring of sympathy from family members, and not infrequently empathy from others who had themselves experienced similar phenomena, usually not diagnosed or treated. Index patients tended to disclose many more symptoms of schizophrenia than had been previously reported, even during hospital admissions for acute episodes.

Despite fears that such frank discussions might increase scapegoating or lead to destructive labeling, this did not occur. Some families and patients were reluctant to accept the diagnosis, despite validating the schizophrenic symptoms. Over time, however, acceptance increased as their fears, often based on earlier misinformation about the catastrophic prognosis of schizophrenia, tended to diminish. Family members and patients felt liberated to discuss their condition to persons in their social network in an informed, confident manner.

The educational process continued throughout the course of treat-ment. Minor exacerbations prompted revision of this educative material, and anticipated stressors became the focus of planning coping strategies to prevent recrudescence of florid symptoms. Patients and their families read over the written handouts several times and commented on how helpful the information was in their own self-management.

Where patients had suffered only one episode there was a greater tendency to reject the diagnosis and to attribute the illness to a "normal" stress reaction, or to the use of street drugs. However, after an exacerba-tion most doubts regarding the nature of the condition were quashed, and patients and families made the added effort required to apply the be-havioral family therapy wholeheartedly.

AN OPTIMAL THERAPEUTIC PACKAGE?

The contribution of many factors to the good clinical and social outcome of persons receiving family therapy suggests that the comprehensive community treatment approach based on the family support system may be a prototype for community mental health programs. The major in-gredients involved precise diagnosis, analysis of functional assets and deficits of the patient and his or her support system, consumer education, problem solving to reduce stress and enhance coping of the index patient and his or her support system, and the judicious use of minimally sufficient, specific drug therapy. The effect of the therapeutic package showed measurable benefits from many of these components over the careful application of a more traditional patient-oriented approach. Patients and families acquired factual knowledge and understanding about the disorder; their problem solving and coping were enhanced, and compliance was improved with lower dosages of drugs. The outcome of this process could be measured not only in terms of symptom prevention and reduction, but also in terms of enhanced quality of life.

This model of community treatment was applied successfully to the major public health problem of schizophrenia. However, there is reason to expect that similar programs might prove highly effective in the management of other mental and physical disorders—in particular those chronic, disabling conditions that are stress-related. This model differs substantially from most currently practiced in the health and mental health fields in that the basic unit of care is the patient plus his or her family. Although frequently the family have been implicated in the etiology of illnesses, either through genetic links or as major sources of stress, their role in nurturing the sick person back to healthy functioning has been ignored in recent medical history. The enormous benefit of specific drugs in the treatment of many formerly disabling ailments has led to minimizing the role of supportive care givers and psychosocial stressors. However, as the limitations of pure biological intervention are reached, the search for further advances may necessitate greater emphasis on psychosocial interventions. This study emphasizes the value of this holistic approach and offers advances in the technology of stress reduction that may be more widely deployed in medical practice and health promotion.

Furthermore, it may be argued that this form of health care delivery is idealistic and not practicable on account of the added costs of treatment. This was not the case in this study, where the economic costs of treatment were no greater with the family treatment, the social costs in terms of family stress were significantly less, and the burden on clinicians was reduced.

It has been pointed out that many patients with mental illness do not live with their families and are socially isolated. While this is certainly true of patients who have been ill for several years, it is seldom the case at the time of onset of their illness. Rejection by the family usually occurs after several episodes of illness and associated behavior disturbance. Family members are poorly informed about the nature of the illness and its management, and often are unable to recognize the patient's behavior as an outward manifestation of an illness. Their responses to disruptive behavior change substantially when they obtain education about the condition and are offered support in its management. Another factor contributing to patients' separation from their family support systems has been a professional attitude that families are harmful to the mentally ill. This has led to the removal of patients from supportive family environments and their placement in board-and-care homes and residential settings where less support may be provided. Family-based intervention may provide a much better support system for most patients at much lower costs. Application of these methods is most effectively applied at the onset of the illness, and not left until major difficulties have developed.

However, it is important to recognize that the family cannot provide support for the patient entirely and that, although minimized, the role of the hospital and other residential facilities is an integral component of the comprehensive treatment program. In our study few patients required hospital care over the entire 2-year period, but for three of the four cases hospital admission was crucial to the management of acute exacerbations. For the fourth, the admission was for the essentially social reasons of enabling the parents to take a vacation and giving them a respite from the care of a chronically disabled patient. The provision of residential care for the severely handicapped patients to enable families to take a break from their care-giving roles is an important service, but one that does not require the use of expensive hospital beds. Thus, while it is evident that hospital services can be substantially reduced by family-oriented approaches, they remain a vital component of the community care system.

A few patients proved exceptionally difficult management problems. These difficulties often reflected premorbid personality disorders and long-standing family conflicts unrelated to schizophrenia. In such cases alternatives to family management might seem indicated. However, it is doubtful that alternatives such as the establishment of surrogate family settings, or assistance in independent living, would prove more effective with these disturbed individuals. But it is clearly unreasonable for families to remain the sole care givers for these persons, and alternative care is essential.

Another problem we encountered was with single parents. Although single parents who were the sole care givers for their sons or daughters with schizophrenia obtained results equal to those of two-parent families, their need for added support was evident. Special efforts to provide this through persons in their social network such as relatives, friends, and neighbors were made throughout therapy. The provision of relatives' support groups such as those described in the Leff program may assist with this problem.

The multifamily groups we formed after the first 9 months of treatment served to support these single parents but did not enable the parents to share their own feelings freely in the presence of the index patients or to establish close support from other parents. The need for respite was even more evident among single parents with handicapped patients.

TIME-LIMITED OR INDEFINITE TREATMENT

The vogue for indeterminate therapy that was formerly the psychoanalysis prerogative has now found followers in biologically oriented psychiatry. The concept of lifelong drug therapy for persons who have suffered an episode of schizophrenia has been supported by studies that have shown that within a year of withdrawing the drugs, a large percentage of patients in remission at the point of withdrawal suffer a clinical relapse of symptoms. Psychosocial interventions, however, promise long-term effectiveness that continues after the intervention has been completed. It is evident that neuroleptic drugs have no effect on the underlying vulnerability of the patient's neurochemistry and are effective only when present in the brain in sufficient quantities. This condition may continue for several weeks or even months after the last dosage of the drug is administered. Psychosocial interventions that aim to bolster the potential of a person to cope effectively with stress may be able to alter the impact of such stress for an indefinite period after the intervention has been completed. However, like all newly acquired complex skills, a lack of continued practice may lead to a rapid loss of these skills. Thus, while it is possible that effective problem-solving behavior can be acquired by patients and their families after several family sessions, it is doubtful that many families would maintain adequate performance of these skills without continued "booster" sessions.

Two-thirds of our families showed evidence of spontaneous application of the problem-solving method after 3 months of behavioral family therapy, and several others had mastered the method after 9 months. Monthly sessions served to revise the methods and to continually upgrade families' skills. At the end of 2 years most families showed considerable poise and skill in conducting their own problem-solving discussions when the need arose, and the therapists served as consultants to assist with special management problems. However, there is a substantial difference between minimal therapy and no therapy, as we came to realize when we began to fade out contact with families at the 2-year point. This termination process engendered considerable stress in almost every family, with many patients showing warning signs of decompensation. Rather than discontinue family therapy entirely, spacing sessions at greater intervals or inviting families to make contact when a further family session might seem necessary appeared preferable.

Almost half the family therapy patients were able to discontinue low-dosage daily neuroleptic drug therapy successfully after 2 years of treatment. The modal dose for the remainder was 100 mg chlorpromazine (or its equivalent). In some cases an intermittent drug regimen was instituted with the patient taking the medication when he or she felt stressed. To date no major exacerbations have resulted from this procedure. Two individually treated, first-episode cases had their drugs withdrawn after 2 years, but one suffered a florid relapse within 2 weeks. It seems possible that the strengthening of coping behavior through the family therapy may enable patients to be managed without long-term medication, or at least on minimal or intermittent dosages. Further study is under way to explore this issue in a controlled fashion.

Despite optimism that persons who have suffered schizophrenia may be helped to attain stable remissions of their illness and to return to unimpaired life-styles, it is doubtful that their vulnerability to further episodes is permanently reduced. At this juncture it is important that they be followed closely and encouraged to make contact with their case managers at any time they experience warning signals that may herald a return of symptoms. Episodes may be less frequent and less severe, but they are likely to recur in a high proportion of cases. It is hoped that future developments in biological studies may reveal clinically useful vulnerability markers to aid in predicting the probability of exacerbations.

POOR RESPONSE TO TREATMENT

Every family treated with behavioral family therapy appeared to derive some benefit from the program. There were no major adverse effects that could be associated with the treatment. However, it could be argued that in some cases the family members were overly burdened by being expected to care for a particularly difficult index patient, and that residential care may have been a more appropriate arrangement for several persistently symptomatic patients. In one case a burly patient, who was very difficult to communicate with verbally, made several assaults on his father, threatened his mother, and destroyed two glass doors, a television set, and an expensive hi-fi system. Attempts by the family to modify this unprovoked aggression were only partially successful, and after 9 months residential care was recommended. However, the same violent behavior persisted and resulted in immediate expulsion from several board-and-care homes and subsequent return home to the more tolerant and effective family management. This patient showed little evidence of florid delusions or hallucinations, and much of his behavior appeared directed toward maximizing parental attention. It is doubtful that psychosocial interventions could effect behavior change in such an individual in a community environment unless severe sanctions could be imposed. Behavior modification in a controlled environment may be more likely to succeed. However, only the legal system has the ability to impose such environments on the unwilling individual. Few parents are willing to press charges in such cases, and in the presence of clear mental illness such efforts are usually unrewarding. The violent or antisocial person who also suffers from schizophrenia presents a major problem for community management, and one that we were unable to solve. However, we did support the notion that antisocial behavior is never acceptable in the community regardless of the mental status of the patient, and that the same social sanctions should be imposed on the mentally ill offender as on any other member of the community. In other words, punishment should fit the crime. Dramatic improvement in destructive behavior followed arrests, court appearances, and jail sentences in those few instances of police intervention. One patient summarized our posture when he said, "It doesn't matter how far gone you get, you always know what is right and wrong." Too often a diagnosis of schizophrenia provides license for inappropriate behavior and a lack of self-control. Such attitudes are antithetical to successful community adaptation of persons with mental illness and should probably be abandoned.

Inadequate compliance with the treatment program was probably the major factor limiting the success of behavioral family therapy. These methods focus on the family conducting its own family discussions between therapy sessions. Families that avoid carrying out these tasks are less likely to master the problem-solving approach and to derive full benefit from the training. The tendency to leave vital discussions until the next therapy session was evident in several families, and future development of these methods may be needed to counter this problem more effectively.

Two features that appeared common to the less compliant families were high communication deviance scores and low literacy skills of one or more parents. Parents who showed evidence of disordered associations on a TAT administered before treatment, or who had limited reading and writing abilities, seemed less likely to convene family meetings. This may have reflected a lack of structured thinking and planning on the one hand, and an avoidance of a task that involved verbal comprehension and note taking on the other. The prescription of structure to family routines is essential for the effective management of stress, and more attention to arranging regular family meetings may be necessary. Our approach, which depends heavily on verbal instructions and note taking, may require further adaptation for less literate families.

Cultural variables presented some problems. Black fathers were very difficult to involve in family sessions. In several cases illiteracy appeared to account for this reluctance. Others seemed to fear that close scrutiny would reveal their own problems, such as alcoholism. Hispanic families experienced difficulties accepting the equal participation of all family members in the problem solving, and the cultural domination of parents, especially fathers, in family decision making was at odds with the strategies employed. This was usually resolved by preserving the dominant parent as the instigator of family meetings, who then delegated responsibilities for problem solving to other family members. It is important that family therapy approaches preserve flexibility to accommodate to social and cultural differences. Careful analysis of these aspects of the family systems avoided major problems, and we do not believe that any substantial modifications of the approach are necessary in large-scale applications of behavioral family therapy in different cultures.

Families that responded least to the family intervention did not appear reluctant to change their patterns of problem-solving interaction. In a few cases with well-established patterns of coping, the process was slower than expected, with family members reverting to former strategies under stress. However, as the new problem-solving methods were gradually mastered, they took precedence. Once established, these methods tended to be maintained successfully. Earlier notions that families with offspring who develop schizophrenia are resistant to change were not supported by our observations.

COMPARISON OF "BEHAVIORAL" AND "FAMILY SYSTEMS" THERAPIES

There is a tendency to contrast the major varieties of family therapy in current practice. In the absence of studies of comparative effectiveness this exercise seems relatively fruitless. However, it may be important to recognize the essential similarities of behavioral family therapy to the systems approaches that have yet to be empirically tested in the treatment of schizophrenia. The major points of similarity are an emphasis on problem-solving discussion involving all family members and the prescribing of homework tasks designed to foster continued problem solving in the home environment. Both methods consider the family as a dynamic interacting system, in which stresses are shared and changes in any member involve the adjustment of every other member. Everyday problems of living generally take precedence over developmental issues, and change of interaction behavior is emphasized over understanding of the psychodynamics associated with that behavior.

The major differences are associated more with the style of therapy. The goals of achieving effective communication, particularly of emotional expression, and collaborative problem solving are shared by most family therapists. Although there is considerable variation in the nonbehavioral methods, it is probably fair to conclude that they tend to focus on broader problem issues than the behavioral approach. Interpersonal boundaries, leadership, role conflict, alliances of family subunits, metaphoric issues of communication, and emancipation serve as the basis for problem definition in most approaches based on family systems theory. Behavioral family therapy begins after an extensive analysis of family functioning that defines clear-cut, operational goals for each family member and the family as a whole. Functional limitations in the family's ability to assist in achieving these goals are identified. Efforts to overcome these goals usually, but not always, involve enhancement of the communication and problem-solving skills of the family unit. The therapy sessions are training workshops in which family members are coached in alternative strategies, including basic skills, where these appear deficient. The homework tasks are designed to maximize practice of these newly acquired skills in the home environment. The systems approaches tend to focus less on training basic skills, assuming that family members already possess the necessary communication and problem-solving repertoires, but are blocked from employing them effectively by conflicting patterns of family transaction. Thus the therapist's task is to identify these dysfunctional patterns, to devise strategies to untangle them, and to release family members to achieve their mutual goals. Role playing, feedback, and therapist modeling concerning specific interactions observed in the sessions and reported at home are employed in behavioral as well as systems approaches. The homework tasks of systems therapists tend to be strategically aimed at conflict resolution rather than direct skill training. However, there are exceptions to every generalization made here, and in recent years several nonbehavioral approaches have tended to develop strategies remarkably similar to behavioral methods and *vice versa*. The pinpointing of micro-events by Carl Whitaker is almost identical to the ongoing functional analysis of behavioral family therapy (Metcoff & Whitaker, 1982), and the problem-solving approaches of Epstein, Reiss, and Pinsof employ a similar multistep analysis of problem resolution (Epstein & Bishop, 1981; Reiss & Oliveri, 1980; Pinsof, 1983). Birchler has led the synthesis of effective strategies from the behavioral side through incorporating several aspects of systems therapy in his methods (Birchler & Spinks, 1980). Indeed, the convergence of family therapy approaches is perhaps more striking than their differences.

One substantive difference in the current behavioral family approach involves conducting sessions in the home. Behavioral therapists do not assume that behavior learned in the clinic will generalize to the everyday home environment, nor do they assume that family interaction and problem solving in the clinic are similar to those observed at home. How often do families sit in a circle, without distractions, and discuss their problems for an hour? Conducting sessions at home, where family members can reenact family disputes and rehearse more effective communication and problem solving in the natural setting, fosters generalization of these changes. Indeed, in our research study we noted several families that were excellent problem solvers at home, which under the stress of the clinic environment performed quite poorly in the more structured problem-solving assessments. Although travel to the home increases the expense of therapy, missed appointments—even when family members are ill—are negligible, a wider range of family and social network members become involved, and the effectiveness of the approach is probably enhanced. Thus the benefits appear to outweigh the inconvenience. The therapist becomes a part of the family in a warm and welcome manner. A few families perceived the home visiting as an intrusion. However, this resentment tended to dissipate after a few sessions and was generally relegated to a self-consciousness about their living conditions. In several cases families lived in undesirable and crime-infested neighborhoods. We generally avoided traveling to such places after nightfall, and family members escorted us to our cars. But there appears to be an unwritten law of the ghetto that health professionals are cared for, and we have not encountered any assaults or threats in several hundred visits.

It may be concluded that other family therapy approaches in which family problem solving is a major feature might prove equally effective in the management of schizophrenia and other stress-related disorders. Care not to provoke undue family stress in the course of therapy itself is important. Family systems approaches tend to employ somewhat different strategies, but their goals tend to be very similar to the behavioral approach. The differential effectiveness of these methods would seem an excellent topic for a future research study.

WHAT ARE THE BENEFITS OF FAMILY THERAPY?

The focus of our work has been on improving the course of schizophrenia through reducing the ambient stress in the index patient's immediate family milieu and enhancing the support of family members in coping with threatening life events. However, apart from successful achievement of

CONCLUSIONS AND FUTURE DIRECTIONS

sustained improvement in the illness of the afflicted family member, behavior family therapy had several further benefits for the patient and his or her family. Not only did effective family problem solving reduce the risk of recurrence of schizophrenia, but index patients also improved their social functioning—in many cases they exceeded their premorbid levels of achievement. An additional patient-related benefit was a reduction in the amount of neuroleptic medication needed to maintain stability. Several cases remained stable when the medication was discontinued after 2 years of treatment. Thus, it appears that the harmful effects of long-term ingestion of high doses of neuroleptic drugs may be substantially reduced by this psychosocial intervention. In a substantial proportion of cases, very few low doses may be sufficient, and in a few cases it is possible that the use of prophylactic medication could be avoided entirely throughout aftercare management. Attempts to employ drugs on an intermittent basis when patients appeared threatened by overwhelming stress have been relatively successful where adequate psychosocial support has been provided (Heinrichs & Carpenter, 1982; Matthews *et al.*, 1979). However, *low dose* may be more readily administered than *no dose*, and avoids the problem of providing continuous supervision of less reliable patients and monitoring for early warning signals of impending deterioration.

Family members appeared to benefit from the family therapy in a number of ways. First, they experienced a reduction in the distress and burden associated with living with a mentally disordered family member. This may have been partly the result of improvements in patients' clinical and social status, but also appeared to reflect an enhanced ability to cope with difficulties associated with the illness. The patients were less disruptive on family life, and their assets often outweighed their deficits. In several families the index patients appeared to provide considerable support for other family members and were a tower of strength during times of family adversity.

The benefits accrued by family members were not restricted to those associated with the patient and his or her illness. Almost all the family members who were themselves suffering from significant psychological distress and symptoms at the start of treatment experienced relief of their symptoms after 9 months of family therapy. These included parents with depression, anxiety, somatic complaints, and alcohol dependence. A number of siblings with substance-abuse problems and personality disorders showed little change in their socially disruptive behaviors. They tended to avoid family discussions and therapy sessions, and family problem solving tended to focus on strategies to set limits and to find them alternative living arrangements. Most families were able to expand their social activities, to increase their networks of friends and associates, and to improve their work functioning. Caring for a son or daughter who had suffered from schizophrenia was no longer a reason for leading a restricted life-style, and in some cases substantial changes were observed. Overinvolved parents were relieved that they could stop worrying constantly about their afflicted sons and daughters and treat them as normal human beings. They were able to begin to think about themselves again without any sense of guilt. The problem-solving strategies were useful in promoting the effective functioning of all family members and reducing stress in their lives. Family members reported using the same problem-solving methods in their jobs and in other situations outside the family.

However, in a few families enduring stressors over which they had very limited control tended to provide considerable hardship despite their repeated problem-solving efforts. Lack of adequate education, high unemployment, and the ravages of poverty were issues that could not be resolved by family intervention alone. In many cases minor improvements were noted, but for the most part major difficulties persisted and provided an unremitting source of stress to the family which limited the benefits that could be achieved by family therapy. In the one family therapy case where clinical and social deterioration occurred, there was a persistence of enduring stressors of severe proportions that continually threatened to overwhelm the family. Thus, while behavioral family therapy was effective in both well-educated, affluent, and deprived, semiliterate families, it is important to recognize that sociological change may be necessary to ameliorate the stress associated with low socioeconomic status and that psychosocial interventions have only limited efficacy in dealing with such circumstances.

THERAPIST TRAINING

It is too early to suggest that this family management approach is the treatment of choice for the community treatment of schizophrenia in single adults. The cost-effectiveness of the method is persuasive. However, one other major step that limits the widespread clinical application of a new psychotherapeutic approach is the ability to train therapists. Field trials of empirically validated treatments are crucial to their development, yet are all too often neglected by innovative researchers and funding agencies. Fortunately in our case support for field studies from the National Institute of Mental Health Community Support Program, Psychopharmacology Research Branch, and Center for Studies of Schizophrenia as well as the Los Angeles County Department of Mental Health, has enabled us to begin widespread dissemination of the behavioral family therapy methods in community mental health programs throughout the United States.

The behavioral method has the advantage of being clearly operationalized with straightforward, commonsense intervention procedures. But such clarity of purpose should not be equated with ease of application. Indeed, the prerequisites for a competent therapist are similar to those for other forms of psychotherapy. The humanistic qualities of warmth, genuine concern, and empathy are as important to the behavioral therapies as to any other approaches. In the same manner that proponents of psychoanalytic therapies are considered qualified therapists only after they have freed themselves of major intrapsychic conflicts, it is important that persons working with families be able to free themselves from any unresolved family conflicts of their own that may limit their ability to assess objectively the family processes of families with which they work.

While not an absolute essential, a working knowledge of behavioral analysis and basic operant and respondent intervention methods is an advantage for the prospective behavioral family therapist. Experience with role-playing methods and in the nursing management of behaviorally impaired individuals is another feature that enhances the trainee's potentials. In our opinion psychiatric nurses tend to be the group most readily trained for the behavioral family management of schizophrenia, although psychiatrists, psychologists, and social workers have been successfully trained in the procedures.

To date, our training methods have consisted of workshop training with the aid of a detailed training manual, and ongoing supervision of cases. The workshop training requires between 30 and 40 hours of modeling, role rehearsal, and feedback to teach the communication and problem-solving training procedures in an experiential manner. Trainees role-play simulated family sessions and experience the interventions from the point of view of both a therapist and a family member in treatment. Wherever possible, trainees work as cotherapists with experienced behavioral family therapists. Audio-taped recordings of the trainee's family therapy sessions are examined by the trainers as the basis for ongoing supervision until the trainee has mastered the method. At times trainers accompany the trainees on family therapy visits, particularly when the trainee is experiencing difficulty with the application of the intervention.

A feature of the training is the adherence of participants to the communication and problem-solving methods that are disseminated to the families in treatment. Feelings are communicated in the specific and open manner advocated in therapy, and when problem issues are discussed the brainstorming, six-step approach is employed during supervision meetings. The value of these methods has thus been validated by the therapists themselves, who find that the training setting is less fraught with tension, and allows learning to proceed in a clear, orderly fashion. Unfortunately, this lack of tension has sometimes provided a somewhat understimulating environment, and participants have often expressed a yearning for a good, old-fashioned, heated debate or two. Effective psychotherapy is not always exciting and stimulating. It is more often a little tedious and mundane. This is true of most fields of medical practice from heart surgery to endocrinology. The rewards are not obtained through the process of treatment, but from the successful outcome achieved after painstaking effort. Achieving competence in the family treatment of schizophrenia requires several months of sustained, patient effort, but in our experience the end results make the undertaking very worthwhile.

CONCLUSIONS

This volume describes the formulation, development, and effective implementation of behavioral family therapy in the community treatment of schizoj .renia. This approach has been used to improve the problem-solving efficacy of families under stress. The same methods have been employed in the treatment of a wide range of psychiatric conditions, although extensive outcome evaluation has not been undertaken in other conditions. It is probable that the same behavioral methods may prove beneficial in the management of any stress-related conditions including many medical conditions. The dramatic effectiveness of this psychosocial intervention when employed in close association with excellent medical care supports the view that the patient's environmental support system is an essential ingredient in the promotion of optimal health. The trend toward viewing the patient as the unit of pathology should be reversed as evidence that environmental stress plays a substantial role in the breakdown of healthy functioning. The practice of family management in the prevention, treatment, and rehabilitation of mental and physical disorders is strongly supported.

   Furthermore, the family approach not only appeared to prevent the recurrence of symptoms, but also provided enhanced social role functioning and a reduction of the distress and burden experienced by all family members. The goal of an effective treatment is not merely the reduction of pathology, but also the enhancement of the quality of life. Finally, the approach met the criteria of cost-effectiveness, proving somewhat less expensive to implement than the standard approach with which it was rigorously compared.

It is too early to say whether this innovative treatment will gain widespread acceptance and implementation. Work is currently under way to provide efficient training for mental health professionals, in addition to refining the procedures and their clinical application. The methods employed are appealing for the commonsense principles they espouse. However, successful dissemination of a research-validated psychotherapy approach is a major challenge in a field where charisma, intellectual stimulation, and fads have often taken precedence over carefully conceived, unpretentious, highly effective interventions.

REFERENCES

Ackerman, N. *Treating the troubled family.* New York: Basic Books, 1966.

Alexander, J. F., & Parsons, B. V. Short-term behavioral intervention with delinquent families: Impact on family process and recidivism. *Journal of Abnormal Psychology,* 1973, *81,* 219–225.

Al-Issa, I. Behavior therapy and hallucinations: Sociocultural approach. *Psychotherapy: Theory, Research and Practice,* 1976, *13,* 156–159.

Al-Khayyal, M. *Healthy parental communication as a predictor of child competence in families with a schizophrenic and psychiatrically disturbed nonschizophrenic parent.* Unpublished doctoral dissertation, University of Rochester, 1980.

American Psychiatric Association. *Diagnostic and statistical manual of mental disorders* (3rd ed., DSM-III). Washington, D.C.: APA, 1980.

Anderson, C. M., Hogarty, G. E., & Reiss, D. J. Family treatment of adult schizophrenic patients: A psychoeducational approach. *Schizophrenia Bulletin,* 1980, *6,* 490–505.

Anderson, C. M., Hogarty, G. E., & Reiss, D. J. The psychoeducational family treatment of schizophrenia. In M. J. Goldstein (Ed.), *New developments in interventions with families of schizophrenia.* San Francisco: Jossey-Bass, 1981.

Andrews, G., Tennant, C., Hewson, D. M., & Vaillant, G. Life event stress, social support, coping style, and risk of psychological impairment. *Journal of Nervous and Mental Disease,* 1978, *166,* 307–316.

Andrews, W. N. Long-acting tranquilizers and the amotivational syndrome in the treatment of schizophrenia. In M. H. King (Ed.), *Community management of the schizophrenic in chemical remission.* Amsterdam: Excerpta Medica, 1973.

Angrist, S., Dinitz, D., & Pasamanick, B. *Women after treatment: A study of former mental patients and their normal neighbors.* New York: Appleton–Century–Crofts, 1968.

Anthony, E. J. The developmental precursors of adult schizophrenia. *Journal of Psychiatric Research,* 1968, *6* (Suppl. 1), 293–316.

Anthony, W. A., Buell, C. J., Sharratt, S., & Althoff, M. E. Efficacy of psychiatric rehabilitation. *Psychological Bulletin,* 1972, *78,* 447–456.

Asarnow, R. F., & Asarnow, J. R. Attention–information processing dysfunction and vulnerability to schizophrenia: Implications for preventive intervention. In M. J. Goldstein (Ed.), *Preventive intervention in schizophrenia: Are we ready?* Rockville, Md.: National Institute of Mental Health, 1982.

Asarnow, R. F., Steffy, R. A., MacCrimmon, D. J., & Cleghorn, J. M. An attentional assessment of foster children at risk for schizophrenia. In L. C. Wynne, R. L. Cromwell, & S. Matthysse (Eds.), *The nature of schizophrenia.* New York: Wiley, 1978.

Austin, N. K., Liberman, R. P., King, L. W., & DeRisi, W. J. A comparative evaluation of two day hospitals: Goal attainment scaling of behavior therapy vs. milieu therapy. *Journal of Nervous and Mental Disease*, 1976, *163*, 253–262.

Ayllon, T., & Azrin, N. H. *The token economy*. New York: Appleton–Century–Crofts, 1968.

Bateson, G., Jackson, D. D., Haley, J., & Weakland, J. Toward a theory of schizophrenia. *Behavioral Science*, 1956, *1*, 251–264.

Beck, A. T., Rush, A. J., Shaw, B. F., & Emery G. *Cognitive therapy of depression*. New York: Guilford, 1979.

Becker, J., & Finkel, P. Predictability and anxiety in speech by parents of female schizophrenics. *Journal of Abnormal Psychology*, 1969, *74*, 517–523.

Behrens, M. L., Rosenthal, A. J., & Chodoff, P. Communication of lower class families of schizophrenics: II. Observations and findings. *Archives of General Psychiatry*, 1968, *18*, 680–696.

Beigel, A., & Feder, S. L. Patterns of utilization in partial hospitalization. *American Journal of Psychiatry*, 1970, *126*, 1267–1274.

Bell, J. E. A theoretical position for family group therapy. *Family Process*, 1963, *2*, 1–14.

Berkowitz, R., Kuipers, E., Eberlein-Vries, R., & Leff, J. Lowering expressed emotion in relatives of schizophrenics. In M. J. Goldstein, (Ed.), *New developments in interventions with families of schizophrenics*. San Francisco: Jossey-Bass, 1981.

Birchler, G. R., & Spinks, S. H. Behavioral-systems marital and family therapy: Integration and clinical application. *American Journal of Family Therapy*, 1980, *8*, 6–28.

Birley, J. L. T., & Brown, G. W. Crises and life changes preceding the onset or relapse of acute schizophrenia: Clinical aspects. *British Journal of Psychiatry*, 1970, *116*, 327–333.

Bleuler, E. *Dementia praecox: Or the group of schizophrenias* (J. Zinkin, trans.). New York: International Universities Press, 1950. (Originally published, 1911.)

Bleuler, M. The long term course of the schizophrenic psychoses. *Psychological Medicine*, 1974, *4*, 244–254.

Blumenthal, R., Kreisman, D., & O'Connor, P. A. Return to the family and its consequence for rehospitalization among recently discharged mental patients. *Psychological Medicine*, 1982, *12*, 141–148.

Böök, J. A. A genetic and neuropsychiatric investigation of a north-Swedish population. *Acta Genetica*, 1953, *4*, 345–414.

Bowen, M. Family concept of schizophrenia. In D. D. Jackson (Ed.), *The etiology of schizophrenia*. New York: Basic Books, 1960.

Bowen, M. The family as the unit of study and treatment. *American Journal of Orthopsychiatry*, 1961, *31*, 40–60.

Brown, G. W., & Birley, J. L. T. Crises and life changes and the onset of schizophrenia. *Journal of Health and Social Behavior*, 1968, *9*, 203–214.

Brown, G. W., Birley, J. L. T., & Wing, J. K. Influence of family life on the course of schizophrenia disorders: A replication. *British Journal of Psychiatry*, 1972, *121*, 241–258.

Brown, G., Bone, M., Dalison, M., & Wing, J. *Schizophrenia and social care*. London: Oxford University Press, 1966.

Brown, G. W., Carstairs, G. M, & Topping, G. G. Post-hospital adjustment of chronic mental patients. *Lancet*, 1958, *2*, 685–689.

Brown, G. W., & Harris, T. O. *Social origins of depression: A study of psychiatric disorder in women*. London: Tavistock, 1978.

Brown, G. W., Harris, T. O., & Peto, J. Life events and psychiatric disorders: 2. Nature of causal link. *Psychological Medicine*, 1973, *3*, 159–176.

Brown, G. W., Monck, E. M., Carstairs, G. M., & Wing, J. K. Influence of family life on the course of schizophrenic illness. *British Journal of Preventive and Social Medicine*, 1962, *16*, 55–68.

Brown, G. W., & Rutter, M. The measurement of family activities and relationships: A methodological study. *Human Relations*, 1966, *19*, 241–263.

Caputo, D. V. The parents of the schizophrenic. *Family Process*, 1963, *2*, 339–356.

Cardin, V., McGill, C. W., & Falloon, I. R. H. The cost of effective family management for schizophrenia. (In preparation.)

Carroll, R. S., Miller, A., Ross, B., & Simpson, G. M. Research as an impetus to improved treatment. *Archives of General Psychiatry*, 1980, *37*, 377–380.

Cheek, F. E. The father of the schizophrenic. *Archives of General Psychiatry*, 1965, *13*, 336–345.

Christensen, A. Naturalistic observation of families: A system for random audio recordings in the home. *Behavior Therapy*, 1979, *10*, 418–422.

Claghorn, J. L., Johnston, E. E., Cook, T. H., & Itschner, L. Group therapy and maintenance of schizophrenics. *Archives of General Psychiatry*, 1974, *31*, 361–365.

Cohen, C., & Sokolovsky, J. Schizophrenia and social networks: Ex-patients in the inner city. *Schizophrenia Bulletin*, 1978, *4*, 546–560.

Creer, C., & Wing, J. K. *Schizophrenia at home*. Surrey: National Schizophrenia Fellowship, 1974.

Crowe, M. J. Conjoint marital therapy: A controlled outcome study. *Psychological Medicine*, 1978, *8*, 623–636.

Cumming, J., & Cumming, E. *Ego and milieu*. New York: Atherton, 1962.

Davis, J. M., Schaffer, C. B., Killian, G. A., Kinard, C., & Chan, C. Important issues in the drug treatment of schizophrenia. *Schizophrenia Bulletin*, 1980, *6*, 70–87.

Day, R. Research on the course and outcome of schizophrenia in traditional cultures: Some potential implications for psychiatry in the developed cultures. In M. J. Goldstein (Ed.), *Preventive intervention in schizophrenia: Are we ready?* Rockville, Md.: National Institute of Mental Health, 1982.

Dell, P. F. Beyond homeostasis: Toward a concept of coherence. *Family Process*, 1982, *21*, 21–41.

Derogatis, L. R., Lipman, R. S., Rickels, K., Uhlenhuth, E. H., & Covi, L. The Hopkins symptom checklist (HSCL). In P. Pichot (Ed.), *Modern problems in pharmacopsychiatry*. Basel: Karger, 1974.

Dincin, J., Selleck, V., & Streicker, S. Restructuring parental attitudes—Working with parents of the adult mentally ill. *Schizophrenia Bulletin*, 1978, *4*, 597–608.

Doane, J. A. *Affective style coding manual*. UCLA Department of Psychology, Los Angeles, 1978.

Doane, J. A., Miklowitz, D., Goldstein, M. J., & Falloon, I. R. H. *Interaction characteristics of high and low expressed emotion families: A pilot study*. Unpublished report, 1981.

Doane, J. A., West, K. W., Goldstein, M. J., Rodnick, E. H., & Jones, J. E. Parental communication deviance and affective style: Predictors of subsequent schizophrenia spectrum disorders in vulnerable adolescents. *Archives of General Psychiatry*, 1981, *38*, 679–685.

D'Zurilla, T. J., & Goldfried, M. R. Problem solving and behavior modification. *Journal of Abnormal Psychology*, 1971, *78*, 107–126.

Eaton, J. W., & Weil, R. J. *Culture and mental disorders*. Glencoe, Ill.: Free Press, 1955.

Eaton, J. W., & Weil, R. J. The mental health of the Hutterites. *Scientific American*, 1953, *189*, 31–37.

Epstein, N. B., & Bishop, D. S. Problem-centered systems therapy of the family. In

A. Gurman & D. Kniskern (Eds.), *Handbook of family therapy*. New York: Brunner/ Mazel, 1981.

Erlenmeyer-Kimling, L. Studies on the offspring of two schizophrenic parents. In D. Rosenthal & S. S. Kety (Eds.), *The transmission of schizophrenia*. Oxford: Pergamon, 1968.

Esterson, A., Cooper, D. G., & Laing, R. D. Results of family-oriented therapy with hospitalized schizophrenics. *British Medical Journal*, 1965, *2*, 1462–1465.

Evans, A. S. Social casework with chronic schizophrenic patients and their families. In M. Greenblatt, M. H. Solomon, A. S. Evans, & G. W. Brooks (Eds.), *Drug and social therapy in chronic schizophrenia*. Springfield, Ill.: Thomas, 1965.

Evans, A. S., Bullard, D. M., & Solomon, M. H. The family as a potential resource in the rehabilitation of the chronic schizophrenic patient. *American Journal of Psychiatry*, 1960, *117*, 1075–1083.

Eysenck, H. J. Extraversion and the acquisition of eyeblink and GSR conditioned responses. *Psychological Bulletin*, 1965, *63*, 258–270.

Fairweather, G. W., Sanders, D. H., Maynard, H., & Cressler, D. L. *Community life for the mentally ill: An alternative to institutional care*. New York: Aldine, 1969.

Falloon, I. R. H. The treatment of depression: A behavioural approach. *Psychotherapy and Psychosomatics*, 1975, *25*, 69–75.

Falloon, I. R. H. Social skills training for community living. *Psychiatric Clinics of North America*, 1978, *1*, 291–305.

Falloon, I. R. H. Communication and problem solving skills training with relapsing schizophrenics and their families. In M. R. Lansky (Ed.), *Family therapy and major psychopathology*. New York: Grune & Stratton, 1981.

Falloon, I. R. H. *The course of schizophrenia*. Paper presented at NIMH workshop on Preventive Family Interventions for Schizophrenia, La Jolla, Calif., May 1982.

Falloon, I. R. H., Boyd, J. L., & McGill, C. W. Behavioral family therapy for schizophrenia. In J. P. Curran & P. M. Monti (Eds.), *Social skills training: A practical handbook for assessment and treatment*. New York: Guilford, 1982.

Falloon, I. R. H., Boyd, J. L., McGill, C. W., Razani, J., Moss, H. B., & Gilderman, A. M. Family management in the prevention of exacerbations of schizophrenia: A controlled study. *New England Journal of Medicine*, 1982, *306*, 1437–1440.

Falloon, I. R. H., Boyd, J. L., McGill, C. W., Strang, J. S., & Moss, H. B. Family management training in the community care of schizophrenia. In M. J. Goldstein (Ed.), *New developments in interventions with families of schizophrenics*. San Francisco: Jossey-Bass, 1981.

Falloon, I. R. H., & Liberman, R. P. Behavioral family interventions in the management of chronic schizophrenia. In W. R. McFarlane (Ed.), *Family therapy in schizophrenia*. New York: Guilford, 1983a.

Falloon, I. R. H., & Liberman, R. P. Interactions between drug and psychosocial therapy in schizophrenia. *Schizophrenia Bulletin*, 1983b, *9*, 543–554.

Falloon, I. R. H., Liberman, R. P., Lillie, F. J., & Vaughn, C. E. Family therapy for relapsing schizophrenics and their families: A pilot study. *Family Process*, 1981, *20*, 211–221.

Falloon, I. R. H., Lindley, P., McDonald, R., & Marks, I. M. Social skills training of outpatient groups: A controlled study of rehearsal and homework. *British Journal of Psychiatry*, 1977, *131*, 599–609.

Falloon, I. R. H., Lloyd, G. G., & Harpin, R. E. The treatment of social phobia: Real-life rehearsal and non-professional therapists. *Journal of Nervous and Mental Disease*, 1981, *169*, 180–184.

Falloon, I. R. H., Marshall, G. N., Boyd, J. L., Razani, J., & Wood-Siverio, C. Relapse: A review of the concept and its definitions. *Psychological Medicine*, 1983, *13*, 469–477.

Falloon, I. R. H., Pederson, J., McGill, C. W., & Boyd, J. L. The social outcome of family management of schizophrenia. (In preparation.)

Falloon, I. R. H., Pederson, J., Moss, R. B., & Shirin, K. Life events in schizophrenia. (In preparation.)

Falloon, I. R. H., & Talbot, R. E. Persistent auditory hallucinations: Coping mechanisms and implications for management. *Psychological Medicine,* 1981, *11,* 329–339.

Falloon, I. R. H., & Talbot, R. E. The goals of day treatment. *Journal of Nervous and Mental Disease,* 1982, *170,* 279–285.

Falloon, I., Watt, D. C., & Shepherd, M. A comparative controlled trial of pimozide and fluphenazine decanoate in the continuation therapy of schizophrenia. *Psychological Medicine,* 1978a, *7,* 59–70.

Falloon, I., Watt, D. C., & Shepherd, M. The social outcome of patients in a trial of long-term continuation therapy in schizophrenia: Pimozide vs. fluphenzine. *Psychological Medicine,* 1978b, *8,* 265–274.

Farina, A. Patterns of role dominance and conflict in parents of schizophrenic patients. *Journal of Abnormal and Social Psychology,* 1960, *61,* 31–38.

Farina, A., & Holzberg, J. Interaction patterns of parents and hospitalized sons diagnosed as schizophrenic or non-schizophrenic. *Journal of Abnormal Psychology,* 1968, *73,* 114–118.

Fenton, F. R., Tessier, L., & Struening, E. L. A comparative trial of home and hospital psychiatric are. *Archives of General Psychiatry,* 1979, *36,* 1073–1079.

Ferreira, A. J., & Winter, W. Stability of interactional variables in family decision-making. *Archives of General Psychiatry,* 1966, *14,* 352–355.

Fontana, A., Marcus, J., Noel, B., & Rakusin, J. Prehospitalization coping styles of psychiatric patients: The goal-directedness of life events. *Journal of Nervous and Mental Disease,* 1972, *155,* 311–321.

Freeman, H. E., & Simmons, O. G. *The mental patient comes home.* New York: Wiley, 1963.

Friedman, A. S., Boszormenyi-Nagy, I., Jungreis, S., Lincoln, G., Mitchell, H., Sonne, J., Speck, R. L., & Spivack, G. *Psychotherapy for the whole family.* New York: Springer, 1965.

Friedman, C. J., & Friedman, A. S. Characteristics of schizogenic families during a joint story-telling task. *Family Process,* 1970, *9,* 333–353.

Friedman, T. T., Rolfe, P., & Perry, S. E. Home treatment of psychiatric patients. *American Journal of Psychiatry,* 1960, *116,* 807–809.

Fromm-Reichmann, F. Notes on the development of treatment of schizophrenics by psycho-analytic psychotherapy. *Psychiatry,* 1948, *11,* 263–73.

Garmezy, N. Models of etiology for the study of children who are at risk for schizophrenia. In M. Rolf, L. Robins, & M. M. Pollack (Eds.), *Life history research in psycho-pathology* (Vol. II). Minneapolis: University of Minnesota Press, 1972.

Goldberg, S. C., Klerman, G. L., & Cole, J. O. Changes in schizophrenic psychopathology and ward behavior as a function of phenothiazine treatment. *British Journal of Psychiatry,* 1965, *111,* 120–133.

Goldstein, M. J. (Ed.). *New developments in interventions with families of schizophrenics.* San Francisco: Jossey-Bass, 1982.

Goldstein, M. J. Further data concerning the relation between premorbid adjustment and paranoid symptomatology. *Schizophrenia Bulletin,* 1978, *4,* 236–243.

Goldstein, M. J., Judd, L. L., Rodnick, E. H., Alkire, A. A., & Gould, E. A method for studying social influence and coping patterns within families of disturbed adolescents. *Journal of Nervous and Mental Disease,* 1968, *147,* 233–251.

Goldstein, M. J., Rodnick, E. H., Evans, J. R., May, P. R., & Steinberg, M. Drug and family therapy in the aftercare treatment of acute schizophrenia. *Archives of General Psychiatry*, 1978, *35*, 1169–1177.

Goldstein, M. J., Rodnick, E. H., Jones, J. E., McPherson, S. R., & West, K. L. Familial precursors of schizophrenia spectrum disorders. In L. C. Wynne, R. L. Cromwell, & S. Matthysse (Eds.), *The nature of schizophrenia.* New York: Wiley, 1978.

Golner, J. H. Home family counseling. *Social Work*, 1971, *16*, 63–71.

Gordon, T. Parent effectiveness training: A preventive program and its delivery system. In A. W. Albee & J. M. Jaffe (Eds.), *Primary prevention of psychopathology.* Hanover, N.H.: University Press of New England, 1977.

Gottesman, I. I., & Shields, J. Schizophrenia in twins: 16 years' consecutive admissions to a psychiatric clinic. *British Journal of Psychiatry*, 1966, *112*, 809.

Gottesman, I. I., & Shields, J. *Schizophrenia and genetics: A twin vantage point.* New York: Academic Press, 1974.

Gottesman, I. I., & Shields, J. A. A critical review of recent adoption, twin, and family studies of schizophrenia: Behavioral genetics perspectives. *Schizophrenia Bulletin*, 1976, *2*, 360–401.

Gould, E., & Glick, I. D. The effects of family presence and brief family intervention on global outcome for hospitalized schizophrenic patients. *Family Process*, 1977, *4*, 503–510.

Grad, J., & Sainsbury, P. Mental illness and the family. *Lancet*, 1963, *1*, 533–547.

Grad, J., & Sainsbury, P. The effects that patients have on their families in a community care and a control psychiatric service—A two year follow-up. *British Journal of Psychiatry*, 1968, *114*, 265–278.

Greenley, J. R. Family symptom tolerance and rehospitalization experiences of psychiatric patients. *Research in Community Mental Health*, 1979, *1*, 357–386.

Griffiths, R. D. Rehabilitation of chronic psychotic patients. *Psychological Medicine*, 1974, *4*, 316–325.

Grinspoon, L., Ewalt, J. R., & Shader, R. I. *Schizophrenia, pharmacotherapy and psychotherapy.* Baltimore: Wilkins & Wilkins, 1972.

Guttman, H. A. A contraindication for family therapy: The prepsychotic or postpsychotic young adult and his parents. *Archives of General Psychiatry*, 1973, *29*, 352–357.

Haase, H. J. Follow-up treatment and aftercare of discharged schizophrenic patients. *Schizophrenia Bulletin*, 1980, *6*, 619–626.

Hafner, R. J. The husbands of agoraphobic women: Assortative mating or pathogenic interaction? *British Journal of Psychiatry*, 1977, *130*, 233–239.

Hafner, R. J., & Marks, I. M. Exposure *in vivo* of agoraphobics: Contributions of diazepam, group exposure, and anxiety evocation. *Psychological Medicine*, 1976, *6*, 71–88.

Haley, J. The family of the schizophrenic: A model system. *Journal of Nervous and Mental Disease*, 1959, *129*, 357–374.

Hammer, M. Influence of small social networks as factors on mental hospital admission. *Human Organization*, 1964, *22*, 243–251.

Hatfield, A. B. The family as partner in the treatment of mental illness. *Hospital and Community Psychiatry*, 1979, *30*, 338–340.

Heinrichs, D. W., & Carpenter, W. T. The psychotherapy of the schizophrenic disorders. In L. Grinspoon (Ed.), *Psychiatry 1982: Annual review.* Washington, D.C.: American Psychiatric Press, 1982.

Hell, D., & Korpela, K. Observations of the family life of schizophrenics on home visits. *Psychotherapie–Medizinische Psychologie (Stuttgart)*, 1978, *28*, 16–21.

Hemmings, G. The problems of relatives. *Newsletter*, Schizophrenia Association of Great Britain, September 1981.

Herman, B. F., & Jones, J. E. Lack of acknowledgement in the family Rorschachs of families with a child at risk for schizophrenia. *Family Process*, 1976, *15*, 289–302.

Hersen, M., & Bellack, A. S. Social skills training for chronic psychiatric patients: Rationale, research findings, and future directions. *Comprehensive Psychiatry*, 1976, *17*, 559–580.

Herz, M. I., & Melville, C. Relapse in schizophrenia. *American Journal of Psychiatry*, 1980, *137*, 801–805.

Herz, M. I., Spitzer, R. L., Gibbon, M., Greenspan, K., & Reibel, S. Individual versus group aftercare treatment. *American Journal of Psychiatry*, 1974, *131*, 808–812.

Heston, L. L. Psychiatric disorders in foster home reared children of schizophrenic mothers. *British Journal of Psychiatry*, 1966, *112*, 819–825.

Hirsch, S. R. Depression "revealed" in schizophrenia. *British Journal of Psychiatry*, 1982, *140*, 421–424.

Hirsch, S. R., Gaind, R., Rohde, P. D., Stevens, B. C., & Wing, J. K. Outpatient management of chronic schizophrenic patients with long-acting fluphenazine: Double-blind placebo trial. *British Medical Journal*, 1973, *1*, 633–637.

Hirsch, S. R., & Leff, J. P. *Abnormalities in the parents of schizophrenics.* London: Oxford University Press, 1975.

Hoenig, J. The schizophrenic patient at home. *Acta Psychiatrica Scandinavica*, 1974, *50*, 297–308.

Hoffman, L. *Foundations of family therapy.* New York: Basic Books, 1981.

Hogarty, G. E., Goldberg, S. C., Schooler, N. R., & Ulrich, R. F. The collaborative study group: Drug and sociotherapy in the aftercare of schizophrenic patients: II. Two year relapse rates. *Archives of General Psychiatry*, 1974, *31*, 603–608.

Hogarty, G. E., Guy, W., Gross, M., & Gross, G. An evaluation of community-based mental health programs. *Medical Care*, 1969, *7*, 271–280.

Hogarty, G. E., Schooler, N. R., Ulrich, R. F., Mussare, F., Ferro, P., & Herron, E. Fluphenazine and social therapy in the aftercare of schizophrenic patients: Relapse analyses of a two-year controlled trial. *Archives of General Psychiatry*, 1979, *36*, 1283–1294.

Jackson, D. D. Family interaction, family homeostasis and some implications for conjoint family psychotherapy. In J. Masserman (Ed.), *Individual and family dynamics.* New York: Grune & Stratton, 1959.

Jackson, D. D. (Ed.). *The etiology of schizophrenia.* New York: Basic Books, 1960.

Jackson, D. D. The study of the family. *Family Process*, 1965, *4*, 1–20.

Jackson, D. D., & Weakland, J. H. Conjoint family therapy: Some consideration on theory, technique, and results. *Psychiatry*, 1961, *24*(2), Supplement, 30–45.

Jacobs, L. I. A cognitive approach to persistent delusions. *American Journal of Psychotherapy*, 1980, *34*, 556–563.

Jacobs, S., & Myers, J. Recent life events and acute schizophrenic psychosis: A controlled study. *Journal of Nervous and Mental Disease*, 1976, *162*, 75–87.

Jacobson, N. S. Specific and non-specific factors in the effectiveness of a behavioral approach to the treatment of marital discord. *Journal of Consulting and Clinical Psychology*, 1978, *46*, 442–452.

Jacobson, N. S., & Margolin, G. *Marital therapy: Strategies based on social learning and behavior exchange principles.* New York: Brunner/Mazel, 1979.

Johnson, D. A. W. Studies of depressive symptoms in schizophrenia: I. The prevalence of depression and its possible causes; II. A two-year longitudinal study of symptoms; III. A double-blind trial of orphenadrine against placebo; IV. A double-blind trial of nortriptyline for depression in chronic schizophrenia. *British Journal of Psychiatry*, 1981, *139*, 89–101.

Jones, J. E., Rodnick, E. H., Goldstein, M. J., McPherson, S. R., & West, K. L. Parental transactional style deviance as a possible indicator of risk for schizophrenia. *Archives of General Psychiatry*, 1977, *34*, 71-74.

Kallmann, F. J. *The genetics of schizophrenia*. New York: Augustin, 1938.

Kanfer, F. H., & Saslow, G. Behavioral analysis: An alternative to diagnostic classification. *Archives of General Psychiatry*, 1965, *12*, 529-538.

Karlsson, J. L. *The biologic basis of schizophrenia*. Springfield, Ill.: Thomas, 1966.

Kayton, L., Beck, J., & Koh, S. D. Postpsychotic state, convalescent environment, and therapeutic relationship in schizophrenic outcome. *American Journal of Psychiatry*, 1976, *133*, 1269-1274.

Kazdin, A. E. Covert modeling, imagery assessment and assertive behavior. *Journal of Consulting and Clinical Psychology*, 1975, *43*, 716-724.

Kellam, S. G., Ensminger, M. E., & Turner, R. J. Family structure and the mental health of children. *Archives of General Psychiatry*, 1977, *34*, 1012-1022.

Kety, S. S., Rosenthal, D., Wender, P. H., & Schulsinger, F. The types and prevalence of mental illness in the biological and adoptive families of adopted schizophrenics. In D. Rosenthal & S. S. Kety (Eds.), *The transmission of schizophrenia*. Oxford: Pergamon, 1968.

Kety, S. S., Rosenthal, D., Wender, P. H., Schulsinger, F., & Jacobsen, B. The biologic and adoptive families of adopted individuals who became schizophrenic: Prevalence of mental illness and other characteristics. In L. C. Wynne, R. L. Cromwell, & S. Matthysse (Eds.), *The nature of schizophrenia*. New York: Wiley, 1978.

Kinney, D. K., & Jacobsen, B. Environmental factors in schizophrenia: New adoption study evidence. In L. C. Wynne, R. L. Cromwell, & S. Matthysse (Eds.), *The nature of schizophrenia*. New York: Wiley, 1978.

Kraepelin, E. *Clinical psychiatry*. New York: William Wood, 1913.

Kretschmer, E. *Der sensitive Bezeihungswahn*. Berlin: Springer, 1927.

Kulhara, P., & Wig, N. N. The chronicity of schizophrenia in north-west India: Results of a follow-up study. *British Journal of Psychiatry*, 1978, *132*, 186-190.

L'Abate, L. *Enrichment: Structured interventions with couples, families, and groups*. Washington, D.C.: University Press of America, 1977.

Laing, R. D. *The politics of experience*. New York: Pantheon, 1967.

Laing, R. D., & Esterson, A. *Sanity, madness and the family*. London: Tavistock, 1964.

Lamb, H. R. New asylums in the community. *Archives of General Psychiatry*, 1979, *36*, 129-134.

Lamb, H. R., & Goertzel, V. Discharged mental patients—Are they really in the community? *Archives of General Psychiatry*, 1971, *24*, 29-34.

Lamb, H. R., & Oliphant, E. Schizophrenia through the eyes of families. *Hospital and Community Psychiatry*, 1978, *29*, 803-806.

Langsley, D. C., Kaplan, D. M., Pittman, F. S., Machotka, R., Flomenhaft, K., & DeYoung, C. D. *The treatment of families in crisis*. New York: Grune & Stratton, 1968.

Langsley, D., Machotka, R., & Flomenhaft, K. Family crisis therapy—Results and implications. *Family Process*, 1968, *7*, 145-158.

Langsley, D., Machotka, R., & Flomenhaft, K. Avoiding mental hospital admission: A follow-up study. *American Journal of Psychiatry*, 1971, *127*, 1391-1394.

Langsley, D. G., Pittman, F. S., & Swank, G. E. Family crises in schizophrenics and other mental patients. *Journal of Nervous and Mental Disease*, 1969, *149*, 270-276.

Lansky, M. R., Bley, C., McVey, G. G., & Brotman, B. Multiple family groups as aftercare. *International Journal of Group Psychotherapy*, 1978, *28*, 211-224.

Laqueur, H. P. Mechanisms of change in multiple family therapy. In C. J. Sager & H. S. Kaplan (Eds.), *Progress in group and family therapy.* New York: Brunner/ Mazel, 1972.

Laqueur, H. P., La Bart, H. A., & Morony, E. Multiple family therapy. *Current Psychiatric Therapy,* 1964, *4,* 150–154.

Laqueur, H. P., & Lebovic, D. Correlation between multiple family therapy, acute crises in a therapeutic community and drug levels. *Diseases of the Nervous System,* 1968, *29,* 188–192.

Lassner, R., & Brassea, M. Family centered group therapy with chronic schizophrenic patients: A five-year follow-up study. *Group Psychotherapy,* 1968, *21,* 247–258.

Leff, J. P. Developments in family treatment of schizophrenia. *Psychiatric Quarterly,* 1979, *51,* 216–232.

Leff, J. P., Hirsch, S. R., Gaind, R., Rohde, P. D., & Stevens, B. C. Life events and maintenance therapy in schizophrenic relapse. *British Journal of Psychiatry,* 1973, *123,* 659–660.

Leff, J., Kuipers, L., Berkowitz, R. Eberlein-Vries, R., & Sturgeon, D. A controlled trial of social intervention in the families of schizophrenic patients. *British Journal of Psychiatry,* 1982, *141,* 121–134.

Leff, J. P., & Vaughn, C. E. The interaction of life events and relatives' expressed emotion in schizophrenia and depressive neurosis. *British Journal of Psychiatry,* 1980, *136,* 146–153.

Leff, J. P., & Vaughn, C. E. The role of maintenance therapy and relatives' expressed emotion in relapse of schizophrenia: A two year follow-up. *British Journal of Psychiatry,* 1981, *139,* 102–104.

Lennard, H. L., Bernstein, A., & Beaulieu, M. R. Interaction in families with a schizophrenic child. *Archives of General Psychiatry,* 1965, *12,* 166–183.

Lerner, P. M. Resolution of interfamilial role conflict in families of schizophrenic patients: I. Thought disturbance. *Journal of Nervous and Mental Disease,* 1945, *141,* 342–351.

Levene, H. I., Patterson, V., Murphy, B. G., Overbeck, A. L., & Veach, T. L. The aftercare of schizophrenics: An evaluation of group and individual approaches. *Psychiatric Quarterly,* 1970, *44,* 296–304.

Lewinsohn, P. M., Biglan, A., & Zeiss, A. M. Behavioral treatment of depression. In P. O. Davidson (Ed.), *The behavioral management of anxiety, depression and pain.* New York: Brunner/Mazel, 1975.

Liberman, R. P. Behavioral approaches to family and couple therapy. *American Journal of Orthopsychiatry,* 1970, *40,* 106–118.

Liberman, R. P. *A guide to behavioral analysis and therapy.* New York: Pergamon, 1972.

Liberman, R. P. Behavior therapy for schizophrenia. In L. J. West & D. E. Flinn (Eds.), *Treatment of schizophrenia: Progress and prospects.* New York: Grune & Stratton, 1976.

Liberman, R. P., Aitchison, R. A., & Falloon, I. R. H. *Family therapy in schizophrenia: Syllabus for therapists.* Brentwood, Calif.: Mental Health Clinical Research Center, UCLA/VA Brentwood, 1978.

Liberman, R. P., & Bryan, E. Behavior therapy in a community mental health center. *American Journal of Psychiatry,* 1977, *134,* 401–406.

Liberman, R. P., Falloon, I. R. H., & Aitchison, R. A. *Family therapy for relapsing schizophrenics: A multifamily workshop approach.* Unpublished manuscript, 1978.

Liberman, R. P., King, L. W., DeRisi, W. J., & McCann, M. *Personal effectiveness: Guiding people to assert themselves and improve their social skills.* Champaign, Ill.: Research Press, 1975.

Liberman, R. P., Levine, J., Wheeler, E., Sanders, N., & Wallace, C. J. Marital therapy in groups: A comparative evaluation of behavioral and interactional formats. *Acta Psychiatrica Scandinavica*, 1976, Suppl. 266.

Liberman, R. P., McCann, M. J., & Wallace, C. J. Generalization of behavior therapy with psychotics. *British Journal of Psychiatry*, 1976, *129*, 490–496.

Liberman, R. P., Wallace, C. J., Falloon, I. R. H., & Vaughn, C. E. Interpersonal problem-solving therapy for schizophrenics and their families. *Comprehensive Psychiatry*, 1981, *22*, 627–629.

Lidz, R. W., & Lidz, T. The family environment of schizophrenic patients. *American Journal of Psychiatry*, 1949, *106*, 332–345.

Lidz, T. *The origin and treatment of schizophrenic disorders.* New York: Basic Books, 1973.

Lidz, T., Cornelison, A. R., Fleck, S., & Terry, D. The intrafamilial environment of schizophrenic patients: II. Marital schism and marital skew. *American Journal of Psychiatry*, 1957, *114*, 241–248.

Lidz, T., Cornelison, A., Singer, M., Schafer, S., & Fleck, S. The mothers of schizophrenic patients. In T. Lidz, S. Fleck, & A. Cornelison (Eds.), *Schizophrenia and the family*. New York: International Universities Press, 1965.

Lidz, T., Cornelison, A., Terry, D., & Fleck, S. Intrafamilial environment of the schizophrenic patient: VI. The transmission of irrationality. *Archives of Neurology and Psychiatry*, 1958, *79*, 305–316.

Lidz, T., Fleck, S., & Cornelison, A. (Eds.). *Schizophrenia and the family*. New York: International Universities Press, 1965.

Lieber, D. Parental focus of attention in a videotape feedback task as a function of hypothesized risk for offspring schizophrenia. *Family Process*, 1977, *16*, 467–475.

Linn, M. W., Caffey, E. M., Klett, J. C., Hogarty, G. E., & Lamb, H. R. Day treatment and psychotropic drugs in the aftercare of schizophrenia patients: A Veterans Administration cooperative study. *Archives of General Psychiatry*, 1979, *36*, 1055–1066.

Lovaas, I. A behavioral therapy approach to the treatment of childhood schizophrenia. In J. T. Hill (Ed.), *Minnesota symposia on child psychology*. Minneapolis: University of Minnesota Press, 1967.

Lurie, A., & Ron, H. Multiple family group counseling of discharged schizophrenic young adults and their parents. *Social Psychiatry*, 1971, *6*, 88–92.

Malhotra, H. K., & Olgiati, S. G. Fluphenazine therapy in groups. *Comprehensive Psychiatry*, 1977, *18*, 89–92.

Marks, I. M. Behavioral treatments of phobic and obsessive–compulsive disorders: A critical appraisal. In M. Hersen, R. Eisler, & P. Miller (Eds.), *Progress in behavior modification* (Vol. 1). New York: Academic Press, 1975.

Marks, I. M. The current status of behavioral psychotherapy: Theory and practice. *American Journal of Psychiatry*, 1976, *133*, 253–261.

Mathews, A. M., Gelder, M. G., & Johnston, D. W. *Agoraphobia: Nature and treatment*. New York: Guilford, 1981.

Matthews, S. M., Roper, M. T., Mosher, L. R., & Menn, A. Z. A non-neuroleptic treatment for schizophrenia: Analysis of the two-year postdischarge risk of relapse. *Schizophrenia Bulletin*, 1979, *5*, 322–333.

May, P. R. A. *Treatment of schizophrenia*. New York: Science House, 1968.

McCabe, M. S., Fowler, R. C., Cadoret, R. J., & Winokur, G. Familial differences in schizophrenia with good and poor prognosis. *Psychological Medicine*, 1972, *1*, 326–332.

McFall, R. M., & Twentyman, C. T. Four experiments on the relative contributions of rehearsal, modeling and coaching to assertion training. *Journal of Abnormal Psychology*, 1973, *81*, 199–218.

McGill, C. W., Falloon, I. R. H., Boyd, J. L., & Wood-Siverio, C. Family educational intervention in the treatment of schizophrenia. *Hospital and Community Psychiatry*, 1983, *34*, 934–938.

McGlashan, T. H., & Carpenter, W. T. Postpsychotic depression in schizophrenia. *Archives of General Psychiatry*, 1976, *33*, 231–241.

McNeil, T. F., & Kaij, L. Obstetric factors in the development of schizophrenia: Complications in the births of preschizophrenics and in reproduction by schizophrenic parents. In L. Wynne, R. L. Cromwell, & S. Matthysse (Eds.), *The nature of schizophrenia*. New York: Wiley, 1978.

Mednick, B. R. Breakdown in high risk subjects: Familial and early environmental factors. *Journal of Abnormal Psychology*, 1973, *82*, 469–475.

Mednick, S. A. A learning theory approach to research in schizophrenia. *Psychological Bulletin*, 1958, *55*, 316–327.

Mednick, S. A. Berkson's fallacy and high-risk research. In L. C. Wynne, R. L. Cromwell, & S. Matthysse (Eds.), *The nature of schizophrenia*. New York: Wiley, 1978.

Mednick, S. A., & Schulsinger, F. Some premorbid characteristics related to breakdown in children with schizophrenic mothers. *Journal of Psychiatric Research*, 1968, *6*, 267–291.

Meichenbaum, D. H., & Cameron, R. Training schizophrenics to talk to themselves: A means of developing attentional controls. *Behavior Therapy*, 1973, *4*, 515–534.

Meichenbaum, D. H., Gilmore, J. B., & Fedoravicius, A. Group insight versus group desensitization in treatment of speech anxiety. *Journal of Consulting and Clinical Psychology*, 1971, *36*, 410–421.

Mendel, W. *Schizophrenia: The experience and its treatment*. San Francisco: Jossey–Bass, 1976.

Metcoff, J., & Whitaker, C. A. Family microevents: Communication patterns for problem solving. In F. Walsh (Ed.), *Normal family processes*. New York: Guilford, 1982.

Meyer, A. *Collected papers of Adolph Meyer* (Vols. 1–4). Baltimore, Md.: Johns Hopkins University Press, 1948–1952.

Michaux, M. H., Chelst, M. R., Foster, S. A., Pruim, R. J., & Dasinger, E. M. Postrelease adjustment of day and full-time psychiatric patients. *Archives of General Psychiatry*, 1973, *29*, 647–651.

Milton, F., Patwa, V. K., & Hafner, R. J. Confrontation vs. belief modification in persistently deluded patients. *British Journal of Medical Psychology*, 1978, *51*, 127–130.

Mishler, E. G., & Waxler, N. E. *Interaction in families*. New York: Wiley, 1968.

Morgan, R. Industrial therapy. *British Journal of Hospital Medicine*, 1974, 231–242.

Mosher, L. R. Family therapy for schizophrenia: Recent trends. In L. J. West & D. E. Flinn (Eds.), *Treatment of schizophrenia*. New York: Grune & Stratton, 1976.

Mosher, L. R., Menn, A., & Matthews, S. M. Soteria: Evaluation of a home-based treatment for schizophrenia. *American Journal of Orthopsychiatry*, 1975, *45*, 455–467.

Murphy, H. B. M., & Raman, A. C. The chronicity of schizophrenia in indigenous tropical people: Results of a twelve-year follow-up survey in Mauritius. *British Journal of Psychiatry*, 1971, *118*, 489–497.

Myers, J. K., & Bean, L. L. *A decade later: A follow-up of social class and mental illness*. New York: Wiley, 1968.

Myers, J. K., & Roberts, B. H. *Family and class dynamics*. New York: Wiley, 1959.

Neale, J. M., & Weintraub, S. Children vulnerable to psychopathology: The Stony Brook high risk project. *Journal of Abnormal Child Psychology*, 1975, *3*, 95–113.

Norton, N., Detre, T., & Jarecke, H. Psychiatric services in general hospitals: A family-oriented redefinition. *Journal of Nervous and Mental Disease*, 1963, *136*, 475–484.

Nuckolls, K. B., Cassel, J., & Kaplan, B. H. Psychosocial assets, life crisis and the prognosis of pregnancy. *American Journal of Epidemiology,* 1972, *95,* 431–441.

O'Brien, C. P., Hamm, K. B., Ray, B. A., Pierce, J. F., Luborsky, L., & Mintz, J. Group vs. individual psychotherapy with schizophrenics: A controlled outcome study. *Archives of General Psychiatry,* 1972, *27,* 474–478.

O'Connor, N., Heron, A., & Carstairs, G. M. Work performance in chronic schizophrenics. *Occupational Psychology,* 1956, *30,* 1.

O'Connor, N., & Rawnsley, K. Incentives with paranoid and non-paranoid schizophrenics in a workshop. *British Journal of Medical Psychology,* 1959, *32,* 133.

Ødegaard, Ø. Emigration and insanity; study of mental disease among Norwegian population of Minnesota. *Acta Psychiatrica et Neurologica,* 1932, Suppl. *4,* 1–206.

O'Leary, K. D., & Turkewitz, H. The treatment of marital disorders from a behavioral perspective. In T. J. Paolino & B. S. McCrady (Eds.), *Marriage and marital therapy.* New York: Brunner/Mazel, 1978.

Parkes, C. On the use of psychiatric resources for indirect service. *Bulletin, Royal College of Psychiatrists,* 1978, 29–33.

Pasamanick, B., Scarpitti, F., & Dinitz, S. *Schizophrenics in the community: An experimental study in the prevention of hospitalization.* New York: Appleton–Century–Crofts, 1967.

Patterson, D. Y. *Living with schizophrenia.* New Jersey: Squibb, 1980.

Patterson, G. R. Interventions for boys with conduct problems: Multiple settings, treatments, and criteria. *Journal of Consulting and Clinical Psychology,* 1974, *42,* 471–481.

Patterson, G. R., McNeal, S., Hawkins, N., & Phelps. R. Reprogramming the social environment. *Journal of Child Psychology and Psychiatry,* 1967, *8,* 181–195.

Patterson, G. R., & Reid, J. B. Reciprocity and coercion: Two facets of social systems. In C. Neuringer & J. Michael (Eds.), *Behavior modification in clinical psychology.* New York: Appleton–Century–Crofts, 1970.

Pattison, E. M., de Francisio, D., & Wood, P. A psychological kinship model for family therapy. *American Journal of Psychiatry,* 1975, *32,* 1246–1251.

Paul, G. L. The chronic mental patient: Current status, future directions. *Psychological Bulletin,* 1969, *71,* 81–94.

Pilsecker, C. Hospital classes educate schizophrenics about their illness. *Hospital and Community Psychiatry,* 1981, *32,* 60–61.

Pinsof, W. M. Integrative problem-centered therapy: Toward the synthesis of family and individual psychotherapies. *Journal of Marital and Family Therapy,* 1983, *9,* 19–36.

Platt, S., Weyman, A., Hirsch, S., & Hewett, S. The social behaviour assessment schedule (SBAS): Rationale, contents, scoring and reliability of a new intervention schedule. *Social Psychiatry,* 1980, *15,* 43–55.

Polak, P. R., Deever, S., & Kirkby, M. W. On treatment the insane in sane places. *Journal of Community Psychology,* 1977, *5,* 380–387.

Powell, B. J., Othmer, E., & Sinkhorn, C. Pharmacological aftercare for homogeneous groups of patients. *Hospital and Community Psychiatry,* 1977, *28,* 125–127.

Reiss, D. Individual thinking and family interaction: II. A study of pattern recognition and hypotheses testing in families of normals, character disordered and schizophrenics. *Journal of Psychiatric Research,* 1967, *5,* 193–211.

Reiss, D. Individual thinking and family interaction: III. An experimental study of categorization performance in families of normals, character disordered and schizophrenics. *Journal of Nervous and Mental Disease,* 1968, *146,* 384–403.

Reiss, D. Individual thinking and family interaction: IV. A study of information exchange in families of normals, character disordered and schizophrenics. *Journal of Nervous and Mental Disease*, 1969, *149*, 473–490.

Reiss, D., & Oliveri, M. E. Family paradigms and family coping: A proposal for linking the family's intrinsic adaptive capacities to its responses to stress. *Family Relations*, 1980, *29*, 431–444.

Richardson, H. B. *Patients have families*. New York: Commonwealth Fund, 1948.

Ringuette, E. L., & Kennedy, T. An experimental study of the double bind hypothesis. *Journal of Abnormal Psychology*, 1966, *71*, 136–141.

Riskin, J., & Faunce, E. E., Family interaction scales: I. Theoretical framework and method. *Archives of General Psychiatry*, 1970, *22*, 504–512.

Robin, A. L., Kent, R., O'Leary, K. D., Foster, S., & Prinz, R. An approach to teaching parents and adolescents problem-solving communication skills: A preliminary report. *Behavior Therapy*, 1977, *8*, 639–643.

Robins, L. N. *Deviant children grow up*. Baltimore: Williams & Wilkins, 1966.

Rosenthal, D. *The Genain quadruplets*. New York: Basic Books, 1963.

Rosenthal, D., Wender, P. H., Kety, S. S., Schulsinger, F., Welner, J., & Ostergaard, L. Schizophrenics' offspring reared in adoptive homes. In D. Rosenthal & S. S. Kety (Eds.), *The transmission of schizophrenia*. Oxford: Pergamon, 1968.

Rosenthal, T. L., & Kellogg, J. S. Demonstration versus instructions in concept attainment by mental retardates. *Behaviour Research and Therapy*, 1973, *11*, 299–302.

Ro-Trock, G. K., Wellisch, D. K., & Schoolar, J. C. A family therapy outcome study in an inpatient setting. *American Journal of Orthopsychiatry*, 1977, *47*, 514–522.

Rubinstein, D. Clinical issues in family therapy of schizophrenia. In D. Rubinstein & Y. O. Alamen (Eds.), *Psychotherapy of schizophrenia*. Amsterdam: Excerpta Medica, 1972.

Rutter, M. *Children of sick parents: An environmental and psychiatric study*. London: Oxford University Press, 1966.

Ryan, P. Residential care for the socially disabled. In J. K. Wing & R. Olsen (Eds.), *Social care for the mentally disabled*. London: Oxford University Press, 1979.

Sameroff, A. J. *Infant risk factors in developmental deviance*. Paper presented to the International Association for Child Psychiatry and Allied Professions, Philadelphia, 1974.

Sameroff, A. J., & Zax, M. Perinatal characteristics of the offspring of schizophrenic women. *Journal of Nervous and Mental Disease*, 1973, *157*, 191.

Schatzman, M. Paranoia or persecution: The case of Schreber. *Family Process*, 1971, *10*, 177–212.

Schooler, N. R., Levine, J., Severe, J. B., Brauzer, D., DiMascio, A., Klerman, G. L., & Tuason, V. B. Prevention of relapse in schizophrenia: An evaluation of fluphenazine decanoate. *Archives of General Psychiatry*, 1980, *37*, 16–24.

Schuham, H. I. The double-bind hypothesis a decade later. *Psychological Bulletin*, 1967, *68*, 409–416.

Schulsinger, H. A ten-year follow-up of children of schizophrenic mothers: Clinical assessment. *Acta Psychiatrica Scandinavica*, 1976, *53*, 371–386.

Schwartz, C. C., & Myers, J. K. Life events and schizophrenia: I. Comparison of schizophrenics with a community sample. *Archives of General Psychiatry*, 1977, *34*, 1238–1241.

Scott, R. D. Cultural frontiers in the mental health service. *Schizophrenia Bulletin*, 1974, *10*, 58–73.

Segal, S. P., & Aviram, V. *The mentally ill in community based sheltered care: A study of community care and social integration*. New York: Wiley, 1978.

Selvini-Palazzoli, M., Cecchin, A., Prata, G., & Boscolo, L. *Paradox and counterparadox.* New York: Jason Aronson, 1978.

Serban, G. Stress in schizophrenics and normals. *British Journal of Psychiatry*, 1975, *126*, 397–407.

Sharan, S. N. Family interaction with schizophrenics and their siblings. *Journal of Abnormal Psychology*, 1966, *71*, 345–353.

Simpson, G. M., & Pi, E. H. The treatment of refractory schizophrenia. In B. Angrist *et al.* (Eds.), *Recent advances in neuropsycho-pharmacology.* New York: Pergamon, 1981.

Singer, M. T. The consensus Rorschach and family transaction. *Journal of Projective Techniques and Personality Assessment*, 1968, *32*, 348–350.

Singer, M. T., & Wynne, L. C. Differentiating characteristics of the parents of childhood schizophrenics, childhood neurotics, and young adult schizophrenics. *American Journal of Psychiatry*, 1963, *120*, 234–243.

Singer, M. T., & Wynne, L. C. Thought disorder and family relations of schizophrenics: IV. Results and implications. *Archives of General Psychiatry*, 1965, *12*, 201–212.

Singer, M. T., Wynne, L. C., & Toohey, M. L. Communication disorders and the families of schizophrenics. In L. C. Wynne, R. L. Cromwell, & S. Matthysse (Eds.), *The nature of schizophrenia.* New York: Wiley, 1978.

Sloane, R. B., Staples, F. R., Cristol, A. H., Yorkston, N., & Whipple, K. *Psychotherapy versus behavior therapy.* New York: Harvard University Press, 1975.

Snyder, K. S., & Liberman, R. P. Family assessment and intervention with schizophrenics at risk. In M. J. Goldstein (Ed.), *New developments in interventions with families of schizophrenics.* San Francisco: Jossey-Bass, 1981.

Snyder, S. H., Banerjee, S. P., Yamamuro, H. L., & Greenberg, D. Drugs, neurotransmitters and schizophrenia. *Science*, 1974, *184*, 1243–1253.

Sølvberg, H., & Blakar, R. Communication efficiency in couples with and without a schizophrenic offspring. *Family Process*, 1975, *14*, 515–534.

Soskis, D. A. Schizophrenic and medical inpatients as informed drug consumers. *Archives of General Psychiatry*, 1978, *35*, 645–647.

Speck, R., & Attneave, C. *Family networks.* New York: Pantheon Books, Random House, 1973.

Spitzer, R. L., Endicott, J., Cohen, J., & Fliess, J. L. Constraints on the validity of computer diagnosis. *Archives of General Psychiatry*, 1974, *31*, 197–203.

Spitzer, R. L., Endicott, J., & Robins, E. Research diagnostic criteria. *Psychopharmacology Bulletin*, 1975, *11*, 22–25.

Spivack, G., Platt, J. J., & Shure, M. B. *The problem-solving approach to adjustment.* San Francisco: Jossey-Bass, 1976.

Stabenau, J. R., Tupin, J., Werner, M., & Pollin, W. A comparative study of families of schizophrenics, delinquents, and normals. *Psychiatry*, 1965, *28*, 45–59.

Stein, L. I., & Test, M. A. An alternative to mental hospital treatment: I. Conceptual model, treatment program, and clinical evaluation. *Archives of General Psychiatry*, 1980, *37*, 392–399.

Stein, L. I., Test, M. A., Knoedler, W. H. *Cessation of a treatment program for schizophrenia.* Paper read at American Psychiatric Association Convention, Atlanta, 1978.

Stein, L. I., Test, M. A., & Marx, A. J. Alternative to the hospital: A controlled study. *American Journal of Psychiatry*, 1975, *132*, 517–522.

Stevens, B. C. Role of fluphenazine decanoate in lessening the burden of chronic schizophrenics on the community. *Psychological Medicine*, 1973, *3*, 141–158.

Strang, J. S., Falloon, I. R. H., Moss, H. B., Razani, J., & Boyd, J. L. The effects of family therapy on treatment compliance in schizophrenia. *Psychopharmacology Bulletin*, 1981, *17*, 87–88.

Strauss, J., & Carpenter, W. Prediction of outcome in schizophrenia. III: Five year outcome and its predictors. *Archives of General Psychiatry*, 1977, *34*, 159–163.

Strelnick, A. H. Multiple family group therapy: A review of the literature. *Family Process*, 1977, *16*, 307–325.

Strodtbeck. F. Husband–wife interaction over revealed differences. *American Sociological Review*, 1951, *16*, 468.

Stuart, R. B. Operant–interpersonal treatment for marital discord. *Journal of Consulting and Clinical Psychology*, 1969, *33*, 675–682.

Sturgeon, D., Kuipers, L., Berkowitz, R., Turpin, G., & Leff, J. Psychophysiological responses of schizophrenic patients to high and low expressed emotion relatives. *British Journal of Psychiatry*, 1981, *138*, 40–45.

Sullivan, H. S. The onset of schizophrenia. *American Journal of Psychiatry*, 1927, *7*, 105–134.

Sullivan, H. S. *Schizophrenia as a human process*. New York: W. W. Norton, 1962.

Talovic, S. A., Mednick, S. A., Schulsinger, F., & Falloon, I. R. H. Schizophrenia in high risk subjects: Prognostic maternal characteristics. *Journal of Abnormal Psychology*, 1980, *89*, 501–504.

Tarrier, N., Vaughn, C. E., Lader, M. H., & Leff, J. P. Bodily reactions to people and events in schizophrenia. *Archives of General Psychiatry*, 1979, *36*, 311–315.

Thompson, R. W., & Wiley, E. Reaching families of hospitalized mental patients: A group approach. *Community Mental Health Journal*, 1970, *6*, 22–30.

Thornton, J. F., Plummer, E., Seeman, M. V., & Littmann, S. K. Schizophrenia: Group support for relatives. *Canadian Journal of Psychiatry*, 1981, *26*, 341–344.

Tiernari, P., Sorri, A., Naarala, M., Lahti, I. Boström, C., & Wahlberg, E. The Finnish adoptive family study. *Psychiatry and Social Science*, 1981, *1*, 107–116.

Tolsdorf, C. C. Social networks, support and coping: An exploratory study. *Family Process*, 1976, *15*, 407–418.

Truax, C. B., & Carkhuff, R. R. *Toward effective counseling and psychotherapy*. Chicago: Aldine, 1967.

Tsuang, M. T. A study of pairs of siblings both hospitalized for mental disorder. *British Journal of Psychiatry*, 1967, *113*, 283–300.

Van Putten, T. Drug refusal in schizophrenia: Causes and prescribing hints. *Hospital and Community Psychiatry*, 1978, *29*, 110–114.

Vaughn, C. E. Interaction characteristics in families of schizophrenic patients. In H. Katschnig (Ed.), *Die Andere Seite der Schizophrenie*. Vienna: Urban & Schwarzenberg, 1977.

Vaughn, C. E., & Leff, J. P. The influence of family and social factors on the course of psychiatric illness: A comparison of schizophrenic and depressed neurotic patients. *British Journal of Psychiatry*, 1976a, *129*, 125–137.

Vaughn, C. E., & Leff, J. P. The measurement of expressed emotion in families of psychiatric patients. *British Journal of Social and Clinical Psychology*, 1976b, *15*, 157–165.

Vaughn, C. E., Snyder, K. S., Jones, S., Freeman, W. B., & Falloon, I. R. H. Family factors in schizophrenic relapse: A California replication of the British research on expressed emotion. *Archives of General Psychiatry*, 1984.

Venables, P. H. Input dysfunction in schizophrenia. In B. Maher (Ed.), *Progress in experimental personality research* (Vol. 1). New York: Academic Press, 1964.

Wallace, C. J., Nelson, C. J., Liberman, R. P., Aitchison, R. A., Lukoff, D., Elder, J., &

Ferris, C. A review and critique of social skills training with schizophrenic patients. *Schizophrenia Bulletin*, 1980, *6*, 42–64.

Weisbrod, B. A., Test, M. A., & Stein, L. I. An alternative to mental hospital treatment: III. Economic benefit–cost analysis. *Archives of General Psychiatry*, 1980, *37*, 400–405.

Weiss, R. L., Hops, H., & Patterson, G. R. A framework for conceptualizing marital conflict, a technology for altering it, some data for evaluating it. In L. A. Hamerlynck, L. C. Handy, & E. J. Mash (Eds.), *Behavior change: Methodology, concepts and practice*. Champaign, Ill.: Research Press, 1973.

Weissman, M. M., Prusoff, B. A., Thompson, W. D., Harding, P. S., & Myers, J. K. Social adjustment by self-report in a community sample and psychiatric outpatients. *Journal of Nervous and Mental Disease*, 1978, *166*, 317–326.

Wender, P. H., Rosenthal, D., Rainer, J. D., Greenhill, L., & Sarlin, M. B. Schizophrenics' adopting parents: Psychiatric status. *Archives of General Psychiatry*, 1977, *34*, 777–784.

Whitmer, C. A., & Conover, G. C. A study of critical incidents in the hospitalization of the mentally ill. *Journal of the National Association of Social Work*, 1959, *4*, 89–94.

Wild, C. M., & Shapiro, L. Mechanisms for change from individual to family performance in male schizophrenics and their parents. *Journal of Nervous and Mental Disease*, 1977, *165*, 41–56.

Wild, C., Singer, M., Rosman, B., Ricci, J., & Lidz, T. Measuring disordered styles of thinking. *Archives of General Psychiatry*, 1965, *13*, 471–476.

Wincze, J. P., Leitenberg, H., & Agras, W. S. The effects of token reinforcement and feedback on the delusional verbal behavior of chronic paranoid schizophrenics. *Journal of Applied Behavior Analysis*, 1972, *5*, 247–262.

Wing, J. K. A pilot experiment on the rehabilitation of long-hospitalized male schizophrenic patients. *Journal of Preventive and Social Medicine*, 1960, *14*, 173.

Wing, J. K. Social treatments of mental illness. In M. Shepherd & D. L. Davies (Eds.), *Studies of psychiatry*. London: Oxford University Press, 1968.

Wing, J. K. Social influence on the course of schizophrenia. In L. C. Wynne, R. L. Cromwell, & S. Matthysse (Eds.), *The nature of schizophrenia*. New York: Wiley, 1978.

Wing, J. K., Bennett, D. H., & Denham, J. *The industrial rehabilitation of long-stay schizophrenic patients*. London: Medical Research Council Memo No. 42, H.M.S.O., 1964.

Wing, J. K., & Brown, G. W. *Institutionalism and schizophrenia*. London: Cambridge University Press, 1970.

Wing, J. K., Cooper, J. E., & Sartorius, N. *The measurement and classification of psychiatric symptoms*. London: Cambridge University Press, 1974.

Wing, J. K., & Freudenberg, R. K. The response of severely ill chronic schizophrenic patients to social stimulation. *American Journal of Psychiatry*, 1961, *118*, 311–322.

Wolpe, J. *The practice of behavior therapy*. New York: Pergamon, 1969.

Wood, E. C., Rakusin, J. M., & Morse, E. Interpersonal aspects of psychiatric hospitalization. *Archives of General Psychiatry*, 1960, *3*, 632–641.

Woodward, J. A., & Goldstein, M. J. Communication deviance in the families of schizophrenics: A comment on the misuse of analysis of covariance. *Science*, 1977, *197*, 1096–1097.

Wynne, L. C. Consensus Rorschachs and related procedures for studying interpersonal patterns. *Journal of Projective Techniques and Personality Assessment*, 1968, *32*, 352–356.

Wynne, L. C. Methodologic and conceptual issues in the study of schizophrenics and their families. *Journal of Psychiatric Research*, 1968, *6*, 185-199.

Wynne, L. C., Jones, J. E., & Al-Khayyal, M. Healthy family communication patterns: Observations in families "at risk" for psychopathology. In F. Walsh (Ed.), *Normal family processes*. New York: Guilford, 1982.

Wynne, L. C., Ryckoff, I., Day, J., & Hirsch, S. Pseudo-mutuality in the family relations of schizophrenics. *Psychiatry*, 1958, *21*, 205-220.

Wynne, L. C., & Singer, M. T. Thought disorder and family relations of schizophrenics: I. Research strategy. *Archives of General Psychiatry*, 1965, *9*, 191-198.

Wynne, L. C., Singer, M. T., Bartko, J. J., & Toohey, M. L. Schizophrenics and their families: Recent research on parental communication. In J. M. Tanner (Ed.), *Developments in psychiatric research*. London: Hodder & Stoughton, 1977.

Wynne, L. C., Singer, M. T., & Toohey, M. L. Communication of the adoptive parents of schizophrenics. In J. Jørstad & E. Ugelstad (Eds.), *Schizophrenia 75: Psychotherapy, family studies, research*. Oslo: Universitetsforlaget, 1976.

Zigler, E., & Phillips, L. Social competence and outcome in psychiatric disorder. *Journal of Abnormal and Social Psychology*, 1961, *63*, 264.

Zolik, E. S., DesLauriers, A., Graybill, J. A., & Hollon, T. Fulfilling the needs of "forgotten" families. *American Journal of Orthopsychiatry*, 1962, *32*, 176-185.

Zubin, J., & Spring, B. Vulnerability: A new view of schizophrenia. *Journal of Abnormal Psychology*, 1977, *96*, 103-126.

AUTHOR INDEX

437

SUBJECT INDEX

Adoptive parents, 29
Affective disorder (*see also* Suicidal
    behavior)
    associated with schizophrenia, 304
    and family education, 179
    in parents, 309
    management of, 304, 305
    manic–depressive disorder, 23, 24, 26, 181
    neurotic, reactive depression, 177, 188, 303
    versus schizophrenia, 181, 182
Affective Style (AS) coding, 160
    and changes with family management, 401
Alcohol abuse, 177
    and disulfiram, 170
    in parents, 25, 148, 153, 154
    in schizophrenia, 203
Amotivational syndrome, 303, 304
Antidepressant drugs, 303, 304
Antipsychotic drugs (*see* Neuroleptic
    medication)
Anxiety
    behavioral treatment of, 174, 301–303
    educational approaches, 179
    social, 32, 60
Arousal, physiological,
    and effects of medication, 61, 109
    and expressed emotion, 45
    and rehabilitation, 56, 61
    and stress, 56, 60, 64, 108, 109
    and symptoms, 61, 64, 108
    and vulnerability, 56, 60, 64, 66, 76, 108,
        109
Autism, childhood, 6, 14

Behavior disturbance, 187, 188, 308, 334, 340
    aggressive, 21, 33, 37, 123, 187, 188, 318,
        408

bizarre/embarrassing, 123
lack of communication, 21, 22, 32, 33, 44,
    47, 63, 78
passive/negativistic, 21, 123, 187
and reduction with family management,
    343, 344
sexual, 33
suicidal, 33, 34, 37, 316, 340
Behavior rehearsal, 173, 174, 217, 292,
    293
    and communication training, 208–211
    covert, 173, 193, 281
    and problem-solving training, 280, 281
    and role reversal, 235
Behavioral analysis of family functioning,
    120–122, 144–163, 356, 357, 367, 368,
    386, 387
    and continuity of assessment, 142, 161, 162
    and functional analysis, 149–154, 345, 411
    and home observations, 147, 179
    and homework compliance, 290–292
    and journal recording, 157, 158
    and problem solving, 147, 159, 160, 264
    and reinforcement survey, 156–158
    and use of charting, 158, 159
Behavioral psychotherapy
    of anxiety, 301–303
    and assertiveness training, 74
    of depression, 304, 305
    of marital conflict, 119, 120, 122, 167,
        309–311
    and parent effectiveness training, 119, 120
    for persistent psychotic symptoms, 74
    and relaxation training, 74
    and token economy, 80, 288
Bethlem Royal Hospital, 126
Boundaries, family, 6, 14, 101
Brainstorming, 262, 270–272

445